THE
EARLY PLANTERS
of
SCITUATE
M A S S A C H U S E T T S

A History of the Town of Scituate, Massachusetts
from Its Establishment to the End
of the Revolutionary War

Harvey Hunter Pratt

HERITAGE BOOKS
2012

HERITAGE BOOKS
AN IMPRINT OF HERITAGE BOOKS, INC.

Books, CDs, and more—Worldwide

For our listing of thousands of titles see our website
at
www.HeritageBooks.com

A Facsimile Reprint
Published 2012 by
HERITAGE BOOKS, INC.
Publishing Division
100 Railroad Ave. #104
Westminster, Maryland 21157

Copyright © 1929 The Scituate Historical Society

— Publisher's Notice —
In reprints such as this, it is often not possible to remove blemishes from the original. We feel the contents of this book warrant its reissue despite these blemishes and hope you will agree and read it with pleasure.

International Standard Book Numbers
Paperbound: 978-0-7884-0885-4
Clothbound: 978-0-7884-9239-6

TO THE MEMORY OF
THE HONORABLE PEREZ SIMMONS—
ABLE COUNSELLOR AND TRUE FRIEND,
WHOSE LOVE FOR THE
PILGRIM LORE
EARLY INSTILLED INTO THE MIND OF THE WRITER
OF THESE PAGES, HAS FURNISHED THE
INSPIRATION FOR THE WORK—
THIS VOLUME IS
AFFECTIONATELY DEDICATED

OFFICERS:
Scituate Historical Society

Thomas Hatch Farmer, *President*

Arthur H. Damon, *Vice-President*

Hamilton W. Welch, *Treasurer*

Emma Allen Farmer, *Secretary*

TRUSTEES:

Henry Turner Bailey   Katherine Ellis

Edith W. James   Chas. H. Tilden

Adair Yenetchi

ILLUSTRATIONS

Portrait of Harvey H. Pratt .... *Frontispiece*

Memorial to the First Minister of Scituate 26

Lincoln Pond and Mill, Lower Bound Brook 36

Litchfield Stones in the old Cemetery, ... 48

"The Old Sloop"—The Unitarian Church 72

Bound Brook Glen 114

Old Scituate, Undivided 148

The Old Oaken Bucket Place, Greenbush 182

North River Valley 184

"The Two Stack," North Scituate 196

Old Cudworth House, 1723, Scituate 210

The Judge William Cushing Memorial 258

The Timothy Hatherly Memorial 284

The Humphrey Turner Monument, ... 314

The Old Stockbridge Mill, Greenbush 330

The Old Scituate Lighthouse, ... 348

CONTENTS

CHAPTER I
CAUSES OF EMIGRATING—EARLY PATENTS ....1—15

CHAPTER II
MERCHANT ADVENTURERS .... 16—24

CHAPTER III
INCORPORATION OF TOWN .... 25—33

CHAPTER IV
CONTROVERSEY OVER TOWN LINES .... 34—41

CHAPTER V
CONIHASSET .... 42—62

CHAPTER VI
DIVISION OF STATE AND CHURCH .... 63—86

CHAPTER VII
QUAKERS IN SCITUATE .... 87—98

CHAPTER VIII
TOWN GOVERNMENT AND FREEMEN .... 99—126

CHAPTER IX
TOWN GOVERNMENT AND FREEMEN .... 127—149

CHAPTER X
THE INDIANS .... 150—179

CHAPTER XI
CUSTOMS PREVIOUS TO THE REVOLUTION ...... 180—192

CHAPTER XII
TOWN ACTS AGAINST TORIES .... 193—209

CHAPTER XIII
BIOGRAPHICAL SKETCHES .... 210—386

NOTE

The publishers disclaim any responsibility for peculiar spelling and historical facts as they have endeavored to literally follow the text of the author.

S. H. S.

PREFACE

No accurate historian in writing of the early settlers of the Old Colony will be led, however great his respect for their motives, his veneration of their ideals and his sympathies in their hardships and sufferings, into idealizing them as a whole. The virtues of Brewster, Bradford, Carver, Standish, Hatherly, Cudworth and Tilden stand out prominently in comparison with their errors. To their determination, stubborn courage and fixedness of purpose, we owe the origin and existence of our present stable autonomy.

That they brought with them some less worthy, less devoted and less moral than themselves, is true. Nevertheless these persons formed part and parcel in the establishment both of the church and government. In any true chronicle they must be given their proper place, for obviously their presence had its influence in the working out of an eminently satisfactory whole. The Pilgrims themselves, fully realized and appreciated the effects of the residence of this class in their community. They believed it to be baneful. Bradford in his History frequently refers to them. † In 1642 he writes in his manuscript, ‡ "But it may be demanded how came it to pass that so many wicked persons and profane people should so quickly come over into this land and mixe themselves amongst them? Seeing it was religious men yt began yt work and they came for religious sake. I confess this may be marveilled at, at least in time to come, when the reasons

---

† The Bradford History pps. 171, 329, 437.
‡ Ib. pps. 476, 477.

thereof should not be knowne; and ye more because here was so many hardships and wants mett withall. I shall therefore indeavor to give soms answer hereunto. And first according to yt in ye gospell, it is ever to be remembered that wher ye Lord begins to sow good seed, ther ye envious man will endeavore to sow tares. 2. Men being to come over into a wilderness, in which much labour and servise was to be done aboute building and planting, etc., such as wanted help in yt respecte, when they could not have such as yey would, were glad to take such as they could; and so, many untoward servants, sundry of them proved, that there was brought over, both men and women kind; who when their times were expired, became families of themselves, which gave increase hereunto. 3. An other and a maine reason hearof was, that men, finding so many godly disposed persons willing to come into these parts, some beganne to make a trade of it, to transport passengers and their goods, and hired ships for that end, and then, to make up their fraight and advance their profite, cared not who ye persons were, so they had money to pay them. And by this means the cuntrie became pestered with many unworthy persons, who, being come over, crept into one place or other. 4. Againe, the Lords blessing usually following his people, as well in outward as spirituall things, (though afflictions be mixed withall,) do make many to adhear to ye people of God, as many followed Christ, for ye loaves sake, John 6, 26, and a mixed multitud came into ye wilderness with ye people of God out of Eagipte of Old, Exod. 12. 38; So allso ther were sente by their friends, some under hope yt they would be made better; others that they might be eased of such burthens, and they kept at home yt would necessarily follow their dissolute courses. And thus by one means or other, in 20 years time, it is a question whether ye greater part be not growne ye worser."

Possessing the advantage of a larger horizon afforded by the passing years since the above was written, it cannot be agreed that the pessimistic view expressed in the last sentence, was prophetic of the future. The immediate descendants of the emigrants in the Mayflower, Fortune and Anne with those who later joined them fresh from the old country, conscientiously continued the work which the fathers had begun. The interests of the church and government in New England were still safe in the hands of Benjamin Church, the Indian Fighter, Benjamin Lincoln of Hingham, Col. Edmund Quincy of Braintree, John Cushing of Scituate, Abraham Shaw of Dedham and Anthony Thacher of Yarmouth.

Whatever may have been the shortcoming and weaknesses of some, the best that was in them has survived, and so in the following pages the meritorious acts, as well as the errors of the early settlers are unreservedly and impartially recorded.

No apology is made for the free use of material found in other publications.

Many original manuscripts, documents and records have been examined. The work has extended over a period of years when the author had no thought of collecting them in this form; but rather in the preparation of cases in the practice of his profession, wherein ancient titles have been involved. Wherever there has been disagreement with others who have written concerning the same event, the conclusions herein stated have been reached only when they have been readily deducible from facts ascertained, beyond all question, to be true. The dominant purpose, which has been constantly kept in mind, is to compile a trustworthy record of the lives and achievements of the early planters of Scituate.

COLONIAL SCITUATE

CHAPTER I

CAUSES OF EMIGRATING—EARLY PATENTS

"The Lord Christ intends to atchieve greater matters by this little handful of men than the World is aware of."
Edward Johnson, "Wonder-Working Providence of Zion's Saviour in New England, 1628."

IN 1604 before James Stuart had been a year on the throne of England, he called the Bishops and the Puritan Clergymen together at the Hampton Court conference for the ostensible purpose of discussing the millenary † petition, which, signed by some eight hundred clergymen, had been presented to him upon his accession. The Puritan demands in this petition were mild in temper and reasonable in remedy. They asked for no change in the government or organization of the church, but for a reform of its courts, the removal of superstitious usages from the Book of Common Prayer, the disuse of lessons from the apocryphal books of Scripture, a more rigorous observance of Sundays and the provision for training and teaching ministers. Whatever his real purpose in calling this gathering together, he had not in the least altered his opinions concerning the rights and prerogatives of the crown. Before his accession these had found expression

---

† So called because it was supposed to have been signed by a thousand of the English Clergy. It however, bore the signatures of only eight hundred or about one-tenth of the whole. Greenes English People.

in his "The True Law of Free Monarchy" wherein he promulgated the doctrine that "although a good King will frame his actions to be according to law, yet he is not bound thereto, but of his own will and for example-giving to his subjects." He held that in his actions as soverign his will was supreme, he himself unfettered of all control of law, and responsible to nothing save his caprice. Not without natural ability, a great reader upon theological matters, a man of shrewdness, and more than ordinary learning for his time, he was yet without personal dignity or political balance.

When he had gathered the conference about him the petition was not discussed. Rather, he regaled the conferees with a display of his own theological reading and his views upon witchcraft, predestination and the noxiousness of tobacco. Preparing thus early in his reign for a battle with the Houses of Parliament rather than a policy of concession, this meeting with the petitioners afforded the opportunity for display of that intention. When one of the conferees suggested that however interesting his views upon these subjects were, they were not what they had come together to discuss, he lost his temper and retorted "A Scottish presbytery agreeth as well with a monarch as God with the Devil. Then Jack and Tom and Will and Dick shall meet, and at their pleasure censure me and my council and all our proceedings. Stay I pray you, for one seven years, and if then you find me pursy and fat and my windpipes stuffed, I will perhaps hearken to you. Until you find that I grow lazy let that alone. I will make them conform, or I will harry them out of the land." This stormy ending of what the Puritans had hoped would result in religious concessions, fully convinced them to the contrary. The expectation that the presentation of the petition would bring about radical changes in both church and government was not to be realized, and the conflict was on. The benches of the Commons, save only for the lawyers, who were subservient,—were filled with members who were in sympathy with the Puritans. The Parliament had met, inspired by the same faith that filled the hearts of the ministers when they met James and his Bishops at the Hampton conference. "Our desires were of peace only, and our device of unity" it said. Its desire was to reform certain ecclesiastical abuses by the abandonment of "a few ceremonies of small importance" and by "the establishment of an efficient training for a preaching clergy." But James had not so soon forgotten the insults and humilities that had been heaped upon him by the Presbyterians in Scotland. He saw no distinction between Puritanism and Scotch Presbyterianism.

The House of Commons addressed him in these words "Let your Majesty be pleased to receive public information from your Commons in Parliament, as well of the abuses in the Church as in the civil state and government. Your Majesty would be misinformed if any man should deliver that the Kings of England have any absolute power in themselves, either to alter religion or make laws concerning the same, otherwise than as in temporal causes by consent of Parliament."

James the 1st paid little heed to these representations of his Parliament. The rebuff given by him to the House of Commons was but one of the remote causes which made the exodus of the colonists from the realm, possible nearly two hundred years later.

This attitude toward both the Hampton conferees and the Commons gained recruits for the Separatists. The wise and cautious William Brewster, although firm in the faith, had hoped to bring about redress of the abuses through purely peaceful measures. He now saw that this was vain. He summoned a congregation to meet in his own home—Scrooby Manor. Here he was joined by that man "of great learning and sweetness of temper," John Robinson, whose influence over the Separatists was at all times beneficent and great.

Associated with Brewster and Robinson in this independent congregation was William Bradford of Austerfield, then only seventeen years of age, but later to be the revered and long continued Governor of the Colony of New Plymouth. In the brief years following its formation, it gathered to itself Separatists from Lincolnshire, Devonshire, Essex, Kent and other southeastern counties. Assiduously it was hunted out of its meeting places; its individual members were hounded by the officers of the law, and both were harassed upon all pretences and occasions. It grew nevertheless and soon numbered over three hundred. An unsuccessful attempt to escape from these persecutions was made in the later part of 1607. Failing this, the Separatists fled to Amsterdam and thence to Leyden in 1609. Here they remained for eleven years, their numbers being constantly augmented until they had increased to a thousand.

In Leyden they found a broad tolerance of all tongues and creeds so long as the latter embraced Christianity and the former gave utterance to the belief in Christ. This very mixture of tongues and races was, however, a constant source of disturbance and unrest to them. Their children were growing up among alien people, and might learn the language and adopt the ways of the foreigners.

"They had come to Leyden as an organized community, and absorption into a foreign nation was something to be dreaded. They wished to preserve their English speech and traditions, to keep up their organization, and find some favored spot where they might lay the corner-stone of a great Christian state. The spirit of nationality and self government was strong within them. The only thing which could satisfy these feelings was such a migration as had not been seen since ancient times." †

Where then should they turn? The New World discovered by Columbus only one hundred and thirty-eight years before was already populated in part by English speaking people. The colonization of the Atlantic coast of North America was encouraged by the government. In the reign of Elizabeth, the virgin queen, the valorous Raleigh had explored Pamlico Sound and given her name to the territory which he seized,—Virginia. Johnstown had been founded and its success assured. John Smith had discovered the Potomac and the Susquehanna, and some of his band were tilling the soil at New Sweden. Bartholomew Gosnold had already sailed into Vineyard Sound and Buzzards Bay. He had taken possession of the headland, which he named Cape Cod, and of Martha's Vineyard. Likewise he seized the group composed of Naushon, Cuttyhunk and Nashawena. They were re-christened the Elizabeth Islands. In 1605 George Weymouth had sailed up the Kennebec River, to be followed two years later by George Popham, who founded there an ill-started and short-lived colony.

In these widely separated settlements the speech, laws and institutions were all English. Although far from home, all the traditions were those of England. The policy of the government was toward the settlement and colonization of these shores by British subjects. It did not seek to interfere, nor did it actually intrude upon the observance of such forms of religious worships as the colonists themselves should adopt. It demanded simply fealty to the Crown.

Robinson resolved that his congregation should quit Holland and set up an autonomy in the new world. He wrote:—

"We are well weaned from the delicate milk of the

---

† John Fiske's "The Beginnings of New England," pp 74 and 75.

mother country, and inured to the difficulties of a strange land; the people are industrious and frugal. We are knit together as a body in a most sacred covenant of the Lord, of the violation whereof we make great conscience and by virtue whereof we hold ourselves strictly tied to all care of each others good and of the whole. It is not with us as with men whom small things can discourage."

The decision to emigrate having been reached, it remained to devise means and method. At the time Thomas Weston, one of the Merchant Adventurers of London, had sent out one or more companies which had exploited the shores of Newfoundland and New England. He was an adventurous, self-willed, domineering person, of generous wealth for the time, and bent on further accumulations by achievements in the new territory. It was said of him by one of his associates that he was "a man that thought himselfe above the generall, and not expressing so much the fear of God as was meete." With his associates he had obtained a patent from King James in very general and comprehensive language, which professed to cover all the Atlantic coast of America from the grant to the Virginia company on the south, to and including Newfoundland. Little was accurately known of the real extent of the grant, or in truth, of the territory out of which it was made. It did, however, extend fifty miles inland.

In 1619 Weston was the treasurer of and the dominating mind among the Merchant Adventurers. To him Robinson applied to fit out ships, stores, and necessaries for founding a settlement, and homes for himself and his fellow Brownists. Weston had nothing in common with them. Their purpose was to found a new state of which freedom of religious thought and worship should be the corner stone:— his was to colonize plantations to the end that wealth and his own personal aggrandizement, should follow.

CAUSES OF EMIGRATING

Yet he was not adverse to Robinson's proposal. Robert Cushman, the agent of Robinson, was sent to London to make terms with him. The negotiations were in progress for months and finally culminated in the chartering of the Mayflower and Speedwell.

Although the exiles in Leyden had been industrious during their residence there, but little could be, and actually was contributed by them to the finances of the expedition. Weston had driven a hard bargain. His associates in the Merchant Adventurers had, during the period of negotiations, abandoned him in his support of the project, and the expense, some £7000, was largely borne by him. In return he expected from the Pilgrims not only the results of their own toil but the wealth of the new territory which they were to colonize. The failure to achieve the latter and to satisfy the large demands of their financial sponsor caused sore trials to the leaders in the years which were to follow.

No trouble was anticipated, however, on the score of land tenure when the other side of the Atlantic should be reached. It was the intention to settle upon the grant of land in the country about the Delaware River which had been obtained from the Crown by the London Company. A charter had been sought but refused, and on the sixth of September 1620, Brewster, Bradford, Carver, Myles Standish, and their fellow voyagers, one hundred in all, sailed aboard the Mayflower, leaving a part of the passengers in the unseaworthy Speedwell at Plymouth.

The passage was a rough one; the reckoning was lost †

---

† Some of the earlier historians claim that Capt. Jones of the Mayflower had at all times during the voyage complete and accurate knowledge of his position. They aver, with some show of truth, that the Dutch, already contemplating the colonization of the territory recently explored by Hudson about Chesapeake Bay, bribed Jones to take his passengers farther north. Hutchinson's History of Massachusetts (London Ed. 1768). Vol. II Page 452.

and instead of reaching the Delaware Capes, the clearing weather of the morning of November ninth found them in the vicinity visited by Gosnold, fourteen years before,—the shores of Cape Cod. Here they cruised about for weeks, landing at Provincetown and signing, while in its harbor, the compact in the Mayflower's cabin. Finally on the twenty-first day of December, Plymouth was chosen as the point for disembarkation and the site for the new settlement.

It is not the purpose of this chronicle to follow the perils, adventures, privations and heroic devotion to principle, which marked the three years following the establishment of the town of Plymouth.

Before the Pilgrims had become fairly established here, in the mother-country Sir Ferdinando Gorges with the Council for New England, had obtained another patent which covered that part of New England upon which the forefathers had settled; and the Merchant Adventurers in 1621, sought and received a patent from this company. It was taken in the name of one John Peirce, a member of and for the benefit of the whole company of Merchant Adventurers.

"The indenture made the First Day of June 1621 and in the yeeres of the reigne of our souaigne Lord James by the grace of God King of England Scotland Fraunce and Ireland defender of the faith &c That is to say of England Fraunce and Ireland the Nynetenth and of Scotland the fowre and fiftieth. Betweene the President the Counsell of New England of the one ptie And John Peirce Citizen and Clothworker of London and his Associats of the other ptie WITNESSETH that whereas the said John Peirce and his Associats haue already transported and vndertaken to transporte at their cost and chardges themselves and dyvers psons into New England and there to erect and build a Towne and settle dyvers Inhabitants for the advansemt of the genall plantacon of that Country of New England NOW THE SAYDE President and Counsell in consideracon thereof and for the furtherance of the said plantacon and incoragement of the said Vndertakers haue agreed to graunt assigne allott and appoynt to the said John Peirce and his associats and euy of them his and their heires and assignes one hundred acres of ground for euy pson so to be transported besides dyvers other pryviledges Liberties and comodyties hereafter menconed. And to that intent they haue graunted allotted assigned and confirmed. And by theis pnts doe graunt allott assigne and confirme vnto the said John Peirce and his Associats his and their heires & assignes and the heires & assignes of euy of them seully & respectyvelie one hundred seuall acres of grownd in New England for euy pson so transported or to be transported. (Yf the said John Peirce or his Associats contynue there three whole yeeres either at one or seuall tymes or dye in the meane season after he or they are shipped with intent there to inhabit the Same Land to be taken & chosen by them their deputies or assignes in any place of places wheresoeu not already inhabited by any English and where no English pson or psons are already placed or settled or haue by order of the said President and Councell made choyce of, nor within Tenne Myles of the same (unless it be on the opposite syde of some great or Navigable Ryver to the former pticuler plantacon, together with the one half of the Ryver of Ryvers, that is to say to the middest thereof as shall adjoyne to such lands as they shall make choyce of together with all such Liberties pryviledges pffitts & comodyties as the said Land and Ryvers which they shall make choyce of shall yeild together with free libtie to fishe in and upon the Coast of New England and in all havens ports and creekes Therevnto belonging and that no pson or psons whatsoeu shall take any benefitt or libtie of or to any of the grownds or the one half of the Ryvers aforesaid (excepting the free vse of highways by land and Navigable Ryvers, but that the said vndertakers & planters their heires & assignes shall haue the sole right and vse of the said grownds and the one half of the said Ryvers with all their pffitts & apptennes. AND forasmuch as the said John Peirce and his associats intend and haue undertaken to build Churches, Schooles, Hospitalls, Town howses, Bridges and such like workes of Charytie As also for the maynteyning of Magistrats and other inferior Officers. In regard whereof and to the end that the said John Peirce and his Associats his & their heires & assignes may haue wherewithall to beare & support such like charges. THEREFORE the said President and Councell aforesaid do graunt unto the said Vndertakers their heires & assignes Fifteene hundred acres of Land moreover and aboue the aforesaid proporcon of the one hundred acres for euy vndertaker & Planter to be ymployed vpon such publiq vses as the said Vndertakers & Planters shall thinck fitt. AND they do further graunt vnto the said John Peirce and his Associates their heirs and assigns, that for euy pson that they or any of them shall transport at their owne propr costs & charges into New England either vnto the Lands hereby graunted or adjoyninge to them within Seven Yeeres after the feast of St. John Baptist next coming Yf the said pson transported contynue there three whole yeeres either at one or seuall tymes or dye in the meane season after he shipped with intent there to inhabit that the said pson or psons that shall so at his or their owne charges transport any other shall haue graunted and allowed to him & them and his & their heires respectyvelie for euy pson so transported or dyeing after he is shipped one hundred acres of Land, and also that euy pson or psons who by contract & agreamt to be had & made with the said Vndertakes shall at his & their owne charge transport him & themselves or any other and setle and plant themselves in New England with the said Seven Yeeres for three yeeres space as aforesaid or dye in the meane tyme shall haue graunted & allowed to him & them and his & their heires respectyvelie for euy pson so transported or dyeing after he is shipped one hundred acres of Land, and also that euy pson or psons who by contract & agreamt to be had & made with the said Vndertaker shall at his & their owne charge transport him & themselves or any other and setle and plant themselves in New England with the said Seven Yeeres for three yeeres space as aforesaid or dye in the meane tyme shall haue graunted & allowed vnto euy pson so transporting or transported and their heires & assignes respectyvely the like nomber of one hundred acres of Land as aforesaid the same to be by him & them or their heires & assignes respectyvely the like number of one hundred acres of Land as aforesaid the same to be by him & them or their heires & assignes chosen in any entyre place together and adioyning to the aforesaide Lande and not straglingly not before the tyme of such choyce made possessed or inhabited by any English Company or within tenne myles of the same (except it be on the opposite side of some great Navigable Ryver as aforesaid YIELDING and paying vnto the said President and Counsell for euy hundred acres so obtenyed and possessed by the said John Peirce and his Associats and by those said other psons and their heires & assignes who by Contract as aforesaid shall at their owne charge transport themselves or others the Yerely rent of Two shillings at the feast of St. Michaell Tharchaungell to the hand of the Rentgatherer of the said President & Counsell and their successors foreu the first paymt to begyn after the expiracon of the first seaven Yeeres next after the date hereof AND further it shalbe lawfull to and for the said John Peirce and his Associats and such as contract with them as aforesaid their Tennte & srvante vpon dislime of or in the Country to returned for England or elsewhere with all their goods & chattels at their will & pleasure without lett or disturbance of any paying all debts that iustly shalbe demaunded AND likewise it shalbe lawful and is graunted to and for the said John Peirce and his Associats & Planters their heires & assignes their Tennts & srvants and such as they or any of them shall contract with as aforesaid and send and ymploy for the said plantacon to goe & returne trade traffiz import or transport their goods & mchaundize at their will & pleasure into England or elsewhere paying only such duties to the Kings matie his heires & successors as the President and Counsell of New England doe pay without any other taxes Imposicons burthens or restrains whatsoeu vpon them to be ymposed (the rent hereby resved being onely excepted) AND it shalbe lawful for the said Vndertakers & Planters, their heires & successos freely to truck & traffiq with the Salvages in New England or neighboring theareabouts at their wills & Pleasures without lett or disturbance. As also to haue libtie to hunt hauke fish or fowle in any place or places not now or hereafter by the English inhabited. AND THE SAID President & Counsell do covennt & promyse to and with the said John Peirce and his Associats and others contracted wth as aforesaid his and their heires & assignes. That vpon lawful srvey to be had & made at the charge of the said Vndertakers & Planters and lawful informacon geven of the bownds, meete, and quantytie of Lands so as aforesaid to be by them chosen & possessed they the said President & Counsell vpon srender of this pnte graunt & Indenture and vpon reasonable request to be made by the said Vndertakers & Planters their heires & assignes within seaven Yeeres now next coming, shall and will be their Deed Indented and vnder their Comon seale graunt infeoffe I confirme all and euy the said lands so sett out and bownded as aforesaid to the said John Peirce and his Associats and such as contract with them their heires & assignes, Letters & Graunts of Incorporacon by some vsuall & fitt name & tytle with Liberty to them and their successors from tyme to tyme to make orders Lawes Ordynaunce & Constitucons for the rule government ordering & dyrecting of al psons to be transported & settled vpon the lands hereby graunted, intended to be graunted or hereafter to be graunted and of the said Lands & proffitt thereby arrysing. And in the meane tyme vntill such graunt made, Yt shalbe lawful for the said John Peirce his Associats Vndertakers & Planters their heires & assignes by cnsent of the greater pt of them & To establish such Lawes & ordynaunces as are for their better government, and by the same by most voyces elect & choose to put in execucon. And lastly the said President and Counsell do graunt and agree to and with the said John Peirce and his Associats and others contracted with and ymployed as aforesaid their heires & assignes. That when they haue planted the Lands hereby to them assigned & appoynted, That then it shalbe lawfull for them with the pryvitie & allowance of the President & Counsell as aforesaid to make choyce of to enter into and to haue an addition of fiftie acres more for euy pson transported into New England with like resvacons condicons & priviledges as are aboue graunted to be had and chosen in such place or places where no English shalbe then setled or inhabiting or haue made choyce of and the same entered into a boke of Acts at the tyme of such choyce so to be made or within tenne Myles of the same (excepting on the opposite side of some great Navigable Ryver as aforesaid. And that it shall and mybe lawfull for the said John Peirce and his Associats their heires and assignes from tyme to tyme and at all tymes hereafter for their seuall defence & savetie to encounter expulse repell & resist by force of Armes as well by Sea as by Land and by all wayes and means whatsoeu such pson & psons as without the especiall lycense of the said President or Counsell and their successors or the greater pt of them shall attempt to inhabit within the seuall psincts & lymyette of their said plantacon. AND THE SAID John Peirce and his associats and their heires & assignes do covennt & promyse to & with the said President & Counsell and their successors That they the said John Peirce and his Associats from tyme to tyme during the said Seaven Yeeres shall make a true Certificat to the said President & Counsell into a Register book for that purpose to be kept. And the said John Peirce and his Associats Jointly and seually for them their heires & assignes do covennt promyes & graunt to and with the said President & Counsell and their successors That the psons transported to this their pticular plantacon shall apply themselves & their Labors in a large & competent mann to the planting setting making & procuring of good & staple comodyties in & vpon the said Land hereby graunted vnto them as Corne & silk-grasse hemp flaxe pitch & tarre sppeashes and potashes Yrn Clapbord and other the like materialls. IN WITNESS WHEREOF the said President and Counsell haue to the one pt of this pnte Indenture sett their seales and to th' other pt hereof the said John Peirce in the name of himself and his said Associats haue sett to his seale geven the day and yeeres first above written."

Less than a year after this patent was issued, April 20, 1622, Peirce clandestinely obtained another similar patent from the Council for New England to himself personally. He did not profit by this perfidy: on May eighteenth, 1623, under compulsion because of it, he sold all his interest in both, to his Associates for five hundred pounds.

How little was known of the extent of this "wilderness" or else how unscrupulous was the aged James in alloting lands on the North American coast which he had previously patented to others, is apparent from the tangle in titles which followed the founding of Scituate in 1636. While the freemen of Plymouth and Duxbury held title to their lands through the grant from the Council for New England, the ownership of the soil of Scituate was, as to a certain part of it, long in dispute. Gorges and his Associates were, however, glad to have this nucleus of a successful colony firmly established north of their holdings in Virginia. They encouraged others to follow. † Some of these "were very useful persons, and became good members to the body; some were the wives and children of such as were here already; and some were so bad as they were fain to be at charge to send them home again the next year." Some came "on their own particular" as it was called. Cushman says of these latter that they "came without my consent, but the importunity of their friends got promise of our Treasurer in my absence. ‡ . All finally had title to the lands improved by them confirmed. §

---

† Georges and his fellow patenties were all loyal Churchmen. They would have preferred for the new colonizers other than Separatists. They took, however, whomsoever they could get. Palfrey's New England Vol. 1, page 216.
‡ Bradford History page 143.
§ The Georges' letters patent were confirmed by the Council for New England to the Plymouth Colony January 13, 1629. Plymouth Colony Records (Laws) Vol. XI page 6.

CHAPTER II

MERCHANT ADVENTURERS

Here, on this rock, and on this sterile soil,
Began the Kingdom not of Kings, but men;
Began the making of the world again.

Here struck the seed—the Pilgrim's roofless town,
Where equal rights and equal bonds were set,
Where all the people equal franchised met;
Where doom was writ of privilege and crown;
Where human breath blew all the idols down;
Where crests were nought, where vulture flags were furled,
And common men began to own the world. †

WHILE the Pilgrims were overcoming the obstacles and hardships incident to their new residence, the Merchant Adventurers of London and the Council for New England were engaged in strife in the mother country. The members of the former also quarrelled amongst themselves. A large number early disagreed with Weston and seem to have withdrawn from all business relations with him, following the dispute over the charters of the Mayflower and Speedwell.

In 1622 the partners, forty-two in number, purchased all of Weston's interest in the Company and thereafter, with the exception of John Beauchamp, who engaged with him in fitting out the Sparrow, their ways diverged.

---

† From the poem "The Pilgrim Fathers" written for and read at the dedication of the Pilgrim Monument at Plymouth by John Boyle O'Reilly, August 1, 1889.

Upon the return of the Mayflower with no cargo, Weston was much incensed and likewise little pleased at the meager lading of barrel staves and furs of the value of £500, which came later in the Fortune on her return to London. Before the arrival of the latter he had sold out to his partners, assigning at the same time the balance of the debt (£6500) still due to him on account of his original investment. With the exception of William Collier, John Revell, Thomas Andrews, Thomas Brewer, Henry Browning, John Knight, Samuel Sharp, Thomas Ward, John White and Timothy Hatherly, none of the Adventurers came to New England.

The latter came to Plymouth in the Anne in 1623 and remained two years. He suffered from fire and probably went back with Isaac Allerton in 1626. In that year Allerton was sent by the colonists to England who "gave him order to make a composition with ye adventurers, upon as goods termes as he could (unto which some way had ben made ye year before by Captain Standish); but yet injoined him not to conclud absolutly till they know ye termes, and had well considered of them; but to drive it to as good an issew as he could, and referr ye conclusion to them."†

Upon his return in 1627 he brought this agreement:—

To all Christian people, greeting, &c. Whereas at a meeting ye 26 of October last past, divers & sundrie persons, whose names to ye one part of these presents are subscribed in a schedule hereunto annexed, Adventures to New-Plimoth in New-England in America, were contented and agreed, in consideration of the sume of one thousand and eight hundred pounds sterling to be paid, (in manner and forme folling,) to sell, and make sale of all & every ye stocks, shares, lands, marchandise, and chatles, whatsoever, to ye said adventurers, and other ther fellow adventurers to New Plimoth aforesaid, any way accruing, or belonging to ye generalitie of ye said adventurers aforesaid; as well by reason of any sume or sumes of money, or marchan-

---

† The Bradford History, page 252.

dise, at any time heretofore adventured or disbursed by them, or other wise howsoever; for ye better expression and setting forth of which said agreements, the parties to these presents subscribing, doe for themselves severally, and as much as in them is, grant, bargan, alien, sell and transfere all & every ye said shares, goods, lands, marchandice, and chatle to them belonging as aforesaid, unto Isaack Alerton, one of ye planters resident at Plimoth afforesaid, assigned, and sent over as agent for ye rest of he planters ther, and to such other planters at Plimoth afforesaid as ye said Isaack, his heirs, or assignes, at his or ther arrivall, shall by writing or otherwise thinke fitte to joyne or partake in ye premisses, their heirs, & assignes, in as large, ample, and beneficiall maner and forme, to all intents and purposes, as ye said subscribing adventurers here could or may doe, or performe. All which stocks, shares, lands &c to the said adven: in severallitie alloted, apportioned, or any way belonging, the said adven: doe warrant & defend unto the said Isaack Allerton, his heirs and assignes, against them, their heirs and assignes, by these presents. And therefore ye said Isaack Allerton doth, for him, his heirs & assigns, covenant, promise & grant too & with ye adven: whose names are here unto subscribed, ther heirs, &c. well & truly to pay, or cause to be payed, unto ye said adven: or 5 of them which were, at yt meeting afforsaid, nominated & deputed, viz. *John Pocock, John Beauchamp, Robart Keane, Edward Base and James Sherley*, marchants, their heirs, &c. too and for ye use of ye generallitie of them, the sume of 1800 £ of lawfull money of England, at ye place appoynted for ye receipts of money, on the west side of ye Royall Exchanig in London, by 200 £ yearly, and every year, on ye feast of St. Migchell, the first payment to be made Ano: 1628. &c. Allso ye said Isaack is to indeavor to procure & obtaine from ye planters of N. P. aforesaid, securitie, by severall obligations, or writings obligatory, to make paiment of ye said sume of 1800 £ in forme afforsaid, according to ye true meaning of these presents. In testimonie whereof to this part of these presents remaining with ye said Isaack Allerton, ye said subscribing adven: have sett to their names, &c. And to ye other part remaining with ye said adven: the said Isaack Allerton hath subscribed his name, ye 15. Novbr. Ano. 1626 *in ye 2 year of his Majesties raigne.*

Hatherly was then in England and subscribed to it in London. It will be noticed that this agreement speaks of the signers as "Adventurers to New Plymouth in New England in America" and that it is proposed to "make sale" and "grant, bargain, sell and transfere all and every ye said shares, goods, lands, marchandice and chatles to them belonging as aforesaid, unto Isaac Allerton, one of ye planters resident at Plimoth aforesaid, assigned, and sent over as agent for ye rest of ye planters ther, and to such other planters at Plimoth, aforesaid, as ye said Isaac, his heirs, or assigns, at his or ther arrivall shall be writing or otherwise think fitte to joyne or partake in ye premises." From this it must be apparent that the lands which had been conveyed to Allerton to be allotted and apportioned among those planters who "by writing or otherwise think ftte to joyne or partake in ye premises" were only those lands upon which the Plymouth men had actually settled and the patent to which, they had received in association with the London Company from Gorge's "Counsell for New England." The point is, that Hatherly, Andrews, Sherley and Beauchamp, who had succeeded to the title of the forty-two Merchant Adventurers of London, thus early claimed the land at Scituate through their original grant with and subsequent purchase from Peirce and Weston. They did not recognize the right of the Colony Court to dispose of it to others. Hence the apparent deference of that body to these gentlemen, when it was ordered July 1, 1633 "that the whole tract of land between the Brooke at Scituate on the Norwest side and Conahasset, be left undisposed of till we know the resolucon of Mr. James Sherley, Mr. John Beauchamp, Mr. Rich. Andrews and Mr. Tymothy Hatherly as also that porcon of land lately made choice of by Mr. Hatherly aforesaid." † "That porcon lately made choice of" by Hatherly was undoubtedly land which had been set off to him as a freeman and the "whole tract" above mentioned was that which he owned in common with his partners Beauchamp, Andrews and Sherley. ‡

Hatherly had been largely concerned in the trading and colonization schemes of the Adventurers, yet he was, not less than Bradford, Winslow and Carver, a Separatist of the most pronounced character, entertaining determined views upon the subject of religious freedom. These views, coupled with a shrewd business instinct, constituted the force that impelled him finally and permanently to a land of unknown hardships.

Also, he and his remaining partners claimed title to a large tract of land. The Governor and Assistants, who together constituted the Colony Court, did not however readily agree to this claim. Although they had deferred to the "resolution" of the partners, in 1635 the Governor (Mr. Prence), Mr. Collier, Mr. Alden, Mr. Brown and Mr. Howland were directed "by the Court to view that portion of the ground on the north side of North River §

---

† Plymouth Colony Records Vol. 1, page 13.

‡ Hon. Perez Simmons, counsel for the plaintiff in the case of Litchfield vs Scituate, held this view, although Justice Field held that "the foundation of Hatherly's title is a grant from the Colony of Plymouth to himself and his three associates." In the determination of this case it was unnecessary for the Court to go back into the years preceding the execution of that deed. Its delivery by the Colony Court was based upon the recognition by that body of the justice of the Hatherly claim to title growing out of the original grant by King James to Gorges and The Counsel for New England, the grantors of the London Company.

§ This is manifestly an error of the Record. Satuit Brook is the stream intended and not the North River. By order of the Court dated April 12, 1633, Annable, Gilson and other men of Kent had already laid out Kent Street and were occupying the land north of the North River.

and if they find it more beneficial for farms to Scituate than to these parts, then to allot it to them; if not to reserve it." They reserved it. On October second 1637 "It is enacted by the Court that the grant of land at Scituate made to Mr. Tymothy Hatherly, Mr. Andrews, Mr. Sherley and Mr. Beauchamp, shall extend three miles up into the woods from heigh water marke, provided that upon the view of Mr. Prince and Mr. Collyer, it do not too much pjudice the town of Scituate." † This time Messrs, Prince and Collier must have been persuaded that the claims of Hatherly and his associates were just, or perchance the court overruled them, for under date of March 6, 1638 the order of the previous October was confirmed, as it was found that it would not too much prejudice the town of Scituate:

"Forasmuch as by former order of this Court Mr. Prince & Mr. Collyer were appoynted to set bounds of lands at Scituate graunted to Mr. Hatherly, Mr. Andrews, Mr. Shurley and Mr. Beauchamp, three miles from the heigh water mark up into the land, which was in parte accordingly performed by them, and they measured aboute two miles from the heigh water mark, and found that by reason of the crookedness of the river, the land will so wynd towards Conahasset that it will not much prejudice the towneship of Scituate, —the Court doth herefore confirme the said lands unto the said Mr. Hatherley, Mr. Andrewes, Mr. Shurley and Mr. Beauchamp, to have and to hold to them and their heires & assignes forever." ‡

"No line appears to have been run at the time except the westerly line the record of which appears in a note to the last order." §

The Scituate freemen were ill content with this situation.

---

† Plymouth Colony Records, Vol. 1, pages 130, 136 and 147.
‡ Plymouth Colony Records, Vol. 1, page 80.
§ Litchfield v Scituate 136 Mass. page 41.
§ Litchfield v Scituate 136 Mass. page 41.

In 1652 they applied for and obtained a review by the Court of its order of October 2, 1637, but upon hearing and argument the Court held that "having seen and heard the review, we cannot but allow and ratify the line done by our order." Notwithstanding this decision the controversy with the town was not quieted. In 1654, the Colony Court, apparently seeking to pacify the inhabitants made an order "In regard to sundry contentions and entanglements betwixt Mr. Hatherly and sundry inhabitants of Scituate, the Court doth grant unto Mr. Hatherly, to satisfy the partners of Conihasset, a certain competency of land, out of the bounds of any particular township, on the westerly side of the town of Scituate aforesaid." Later, in 1656, it ordered "that the Town (Scituate) take some speedy course to run out their head or westerly line between the pond at Indian Head River and Accord Pond, otherwise, if they neglect it, and the Court grant land that may be found to prejudice them, they may blame themselves." Apparently the Colony Court having decided in favor of Hatherly in 1637, was bound to stand with him, for after this plain warning in July 1666, it further granted to him "a tract three miles square, extending from Accord Pond three miles Southerly."

These orders of the Court were acquiesced in during the lifetime of Hatherly. After his death in 1671 another review was had and a committee of eight persons, four from the Conihasset partners and four representing the town sat with the magistrates. It was an abortive attempt, however, to settle the dispute that had gone on for thirty-eight years. Twelve years later, it was accomplished. John Cushing and Samuel Clap were chosen by the town † with such others as the Court should appoint, as a committee ordered by the Court on March 8, 1683 to run the line. This committee, agreed and reported "that the line should extend three miles

---

† Scituate Records Vol VI. The Court named Cushing, Capt. Josiah Standish and William Peabody of Duxbury, Marke Eames of Marshfield and Capt. John Briggs of Scituate. Plymouth Colony Records Vol. VI, page 103.

from the high water mark in Satuit Brook, N. W. and W. then three miles N. and W. to Bound Brook." The Court not only confirmed this report but ordered a deed to be executed by the Governor and delivered to Hatherly's successors in title. This deed signed by Thomas Hinckley, Governor, and Nathaniel Clark, Secretary, was as follows:

"To all peoples to whom these presents shall come. Know ye that Whereas the Governor of the Colony of New Plymouth and his Associates assembled in General Court in June Anno Domini one thousand six hundred and eighty and five did order and empower the Court of Magistrates in said Colony from time to time, at the request of any concerned to view and examine any former grants of land made by Court to any Town, Society or particular person. And upon examination, as aforesaid, to confirm and ratify such grant or grants by causing the public seal of the said Colony to be affixed to such their confirmation, as per said Court Records may appear.

"And Whereas, in the year one thousand six hundred thirty and three Mr. William Bradford and his associates did reserve a tract of land at Conihasset so-called for the use of Mr. James Shirley, Mr. John Beacham, Mr. Richard Andrews and Mr. Timothy Hatherly, and after said reservation did grant and confirm the said lands to the said Gentlemen and their heirs and assigns forever, as per Court Records may appear.

"And Whereas the said Court of Magistrates in pursuance of said order having viewed and examined the Court Records concerning the said reserve and Grant, do therefore by these presents ratify establish and confirm the sd Grant to the now proprietors of sd lands who rightfully stand seized of and to the said in room and stead of the sd Mr. Shirley, Mr. Beacham and Mr. Andrews and Mr. Hatherly, either as heirs or assigns according to each proprietors interest just right and proportion to and in the same, with all and singular the uplands marshes meadows swamps woods waters Rivers Brooks bays ponds coaves creeks &c being standing or growing in the said lands and premises with the rights privileges and appurtences to the same belonging or in anywise appertaining.

"To have and to hold the said lands and premises with the appurtenances to the now true proprietors thereof deriving their title from the said Gentlemen, according to the said proprietors his respective interest in or unto the same and to the heirs and assigns of such proprietor or proprietors forever.

They and every of them yielding and paying to our Soveraigne Lord the King his heirs and successors, and to the President of the Honorable Council for New England such part of the gold and silver oar as shall from time to time be found in the said lands, as in and by our original charter or Patent is prescribed.

"In Testimony Whereof of the said Court of Magistrates, by verty of said power committed to them have ordered the Publique seal of this Colony to be affixed to these presents this fifth day of March Ano 1685-6."

CHAPTER III

INCORPORATION OF TOWN

IN 1623 the last of the so-called new comers arrived in the "goode shippe Anne." Among them were Anthony Annable and Nathaniel Tilden who were granted lands "towards the eele river" † in Plymouth. Each was admitted a freeman and within the next ten years had left these allotments to take up residences on the second and third cliffs here. During this decade they were joined from time to time by William Gilson, who brought with him the minor children of his sister—John and Hannah Damon,—Humphrey Turner, Henry Cobb, all of whom were "Freeman of the Incorporacon of Plymouth in New England," and Thomas Bird, Edward Foster, James Cudworth and Henry Rowley. Gilson was a member of the "counsell" or "assistant to the Govr." and all were well-to-do men of the colony as is shown by their "rating," or taxation for public use. ‡ The locality had already received the name § of Scituate from the Indian "Satuit" or cold brook. Prior to 1634 they laid out Kent Street and erected houses on the westerly side of it. The street itself began at Satuit Brook and ran Southeasterly to the third cliff, upon which Gilson erected a grist mill two years later. Each houselot was eight rods wide upon the street and extended a quarter of a mile back into the woods. Edward Foster's was the

---

† Plymouth Colony Records, Vol. XII, page 6.
‡ Ibidem, Vol. 1, page 9.
§ "At a Generall Court held Jan. 1, 1633,—Acts 6. It. Anthony Annable chosen constable for the ward of Scituate, and to serve the King in that office for the space of one whole yeare & to enter upon the same with the Govr elect." Ibidem, Vol. I, page 21.

most northerly; Gilson's adjoined it on the south; and next came that of Henry Rowley. Humphrey Turner owned the next lot, although the house which he built was under and to the east of Coleman's Hills and James Cudworth's was on the Driftway. The last house was that of Anthony Annable. The meeting house had not been built at this time. Services were held at the house of James Cudworth which he describes in a letter † to his step-father as "but a mean one" and "the biggest." When it was erected a year or so later it stood upon "Meeting house lane," which ran at right angles with Kent Street, and bounded Annable's houselot on the south. The fort or "pallisadoes" was on the easterly side of Kent Street opposite the stile at the end of Greenfield lane and situated just north of the thirty foot way ‡ to the creek which William Crocker sold to Nathaniel Tilden.

On September eighteenth 1634 Reverend John Lothrop with some thirty members of his congregation whom he had brought from Egerton in the County of Kent, arrived in Boston in the "Griffin." They immediately came to Scituate. Others joined them here § notably George Kennerick and George Lewis, who sought and obtained dismissal from the church at Plymouth "in case they join in a body at Scituate."

A farm of twenty acres was alloted to Mr. Lothrop at Colman's Hills adjoining Humphrey Turner's. John Hewes, Walter Woodworth, George Lewis, Richard Foxwell, Samuel Fuller, Barnard Lombard, Simon Hoyt and Isaac Chittenden each had lots equal in size to those of Foster, Gilson and the others, on Kent Street, and similar grants were made to William Hatch, Samuel Hinckley, Nathaniel Tilden, Isaac Stedman, George Kennerick,

---

† Post, page 251.
‡ Plymouth Colony Records, Vol. XII (Deeds) page 104.
§ "At a Generall Court held Jan. 2nd, 1633, it was ordered 12. That whereas by indenture many are bound to give their servts land at the xpiracon of their terms, it is ordered, that they have it at Scituate, or some other convenient place, where it may be useful." Ibidem Vol. I page 23.

MEMORIAL TO THE FIRST MINISTERS OF SCITUATE.
Meetinghouse Lane Cemetery.

Daniel Standlake and John and George Lewis, the last of whom for some reason, obtained two. The highways in addition to Kent Street were Meeting House Lane, and parallel with it, Greenfield Lane. The "Driftway" extended around Colman's hills from Kent Street. The latter did not extend farther than its present junction with the road over the third cliff. The farm of Isaac Robinson who had sold one half of his land at Island Creek, Duxbury, for thirty dollars, and the houselot of John Handmer who afterwards went to Green's Harbor, were around on the southerly side of Colman's hills near the New Harbor Marshes as that part of the North River which constitutes its present mouth, was called. Timothy Hatherly at this time had not built at Musquashcut Pond where he had his farm later, near the road which now appropriately bears his name.

This was the compact little settlement of twenty-seven householders who had gathered themselves and their families into a church and community. The next step was incorporation as a town. † At a general court held on the fourth and fifth days of October 1636 it was ordered "That the towne of Scituate be allowed (vizt, the purchasers and freemen) to dispose of the lands beyond the North River, except that wch was before disposed on to others. And also it be allowed them to make such orders in their township for their convenient & comfortable living as they shall find necessary, provided they have, in case of justice, recourse unto Plymouth, as before."

Timothy Hatherly was already an Assistant and Humphrey Turner was constable, each chosen by the whole body

---

† "At the first settlement of the Colony, towns consisted of clusters of inhabitants dwelling near each other, which, by the effect of legislative acts, designating them by name and conferring upon them the powers of managing their own prudential affairs, electing representatives and town officers, making by-laws and disposing subject to the paramount control of the Legislature, of unoccupied lands within their territory became in effect municipal or quasi corporations, without any formal act of incorporation." Gray, C. J. in Hill vs. Boston 122 Mass. Rep. page 349."

of the freemen of the colony to serve in their respective capacities. In the first year of the incorporation James Cudworth was chosen a constable and Gilson, Foster and Hatch members of the Grand Jury.

The municipal territory was soon found to be too small. Before the incorporation, there had been a suggestion that the land lying between the South River (in Marshfield) and the North River might be "more beneficiall" to Scituate than to Plymouth, and Governor Prence, William Collier, John Alden, Mr. Brown and John Howland had been authorized to allot it if they so found it. They did not; they reserved it; but the freemen of Scituate, especially Hatherly, Turner, Tilden, Cudworth, Gilson and Robinson who were among the best men in the colony, desired one of the banks of the North River upon which to enlarge. Hardly had they begun their corporate existence as a town when they set about the consummation of this wish. They addressed the government at Plymouth complaining that "the place is too straite for them, the lands adjacent being stony, and not convenient to plant upon." Upon these representations a court of Assistants held on the first day of January 1637 passed the following order:—

"Whereas certain freemen of Scituate, vizt Mr. Tymothy Hatherly, Mr. John Lothrop, William Gilson, Anthony Annable, James Cudworth, Edward Foster, Henry Cobb, Isaack Robinson, George Kennerick, Henry Rowley, Samuell Fuller, John Cooper, Bernard Lumbard, George Lewis and Humphrey Turner, have complayned that they have such smale porportions of lands there alloted them that they cannot subsist upon them, the Court of Assistants have this day granted them all that upland & necke of land lying betweene the North & South Rivers, and all the meadow ground from the North River to the Beaver Pond, and all along by the North River side, and to hold the breadth from the South River trey, or passage, by a straight line to the North River, so far up into the land as it shall be marked and set forth unto them. Always provided and upon condition that they make a towneship there & inhabit upon the said land, and that all differences betwixt them and Mr. Vassall or others of Scituate be composed & ended before the next Court, or if any doe then remayne, that they be referred to the consideration of the Governor & Assistants, that their removall from Scituate may be without offance. And also provided and upon condition that whereas a proportion of two or three hundred acres of the lands above said should have been granted to Mr. Vassall, upon condition he should have erected a ferry to transport men and cattell over the North River at these rates, vizt, for a man a penny, for a horse four pence, and for every beast four pence; and to make causes (causeways) or passages through the marshes on both sides the ferry both for man & beast to passe by, which he was willing to doe, and to answer all damages which might happen in default thereof; and the Court in their judgments did conceive it more expedient to prefer the necessities of a number before one private person. That the said freemen of Scituate above named do so erect a ferry over the North River, to transport men and beasts at the rates above said, and make such passages on both sides through the marshes to the ferry, & provide a sufficient man to attend the same, that may answere all damages which may happen through his neglect thereof, or else the graunt abovesaid to be voyde."

Vassall, in 1635 had lands granted to him on the North River for the purpose of a home and plantation. These he called "West Newland" and his residence, the house beautiful,—"Belle house." He was a learned man for the times and ambitious to become a landed proprietor and person of importance in the new colony. His neighbors evidently did not take him at his own valuation. The only public service which he performed among them was to "sett" bounds between disputing land owners and this, probably because he was a competent surveyor and possessed one of the few "instruments" in the colony. The great objection to him was apparently his endeavor to secure so large a tract, containing so much valuable salt marsh, and bordering the river for himself.

The differences which existed between Mr. Vassall and his neighbors who thus took away from him "two or three hundred acres" began almost immediately upon his arrival here. Vassall had been one of the patentees of the Colony of Massachusetts Bay and had been in Boston with Gov. Winthrop in 1630. He had returned to England but had come again in 1634 and located at Scituate. Edward Winslow wrote of him "he is a man never at rest, but when in the fire of contention" † and Governor Winthrop said he was "a man of busy and factious spirit ‡, always opposite to the civil governments of the country and the way of our churches." Deane, on the other hand, records that he united himself harmoniously with Mr. Lathrop's church and enjoyed that place until 1642 when President Chauncey came to be pastor. § Governor Hutchinson says of him:

"Mr. William Vassall, as well as his brother Samuel Vassall, were gentlemen of good circumstances in England, but do not seem to have been fully of the same sentiment in matters of religion with the planters in general: and altho William came over with the first company (to Boston), yet he soon went back to England. He returned a few years after to New England and settled at Scituate in Plimouth Colony, not because they were reputed more rigid than the Massachusetts people. When Jamaica was taken by Cromwell, he laid the foundation of several fine estates there, enjoyed by his posterity to the present time. William Vassell as we have observed came over with the first patenties and was of the Assistants in 1630, but soon after returned to England, and in the year 1635 came back to New England and settled at Scituate in the Colony of New Plimouth. He was a gentleman of

---

† Pamphlet entitled "New England's Salamander Discovered."
‡ II Winthrop 260.
§ Deane's History of Scituate page 367.

a pleasant, affable disposition, but always opposite to the government both in Massachusetts and Plimouth. Scituate in Plimouth is contiguous to Hingham in Massachusetts, and Mr. Vassall had much influence in the latter colony as well as the former and had laid a scheme for petitions of such as were non freemen to the courts of both colonies and upon the petition being refused, to apply to the parliament pretending they were subjected to an arbitrary power, Extra-judicial proceedings, &c."

However correct this latter estimate of him may be it is true that he quarrelled violently with Chauncey over the question of baptism and caused a disruption in his congregation which was not healed until after Vassal's departure in 1646.

While it is true that both sides were capable of making a good fight and that the freemen won in the first encounter before the court, it is not clear that they lived up to the condition imposed upon the grant,—that of maintaining a ferry. On April 2, 1638 Vassall obtained this order from the Court:—

"Two hundred acres of upland and a competency of meadow lands to be layed to that, are granted to Mr. William Vassall to keepe a ferry over the north river where the old indian ferry was, and to transport men & beasts at these rates vizt, for a man, 12 & for a beast 4 d, a horse and his rider 4 d and to make the way passable for man and beast through the marshes on both sides the river at his owne charges, and to keepe them in repaire from tyme to tyme & Captain Standish & Mr. Alden are appoynted to set the land forth to him." † Even assuming that Standish and Alden attended to this duty the land was not immediately given him. The Scituate freemen were still fractious.

---

† Plymouth Colony Records Vol. I Page 82.

They insisted that Vassall take the oath of "fidelitie," † which he did in the following February. This was supposed to settle the whole trouble. Bradford, Winslow and Browne were appointed to view the "neck of land granted unto Mr. William Vassall & to set the same forth to him execept there be some such difficultie therein that will require the further consideration of the Court." ‡ Finally, on the third day of June 1639 he was granted a "parcell of land to lye in forme of a long square" § containing, with the marsh, one hundred and fifty acres, which included his original Newlands.

The inhabitants of Scituate were also appeased. On November 30, 1640, at a sitting of the Court of Assistants it was enacted that:

"Whereas the inhabitants of the towne of Scituate are greatly straitened for lands and there is necessyty that they should be enlarged, and that at the North River, where they desire to have supply for their wants, there is five hundred acres and upwards granted already to divers persons of Plymouth and Duxburrow, the Court doth grant (that those persons to whome said lands are granted, having their several grants layd forth unto them) that the said inhabitants of Scituate shall have two miles ¶ in length from the end of the said graunts, up the said North River, and a mile in breadth (if it be there to be had when the foresaid graunts are layd forth) and if not then to abate of that proportion & Mr. Timothy Hatherly, Edward Foster & Humphrey Turner shall dispose the said lands to such persons of

---

† Plymouth Colony Records Vol. 1, page 103.
‡ Ibidem, page 120.
§ Ibidem, page 124.
¶ In 1788 by mutual agreement between Scituate and Marshfield this tract which was always called "The Two Miles" was released to the latter town.

INCORPORATION OF TOWN

Scituate as they shall think fitt to be supplyed." †

Through these orders all of the boundaries of the town became fixed and settled and were stated by the Court March 7, 1642 to be as follows:—

"It is ordered by the Court that the bounds of Scituate towneship, on the westerly side of the towne shall be up the Indian Head River, to the pond ‡ which is the head of the said river and from thence to Accord Pond, and from thence to the sea by the lyne that is the bound betwixt Massachusetts & Plymouth." §

Its easterly boundary was the sea and its southerly boundary, the North River. ¶ Thus we have a definition of the town boundaries, readily discernible to-day—Bound brook (so-called from the fact that it was the division line between the two provinces) on the North, the sea upon the east; North River and its headwaters, the Indian Head River to Indian Head Pond, upon the south, and a line drawn thence through Ford's Farms to Accord Pond at Hingham on the west. The towns of Pembroke, Hanover, Abington, Rockland and Norwell have all been taken either in whole or in part from this tract.

---

† Plymouth Colony Records, Vol. I, Page 168.
‡ Indian Head Pond, now in Pembroke.
§ Plymouth Colony Records, Vol. II, Page 54.
¶ Ibidem, page 54.

CHAPTER IV

CONTROVERSY OVER TOWN LINES

THE controversy which was going on for a half century between Hatherly and the Conihasset partners on the one side and the freemen of Scituate on the other, had its parallel in the contemporaneous dispute between the colonies of Plymouth and Massachusetts Bay over the division line between the two governments. Beginning with 1637 disputes arose between the people of Hingham and Scituate over the meadows lying on either side of the Gulph. † It may be difficult at the present day to understand the wrangle over what would now appear to be a trifling lot of salt marsh; but it must be remembered that in the years of the early settlement of the colonies of Plymouth and Massachusetts Bay, these meadows had a very material worth. The land occupied by the freemen was rocky; it was well wooded; acres of cleared and ploughed land were not abundant; William Gillson's single wind mill on the Third Cliff sufficed to grind all the indian corn that the planters raised; cattle were constantly being brought by each ship which came from England. The beeves readily ate the meadow grass, though salt, and the marshes upon which it grew had a distinct value. On the Scituate side of "the Gulph" lay the greater expanse. The town very properly held that the Gulph was the natural boundary. Hingham upon the spec-

---

† Bound brook, following its bed, from Accord Pond to Bound Rock, (now marked by a bronze tablet near the Cohasset line,) empties into the marshes lying between Cohasset harbor and Musquashcut pond. The creek winding through these marshes through Brigg's Harbor or Musquashcut harbor, as it was called in 1637, to the harbor of "Little Hingham," was called the Gulph.

ious plea that Bound brook was in reality the Charles River spoken of by Captain John Smith in 1614, claimed that the patent line of the Colony of Massachusetts Bay lay south of it. They caused it to be surveyed, but finding that this assertion would lead them into the very egregious blunder of taking in the town of Scituate itself ("we x x x x found it to come so far southward as would fetch in Scituate and more." †) they abandoned it before commissioners subsequently chosen. In 1637 four commissioners were named, two from each colony. Messrs. William Aspinwall and Joseph Andrews appeared on behalf of Massachusetts Bay and Timothy Hatherly and Nathaniel Tilden on the part of Plymouth. Not much in the way of pacification and agreement ought to have been expected from these gentlemen. Hatherly and Tilden not only lived near the disputed meadows, but the former laid claim individually to their ownership. Each was a determined, not to say pugnacious man, unused, especially when combated, to giving way to others. Andrews, for the other side was as interested as Hatherly and Tilden. He lived in Hingham, William Aspinwall was that unyielding deputy to the General Court from Boston who suffered expulsion therefrom rather than desert his friend Wheelwright and acknowledge the promulgations of the Synod. ‡ They met at Hingham and — — disagreed.

The squabble was kept up. The authorities of Hingham undertook to "allote" certain of these meadows to their

† Another plot the old serpent had against us, by sewing jealousies and differences between us and our friends at Connecticut and Plimouth. This latter was about our bounds. They had planted Scituate, and had given out all the lands to Conyhasset. We desired only so much of the marshes there as might accommodate Hingham, which being denied, we caused Charles River to be surveyed, and found it came so far southward as would fetch in Scituate and more." I Winthrop 283.

‡ Three Episodes in Massachusetts History, Adams, Vol. I, pages 475 to 479.

own inhabitants. They measured and staked them out only to find these temporary monuments destroyed almost as soon as placed.

In 1640 the two governments again made an attempt to settle the dispute. John Endicott and Israel Stoughton, acting for Massachusetts Bay and William Bradford and Edward Winslow representing Plymouth Colony, were commisioned by the two jurisdictions to agree upon a settlement. The character of the men chosen to reach a satisfactory conclusion is the best evidence of the importance the quarrel had assumed in the opinion of the two governments. Endicott, enjoying at this time almost as great a popularity as Winthrop himself, domineering and insulting to those with whom, like Cotton, he disagreed, was calculated to drive everything before him in reaching and securing his end. Stoughton, hero of the Pequot campaign and unrelenting magistrate, was expected to supplement the efforts of Endicott. Against these two were matched the patient and conciliatory Bradford, Governor at the time, and Winslow humane, just, kind, but apt to be impetuously outspoken. The occasion which brought these four strong men together is described by Bradford in his manuscript. †

"And this tracte (the Conihasset grant) extended to their utmoste limets that way, and bordered on their neighbors of ye Massachusetts, who had some years after seated a twone (called Hingham) on their lands next to these parts. So as now ther grue great diferance between these 2 townships, about their grounds, and some meadow grounds that lay betweene them. They of Hingham presumed to allote parte of them to their people, and measure and stack them out. The other pulled up their stacks, and threw them. So it grew to a controversie between the 2 governments, and many letters and passages were betweene them aboute it; and it hunge some 2 years in suspense. The Courte of Massachusetts appointed some to range their line

---

† Bradford's History of Plymouth Plantations, page 439.

LINCOLN POND AND MILL,
Lower Bound Brook, Mordecai Lincoln's "Mansion House" is seen in the distance. From a painting by Walter Sargent.

according to ye bounds of their patente, and (as they wente to worke) they made it to take in all Sityate, and I know not how much more. Againe in ye other hand, according to ye line of ye patente of this place, † it would take in Highame and much more within their bounds. In ye end both Courts agreed to chose 2 commissioners of each side, and to give them full and absolute power to agree and setle ye bounds betwene them; and what they should do in ye case should stand irrevocably. One meeting they had at Hingam but could not conclude; for their commissioners ‡ stoode stffly on a clawse in their graunte, That from Charles-river or any branch or part thereof, they were to extend their limits, and 3 myles further to ye southward; or from ye most southward parte of ye Massachusetts Bay and 3 miles further. But they chose to stand on ye former termes, for they had found a smale river, or brooke rather, that a great way witn in land trended southward and issued into some part of yt river taken to be Charles-river, and from ye most southerly part of this, and 3 mile more southward of ye same, they would rune a line east to ye sea aboute 20 mile; which will say they take in a part of Plimouth itself; Now it is to be knowne yt though this patente and plantation § were much the ancienter, yet this inlargement of ye same (in which Sityate stood) was granted after theirs, and so theirs were first to take place, before this inlargemente. Now their answer was, first, that, however according to their owne plan, they could noway come upon any part of their anciente grante. 2ly, they could never prove yt to be a parte of Charles-river, for they knew not which was Charles-river,

---

† The Plymouth Colony patent.
‡ i. e. Massachusetts.
§ Plymouth.

but as ye people of this place, which came first, imposed such a name upon yt river, upon which, since Charlestown is builte (supposing yt it was it, which Captaine Smith in his mapp so named).

Now they yt first named it have best reason to know it, and to explain which is it. But they only tooke it to be Charles river, as fare as it was by them navigated, and yt was as farr as a boate could goe. But yt every runlett, or small brooke, yt should, farr within land, come into it, or mixe their stremes with it, and were by the natives called by other and differente names from it, should now by them be made Charles-river, or parts of it, they saw no reason for it. And gave instance in Humber, in Old England, which had ye Trente, Ouse, and many other of lesser note fell into it, and yet were not counted to parts of it; and many smaler rivers and broks fell into ye Trente, & Ouse, and no parts of them, but had names aparte, and divisions and nominations of themselves. Againe, it was pleaded that they had no east line in their patente, but were to begin at ye sea, and go west by a line, &c. At this meeting no conclution was made, but things discussed & well prepared for an issue. The next year, ye same commissioners had their power continued or renewed, and meet at Sityate, and concluded ye mater as followeth:—

"Whereas ther were tow commissiones granted by ye 2 jurisdictions, ye one of Massachusetts Governmente, granted unto John Endicote, gent: and Israell Stoughton, gent: the other of New Plimoth Governmente, to William Bradford, Govr. and Edward Winslow, gent: and both these for ye setting out, setting, & determining of ye bounds & limetts of ye lands betweene yr said jurisdictions, whereby not only this presente age, but ye posterities to come may live peaceably & quietly in yt behalfe. And for as much as ye said comissioners on both side have full power so to doe, as appeareth by ye records of both jurisdictions; we therefore, ye said comissioners above named, doe hereby with one consente & agreemente conclude, determine and by these presente declare, that all yt marshes at Conahasett yt ly of ye one side of ye river next to Hingam, shall belong to ye jurisdiction of Massachusetts Plantation; and all ye marshes yt lye on ye other side of ye river next to Sityate, shall belong to ye jurisdiction of New Plimoth; excepting 60 acres of marsh at ye mouth of ye river, on Sityate side next to the sea, which we do hereby agree, conclude, & determine shall belong to ye jurisdiction of Massachusets. And further, we doe hearby agree, determine, and conclude, yt the bounds of ye limites betweene both ye said jurisdictions are as followeth, viz. from ye mouth of ye brook yt runneth into Chonahasett Marches (which we call by ye name of Bound Brooke) with a straight and directe line to ye midle of a great ponde, yt lyeth on ye right hand of ye uiper path, or commone way, yt leadeth between Waimoth and Plimoth, close to ye path as we goe along, which was formerly named (and still we desire may be caled) Acord Pond, lying aboute five or 6 miles from Weimoth southerly. and from thence with a straight line to ye southermost part of Charles-river, and 3 miles southerly inward into ye countrie, according as is expressed in ye patente granted by his Matie to ye Company of ye Massachusetts Plantation. Provided allways, and never ye less concluded and determined by mutuall agreemente betweene ye said comissioners, yt if it fall out yt the said line from Accord pond to ye sothermost parte of Charles-river, & 3 miles southerly as is before expressed, straiten or hinder any parte of any plantation begune by ye Gover^{nt} of New Plimoth, or hereafter to be beggune within 10 years after ye date of these p$_s$^{nts}, that then, notwithstanding ye said line, it shall be lawfull for ye said Gov^{nt} of New Plimoth, to assume on ye northerly side of ye said line, wher it shall so intrench as afforesaid, so much land as will make up yt quantity of eight miles square, to belong to every shuch plantation begune, or to (be) begune as aforesaid; which we agree, determine, & conclude to appertaine & belong to ye Gov^{nt} of New Plimoth. And whereas ye said line, from ye said brooke which runeth into Choahassett saltmarshes, called by us Bound-brooke, and ye pond called Accord pond, lyeth nere ye lands belonging to ye townships of Sityate & Hingam, we doe therefore hereby determine & conclude, that if any devissions allready made and recorded, by either ye said townships, doe crose the said line, that then it shall stand, & be of force according to ye former intents and purposes of ye said townes granting them (the marshes formerly agreed upon excepted). And yt no towne in either jurisdiction shall hereafter exceede, but containe themselves within ye said lines expressed. In witness whereof we, the commissioners of both jurisdictions doe by these presents indented set our hands & seales yr ninth day of yr 4 month in 16 year of our soveraine Lord, King Charles; and in yr year of our Lord, 1640.

WILLIAM BRADFORD, Govr.   Jo: ENDICOTE
   ED. WINSLOW   ISRAELL STOUGHTON"

The agreement by the Plymouth Colony Commissioners to except sixty acres of marsh at the mouth of the river on the Scituate side "next to the sea" was a complete surrender. Indeed, this was practically the only territory in dispute. Although the Massachusetts Bay Colony laid claim through its survey, to much more, it is apparent that this contention was not a serious one. It served as something to trade on; and it is not at all surprising to find that Scituate refused thus to be hoodwinked. The owners of the meadows and the freemen of the town itself, declined to be bound by the determination and conclusion of the commissioners. An abortive attempt was made by the Colony

Court in 1654 to compel recognition of the line thus adjudicated and the reservation thus excepted when Mr. Anthony Eames of Marshfield and Cornet Robert Stetson were appointed, authorized and required "to see that the three score acres of meddow at Conahassett belonging to the town of Hingham bee layed out according to the acte of the comissioners concerning the same." No return was ever made by these gentlemen of the performance of this duty and it is probable that it was never executed for on June 3, 1662 another reference was ordered†. To this commission Josiah Winslow, Capt. Thomas Southworth and Cornet Robert Studson were appointed on behalf of Plymouth and joined the next year by Maj. Ebenezer Lusher, Capt. Roger Clap and Lieut. Joseph Fisher on the part of Massachusetts Bay. They agreed "that the Gulph shall stand as the boundary." And so, it stood to the time of the amalgamation of the two colonies, thirty years later, although contentions and law suits between individuals and the two towns most directly interested were many and violent during that time.

---

† "Whereas notwithstanding all former provision made for the perfecting of the line betwixt the Massachustts and this collonie, from Accord Pond westward, hath bine obstructed, the neglect whereof being soe greivious to them and us, and soe hurtful in sundry respects,—
This Court doth therefore order, that Major Josias Winslow, Capt. Thomas Southworth and Cornett Robert Studson be a comittee fully impowered to acte in the perfecting of he said line, and to conclude the right thereof, according to the graunt of the charter of our collonie: who are to give meeting unto a comittee being in like manner impowered by the honored Court of the Massachusetts to acte therin in their behalfe, that so there may be a finall issue put to that controversy, and what shalbee by the said comittees acted, our said comittee are to returne to out next Generall Court."
Plymouth Colony Records Vol. IV page 24.

CHAPTER V

"CONIHASSET"

In the Indian language—a fishing promontory.
Flint's Century Sermon

"Quonahassit"—*"A Long rocky place"*
E. Victor Bigelow, Historian of Cohasset

BETWEEN the years 1633, when the Colony Court, deferring to the wishes of Hatherly, Beauchamp, Shirley and Andrews, had reserved the land lying between Satuit Brook and Cohasset Harbor until it should be appraised the "resolucon" of those gentlemen, and 1642 when Hatherly purchased the holdings of Beauchamp † the last of the Adventurers to sell to him, a number of persons had settled and built upon this tract without color of title, ownership or authority. In 1646 there were living upon it Thomas Tarte, Rodolphus Ellmes, John Hoar, and Richard Mann

---

† Before Bradford Governor, 1642. The xth of March 1642. Memor. and That Mr. Edmond ffreeman doth acknowledg that for and on behalf of Mr. John Beauchampe of London Merchant by virtue of a warrant of Attorney under the hand of the said John Beauchampe of London Merchant bearing date the tenth day of July Anno Dni 1639 and by other letters also to him directed for the sale of certaine lands of his lying at Scituate, Hath for & in consideration of the sume of fourty pounds absolutely bargained and sold unto Mr. Tymothy Hatherley of Scituate gent All those lands upland and meadow belonging or appertaining unto the said Beauchamp with all and singular thappurtenances unto them belonging and all his Right, Title and interrest of and into the said premises with their appurtenances unto the said Tymothy Hatherley his heirs and Assigns for ever to the onely proper use and behoofe of him the said Tymothy Hatherley his heires and Assignes for ever.

The wordes of Mr. Beauchamp his letter, are these, viz:
"For my ground at Scituate sell it if you can (although it be never so little) which concerne this bargain & sale subscribed thus.
Your loving brother,
JOHN BEAUCHAMP

I, Edmund ffreeman do acknowledge this Record abovesaid to Mr. Hatherley to be my Ackte & Deede.

at or near Mann Hill, John Williams at Cedar Point, John Allen, John Hollet, John Stockbridge and John Woodfield at other locations. These men with Reverend Charles Chauncey, Thomas Chittenden, John Damon, Thomas Ensign, Thomas Hiland, James Cudworth, William Holmes, Edward Jenkins, Henry Merritt, Thomas Rawlins, Joseph Tilden, Richard Sealis, Ann Vinal, John Whiston, Gowan White and John Whitcomb, purchased twenty-seven thirtieths of the land from Hatherly for one hundred and eight pounds. Hatherly retained one fourth of it for himself. Joseph Tilden owned two thirtieths, the others, one each. The land was conveyed on December 1, 1646 and described as follows:

"Bounded with a brook of water lying southerlee of the harbor at Seteat and from hywater marke in yt brook to run three myles west into the woods and from the mouth of the sd brook to run east to the sea having Seteat land on the south border and the north border being att a little neck of land formerly called and knowne by the Indians or natives by the name of Conahaset allies Cohaset and is neare a great fall of water and from hywater mark at the said neck to run three myles on a west lynne up into the woods and from the vtmost extent of sd threemyle west lynn in the woods to run a directe lynn for the west border vnto the vtmost extent of the threemyle west lynn yt Runes from the foresaid Seteat brook into the woods vntell it meets; hauing the common on the west border and the Sea on the east border of the sd land."

The purchasers immediately organized themselves into a voluntary association to which they gave the name of Conihasset Partners. Their first act was to provide for a permanent record of their proceedings. On March 1, 1649 it was "agreed on by the purchasers of Conihasset allies Cohaset, there shall be a book of Records kept for the recording of all such orders as are or shalbe made about the said land and for the inrowling of all such Lands as is or shalbe laide out, and for the inrowling of the sale or Alienation of the said land this booke † is appoynted by the generall agreement of the said purchasers being mett together."

They chose a clerk, surveyors and committees. Richard Garrett, then also town clerk was the first "clarke" chosen by the Partners. This was in 1649. He served until 1656. James Torrey was his successor and held the position for nine years. He was followed by James Cudworth who was kept in office until 1681 when Stephen Vinal, Sr., was elected. He was succeeded by his son Stephen, Jr., on February fourteenth 1709 and for fifty-six years this correct and clerical individual who was a most excellent penman, kept the records. His successor, the last clerk of the Conihasset Partners, was Samuel Jenkins who was chosen clerk on May first 1767. Each clerk, upon being chosen subscribed to this oath:—

"You shall serve in the office of a clarke unto the company of the Purchasers of the shares of Conihassett Land; you shall faithfully keep this their book of records committed to your trust; you shall in it entrye make of such acts and orders and of all such divisions of land as you shall be ordered unto by the company or any whom they shall appoint thereunto; you shall enter all alienations of land that belongs unto Conihassett lands you being paid for your several entries by those whom it doth concern, and you shall return this their book afterwards unto the said company or whom they shall appoint when it shall be by them required. All of which you sweare truly and faithfully to perform, as you look for help from God that is a God of truth and punisher of falsehood; ffurther you doe sweare that since said company chose you to be their clarke you have entered nothing in this book of records but that you weare appointed unto by the

---

† The original—in the Registry of Deeds at Plymouth.

company or such as they did appoint." The fee for making each entry was four pence—"but if he make any larger writing, if he and those by whom he is employed cannot agree about the price, that then, James Cudworth, Joseph Tilden and John Hoare shall determine of the difference and what (they) shall conclude it worth they shall rest satisfied."

Nicholas Litchfield and Anthony Dodson were chosen surveyors. The meetings were originally "warned" by a committee of three persons, chosen from among the partners for the purpose, which issued its warrant eight days in advance of each meeting, in precisely the same manner as town meetings of the freemen were called. In the later years these warrants, were issued by one of the proprietors who was a justice of the peace, upon the petition of eight partners,—an analogy to the same method provided in certain cases, for calling town meetings; and likewise in imitation of the municipal gathering, they were presided over by a moderator. It was early provided that such a "lawful warning" should bind those not attending as well as those present, "except in fee simple of land," or in other words when divisions were made and real property granted. In the beginning it was:—

"Agreed by the Company being met together for the ordering of the said land for the more safe and peaceable enjoying of the said Conihasset land, do for the more speedy despatch of business, order that what shalbe voted by the company, the greater vote shall carry it (except only in the fee simple of lands) and that every thirtyeth part or share shall have one voyce and that two half shares shall have but one voyce."

On the same day, March first 1640, Hatherly received £10:16s: being the balance due him in full-and reserved "for my quarter part of Conihassett lands, two hundred acres of upland at Musquashcut farm; four hundred acres of upland at my farm at Scituate and one hundred and thirty-six acres of salt marsh."

Choice of location among the other partners was made by lot, and four working days were given in which to make a selection. John Booth obtained the first choice and took a tract of land on the hill over which Blossom Street now extends from Gannett's Corner. For many years it was called "Booth's Hill." Major Cudworth was sixth. He made his selection on Mann Hill. Anne Vinal, Rev. Mr. Chauncey and Nathaniel Tilden all came well down in the list, but there being ample acres of both upland and meadow for all, the records do not disclose that there was dissatisfaction.

Having thus become invested with their individual legal titles, the partners proceeded to pass protective measures. It was:—

"Agreed on by the Company that no one or more purchasers shall sell or let any of the Conihassett lands unto any of another town so as to sell the Common, or to make use of the timber or wood as long as he to whome it is sold or let lives out of the town of Scituate" and later—

"Whereas the Purchasers of Conihassett having divers allottments of land each man making choice of his land for his most convenience, both for land and timber, by reason of which it may so fall out that some man's land may be inclosed from all common, so that he cannot have way to his land unless he have passage over some part of his neighbors lot, it is agreed and voted by the Company if any man shall so stand in need of a way to his land so as that he must of necessity go over his neighbors land or else cannot come to his own land, that then, if the party wanting a way and the party whose land he desires to go over cannot agree where he shall goe; that three men of the company be appointed to determine where he shall go, they determining of it where it may be least prejudicial to the party over whose land he is to go, & what damage shall be done by so doing; if the parties concerned in it cannot agree it themselves, the three men shall determine the damage betwixt them to prevent suits at law. † And for as much as three men may be some of them interested persons in the difference, therefore the Company have agreed and chosen five men & so three of the five, those three that are not concerned in the difference are to determine it, and the men chosen are Joseph Tilden, John Hollett, Isacke Chittenden, John Merritt and James Cudworth."

The manner of thus owning and disposing of the Conihasset tract by these partners was unique, even in the Plymouth Colony itself. The grantees did not constitute a corporation, for there was no such land holding device known to the common law which the forefathers brought with them from the mother country. Neither was there any local law up to 1682, authorizing such a combination. They were tenants in common with Hatherly and each other.

This tenancy essentially differed from that of the "commoners," as the inhabitants of the several towns were called, in relation to that part of the municipal territory not individually owned. The Conihasset tract, while it lay within the town limits of Scituate, was absolutely owned by the Partners and although "common" land, the townsmen had no voice in its disposal. Hatherly, Chauncey, Cudworth and the rest as inhabitants of the municipality of Scituate were commoners in the lands of the town not individually owned in fee, and had a voice and vote in town meeting with their neighbors in its disposition or sale; but in the acres between Satuit Brook and the "Gulph" the commoners and freemen of the town, had no community of interest; it belonged to the "Partners" alone.

The courts of Massachusetts, have singularly failed, both to make or recognize the distinction existing between these kinds of ownerships, using the terms "commoners" and

---

† It is interesting to read in this record that when this vote was propounded Walter Briggs and Ensign Williams, each in after years a persistent litigant, "refused to act."

"proprietors" interchangeably and as having an equal status. The *commoners* came into being through municipal incorporation, by the colony court. They might number one hundred or one thousand and increase still further with the growth of the voting population. The *proprietors,* on the other hand, were tenants in common whose numbers could only increase by their own acts of alienation. Neither proprietor or commoner, as the terms were used in Plymouth Colony in 1650 had any standing known to the common law. Each sprang from the same source—the necessities of the situation. It will be remembered that the Pilgrims settling Plymouth without royal charter, erected a government of their own and assumed the most supreme rights and prerogatives of sovereignty. They negotiated treaties with the aborigines, declared and prosecuted wars, levied rates and taxes, made and executed laws and erected townships. In the exercise of the last function their General Court vested absolute and indefeasible title in the municipalities thus created to the lands lying within the limits of the grant, not otherwise held in fee by individual owners. The inhabitants of the town, freemen and townsmen (those who had taken only the oath of fidelity) thus became commoners, and in ordering the affairs of the town, disposed of the common lands.

Proprietors were recognized even before the union of the two colonies in 1692, when the acts of authority of the General Court were directed along the lines permitted by a written charter. Thus in Plymouth Colony in the "Lawes and Orders" made by the Generall Court holden at Plymouth July the 7, 1682, it was enacted "Whereas in divers Townes and Places of this Collonie there are Severall Tracts of land which belong to and are held by divers persons in comon as the proprieator thereof and noe order hath bine yett made for their early meeting together to divide the said land or to make orders for the settlement of the same; it is therefore enacted that when the need doth require in any such place or township if the matter did not concerne the

LITCHFIELD STONES IN THE OLD CEMETERY,
Meetinghouse Lane, Kent street, Scituate.

Towne as a Towne in Generall upon the request made by the said proprietors or some of them to any majestrate of this Collonie an order shalbe graunted them to warne all the proprietors belonging to such Townes to come together att some certaine time and place to transact such matters as may concerne them and what shalbe lawfully enacted at such meeting by the propiators or the major parte of them shalbe vallid and binding." Thus Ann and Stephen Vinall had common lands alloted to them. † William Parker and Joseph Coleman were likewise recipients of Colonial lands "according to their antiquity and desirt" ‡.

After the annexation, under the Provincial Charter the General Court of Massachusetts Bay did the same thing although not always as Chief Justice Parsons said "on conditions of settlement and for the purpose of forming towns to share the public burden" §, but because the grantees either had "lived and made improvements thereon" or "had fought in his majesty's service" or were "ancient freemen" or for money expended in educating Indians. ¶

These proprietaries were spoken of and deemed to be a species of corporation or quasi-corporation. As was said by Justice Strong ❖ "This is a species of corporation different from corporations in general—*this* is intended to *die*, those to *live forever*." In other words, the purpose of the real estate owning proprietaries of colonial times was to hold the land until it had been entirely divided or alienated —then to die. Following a long established policy the General Court of to-day refuses to incorporate a strictly

---

† Town Records Vol V page 6.
‡ Plymouth Colony Vol V page 154.
§ Higby et al vs Rice 5 Mass. at page 349.
¶ Ibidem page 351.
❖ proprietor of Monumoi Great Beach vs Rogers 1 Mass at page 163. See also note by Justice Gray (then Reporter of Decisions) to Comm v Roxbury Gray page 512 and Ipswich vs Proprietor of Jeffries Neck Pasture 218 Mass. 487.

real estate owning body which never dies and in which the title to land may be tied up indefinitely.

But the Conihasset Proprietors were like neither of these. Their muniment of title was only thrice removed in a direct line, through the Council for New England, the London Adventurers and Hatherly, from the royal patent of King James himself, and they recognized no fealty to the colony court so far as this land tenure was concerned. † Indeed, this view of their status seems to have been mutually entertained in the earlier days. For instance, on October fifth 1652 "a petition was preferred to the Court by John Hoare concerning the lands att Conahassett sold by Mr. Hatherley to sundry persons of Scituate, which the Court having heard and considered of, have ordered and doe request Mr. Hatherley to signify unto those whom it conseres that the Court doth hereby require them either to come to an equall devision of the said lands according to the deed or to returne a reason unto the Court wherefore they do not, at the next Generall Court: unless the parties shall see reason and shalbee willing to issue it by refering it unto som endifferent men, that they together with John Hoare, shall think meete by joynt consent to refer it unto; *the which latter wee desire may bee,* as thinking it may be the best way to end the difference about it"‡. No attention whatever was paid to this by the Partners. The next year this neglect was called to the attention of the Court and it solemnly caused this decree to be spread upon its records:

"the Court doth find that through unexpected occations and feares of troubles this hath been neglected, there-

---

† In this grant to the Council for New England James I conveyed not only the soil described, but also all havens, ports, rivers, waters, fishings, mines and minerals, as well royal as other mines, and all and singular other commodities *jurisdictions, royalties, privileges, franchises and preeminencies.* This language was broad enough to justify the Partners in their claim, even had it extended to something far beyond the mere owning and disposing of their land. See Barker vs. Bates 13 Pickering pages 258-260.

‡ Plymouth Colony Records, Vol. III, Page 18.

fore the Court doth hereby order and require them that were first appointed to record these several allotments, or soe many of them as will bring in theire bounds of said allotments unto them, that they forthwith record them, and returne the said records into the Court att the next Court of Assistants, that soe the Court may judge equality of it, and soe confirm the same; and in case any persons doe refuse to bring in their bounds to bee recorded and presented, to the Court, that you return theire names unto the Court of next Assistants, that so theire may bee an end of these controversies."

Notwithstanding this order the Partners, as independent as before, refused compliance with it. They neither brought in "their bounds to be recorded" nor permitted the court to judge of the equality or equity of their own divisions. Their names may have been returned into the next or a subsequent sitting of the Assistants, but if so, no mention was made of it and records of allotments and division of land continued to be entered in the book which they had provided for the purpose.

John Williams was another partner who sought to compel, what he alleged was his fair division, to be set off to him. When he exhibited his petition to the Court of his Majesties government at Plymouth in March 1680, that body well knew the attitude of the Conihasset Partners towards interference by it, in their internecine affairs. It had its own dignity to maintain, yet, it clearly was not positive of its right to adjudicate in the premises. The language of its order shows how diplomatically it sought to propitiate the proprietors and at the same time save its own face. Here it is †

"Whereas Captain Williams and some other exhibited a petition to the Court, requesting that they would grant them a division of the undivided lands of Conahassett, this Court doth order, that it may be signifyed

---

† Plymouth Colony Records Vol VI page 55.

to the purchasers of Conahassett, that they judge it to be rationall that they come to an equall division, and doe advise them speedily soe to doe; and in the meantime judge it meet, that they the petitioners and purchasers, sell noe timber for barke in anywise nor upon any other accoumpt but what shalbe or may be for present necessitie, in order to building or fencing for his or theire own use in Scittuate, and noe otherwise, and the said purchasers sett upon the worke of division before the leaves come forth."

In other words, the order being entered in March the work was to be "sett upon" at once. The leaves came forth; they turned into the sere and yellow but the division was not made. At the sitting of the court in October following, it entered this memorandum. †

This Court have considered the petition of (certain) propriators of Conahassett land, which made theire addresse to the Court for releiffe last March, in reference to the equall devideing of the said Conahasset land, the Court then advised them to come to an equall division of the undivided land of Conahassett before the leaves come forth; but understanding that the advice is not attended unto as to the accomplishment of the said division, doe require the propriators to meet together as speedily as may be, and make an equall devision of all undivided lands of Conahasset according to each persons purchase.

It will be noted that this time the court did not undertake to enter an order; it satisfied itself with the giving of advice. But advice or order it was not heeded. The partners were obdurate. Even Williams himself, a most stubborn litigant, apparently saw the hopelessness of obtaining real relief from the court. Otherwise he would not have made this offer of compromise which he submitted five years later:—

---

† Plymouth Colony Records Vol VI page 79.

"1. To divide the cost (of division).
2. Lands theretofore laid out to be measured and every man to have his just measure and no more.
3. Convenient ways to be laid out on undivided lands.
4. If any of the Proprietors looke at any of said lands more doubtful than the rest, I am willing there should be two divisions, one of that which is thought doubtful and another on that on which is undoubtful; that each proprietor may have his part of both."

It was not accepted. He tried it again in 1683. This time believing that there might be greater strength in numbers he induced Rodolphus Ellms, Israel Cudworth and others to join him, and they sued Israel Chittenden, Stephen Vinal, Jonathan Cudworth and fourteen others of the partners who had voted against Williams' proposed division and blocked it. The suit was for £300. The record † says:—

"all of the aforesaid defendants have been severall times, att severall meetings, desired and pressed soe to doe, not only by the plaintiffes, but alsoe by the honored Court; yet all proveth fruitless and in vaine to the obtaining of soe reasonable and just desire."

The Court was however still timid of taking jurisdiction in the landowning affairs of the partners. The suit was withdrawn.

Far from appealing to or permitting the colony court authority in the settlement of their difficulties, they adjusted them themselves. A committee consisting of Stephen Otis, Benjamin Peirce, Thomas Jenkins, John Barker and John Booth appointed as late as 1714, ordered David Little to remove his stonewall from the highway and gave Benjamin Studley permission (?) to

"change the course of the highway through his land provided said land that said Studley removes said highway to, be not worse in its own nature for a highway than the land was in its own nature, where the

---

† Plymouth Colony Records Vol III page 259.

highway was first laid out; and if it be worse land as aforesaid then said Studley to make it so good at his own proper charge. And all to be done between this day and the last day of October next."

The order provided that Studley should pay the committee seven shillings and sixpence for "their time." Like authority was also given to Nicholas Litchfield.

There was one exception to this refusal of the Conihasset Partners to recognize the jurisdiction of the court of Assistants over their land titles. This was a suit brought by Samuel Clapp and John Cushing, Jr., as agents, on behalf of the town against them. The reason for the submission by the partners to the authority of the court in this case, is probably to be found in the fact that it related to the original title of Hatherly to the whole tract of Conihasset land. It will be remembered that the question of the Hatherly title had been settled upon an award made by Gov. Prence and William Collier in favor of Hatherly's grantees, the Conihasset Partners. This suit, although it related to but five acres of upland near Merritt's Swamp, was an attempt to revive the old controversy and put the title of the entire acreage again in issue. After setting forth the claim of the town, in the quaint pleading of the time, the record goes on to say:

"Both parties by their Agents appeared in Court. The Defendants deny ye things charged in ye writ, claiming the sd land to be their own; and say they will defend their title to ye same. And further say, ye line formerly ran by Mr. Prence and Mr. Collyer is their bounds &c. And disown ye line made by Mr. Paybody in March 1682—

Which case after pleas made and evidences on both sides given in was committed to ye jury who brought in their verdict as followeth, vizt: We find ye line ran by Mr. Prence and Mr. Collyer to be the bounds between Conahasset and Scituate and therefore find for ye Defendants & ye costs of ye suit."

As has been said above, because of the fact that the grant to which they succeeded had originally come directly from the Crown, it is probable that the partners believed that they were invested with something like sovereign power within their prescribed territory. They laid out church lands which were never used for that purpose. This was due perhaps to their fealty to Rev. Mr. Chauncey, one of their number who held the first church together despite the aggressions of Vassall. It also may have been due to a desire to establish a parish of their own. In 1702 and again in 1709 and 1710, the Chauncey-Vassall controversy having long since been forgotten, they appropriated lands for parish purposes, but nothing further than the "lay out" eventuated and the land so appropriated was finally divided among the partners.

Next in importance to the division of the land itself was the laying out of highways over it. The first action is recorded in the following vote:

"Whereas it is supposed that it may be much more beneficial than it can be prejudicial to hang gates thwart the highwayes which passeth through or between men's lands, where the proprietors have not taken up for such highways passing over or between their sd lands, do grante the same. This was voted."

When Hatherly had built his house on the north shore of Musquashcut Pond there was a path or way that lead therefrom in a southerly direction, by little Musquashcut, or Little Pond as it was called, to the Harbor. Another way or path went from Mann Hill westerly over Hooppole neck dividing the marshes and connecting with the Country Road as Main Street was then called and also with the "stepping stones" to "Farm Necke." In 1661 the partners voted that there should be a highway left both for cart and cattle from the Little Pond unto the way that goes to Hooppole Necke upon the undivided land and from the Little pond to the seaside "where the way did formerly lie between 2 slows."

A more or less comprehensive plan for the creation of

highways within and over the tract to connect with those of the town was adopted in 1695. There was one:—

"From Mr. Cushing's Bridge down to the Gulfe, or some other convenient place about the westerly end of the farme neck or great neck.

And from the aforesaid way There be a way laid unto Hooppole neck;

And that the road from Lieut. Buck's unto Bound brook to be continued.

And that there be a highway laid out of said country way somewhere near William Jameses unto the Cedar Swamp or to the town common.

To be built two rods in breadth."

A committee consisting of John Vinal, Sr., Benjamin Peirce, Thomas Jenkins, Stephen Otis, John Peirce and Israel Cousing, was chosen to build.

John Booth early persuaded his partners that a highway was needed over his hill to reach Accord pond. It was called "Booth Hill road," Gannet Street from the intersection of Booth Hill road and the "country way," soon followed to the "stepping stones." On November eighth, 1704 the partners confirmed "all other highways formerly reserved by Mr. Hatherly or the proprietors upon their own propriety. This act was voted by the company." At the same time "the land from John Tilden's, Thomas Jenkins, the new minister's house †, Jonathan Jackson's and Capt. Otis' house lot as the cart path goeth to the landing was "laid out as a highway" and "from William Ticknor's to Stoney Brook, also a highway." These votes and actions did not mean that thereupon roads "two rods in width" were immediately built, over the locations designated. They still remained cartpaths; but they had been lawfully established so far as the Conihasset Partners were concerned and this establishment was deemed necessary and effectual to prevent law suits and vexatious controversies. Indeed,

---

† Rev. Nathaniel Eels, pastor of the Second Church.

it is within the memory of persons now living that in going from the Glades to the stepping stones as late as 1840, it was necessary to 'take down' as many as five pairs of bars; and a daughter of Isaac Collier who lived in the old Collier house, still standing at 'Farm Neck' describes her journey to church in 1800 over the cart path 'between too slows,' at the foot of Mann Hill, and through the Egypt Road to the meeting house.

For twelve years after Hatherly had conveyed the Conihasset tract to the Partners, he kept up a sporadic controversy with the town over what he claimed was the insufficiency of the acreage awarded to him as the successor in title to the London Adventurers. In 1654 the Colony Court passed this order. †

"In regard to sundry contentions and intenglements betwixt Mr. Hatherley and some of the inhabitants of the towne of Scituate, the Court doth grant unto Mr. Hatherley for to satisfy the partners att Conahassett, a certain competencye of land out of the bounds of any particular township, on the westerly side of the town of Scituate aforesaid."

Two years later it described this tract as "beginning at Accord Pond ‡ on the souther side of the line, § and to run three miles southerly towards the Indian Head Pond and to bee layed out three miles square."

It was not until three years thereafter that commissioners

---

† Plymouth Colony Records Vol. III page 52.

‡ There are two traditions as to how this sheet of water obtained its name–one to the effect that when the commissioners from the two colonies finally fixed the boundary line between the two patents, they were in accord as to the pond being a monument of that boundary. The other, that it served as a northeast corner boundary of the land that had been awarded Hatherly in "accord and satisfaction" of his demand for more land in Scituate. Either may be right. Both may be wrong. The curious reader is left to his election.

§ The boundary line between the colonies of Plymouth and Massachusetts Bay.

were appointed to lay it out. John Alden and William Bradford were then appointed by the Court, to "join with such as Mr. Hatherley shall procure," but they did not act. In 1662 Lieutenant Torrey, Cornett Studson and .Mr Joseph Tilden were "appointed by the Court to lay out the tract of land granted to Mr. Hatherley above Scituate, according to the graunt, viz: to begine att the southermost end of Accord Pond and to goe noe further northerly least it entranch upon the Bay Line." For some unexplained reason these gentlemen likewise did not act. It could not have been that they were unacceptable to Hatherly for Torrey and Tilden were both Conihasset partners and the latter was his step-son and beneficiary. Whatever the cause of their inaction, it is the fact that the next year Torrey, John Bryant and William Barstow were appointed to perform the service. Their report follows:—

"Wee, James Torrey, and William Barstow, and John Bryant, being appoynted by the Court to lay out a tract of land granted to Mr. Hatherley by Accord Pond, which parcells of land was to bee layed out three mile square on the head line of the towne of Scituate, wee, James Torrey and William Barstow, attending to our order for the time and place appointed, have measured the aforesaid land, which begines att the utmost southerly part of Accord Pond, and runs west on a third part of a point Southerly three miles, then turning with a square line south and a third part of a point easterly to the end of three miles, then turning with another square line east and a third part of a point northerly three miles, then turning with another square line north and a third part of a point westerly in the headline of the township of Scituate three miles, which said line ends att Accord Pond, att the place where it began. †

per me, JAMES TORREY,

WILLIAM BARSTOW."

This being accomplished, the land was divided into ninety-two shares of which Hatherly retained twelve. He soon however acquired two shares from John Williams, Jr., one share each from Rev. Charles Chauncey, John Damon, Edward Jenkins, Rodolphus Ellms, Mr. Tarte and John Hoar; one and one-half shares each from Isaac Chittenden, Samuel House and Samuel Jackson.

At about this time "sundry of the towne of Hingham appiered" at Court, says the Colony Record, "and desired to buy a parcell or tract of land of the countrey lying betwixt the Bay Line and Accord Pond and the land granted to Mr. Hatherley; and the Court declared themselves willing to sell it, and pitched a prise and refered the agreement to the Treasurer in the countreyes behalf." These 'sundry of the town of Hingham' were probably John Thaxter, John Jacob, Matthew Cushing and Edward Wilder for on December 1664 Hatherley sold the twenty-three shares which he had acquired as set forth above to these gentlemen and John Otis of Scituate.

In other pages of this chronicle it is stated that the Scituate forefathers were particular in extinguishing the Indian title to the lands upon which the township was founded. The Conihasset partners were not behind them in this particular. When the Court granted the "three miles square" to Hatherly, Josiah Wampatuck "came into the Court and owned that the three miles square of land by Accord Pond, which was graunted by the Court to Mr.

---

† This three square miles was a part of a locality called afterward "Foardes Farms." On the incorporation of the town of Abington it was set off from Scituate and included in the limits of that town. It is now in Rockland and has a Post Office which perpetuates the Hatherly name.

Hatherley, that hee hath sold it to Mr. Hatherley and is by him fully satisfyed for it" †. In 1686, a suggestion having arisen that young Josiah son of the above claimed it, the partners paid him eighteen pounds and received this deed ‡.

To all Christian People to whom these presents shall come Josiah Wampatucke, son & heir of Josiah Wampatucke Indian deceased Sachem in New England sendeith Greeting— Know ye that the foresd Josiah Wampatucke for and in consideration of eighteen pounds in current money of New England paid unto ye foresd Josiah Wampatucke & his father by yer former proprietors of Coney Hasset and now by Capt. Jno. Williams all of Scituate in ye Colony of New Plymouth in New England, the contents whereof being fully satisfied contented & paid the sd Josiah Wampatucke doth hereby acknowledge himself fully satisfied & paid and of all and every parcel thereof doth clearly acquit exonerate and discharge the sd purchasers and Captain Williams and every of ye heirs forever by these presents, doth clearly and fully and absolutely give grant bargain sell alien infeoffe & confirm unto ye sd Capt. Jno. Williams and his heirs for ye proper use and behoof and for the purchasers of ye sd Coney hasset and their heirs forever, all ye sd Coney hasset land according to ye Records of Plymouth concerning sd land and deed given by Mr. Timothy Hatherly to the Purchasers of the sd Coney hasset land as may appear by a deed under the sd Timothy Hatherley's hand & seal bearing date the first of December 1646; together with all woods, trees & rocks ponds rivers swamps meadows and all appurtenances and privileges thereunto belonging whatsoever and all profits thence to be had made or raised. And also all his right title interest possession claim propriety in or to the above sd bargained tract of land or any part of parcel thereof. To have & to hold and peaceably to enjoy all the said tract of land

---
† Plymouth Colony Records Vol IV page 185.
‡ Conihasset Records page 486.

with all the appurtenances thereof bounded as aforesd; and to the sale and proper use and behoof of ye sd Capt. John Williams and the purchasers of ye sd Coney hasset land as aforesaid & to every of ye heirs forever. And ye sd Josiah Wampatucke doth for himself his heirs exors admrs & assigns covenant promise and grant by these presents that the sd Capt. Jn. Williams and sd purchasers shall & may by virtue hereof from time to time and forever hereafter enjoy and possess all ye sd premises without any molestation or limitation whatsoever by any such person or persons. And doth hereby engage and promise to keep harmless and warrant and defend ye sd Capt. John Williams and purchasers from all former bargains sales titles & incumbrances, had made committed or done or suffered to be done whatsoever. And further doth hereby acknowledge that he hath given full possession of all ye above sd prems that are contained in this instrument and doth promise to do any further act or acts for ye perfecting of assurance unto ye sd Capt. Williams and sd Purchasers as the law do or may require   In witness whereof ye sd Josiah Wampatucke hath hereunto set his hand and seal this twenty-third day of February Ano Dom one thousand six hundred eighty & 6-7 Anno qi Regui Regis Jacobi, Secundi Secundo.

Signed sealed and delivered
in presnece of us Testes
this the marke of
   x
frances Garnet
  John F. Thrasher
  Nathainel N. Johnson
  Nathanaill Johnson

this is the marke of
   x
Josiah Wampatucke

Josiah Wampatucke whose name is above mentioned coming before me the 15 June 1687 did freely own the above written instrument to be his act and deed. William Bradford one of his Majesties Counsel for this territory of New England.

Roxbury March 6, 1686. Francis Garnert & Nathanaell Johnson made oath that they were present upon ye day of ye date of these presents & saw Josiah Wampatuck sign, seal & deliver this instrit as his act & deed & gave possession accordingly.

Before J. Dudley

By the year 1719 most of the lands had been divided. On March fifteenth at a meeting over which John Barker presided as moderator, he, with Capt. Benjamin Peirce and Captain Stephen Otis were chosen to "Lay out what is omitted." Before long this was accomplished but the meetings and records of the partners did not thereupon cease. Both were kept up until 1767 when the last meeting was held, the records closed and the partnership that was not a corporation "made to die," became defunct.

CHAPTER VI

DIVISION OF STATE AND CHURCH

"I tell you, sir, there are two kings and two kingdoms in Scotland. There is Christ Jesus the King and his kingdom the Kirk, whose subject James VI is, and of whose kingdom, not a king, nor a lord nor a head; but a member. And that whom Christ hath called to watch over his Kirk and govern his spiritual kingdom have sufficient power and authority so to do both together and severally."

Andrew Melville to King James the Sixth †

THE words of the Puritan preacher above quoted exemplify the theory of the forefathers concerning the attitude of church and state toward each other. They go further; they state the exact belief of the Puritan as to his own standing, as one "whom Christ hath called to watch over his Kirk and govern his spiritual Kingdom." He was one of "the Lord's people;" a people dedicated to Him by solemn covenant, and whose end as a nation was to carry out His will. For such an end it was needful that rulers, as well as people should be 'godly men.' ‡ That this belief was paramount when the new home on these shores was reached is proven by the qualifications which were prescribed for being a "freeman." He must be "a church member, orthodox in his religion and not vicious in his life," and only those who were "orthodox in their judgment concerning the main points of Christian religion as they have been held forth and acknowledged by the generality of the Protestant orthodox writers," had full liberty to gather themselves into a

---

† Green—History of the English people (1890) page 523.
‡ Ibidem, page 606.

church estate. It may be readily assumed therefore that Cobb, Annable and Kendrick who were permitted to withdraw from the church at Plymouth "in case they join in a body at Scituate," were men possessing all of these qualifications. On November 23, 1634 when this "leave" was granted all of the men named had been admitted freemen, George Lewis the other person was "made free and sworne" a little more than a year later. They first met at the house of James Cudworth, it being the largest, but they soon erected a meeting-house on the top of the hill back of Kent Street and named the approach to it Meeting House Lane.

The building itself was probably not unlike that at Plymouth—built of logs, the interstices filled with clay, the light admitted through windows glazed with oiled paper † the thatched roof of flags taken from the marshes and the whole without chimney or other means for heat. Thus it stood for forty-four years. In it, prior to the coming of Rev. John Lothrop, it is said that Giles Sexton or Saxton who had come to Boston from Yorkshire, been admitted a freeman in Massachusetts Bay in 1631 and thence taken up a residence in Scituate, preached for three years. This is purely tradition, however. An exhaustive examination of church, colony and town records does not disclose him as living here at all. Mather ‡ speaks of his removal "from Scituate, first to Boston and so unto England, in his reduced age, because of "the unsettled condition of the Colony, and some unhappy contention in the plantation where he lived." Whether this "unhappy contention" was the discussion going on between Rev. Charles Chauncey and Mr. Vassall, § or the controversy over land titles between the freemen of

---

† Edward Winslow writing on the eleventh day of December 1621 to a friend in England who intended to come to Plymouth said:—"bring Paper and Linced oyle for your Windows and Cotton yarne for your Lamps."
‡ Magnalia 1 page 536.
§ Deane's History of Scituate, 167.

the town, and Hatherly and his Conihasset partners, does not matter. The former did not arise until 1640, and the latter did not become prominent until after the incorporation in 1636. It was certainly not because of either that Saxton ceased his ministrations over the community on Kent Street which were active from 1631 to 1634, if they ever existed at all.

Rev. John Lothrop's coming to Scituate in September 1634 followed his release from a London jail, where he had been imprisoned for two years. This freedom was gained on condition that he emigrate. His incarceration had resulted from the same persecution which sent Rev. John Robinson and his congregation to Leyden. Lothrop was originally a member of the Church of England, ordained as one of its ministers and settled over a congregation at Egerton in Kent. He had become convinced against the "superstitious usages" of the church; had rejected its ceremonies as relics of idolatry and with a desire for the reform in the Liturgy, the abandonment of the use of the surplice, the sign of the cross in baptism, and other outward ceremonials and forms, he had joined hands with the Puritans. He came to London and for eight years clandestinely cared for the religious welfare of his fellow worshippers at Blackfriars. He was apprehended in the Spring of 1632 and cast into prison with a number of his congregation. Coming to Scituate, either with him or at about the time of his arrival were William Vassall, Elder Thomas King, Deacon Thomas Besbeach or Bisby, Thomas Lapham, Henry Rowley and Isaac Robinson, the son of the great Puritan founder. With those already here they formed the first church and Mr. Lothrop was "called to office" as their minister. It must unhappily be recorded that having found here "freedom to worship God" they nevertheless proceeded to quarrel among themselves, largely over the question of baptism. Mr. Lothrop had had a similar controversy in his church while he was pastor in London, and the dispute as to whether baptism should be by total immersion or mere laying on of hands, became rife—this time among his parishioners in the new land.

This spirit of contention sorely troubled the amiable pastor. He wrote to Governor Prence at Plymouth seeking for the latter's good offices in obtaining for himself, Annable, Cudworth, Gilson, Rowley and others a new location for the "seatinge of a township for a congregation," and on January 22, 1638, a grant of a plantation at "Scippekann" (Rochester) was made to them by the General Court. † These local separatists did not, however, accept this location. They went the next year to Barnstable.

This defection left the church at Scituate without a head. It turned to Plymouth for assistance. There was living in Plymouth at the time Charles Chauncy who was associated in the ministry there with Mr. Rayner. He had been graduated at Cambridge in 1613 at the age of twenty; had begun a clerical life at Marston Street, Lawrence, and held the vicarage of Ware from 1627 to 1634. ‡ He was driven from this position in the church by Archbishop Laud for the same reason—non conformity—that had sent Lothrop. from his pastorate at Egerton, and in December 1637 he came to Plymouth. With him came a wife and four children. He was granted § ten acres of "meddowing in the North Meddow by Joanes River" ¶ He remained until the call came to him from Scituate in 1640.

Mr. Chauncey was a scholar, a theologian and skilled in law and medicine as well. After his graduation at Cambridge he had been a professor of Greek there and just before his induction into the ministry, a professor of Hebrew. He was a master at apt expression, resourceful in argument, but impatient of opposition. His advent as

---

† Plymouth Colony Records, Vol I, page 104.
‡ Davis' Ancient Landmarks of Plymouth, page 96.
§ Plymouth Colony Records, Vol. I, page 166.
¶ In Kingston.

the pastor of the church at Scituate found a ready opportunity for the indulgence of these qualities. The church as it existed under Mr. Lothrop for five years, had about evenly divided, one half going with him to Barnstable, the other with Timothy Hatherly at their head remaining here.

It was not long before it became apparent that the persons constituting this remaining half were not entirely in accord. The call to Mr. Chauncy was not unanimous. William Vassall, Elder King, Thomas Lapham ,John Twisden, who had been admitted a freeman in 1639, Sara the wife of Elder King, Judith the daughter of William Vassall and Anna Stockbridge refused to join in the call. They declined to enter upon a new covenant into which they were asked to join by those who had called Mr. Chauncey and declared that they were a church in themselves; they insisted that "by the gracious assistance of Christ, (we) will walke in all the ways of God that are and shall be revealed to us out of His word, to be his ways, so farre as God shall enable us. And to this end, we will do our best to procure and maintaine all such officers as are needful, whereby we may enjoy all His ordinances, for the good of the souls of us and ours; and we shall not refuse into our society such of God's people whose hearts God shall incline to joyne themselves unto us, for the furtherance of the worship of God amongst us, and the good of their souls." Further, they entered a covenant and declaration upon the church record as follows:

"Whereas, since the Covenant above written was made, we have met with many oppositions from Mr. Chauncy and the rest of the church with him, and that at the last meeting of the Elders in the Bay, and this present, it was their judgments that from the tyme that they denied communion with us we were free from them, that their advice to us was, to renew our former Covenant in a publicke manner, which we are contented to do in convenient tyme; yet nevertheless we hope that all the Churches of Christ that shall take notice of our Covenant will acknowledge us to be a true

Church of Christ, and hold commuinon with us the mean tyme; and whereas there was great desire of the Elders manifested that we should divide the Town and become two Towns, as well as two Churches, some alleging that we must give way to let the other church have the larger boundes, because they were the ancient Church.

We answer—that neither in respect of inhabitants in the Town, not yet in respect of Church state in this place, is there much difference, not above two or three men; for when Mr. Lothrop the first Pastor left us, insomuch that of seven male members left by the church that went, we were three.

"2. In regard that they cast us off wrongfully, they ought to be contented that we should be at least equal with them, in the division of lands and commons; although, indeed, the lands are mostly divided already.

"3rd. Whereas some have thought fitting that their towne should come three miles from their Meeting house toward us, we say that such a division would take in all our houses into their towne (nearly) or if they leave us that little necke of land that some of us dwell upon, that is but one hundred rods broad of planting land, and their towne would goe behind our houses and cut us off from fire wood and commons for cattle, for a mile and a half beyond our houses; And therefore the Governor's motion was most equal 'that we should set our Meeting-house a mile further from theirs, so that the members of each church would draw themselves to dwell as neare to each Meeting-house as they can, and the Town need not be divided.'

"Lastly. If that it were needful to divide the town, it were most fitting for them to set their Meeting-house a mile further from us, towards their farms and hay grounds, and then they may use those lands that now they cannot conveniently doe, and so have convenient room to receive more inhabitants and members, and that is the only way to give maintenance to their officers and enlarge themselves."†

Thus it will be seen that Vassall, King and Lapham were, in part, actuated by other than spiritual motives in their quarrel with those who were left after the departure of Mr. Lothrop to Barnstable. The first named was clearly the leader in the controversy. It will be recalled that at this time (1642) his differences with his neighbors at the harbor had been settled by the decree of the Court of June 3, 1639. This order granted him a parcel of land to lie in the form of a long square, containing with marsh, one hundred and fifty acres. It is apparent that he was still dissatisfied. Failing in his fight with Hatherly, Turner and the rest, he shrewdly tacked this matter of a greater plantation on to the doctrinal controversy, joining Elder King, who lived near him, in the hope of getting a "division of lands and commons" which "should be at least equal to them," in which he, King and Lapham should solely participate. It may be that this view of his motive does him an injustice. The evidence, however, is against him. It appears singular from a view-point of two hundred and fifty years that this little handful of men who had undergone hardships on account of their religious beliefs, who were then living isolated lives, should divide themselves not once, but twice over a question purely of form in religious worship, and battle for a greater isolation. The dispute affords an insight into the Puritan character which serves to efface that part of the picture, which has been more or less popularly drawn of them, as men to be idolized.

Chauncy, with whom were the other four men, remnants of the Church, "left by the Church that went," was not slow in picking up the cudgel in behalf of his loyal supporters. He addressed letters to the elders of the churches in Boston, Roxbury, Plymouth and elsewhere in the two colonies. The contest so far as he was concerned was less one of the establishment of a new township of consequential area, than

---

† Deane's History of Scituate, page 61.

"that the name of God and his doctrine be not blasphemed" by this unfortunate division and contention. Replying to the declaration above quoted, in a letter to the elders of the church at Roxbury, which at that time was in charge of Reverend John Elliot the apostle to the Indians he said:

"Now that because other things have fallen out amongst us, that so serve to lay some blemish upon us, we have thought fit to acquaint you and other churches with them.   x   x   x   x

Upon Mr. Lothrop and his brethren's resolution to depart from this to Barnstable, there was a day of humiliation kept at Mr. Hatherly's house, by the rest of the brethren that purposed to stay at Scituate, and as some of them do constantly affirm they entered into Covenant with God and Christ and with one another, to walke together in the whole revealed will of God and Christ.

This meeting the four above named persons account to be the beginning of their Church, and yet two of them (by name William Vassall and John Twisden) were absent from it, and the other two (Thomas Lapham and Thomas King) tho' they were present, yet since, before many witnesses, have resolutely denied that themselves expressed any covenant by word of mouth; but however, they say they made an implicit Covenant, which they judge sufficient to constitute a true Church, whilst we do not, and therefore could not hold communion with them upon any such ground.

Besides, though they have of late renewed Covenant together, yet we judge that it was done surreptitiously without any notice given to our Church beforehand, who had just exception against some of their members that renewed it.   x   x   x   x

Also, (we hear) it was done irreligiously without fasting or prayer needful for so greate a business.

Besides, we cannot excuse the meeting from being factious there being already a Church gathered; and we have offered them several tymes, that in case we saw cause, they might joyne with us, which they still refused.   x   x   x   x

And these things we desire you, as you have opportunity, to acquaint at least the elders of our neighbor Churches withal, that neither yourselves nor they may have communion defiled by any of them offering to communicate with you."

The request in this letter that the elders of the neighboring churches be acquainted with Mr. Chauncy's version, provided the occasion for Vassall likewise to address them. He sent many letters. He was obsessed of a town division; of a still larger grant of land, and in these communications he continually joined the two issues. The Conihasset grant to Hatherly disturbed him no less than his aversion to Mr. Chauncy. Here are excerpts from a letter written by him to Rev. John Wilson at Boston.   x   x   x   x:—

"but the truth is that before we came hither, which is more than seven years since, the old Church were at difference about moving the Meeting-house toward that end of the Town where our hay grounds and most of our lands lie, it being set, for Mr. Hatherly's ease, at the very outside of our plantation; Mr. Hatherly and some of London, having by estimation eight if not ten thousand acres of land beginning very near our Meeting-house, in which Mr. Hatherly makes farms, one of which is three miles northward from the Meeting-house, and our lands lie ten miles or more to the southward, by which runneth a faire River, † navigable for boats ten miles, and hay grounds on both sides, and hath an outlet into the sea about four miles from the Meeting-house, with lands sufficient for a Towneship to settle upon; by that river lieth most of our land, and there is little hay ground near the Meeting-house, but east and west remote from it, lieth good store; so that if all other differences were reconciled, yet it were the

---

† The North River.

undoing of us and them both, if we do not become two congregations, and take in more to them and us."

The matter was referred to the Elders of both Plymouth and Massachusetts Bay. Even their good offices failed to effect a reconciliation. After further trouble, this time with the church at Duxbury over the dismissal of William Witherell from that society for the purpose of effecting his pastorate over the Vassall faction at Scituate, the four antagonists of Mr. Chauncy gathered into a church estate and Mr. Witherell was inducted into office as their minister. They built a church (necessarily a small structure) on the road near "King's Landing" † and established a burial ground near it.

The dissensions were kept up. The discussion was acrimonious and the feeling intense, especially between Chauncy and Vassall. Mr. Witherell does not seem to have publicly joined in the squabble—certainly later on, his efforts were for peace. For six years, not only the two societies, but the town itself and the two colonies, saw this unfortunate condition continue and were necessarily drawn, more or less into it. In 1646 Mr. Vassall went to England. ‡ Upon his departure Mr. Chauncy became less bitter and in 1654, he himself left Scituate upon the invitation of the overseers of Harvard College to be its president. He died in that office after serving seventeen years.

Mr. Chauncy was succeeded by Henry Dunster, who had been his immediate predecessor as the head of the college at Cambridge. Like Mr. Chauncy he was one of the learned men in New England. Besides the good name which he had earned as president of The College, he had become well known for his work with Richard Lyon in revising the New England version (1640) of "The Psalms ,Hymns and Spiritual Songs of the Old and New Testament, Faithfully Translated into English Meeter." He came to Scituate, not as an ordained preacher of the gospel, but as a "teacher,"

---

† On North River near the present Union bridge in Norwell.
‡ Winthrop, Vol. II, page 321.

"THE OLD SLOOP"—THE UNITARIAN CHURCH,
Scituate Center, Burned July 4th, 1879. From
a drawing by unknown artist.

an office in the church provided by the Congregational churches of the time. He continued to act in this capacity until his death in Scituate in 1659. Just before this occurred the colony was in a state of upheaval over the presence of the Quakers in its midst and their activities in denouncing the religious doctrines which the forefathers had come here to establish. Unlike the majority of his fellow Congregationalists Dunster was extremely tolerant of the Quakers. James Cudworth, at the time he was being ostracised for his attitude toward the sect wrote of him, "Through mercy, we have yet among us, the worthy Mr. Dunster, whom the Lord hath made boldly to bear testimony against the spirit of persecution."†

Following him, Nicholas Baker of Hingham came to the first church and was ordained here in 1660. Through his amiable efforts, coupled with those of Mr. Witherell, pastor of the second church or "South Society," or "Church up the River" as it was variously called, the feud which had existed for years between the two congregations was settled and the members participated together in that communion which according to Chauncy, the Witherell followers had defiled. They did not, however, amalgamate the societies. The town generally was in favor of such action ‡, but the General Court at Plymouth, which had been appealed to, did not advise it. §

---

† Baylies on the other hand says that "his dislike and hatred of the Quakers was unrelenting and vindicative. Memoires of Plymouth Colony, Vol. I, page 50.
‡ Scituate Town Records, Vol. VI.
§ "At the Court of his Majesties holden att Plymouth, for the Jurisdiction of New Plymouth, the first of November 1679.

In answare to the petition of several of our brethren and naighbours residing att the North River in Scittuate bearing date October 1679, as followeth:—

Beloved Brethren and Naighbours: Wee, haveing seriously as our opportunity would permit, amidse (amidst) our many and pressing occations, considered of the declaration of youer minds, and reasons annexed in youer said petition, desire to be sensible of

It is apparent from the language of the Court's communication that the members of the South Society looked to profit by such a union materially, as well as spiritually. Their church building was in a state of decay. Their pastor was old and they were compelled to appoint an assistant

your present state, which is as you say, sadly desolate, as concerning the uniteing of the two societies together; wee looke att it (in itselfe considered) to be the best expedient for the obtaining of mutuall strength in the wayes of God, in communication of the gifts and graces of his Holy Spirit, for generall and speciall welfare of all, and for the support of ministerial administrations. Notwithstanding, wee conceive, by reason of remote distance of place and other considerations, that if it were effected it would not have a tendencye to the effecting of the ends proposed to induce unto the same, but rather the contrary; and therefore our advice is to a continuance in two distinct bodyes, retaining a brotherly affection each to other, and indeavoring to promote the good of each other what you can, as many years you have don; and as for and in reference unto such of the society of youer end of the towne whoe have lately repaired to the other congregation to heare the word of God, wee see no reason to blame them for so doing, considering the defisiensye of youer reverend pastour (Mr. Witherell, then in his eightieth year) by reason of age, and other infeirmities thereof, as you say, and the able despensation of the words by the other, yett, notwithstanding wee advise and desire that such would looke backe with a single eye to the societie of which particularly they are, so as to put forth theire best and streniouse indeavors for the promoteing of theire sperituall good and edification, both in seeking unto God for help in the minnestry of his word, and otherwise for the obtaining of soe great a favor; and whereas wee are informed that youer meeting house is fallen much to decay, wee require you, (according to order of Court) that you all, both those above last mensioned, with theire brethen and naighbours, doe mutually joyne together in the erecting of another, such an one as may be a fitt and meet place for you to meet in together to worship; and for as much as we understand that there are different apprehensions amongst you in reference unto contributing or collecting the charge thereof, and the place whereon to erect it, wee have appointed a committee viz, Elder Kinge, Cornett Robert Studson, John Bryant, Sen'r, and John Turner, Sen'r., these four or any three of them, acte in those affaires whoe wee hope will determine therein so as tend to youer mutuall good. Thuse hartily desiring youer present and future happiness, we commend you and all youer piouse concernes to the wise guidance and direction of our Good God. Restng, &c.

Wee have appointed and impowered another committee, viz. our honored Governor (Josiah Winslow), Mr. Hinckley, Major Bradford, Mr. Arnold, Mr. Cotton and Mr. Wiswell, to acte and determine in reference to the premises as they shall see reason, upon hearing of the case or cases respecting the same."

—Mr. Mighill—to aid him. It would have been quite to their advantage if they could have been assisted in erecting a new church by the congregation at the Harbor and that edifice placed "at Walter Woodworth's hill, or the center of the present inhabitants of the Town." † The conclusion of the Court does not appear to have been illy founded. Each society had a goodly number of members. Cudworth and some of those who had gone to Barnstable with Mr. Lothrop had returned and rejoined the first church, whose membership had been further augemented by the Tildens, Vinals, Damons, Briggs and Litchfields. To the second church had been added the families of Hatch, Stockbridge, Torrey, Stetson, Clapp and Barstow.

The matter of the maintenance of the church, which was accomplished by the imposition and collection of rates or taxes, probably also entered into the conclusions of the Court. These rates were assessed by committees chosen by the town and not by the parish:—

"Nov. 1, 1667. Thomas King, Isaac Chittenden and Isaac Buck were chosen ratirs to make a rate for the maintenance of the ministers. They put the rate at £107 s. 10, payable to Mr. Baker 57 £ 10 s: and to Mr. Witherell £50 payable the one half in corne and the other half in clothing, provisions or cattle."

A vigorous protest was entered by the members through a petition ‡ from John Bailey and twenty-six others who objected to being "rated for the erection and maintenance of a church in which they did not worship:—

To The Honorable General Court now assembled at Plymouth, June 1680. *Humbly Showeth, etc.*

That we whose names are here underwritten, being inhab-

---

† Vote of October 24, 1679, Scituate Town Records, Vol. VI.
‡ Mass. Hist. Soc. Coll. (Fourth Series) Hinckley Papers, Vol. V, page 38.

itants of the town of Scituate and members of this Commonwealth, cannot but acknowledge it as to be our great privilege to enjoy, so to be our bond and duty to support and uphold, the present government under which we live, by all due means; acknowledging it to be the great and underserved favor of our gracious God to us, that our judges may proceed of ourselves, and that strangers rule not over us; and that we have such fundamental law and constitutions, so carefully revised and so essentially good, and suitable to the well-being of this Commonwealth, that they ought to be, as they are declared, for ever preserved unviolable; so that, although succeeding laws and orders, through change of time and choice of psons may infringe upon the due liberty of the subject; and if the judges themselves (though the best of men), yet being but men, may through ignorance or mistake err in the dispensation of justice, as holy records gives us examples of for our instruction,—yet those just constitutions, the defense of our due liberties, may recover the subject's rights, whom the law says shall not be damnified in any respect, through color of law or countenance of authority, without legal conviction by due process. The consideration of the above-written premises, duly weighed, both doth embolden and encourage us to present our grievances to this Honored Court, who are yet unconcerned in the grounds of our present complaint; and, having no Court of Appeal nor higher power within our jurisdiction, we crave your serious consideration and application to our redress as the Lord shall direct in a case of so great moment, not only, as to our own particular who take ourselves to be greatly wronged and oppressed, but also, and that more especially, as it hath so deep an influence into the general liberties of the whole inhabitants of this jurisdiction; the case of each plantation in this Colony being, or liable to be, parallel with ours, who have our own goods liable to be taken from us, as delinquents, for not performing a duty, who were never yet convicted by any law of God or man of any duty incumbent upon us to do the thing required of us to that purpose, in reference to the building a new meetinghouse in o (ur) town, as appears enjoined by an order of Court bearing date October, 1679; it being, as we conceive, so directly contrary to the due liberties of our town, who, with the concurrence of the churches, preferred their minds to the Honored Court at March last past; so that if there were either law or reason for the merit of the case, as it is required, which we cannot apprehend of, yet it could not appertain to us, the most of whom never appertained to that society, but do judge that we are, according to the rule both of law and gospel, in a regular way for the maintaining the worship of God Without any such forcible means as is uncomfortable for us to yield to. But yet further; suppose it should be imagined that the towns have not a regular power within themselves to order their own prudential matters, which the law allows them, and that this were a just injunction laid upon us so to act in and with that society; yet could it be in reason denied us, as here it is, our own free vote and approbation in our own concerns, but must be as children under age, under tutor, only to be appointed what to do, on which account, there has been such unusual austerity used about this rate as we have not been exercised with before. Our case being thus dubious and difficult, finding no rule nor reason quietly to submit to it, and seeing ourselves barred of all usual methods of law for any trial by due process, doe yet further crave of this Honored Court some satisfaction, either by your own determination as it may stand with the general interest of the Colony, or by making way for our due Process in the premises, and for your help and direction therein. We earnestly implore the guidance of His good Spirit in whose hand is our breath and all our ways; and so rest your humble petitioners,

John Bayley	John Barstow
Daniel Staycy	Jonathan Jackson
Thomas Pinchin, Sen.	Jonathan Cudworth

John Curtis
Josiah Palmer
Zachariah Dimmon
Henry Chittenden
Anthony Dodson
Benjamin Pirce
Peter Worthylake
Samuel Holbrook
John Booth
John Allin
Thomas Wood
Nathaniel Turner

Joseph White
Benjamin Woodwarth
John Buck, Sen.
Steven Vinall
Daniel Daman
Matthew Gannet
Peter Collimore
William x Randall, Sen. (His mark)
Joseph Woodwarth

(*In the above signatures, the original orthography is retained.*)

When the court, therefore, undertook to settle the differences between the two congregations, the making of a rate by a committee of the town was changed (at least so far as the second society was concerned), by the following order:

"Plymouth the 29 October, 1680

Whereas the Generall Court incurraged and ordered the church and society att the North River, att Scituate, to erect a new meeting house for the worship of God, and sett the bounds how farr they should rate for the defraying the charges thereof, namely, upon all the inhabitants thereof from the mill brooke upwards further explained by the Court and declared to be their full intent and purpose that the said order should be observed, with this proviso namely, that the particular persons heer named, that live above the mill brooke, namely Jeremiah Hatch, Thomas Hatch, Thomas Palmer, Samuel Clapp, being of the lower societie, should be exempted out of the said rate; and that these persons heer named who live below the mill brooke namely, Mistris Elizabeth Tildin, Richard Curtice, John Turner, Charles Stockbridge should be put into the said rate; this Court doth declare and rattify this theire said acte, and doe require and expect, that according to this rule, the rate be made and collected by the congregation and societie up the river for finishing the meetinghouse, and for the maintenance of the minestry, and all necessarie charges for incurragement and support of the worke of God amongst them; and this Court doth promise and resolve, according to theire power and interest, to strengthen the hands of that church and societie in theire due attendance to this order."

The meeting house was built on the site of the one it replaced. It could have been neither commodious nor substantial, however, for, twenty-six years later a new building was erected upon common lands of the town. † This was a frame structure "fifty feet in length and forty in breadth, and twenty feet between joints and a flat roof of about ten feet rise." ‡

The first society meanwhile was worshipping in the building in Meeting House Lane. This structure, too, had become out of repair and unfitted to the use of the increased congregation. After Mr. Baker's death in 1678 it was razed and replaced by a new one of much the same construction, on the same site. It is interesting to note how nearly contemporaneous were the apparent necessities for new houses of worship by the two societies. While the south parish was occupying its new house erected on the common land, the first society on October 1, 1707 "voted to build a new meeting house upon the same part of the meeting house hill, not to be farther west than where the ways meet below Lieut. Buck's shop;" that the cost "should not exceed £300 with the old meeting house." It contained pews but was not plastered or otherwise substantial. In twenty years it stood so in need of repairs that in 1729

---

† "May 28, 1707. Voted liberty to the South Parish to set up their Meeting-house at or near the place where it is now framed, upon the Town Common, and to use of their common land, a conveniency for a burying place, and also for building a stable or stables."

‡ Deane's History of Scituate, page 37.

it was voted "to take down the said house and remove it to a certain piece or gore of land betwixt two highways, which two highways open from that which goeth by Balch's toward Cohasset, the one by James Cudworth's house, the other by John Otis's which piece of land is the N. W. part of a 20 acre lot, and since exchanged by the town; provided sd gore or land can be obtained."

The gore of land was easily "obtained" but the removal was not to be as readily effected. David Jacob and others objecting to the rebuilding, addressed the General Court setting forth that there was no need of the new structure as the present edifice was "a very commodious House & in a manner new" and that it was proposed to "set it up" in "a Place very inconvenient for the Generality of the People, that the vote upon which they proceed was obtained in a very unfair and illegal manner and passed against the sense of the most substantial People." An order was passed April 8, 1731 by this body enjoining the removal of the Meeting house until the May session and appointing a committee of five of its own members to examine into the situation. This committee reported on June seventeenth that the house should not be removed "from the Place where it now stands for the space of seven years next coming" and that in the meantime the necessary repairs of said house be effected at the charge of the precinct."

Notwithstanding this order the work of tearing down the old structure continued and in August of the same year Deacon Jacob and the other remonstrants again addressed the Legislature through this petition:—

> "shewing that in defiance of the Order of this Court forbidding the removal of their Meeting House, divers persons of said precinct have violently broke into said Meeting house & have erased & demolished it praying that this Court would interpose their authority for punishing those that have disobeyed their Orders, & also direct that satisfaction be made to the aggrieved petitioners."

A committee consisting of Councillor Palmer and Representatives Lewis of Boston, Shore of Dighton, Bourn of Sandwich and Goddard of Framingham was appointed "to examine into the matters complained of and consider and report as soon as may be what is proper for the Court to do in the Affair."

The matter was deemed of sufficient importance to result in a report by this committee only four days later. It is here given in full:—†

"Whereas it appears &c

"The Committee having viewed the Precinct & considsidered the Pleas & Allegations of the Parties relating to the Meeting house, are of Opinion that the Meeting House remain where it now stands until June 1737, & then the same be removed from thence about one mile & a quarter Westward to the Place where the Inhabitants of the said Precinct voted to remove the same Mar. 17. 1729; & in the mean time the necessary repairs of the said house be effected & the Cost thereof with all other Charges that have arisen on account of this Controversy relating to the said Meeting house be paid by the Precinct aforesaid."

Nothing eventuated from this report, for the Legislature adjourned to September twenty-second, on the same day that it was made. The next year, however, David Little who was one of the persistent advocates of a relocation and rebuilding with others of the parishioners who agreed with him, petitioned the Legislature "setting forth the unhappy circumstances of the said Precinct" by reason of the order prohibiting the removal and asking for a revocation of the order against it. Another committee was chosen on which served Oxenbridge Thacher, Esq., of Boston, afterward the brilliant leader of the Massachusetts Bar.

This committee took its time, went into the matter thoroughly, and did not make recommendation until the spring of 1733. It reported as being of the opinion:

† Province Laws 1733-34. Chapter 171 Vol. XI.

"that the Meeting house remain where it now stands until June 1737 and then the same be removed from thence about one mile and a quarter Westward to the place where the Inhabitants of the said Precinct voted to remove the same March 17, 1729; & in the meantime the necessary repairs of the said house to be effected & the Cost thereof, with all other charges that have arisen on account of this controversy relating to the said Meeting house be paid by the Precinct aforesaid."

This settled the controversy. In the designated year a new edifice was built upon the gore of land and Deacon Little and his fellow parishioners prayed the more unctiously.

The new structure was not to be of much greater life than its predecessor on Meeting House Lane. In 1769 it was again "voted to build a new meeting house" which "should be 67 feet by 50." Its location was fixed at this meeting— "that the house should be set on the top of the hill in Mr. Daniel Jenkin's pasture." This site, however was not agreeable to all of the parishioners. Indeed, it was not definitely chosen until arbitrators, (Benjamin Lincoln of Hingham, Robert Bradford of Kingston and James Humphries of Weymouth) fixed it as the most desirable location. The building itself was completed and occupied in the latter part of 1774. Deane, in whose time (1831) it was standing, says that "It had a spire at the westerly end and a portico at the easterly end. It is a building of just proportions and respectable appearance, and with proper attention to repairs, promises to last at least another half century, and exhibit its ancient model to posterity."

Following Mr. Baker, as ministers of the First Parish were Rev. Jeremiah Cushing, Rev. Nathaniel Pitcher and Rev. Shearjashub Bourne, each a graduate of Harvard and Rev. Ebenezer Grosvenor a graduate of Yale. A remonstrance was made to the church authorities at the time of the ordination of the latter, and although unsuccessful it foreboded the dissension which beset his pastorate during seventeen years. Deane, himself a learned divine, says that Mr. Grosvenor "was undoubtedly too mild and catholic in his faith and practice to give universal satisfaction." He resigned in 1780 and for two years up to the time of his death, preached to "the College in Cambridge."

For seven years after Mr. Grosvenor's departure, the First Society was without a settled minister. Many candidates were called but none was able to satisfy both factions. It was the old controversy renewed, although now more doctrinal than relating to mere outward ceremonials and observances. Finally Rev. Ebenezer Dawes of Bridgewater who had been graduated from Harvard in 1785 at an advanced age for the times—he was twenty-nine—was ordained and settled over the society in 1787.

During all this time the Second Parish was not without its troubles. Mr. Witherell had been the minister for nearly forty years. A new meeting house was built in 1790. The previous year it had been,

"Voted to build a new Meeting-house x x x, using what of the old house may be convenient, and that the old pews be set up in the new house, as near as may be where they are in the old house, and that each proprietor enjoy his pew in the new house, saving those who have not agreed to give anything to encourage sd work, or for taking down and setting up their pews. Their pews shall remain for further consideration; x x x x that John Cushing, Nathaniel Clap, Joseph Tolman, Galen Clap and Nathaniel Turner be agents to agree with some suitable person or persons to complete sd work as soon as may be, not to exceed the first Nov'r 1770 "

The agents chose Joseph Tolman, one of their own number, his uncle Elisha and Hawkes Cushing — undertakers, as they were called, — and they proceeded to erect a house of worship senventy-two feet long and forty-eight wide with a spire and belfry at the west end and a porch at the east. It was the most "commodious" church building that had been attempted. The profit enuring to the undertakers out of their work was of such size as to create a mild scandal. On the whole, however, through the influence exerted by Mr. Witherell over his parish, matters progressed smoothly. Upon his death in 1684, Rev. Thomas Mighill who had been his assistant, was called upon to become the pastor. He was ordained on the fifteenth day of October of that year but his occupancy of the pulpit was short—he died five years later. There appears to have been no minister regularly settled over this parish for the next five years. In 1694 Rev. Deodate Lawson was ordained. His tenure of the office was also brief. While his baptismal name indicates that he was God given, his ministry at Scituate showed that he was not at the same time, God serving. He sought his own secular advantages rather than the spiritual welfare of his parishioners. He absented himself, not only from his pulpit, but from his people. He was away for two years from 1696 to 1698, leaving the latter to get along as best they might. In their distress they, as usual, consulted the Elders of neighboring churches and being advised that they were "not to blame if they use all Evangelical endeavors to settle themselves with another Pastor, more spiritually and more fixedly disposed," they secured the services of Rev. Nathaniel Eells of Hingham at "£65 a year and the use of the parsonage." This was in June 1704. He continued his pastorate actively for forty-six years and was probably the best beloved of all the ministers who have lived in Scituate either before or since his time. Judge Samuel Sewall was a frequent visitor at the home of Mr. Eells and often sat an interested and appreciative listener to his preaching. There are many references to him in the former's diary, as for instance:

"Satterday, March 26 (1709) Col. Hathorne, Mr.

Curwin, Mr. Taft and I set out for Plimouth †, get to Job Randalls about sun setting. March 27th. Mr. Eels preaches in the Forenoon; Mr. Taft in the afternoon; sup at Mr. Eels."

"Lords Day March 23. (1712) Heard Mr. Eels. Rain'd hard last night and something this day. Thin meeting." "Midweek, April 2. Congregational meeting at South Church x x x x I was not at the Meeting. x x x x Speaking of Mr. Eels and enquiring how he preach'd, I comended him; and Mr. Pemberton ‡ upon it, with a very remarkable Aer Said, his pupils could do worthily, he was one of them."

"March 27. (1714 at Scituate). Mr. Eels preaches very well. Sup with him. Give Sarah Witherell (now Hubbard) Ten Shillings. Gave Mr. Eels some small books. Earl Sacrament, Wadsworth Catechisme, Colman Providence." April 26, (1719) Heard Mr. Eels. In the afternoon he baptized Sarah Stockbridge, an Orphan."

"April 24, 1720. Set out with Scipio § for Scituate. Baited at Mills's, went forward with Bointon and Read. Dined at Cushins; parted with my company at the foot of the Hill. Got to Mr. Randall's about 1½ hour by Sun; found my Landlady dead.

April 24. Mr. Eels preaches out of Deuteronomy, Hear O, Israel—Cap. 6. 4. p. m. Mr. Eels baptized James Briggs and Israel Silvester and Elisha Silvester." ¶

---

† Judge Sewall was on his way to Plymouth to hold the Spring Term of the Superior Court of Judicature with Judges John Hathorne and Jonathan Curwin who accompanied him, three then constituting a quorum of the court for the transaction of business.

‡ Rev. Ebenezer Pemberton, pastor of the South Church who had been the tutor of Mr. Eells at Cambridge.

§ Judge Sewall's negro servant.

¶ Israel and Elisha Sylvester were sons of Zebulon the grandson of Richard who settled in Scituate in 1642. The latter named was banished from the Massachusetts Bay Colony because he persisted in the then heresy, that "all baptized persons should be admitted to Communion without further trial. Israel deceased at Assinippi in 1812 aged ninety-five years.

Rev. Jonathan Dorby followed Mr. Eells for a brief period. Then came the Rev. David Barnes, a man of much more than local importance. He preached at Harvard and was given its degree of D. D. in 1788; at Derby Academy in Hingham; at Plymouth, Duxbury and Boston. Through all the trying times of the Revolution he was without pay from the society. At the time of his resignation in 1809, it gave him, however, five hundred dollars in recognition of this sacrifice. His annual salary had been £80. He died April 26, 1811.

CHAPTER VII

QUAKERS IN SCITUATE

"No Quaker Rantor or any such corrupt pson shalbee admitted to bee a freeman of this Corporation."
Ancient Laws of Plymouth Colony 1658

WHEN Mary Fisher and Anne Austin landed at Boston on that May morning in 1656, the Scituate planters had small notion of what the coming of these two women portended to them. In the five years which followed, up to the time when Charles II issued his edict requiring Quakers in New England to be sent to old England for trial, and even thereafter, the presence of these followers of George Fox in their community was regarded as a positive menace by the freemen. Whatever may now be said of the feelings which prompted this attitude toward the Quakers, it was far from being without justification at the time.

It is well to bear in mind that the men of importance in Scituate from 1636 to 1661, were stubbornly devoted both to the causes of a stable autonomy and freedom of religious worship. In order to have the latter they must maintain the former. The Quaker would have disrupted both. From the standard of orthodox Christianity, discarding all ceremonial forms, he would have done away with baptism and abandoned all tenets save the one, his own—"Inward Light" —which lay at the very foundation. By this inward light the Quakers in common with all other persons were to be guided in their conduct in life. They held to the most absolute assertion of the right of private judgment. This led them not only to stoicism in persecution, but to exaggerated forms of expressions of fealty to their own faith, and scorn for the authority of those who oppressed them.

Witness the words of William Robinson who with Marmaduke Stevenson, was hanged for his heresy on Boston Common in 1659.

"And when W. Robinson went cheerfully up the Ladder, to the topmost round above the Gallows, and spake to the People,—That they suffered not as Evil Doers, but as those who testified and manifested the Truth, and that this was the Day of their Visitation and therefore desired them to mind the Light that was in them, the Light of Christ, of which he Testified and was now going to Seal it with his Blood." †
And this scene in the session of the court at Plymouth on the third day of June, 1658. ‡

"Moreover att the same time, the said (Humphrey) Norton againe carryed very turbulently, saying to the Governor 'Thy clamorouse tongue I regard noe more than the dust under my feet, and thou art like a scolding woman; and thou pratest and deridest me, or to the like effect, with other words of like nature, and tendered a writing desirouse to read it in the Court;' to which the Governor replyed, that if the paper were directed to him, hee would see it before it should bee openly read; the said Norton refused to deliver the said paper to the Governor and so it was prohibited to bee read."

Witness further, "that Lydia Wardwell and Deborah Wilson were adjudged to the whipping post, for coming into our assemblies, entirely divested of their cloathes." §

It was not alone the hateful doctrine of "Inward Light" and its possible effect upon their own modes of religious observance, which the Pilgrims feared. They were quite

---

† New England Judged (1661) pages 122-136.
‡ Plymouth Colony Records Vol. III, page 140.
§ Mass. His. Soc. Coll. (Fourth Series) Hinckley Papers, Vol. V, page 18.

as much distressed over the possible undermining of their well beloved structure of self government, by the establishment of the anarchical doctrine of the Quakers. This had been built at the cost of great privation and devotion. At the time of the appearance of the Quakers in Plymouth Colony, war with the Indians was not improbable. The individual must bear arms against this enemy for the preservation of the home and Commonwealth. This the Quaker refused to do. No more would he pay any part of the taxes necessary to the support of either church or state.

The Quaker's side of the question, logically put from his own standpoint is contained in a petition drawn by Edward Wanton of Scituate and signed by himself and three others. The naive reference therein to the "liberty upon sufferance" of the forefathers themselves is delicious.

> *"To the Governor and Magistrates, with the rest of the Court of this Colony of New Plymouth, sitting at   , this instant fourth month called June,* 1678.

We whose names are hereunder written, called Quakers in your said jurisdiction, conscientiously and in all tenderness show why we cannot give maintenance to your present established preachers.

We suppose it's well enough known we have never been backward to contribute our assistance in our estates and persons, where we could act without scruple or conscience, nor in the particular case of the country rate, according to our just proportion and abilities, until this late contrivance of mixing your preachers' maintenance therewith, by the which we are made incapable to bear any part of what just charge may necessarily be disbursed for the maintenance of the civil government; a thing we could always readily do until now. And why we cannot in conscience, directly or indirectly, pay any thing to your said preachers as such, we, in true love and tenderness, (not through contention or covetousness, the Lord is our witness,) offer as followeth:—

1. The ground of a settled maintenance upon preachers either must arise from the ceremonial law of the Jews paying tithes to their priests, the Levites; or from the Pope, who first instituted the same (as we find in history) in the Christian Church, so-called, in the year 786, in the time of Offa, King of Mercia, where there was a council held by two legates sent from Pope Adrian to that purpose (see Selden's "History of Tithes"). Now, the first, your preachers say as well as we, is ended, and therefore will not have their maintenance called tithes. The second (viz. the Pope's institution) we suppose they will also disclaim as any precedent or ground for their practice. We must therefore necessarily conclude they have no ground at all; which we further demonstrate as follows:—

2. The gospel ought to be preached freely, according to the injunction of our Lord Jesus to his disciples when he sent them forth to preach. Matt. x. 8: "Freely you have received, freely give." This is far from bargaining for so much a year, and, if it be not paid, take away food, clothes, bedding, and what not, rather than go unpaid. Doubtless those are no true shepherds who mind the fleece more than the flock. The apostles would rather work with their own hands than make the gospel burthensome or chargeable to any (1 Thess. II 9; Acts xx. 34; 1 Cor. xv. 9, 12; 2 Thess. III. 8.) Now, they are otherwise minded than the apostles who would rather make their gospel burthensome than work. The apostle coveted no Man's gold or silver or apparel (Acts xx. 23). What thought will true charity allow us of those, who not only covet, but forcibly take away, either gold, silver, or apparel, and that where it can (not be) well spared, from families, and children? The gospel is the power of God, and therefore neither to be bought or sold. Christ Jesus invites people freely. His ministers ought not to make people pay.

3. Preachers are to receive maintenance but as

other men; viz: when they are poor and want it. And here we are not backward, according to our abilities, to minister to the necessities of any men. Only this ought not to be forced or compelled from any, but ought to be left to the giver's freedom.

4. The true ministers of Christ never received any thing (if they stood in need) but from such who had been benefited by them; and, in that case, they thought it but reasonable (as indeed we do, if there be occasion) that those who from them had received spirituals should (if they stood in need) communicate to them their temporals (1 Cor. IX. 11; Rom. XV. 27). Now therefore, have we been benefited by your preachers? Do we receive of their spirituals? Say they not of us, we are heretics? Let them therefore, first convict us, and put us into a capacity of receiving some advantage from them (if they can), before they receive maintenance from us. It is related (in the book called "Clark's Lives") of one Rothwell, a man famous in England in his day, that a collection having been made for him in his absence, and understanding, at his return, some had given that he was persuaded had not been profited by his preaching he returned their money again. It were well if there were more so honestly minded.

5. We do really believe your preachers are none of the true ministers of Christ. Now, how can it reasonably be expected from us we should maintain or contribute towards the maintenance of such a ministry as we judge not true, without guilty consciences and manifest contradiction of ourselves and principles?

We request, for conclusion, you will please to consider whether you may not prejudice yourselves in your public interest with the king (you yourselves having liberty upon sufferance) if you should compel any to conform in any respect, either by giving maintenance or otherwise to such a church government or ministry as is repugnant to the Church of England.

We leave the whole to your serious consideration, desiring (if it may be) we may be eased in the forementioned case,—viz., that you will please to distinguish between the country rate and your preacher's maintenance, and that we may not be imposed upon against our consciences; that so, under you, we may live a peaceable and quiet life in all godliness and honesty; that so, the end for which you are placed in government being truly answered, in the promotion and propogation of the common benefit, we therein may have our share.

Who are your friends,
EDWARD WANTON,
JOSEPH COLMAN
NATHANIEL FITSRANDAL.
WILLIAM ALLEN."

Driven from England as the Pilgrim had likewise been, the disciple of George Fox did not seek untried shores to build a church whose practices should be to his own liking. Instead he sought out a new and struggling community and immediately commenced to spread dissension among its members. He refused to take the oath of fidelity to the government whose refuge he sought, or become a freeman and share in its responsibilities. Viewed in the light of strict impartiality this seems not only unreasonable—it was despicable.

The forefathers, then, to whose government the Quaker came may be excused if they viewed that coming with alarm. In their own words, this is the way they looked upon it. :—

"Whereas there hath severall persons come into this Government comonly called Quakers, whose doctrine and practises manifestly tends to the Subversion of the foundamentalls of Christian Religion, Church order, and the Civell peace of this Government, as appiers by the Testimonies given in sundry depositions and otherwise; It is therefore enacted by the Court and the

Authoritie thereof that noe Quaker or person comonly soe called bee entertained by any person or persons within this Government under the penaltie of five pounds for every such default or bee whipt; and in case any one shall entertaine any such person Ignorantly if hee shall Testify on his oath that he knew not them to bee such hee shall bee freed of the aforesaid penaltie provided hee upon his first decerning them to bee such doe discover them to the constable or his deputie:

It is also enacted by this Court and the Authoritie thereof that if any Rantor or Quaker or person comonly soe called shall come into any towne within this Government, [any by any person or persons bee knowne to bee such, the person soe knowing or Suspecting him shall forthwith acquaint the Cunstable or his deputie of them on paine of Presentment and soe lyable to cencure in court whoe forthwith on such notice of them or any other Intelegence hee shall have of them; shall diligently endeavor to apprehend him or them and bring them before some one of the magistrates who shall cause him or them to be committed to Goale there to be kept close prisoners with such victualls onely as the Court alloweth until hee or they shall defray the charge both of theire Imprisonment and theire Transportation away; Together with the Engagement to returne into this Government no more or else to be continewed in close durance till further order from the Court]. And forasmuch as the meetings of such persons whether Strangers or others proveth disturbing to the peace of this Government. It is therefore enacted by the Court and the Authoritie thereof that henceforth noe such meetings bee assembled or kept by any person in any place within this Government under the penaltie of forty shillings a time for every speaker and ten shillings a time for every hearer that are heads of families and forty shillings a time for the owner of the place that permits them soe to meet together."

This was not a severe enactment. The appellation of Rantor which it attaches to the objectionable persons, gives a very lucid idea of the tactics adopted by them to gain an audience. It is to the credit of the people of the Plymouth Colony that they did not adopt the severe punishments created by the General Court of Massachusetts Bay. The greatest penalty imposed by Plymouth was whipping not to exceed fifteen stripes while in Massachusetts imprisonment at hard labor was added to this for a first offence. For the second offence the unhappy culprit was to lose both ears, and for the third he was to have his tongue bored with a red hot iron. Nor was this all. At a meeting of the Commissioners for the United Colonies held in Boston on the twenty-third day of September 1658 that body "propounded and seriously comended" that the several General Courts pass laws making it a capital crime for the Quaker to return after banishment. This recommendation was readily signed by Endicott, the President of the Commissioners, who, indeed, probably drew it, and by Governor Prence and Josias Winslow, Commissioners from Plymouth. Massachusetts immediately adopted it with little difficulty. The Plymouth Colony, however, remained satisfied with the milder form.

The "Rantor" or "Quaker" came into Scituate. Here he found some of the best men, Cudworth and Hatherly among their number, as tolerant of their presence and practices, as was Roger Williams in Rhode Island; but who, like Williams, detested their doctrines. Among the first disturbances in Scituate to come to the attention of the Court was that made by Joseph Allen who was one of a conspicuous group of "Rantors" at Sandwich. He had been haled before the court several times for refusal to take the oath of fidelity and each time paid a heavy fine. This did not deter him. On a Sunday morning in the spring of 1660 he appeared in Scituate at a Quaker meeting at the house, probably, of Rodolphus Ellms, who was a sympathizer of the sect. Not content with worshipping among his friends in a way which satisified his conscience and his spiritual longings, he went to the meeting-house of the Congregationalists where they were engaged in their own devotions. There he proceeded to revile both them and their religion. Subsequently, being arraigned in court he was,—"for being att a Quakers meeting, fined ten shillings; and for making a disturbance in the meeting on the Lord's Day att Scituate, fined forty shillings."

The religious activities of the Quakers in Scituate centered about the homes of James Cudworth and Rodolphus Ellms. At the October court 1660 the latter was fined ten shillings for being present at one of their gatherings. His brother-in-law Robert Whitcomb was at this time paying court to Mary, the comely daughter of Captain Cudworth. These two concluded that their marriage should be consummated after the manner of the Quakers, and Henry Hobson of Rhode Island was invited to guide the youthful couple in the observance of the true form. At the ceremony no clergyman or civil magistrate was present. The contracting parties stood up in the presence of witnesses, mutually promised to live faithfully together as man and wife, and the knot was tied. This was rank heresy. Such an irregular union in the covenant of matrimony must be punished, notwithstanding that the bride was the daughter of one of the most popular men in Scituate. Mr. John Browne and Captain Thomas Willitt, two of the important men of the colony, were appointed by the court to apprehend the offending Hobson and take "cecuritie for his appearance before the Court att Plymouth to answere for his derision of authorities in counterfeiting the solemnising of the marriage x x x." † The audacious pair themselves were taken before the same tribunal. Of it, her father had formerly been an Assistant, and on it there now sat the Governor Thomas Prence, John Alden, William Bradford, son of the former Governor, Thomas Southworth, William Collier, Thomas Hinckley and Josias Winslow. It was an impor-

---

† Plymouth Colony Records Vol. III, page 209.

tant occasion both for the culprits and the people of the colony itself. Among the jurymen were Lieut. James Torrey, who was soon to succeed the bride's father as head of the town's military company, Cornet Robert Stetson, who served with him in it, and another townsman, Samuel Hicks. No defense was offered. Of course none was possible; but one verdict could be rendered. The newly made man and wife were found guilty. The court sentenced them to pay a fine of ten pounds; to be imprisoned during its pleasure, and they went to jail. Their confinement was not for long, however. Four days in the rude building on Summer Street in Plymouth, which served as a prison, with a thieving Indian as their co-tenant † convinced them that it was better to bow to the will of the magistrates. On March ninth they announced that they desired "to bee orderly married," and this being accomplished they were released. ‡ A year from that date the court spread this entry upon its records:

Whereas Robert Whitcombe and Mary Cudworth was formerly fined for disorderly coming together without consent of theire parents and lawful marriage the sume of ten pounds, and imprisoned during the pleasure of the Court, having since been orderly married, and liveing orderly together, and following their callings industriously, and attending the worship of God diligently, as is testifyed by some of their naighbors of good report, the Court have seen good to remitt five pounds of the said fine; in respect also of their povertie the Treasurer is ordered likewise to bee slow in demanding the remainder." §

---

† March 5, 1660. Att this Court, a certain Indian called Cancantawashinck appeared before the Court, having bine committed to prison for stealing divers things from divers persons att Taunton, which was proved to his face, and by him owned and confessed. Hee was heard and examined and againe comited to prison." Plymouth Colony Records, Vol. III P. 209.

‡ Ibidem, page 206.

§ Ibidem, Vol. IV, Page 9.

The Court was obviously in error concerning the whole of the offense charged. It could not have been "coming together without the consent of their parents" for this approval was as necessary to the legality of a Quaker ceremony as a Puritan one, and where in Scituate, if not in the home of her father who was a sympathizer, could such a marriage have been consummated. It is probable that the clerk in drawing the presentment strictly followed the words of the statute in which this clause appears, without reference to the real fact.

The magistrates were at least impartial in their prosecutions for violation of this anti-Quaker law. Learning that Isaac Robinson, the son of the Leyden pastor, was suspected of abetting the disturbers they summoned him before them at Plymouth and disfranchised him. But "their being some mistake in this," says the record, "att his request, hee, the said Isaacke Robinson, is reestablished, and by general voat of the Court accepted againe into the association of the body of the freemen of this corporation." They dealt leniently also with Ensign John Williams, who lived in and maintained the garrison house at Cedar Point, and who trained the local military company.

"Ensigne John Williams, for entertaining a foraigne Quaker, fined forty shillings, according to order; and in reference to the offence given by him, by his countenancing or adhering to the Quakers, in hopes of (his) reformation, the Court have suspended what might have bine imposed, in disgrading him of his place for the present."

"William Parker for permitting a Quakers meeting to bee in hise house, fined forty shillings" and "for entertaining a strange Quaker called Wenlocke, into his house, fined five pounds."

Other prosecutions were had, but none which reached either in interest or importance the case against Capt. James Cudworth. When the Quakers began coming to the colony in 1656-7 Cudworth was an Assistant in the Plymouth

Colony. The laws proposed for the punishment of the Quakers and their banishment did not meet with his entire approval. He was not at once convinced that their religious principles were without merit, or their personal presence in the colony undesirable. He was tolerant of them and would not condemn and punish, upon what he considered the frivolous pretexts advanced by the anti-Quakers. His opinions were largely those of his friend Hatherly. Of the men who sat on the magistrate's bench with him Governor Bradford and John Alden were more radical. Thomas Prence, always an enemy of Cudworth, was insultingly aggressive. Josias Winslow was inclined toward him in a friendly way and William Collier held himself in haughty reserve. In the disputations held by these men over the Quaker question Cudworth was well aware of the unpopularity of his position. He wrote:

"This spirit (of intolerance) did work those two years that I was of the Magistracy, during which time, I was, on sundry occasion, forced to declare my dissent in sundry actings of that nature; which altho' done with all moderation of expression, together with due respect unto the rest, yet it wrought great dissatisfaction and prejudice in them against me."

He frankly told his fellow magistrates that he had entertained Quakers at his house, giving as his reason, "thereby that I might be the better acquainted with their principles. I thought it better to do so, than with the blind world to censure, condemn, rail at and revile them, when they neither saw their persons nor knew any of the principles. But the Quakers and myself cannot agree on divers things, and so I signified to the Court; but told them withal, that as I was no Quaker, so I would be no prosecutor."

It was due perhaps to this firm stand by Cudworth, the wisdom of Henry Dunster and the sagacious counsel of Hatherly that the Old Colony was not committed to the drastic and cruel treatment with which the members of the sect were treated by the government of Massachusetts Bay, led by John Endicott.

CHAPTER VIII

TOWN GOVERNMENT AND FREEMEN

"Bee Subject to every
Ordinance of Man for
the Lord's sake
I Peter 2 cond 13th."
Text inscribed upon the fly leaf of "The Booke of Generall Lawes and Liberties."—1658.

IT was not alone religious zeal and enthusiasm which drove the forefathers across seas to "those vast and unpeopled countries of America." They had the desire, equally potent, to establish a democracy which while acknowledging allegiance to the crown should nevertheless, be a stable and permanent autonomy. The Exiles from Leyden did not know upon their embarkation, that they should find a habitat upon territory which was not within the limits of their patent. Although a royal charter which should prescribe their rights, privileges and immunities, had been refused them, the compact † signed in the cabin of the

---

† "In Ye name of God, Amen. We whose names are underwritten, the loyal subjects of our dread sovereigne Lord, King James, by ye grace of God, of Great Britaine, Franc, & Ireland, King, defender of ye faith &c haveing undertaken, for ye glorie of God, and advancemente of ye Christian faith, and honor of our King & countrie, a voyage to plant ye first colonie in ye Northern parts of Virginia, doe by these presents solemnly & mutually in ye presence of God, and one of another, covenant & combine ourselves together in a civill body politick, for our better ordering & preservation & furtherance of ye ends aforesaid; and by virtue hereof to enact, constitute and frame such just and equal lawes, ordinances, acts, constitutions & offices, from time to time, as shall be thought most meete and convenient for ye generall good of ye colonie, unto which we promise all due submission and obedience. IN WITNESS WHEREOF we have hereunder subscribed our names at Cape Cod ye 11 of November, in ye year of ye raigne of our soveraignd lord, King James of England, France & Ireland, ye eigheenth and of Scotland ye fifty-fourth. Ano. Dom. 1620.

Mayflower on the morning of the eleventh day of November 1620, served as a corner stone upon which to build, as permanent as any parchment bearing the seal of royalty.

Carver, who had been chosen Governor *en voyage*, did not long survive. In April 1621 William Bradford was chosen Governor in his place and Isaac Allerton elected an "Assistant." † On the previous twenty-seventh day of February Miles Standish had been chosen captain. This was neither in the sense of a military officer to have supreme command in all affairs, nor yet as a civil constable to serve such processes as might be committed to him. The latter office was to be created later. Standish by reason of his profession of arms was selected as a "military officer" to command in affairs because of the extreme probability of trouble with and attack by the Indians.

Bradford and his one Assistant continued to order the affairs of the colony for three years. Meantime both the Fortune and Anne had arrived at Plymouth bringing new colonists who of course sought participation in governmental affairs.

Of the elections in 1642 Bradford says: ‡

"The time of new election of the officers for this year being come, and ye number of their people increased, and their troubles and occasions therewith, and also to adde more Assistants to ye Govr. for help and counsell, and ye better carrying on of affairs. Showing that it was necessarie it should be so. If it was any honour or benefitte, it was fitte others should be partakers of it; if it was a burthen (as doubtless it was) it was but equal others should help to bear it;

---

† Shortly after William Bradford was chosen Governor in his (Carver's) stead, and being not yet recovered his illness, in which he had been near ye point of death, Isaac Allerton was chosen to be an Assistnte unto him, who, by renewed election every year, continued sundry years together." Bradford History Page 122.

‡ Bradford History, Page 187.

and yet this was ye end of Annual Elections. The issue was, that as before ther was but one Assistante, they now chose 5, giving the Govr. a double voyce; and afterwards they increased them to 7, which course hath continued to this day."

The electorate did not take this broad hint as to the governorship, but re-elected Bradford. They continued to do so up to the year of his death, (1657), save for three years from 1633-1636 and in 1638 and 1644. No record is extant which shows who these first Assistants were.

In 1633 "The Records of the Colony of New Plymouth, in New England" begin. For the first three years they were kept by the Governor. At the General Court held on the third day of January 1636 Nathaniel Souther was elected and sworn as "Clarke of the Court."

The first record happily gives us not only the names of the Governor and "Assistants or Councill" as the body was called, but of all the freemen as well. At this time no property qualification was imposed upon the right of suffrage. It did not attach until 1669 when the General Court enacted "that none shall voate in Town Meetings but ffremen or ffreeholders of twenty pound ratable estate and of good conversation having taken the oath of fidelitie." When the colonies of Plymouth and Massachusetts Bay were united the amount required was "a freehold of 40s per ann. or other property of the value of 40 £ sterling.

The elective franchise was exercised by the freemen, males who had taken the freeman's oath. The "oath of fidelitie" was similar. It was administered to those, not freemen who made "choice at present to reside within the Government of New Plymouth." The freeman's oath was as follows:

> "You shall be truly loyall to our sovereign Lord King Charles, his heires and successors, the state and government of England (as it now stands). You shall not speake or doe, devise or advise any thing or things, act or acts, directly or indirectly by land or water, that

doth, shall or may tend to the destruction or over throw of this present plantacons, colonies or corporacon of New Plymouth. Neither shall you suffer the same to be spoken or done but shall hinder oppose and discover the same to the Governor and Assistants of the said Colony for the time being or some one of them. You shall faithfully submit unto such good and wholesome laws and ordinances as either are or shall be made for the ordering and government of the same and shall endeavor to advance the growth and good of the several plantations within the limits of this Corporacon by all due means and courses. All which you promise and sweare by the name of the Great God of heaven and earth, simply, truly and faithfully to perform as you hope for help from God who is the God of truth and punisher of falsehood."

To this oath, William Gilson, Simon Hoyt, Anthony Annable, Humphrey Turner and Henry Cobb, all of whom lived in the ward of Scituate, had subscribed before 1633. James Cudworth and Timothy Hatherly were admitted as freemen in 1634 and William Hatch and George Kenrick the next year. In 1636, the year of the establishment of the town, George Lewis, Bernard Lombard and Edward Foster were sworn. John Lewis, John Hewes and Samuel Hinckley followed the next year, Isaac Stedman in 1648 and Isaac Chittendon not until 1653. These were all the male residents of the town when it was incorporated.

Only those, of course, who had been admitted as freemen in 1636 or prior thereto had a voice in the affairs of the colony. There were no town affairs then which were ordered by the townspeople themselves. The affairs of both town and colony were governed by the freemen of all of the towns † who assembled for the first few years in "General Court" at Plymouth to that end. At such a gath-

---

† Duxbury was established in 1637; Marshfield in 1640, Sandwich, Taunton, Yarmouth, Barnstable, Rehoboth and Eastham all before 1652 and Bridgewater, which had theretofore been known as Duxburrow New Plantation, in 1656.

ering on the fourth and fifth days of October 1636 "The ordinances of the colony and corporation being read, divers were found wanting the reforming others the rejecting, & others fitt to be instituted and made. It was therefor ordered and agreed, that four from the town of Plymouth, two for Scituate and two for Duxburrow should, as committees for the whole, be added by the Govr. & Assistants, to rectifie & Prepare such as should be thought most convenient, that, if approved, thay may be put in force the next Generall Court." Anthony Annable and James Cudworth on the part of Scituate were chosen for this work. On the fifteenth of the following November this committee reported to the whole body of freemen. The view which they took of their own rights and privileges cannot be better stated than in their own language. In a preamble is recited the facts above stated. It continues:

"Now being assembled according to the said order and having read the combination made at Cape Cod on the 11th of Novbr 1620 in the yeare of the raigne of our late Sov. L. King James of England, Ffrance and Ireland, the eighteenth, and of Scotland the fifty-fourth as also our letters Patents confirmed by the honorable Councill his said Majestie established and granted the 13th of January 1629, in the fifth yeare of the raigne of our Sov. Lord King Charles, and finding that as freeborne subjects of the State of England we hither came indewed with all and singular the privileges belonging to such, in the first place we thinke good that it be established, for an act.

That according to the x x x x due privilege of the subject aforesaid, no imposition, law or ordinance be made or imposed upon us by ourselves or others at present or to come, but shall be made or imposed by consent according to the free liberties of the State of Kingdom of England & no otherwise.

That whereas before expressed, we finde a solemne & binding combination as also letters patent derivatory from his Majestie of England our dread Sovereign, for the ordering of a body politick within the severall limits of this patent vizt from Cowhasset to the utomost bounds of Puckanokick, westward, & all that tract of land southward to the southern ocean with all and singular lands rivers, havens, waters, creeks, ports, fishing, fowling, &c. By vertue whereof we ordaine institute and appoint the first Tuesday of March every yeare for the election of such officers as shall be thought meet for the guiding & government of this Corporation." †

It was provided that upon the day appointed a Governor and seven Assistants should be chosen, "to rule & governe the said plantations within the said limits for one whole yeare & no more. And this election to be made only by the freemen according to the former custome. And that there be also Constables for each part, and other inferior officers to be also chosen." It was further enacted that there should also be elected a treasurer "whose place it shall be to receive in whatsoever sum or sums shall appertain to the Royalty of the place either coming in by way of fine amercement or otherwise."

A "Clarke of the Court" and Coroner were also to be chosen. The duties of all of the elective officers, from the Chief Executive downward, were prescribed and defined. The Governor was responsible for the due execution of all the laws and ordinances. He was to call together and advise with the Assistants "upon such material occasions as time shall bring forth." In such a meeting he had a "double voice." If the Assistants deemed the matter too momentous for an ultimate decision by themselves and the Governor, the latter warned a meeting of the whole body of the freemen—the Great and General Court. The Governor also had the power to arrest and commit to jail,

---

† The original record in a note subsequently made has the following:—"This is altered afterwards to the first Tuesday in June yearly by a General Court" This because of the boisterous March weather and the distance to the place where the election was held.

provided that "with all convenient spede shall bring the cawse to hearing before either of the Assistants or Generall Court according to the nature of the offense." The Assistants or Magistrates, as they afterwards came to be called were required to appear "at the Governor's summons" and give "his best advice both in a public Court and private Councill with the Governor for the good of the Colonyes within the limits of this Government." The individual assistant might examine and commit to jail under like circumstances as the Governor in the latter's absence and he sat with him in the trial of all except trivial causes. These latter were tried usually before three or more Assistants. In this capacity, whether sitting with or without the Governor, the tribunal was known as "the Bench." Capital crimes of which there were five, † felonies, and offences against the government were tried before the whole body of freemen, Governor and Assistants sitting as the General Court. No danger then threatened of encroachment of one branch of the government upon the prerogatives of another. It was not until many years later that the Executive was restrained from interfering with the Legislative and the Judicial, the two latter from coming into collision with the first and all from clashing with each other. Judge Morris regards this as a great achievement.

"But," he says "it remained for our own America to develop the idea of the triple division of the powers of government and their true relation to each other, to the fullest extent. The government which Montesquieu thought he found in England, he would have found more naturally developed even then in our colonies, if he had been better acquainted with them. By reason of their peculiar circumstances the triple division had become the almost universal practice in the thirteen colonies; and what was practice in the colonies became fundamental law when the colonies became

---

† Treason or rebellion against the government, wilful murder, witchcraft, arson and the crime against nature."

independent states. x x x x It has now to a greater or less extent permeated the policy of all civilized nations; although nowhere has it been so thoroughly established as a part of governmental policy as it has been with ourselves. x x x We are a wonderfully inventive people; but the greatest of American inventions is that of an independent judiciary, constituting an equal co-ordinate power in the State with the legislative and executive branches of government. An independent judiciary is the best safeguard of popular liberty that has ever been devised, and the best contribution to jurisprduence that has been made in modern times." †

It was but for two years only that the whole body of freemen sat in the legislative branch of the government. On March fifth 1638 it was enacted that:

"Whereas complaint was made that the freemen were put to many inconveniences and great expenses by their continual attendence at the Courts. It is therefore enacted by the Court for the ease of the severall Colonies and Townes within the Government, that every Towne shall make choice of two of their freemen and the town of Plymouth of four to be Committees or Deputies to joyne with the Bench to enact and make all such lawes and ordinances as shall be judged to be good and wholesome for the whole. Provided that the lawes they doe enact shalbe propounded one Court to be considered upon until the next Court, and then to be confirmed if they shall be approved of (except the case require present confirmation). And if any act shall be confirmed by the Bench and Committees which upon further deliberation shall prove prejudicial to the whole, that the ffreemen at the next election Court after meeting together may repeale the same and enact any other usefull for the whole. And that every Township shall beare their Committees

---

† Morris-History of the Development of Law, page 313 et seq.

charges and that such as are not ffreemen but have taken oath of Fidelitie and are masters of famylies and Inhabitants of the said Townes, as they are to beare their part in charges of their Committees, so to have a vote in the choyce of them. Provided they choose them only of the ffreemen of said Towne whereof they are; but if any such Committees shall be insufficient or troublesome, that then the Bench and the other Committees may dismiss them and the towne to choose other ffreemen in their place. †

That the body of deputies should be made up only of freemen is indicative of the jealousy with which the church was guarded. As has been shown in earlier pages, only he who was church-member, orthodox in religion and not vicious in his life, could be a freeman. While others who had taken the oath of fidelity were permitted to vote, they were restricted in their election to a choice between freemen. While the sole legislative body was composed of this class the church for which it made the laws, was safe from corruption, attack, or disestablishment.

In addition to the officers before mentioned, the code adopted at this meeting provided for presentments by a grand jury or "Great Quest" as it was called. Such presentments were to be made only upon oath, which might be administered by an Assistant. Trial thereof, as well as all causes between individuals wherein the thing in controversy did not exceed forty shillings, was by jury. Misdemeanors and small causes were tried before the Assistants, associates or magistrates as they were variously entitled, and many years later the more trivial disputes were heard and determined by selectmen of the towns.

The covenant of marriage was considered by the Pilgrims as a purely civil contract the consummation of which was to

---

† Plymouth Colony Records Vol. XI (Laws) page 31.

be before a magistrate, and not a function of the church to be solemnized by a man of the cloth. †

The Assistants were authorized to perform this ceremony. Timothy Hatherly was "appointed and deputed by the Court to administer marriage at Scituate as occasion shall require." ‡ Thomas Prince, afterward Governor, with Margaret Collier; Nathaniel Morton, the "Clarke" with Lydia Cooper; and many others were from time to time united in marriage before "the Bench."

Service in all elective offices was compulsory, for the term of the first election at least, and fines for refusal were imposed. Nor was the law less severe in the matter of the actual casting of the ballot by those entitled. At first it was required that the freemen should attend the annual election at Plymouth in person. Later he might prepare his vote in the town meeting, seal and deliver it to the deputy from his town who was required "to observe by a list of their names whoe hath voted and whoe hath not." Failure to exercise the elective franchise in the one way or the other, was punished by the imposition of a fine at first of three, and when the privilege of proxy was granted of ten shillings.

---

† Bradford in his history gives the reason for this at page 122 "May 12, (1621) was ye first marriage in this place, which according to ye laudable custome of ye Low-Countries, in which they had lived, was thought most requisite to be performed by the magistrate, as being a civill thing, upon which many questions about inheritances doe depend with other things most proper to their cognizans, and most consenant to ye scriptures Ruth. 4. and no where found in ye gospel to be layed on ye ministers as a part of their office. This decree or law about mariage was published by ye Stats of ye Low Countries Ano. 1590. That those of any religion after lawful and open publication, coming before ye magistrats, in ye Town or Stat House, were to be orderly by them married one to the other. Petets Hist. fol. 1029. and this practise hath continued amongst, not only them but hath been followed by all ye famous churches of Christ in these parts to this time. Ano. 1646."

‡ Plymouth Colony Records, Vol. III, Page 152.

Plymouth, Duxbury and Barnstable monopolized the office of Governor in the Plymouth Colony from the beginning, to the amalgamation with Massachusetts Bay in 1692. James Cudworth after his restoration to citizenship was made Deputy Governor at about the time of the creation of that office, but that was as near as any Scituate man ever came to the chief magistracy.

This should not be taken as a reflection either on the town or the abilities of the men who were its representative citizens. Bradford early advocated rotation in office, but his advice was not heeded. His successors, Prince, Winslow, and Hinckley were as regularly re-elected as was he, himself. The men whom the town of Scituate sent to Plymouth as Assistants and Deputies were individuals of character and high standing in the colony. Anthony Annable was the first person to hold the office of Assistant, and this before the erection of the town. Upon its incorporation he was continued for two years. Timothy Hatherly, Edward Foster and James Cudworth followed him, Hatherly and Cudworth for many years, Foster but for one. There were no sittings of the General Court at Plymouth during the reign of Andros. After his overthrow John Cushing, the first of that name in Scituate, served until the annexation. Among the deputies to the General Court during this time, were Annable, Foster, Cudworth, Humphrey Turner, Richard Sealis, John Williams, Thomas Chambers, Edmund Edenden, George Kennerick, Thomas Clap, Robert Stetson, James Torrey, Isaac Buck, Isaac Chittenden, John Cushing, John Damon, Jeremiah Hatch, John Bryant Senior, Samuel Clap, Joseph Sylvester and Benjamin Stetson. Upon the establishment of the union between the two colonies of Plymouth and Massachusetts Bay, there were sent from Scituate to the General Court held at Boston, up to the time of the adoption of the state constitution, John Cushing and Samuel Clap, Benjamin Stetson, John Cushing, Jr., son of the Assistant and Deputy, Elder Thomas King, John Barker, Joseph Otis, Thomas

Turner, Stephen Clap, James Cushing, a brother of John Junior, Thomas Bryant, Amos Turner, John Cushing, third, Nicholas Litchfield, Thomas Clap, a great grandson of the early Assistant, Caleb Torrey, Ensign Otis, Joseph Cushing, Gideon Vinal, Nathan Cushing, William Turner, Israel Litchfield, Rev. Charles Turner and Daniel Damon. All of these stood well up among the public men of their times. The three generations of Cushings named above, at different periods also occupied honorable position upon the bench. William Turner was a major in the Revolutionary army and a delegate to the Cambridge convention to prepare a State constitution, and Gideon Vinal was a delegate to the Salem Congress in 1774.

The laws enacted by the legislative branch up to 1692 were both various and numerous. Although they followed in the form of their enactment the "good and wholesome laws of England," the subject matter was that which from time to time arose from and was suited to their necessities and surroundings. They were repeatedly both repealed and revised. Among the earliest laws the crimes in addition to those made capital, were adultery, drunkenness, thefts, selling or lending boats, gear or guns to the Indians; profane swearing and cursing; removing or defacing land marks; burning fences; embezzlement; forgery of deeds; theft of public records and reproaching the Marshal. In 1645, the practice of wearing a domino or mask, the better to prevent recognition while bent upon immoral quests, had grown to such an extent that the General Court took a hand to prevent it. On June 4, 1645 this law † was passed:—

"Whereas some abuses have formerly broken out amongst us by disguiseing, wearing visors and strang(e) apparell, to lascivious ends & purposes, It is therefore enacted That if any person or persons shall hereafter use any such disguisements, visors, strange apparell or the like to such lascivious and evil ends and intents, and be thereof convict by due course of law,

---

† Plymouth Colony Records Vol XI (Laws) page 48.

shall pay fifty shillings for the first offence or else be publickly whipt and for the second tyme five pounds or be publickly whipt and be bound to the behavior, if the Bench shall see cause."

Profanation of the Lord's Day by "doing any servill works" was also punished. Lying, playing at cards or dice, denying the scriptures and villifying the ministers, neglecting to "come to the publick worship of God," travelling on the Lord's day and horse racing "in any street or common road" were denounced and the offenders fined, whipped or placed in the stocks.

Sumptuary laws early occupied the attention of the government. The first legislation was the act of June 2, 1633:—

"That none be sufferred to retale wine, strongwater or biere either within doores or without except in Inns or Victualing howses allowed, And that no beere be sold in any such place to exceed in price two pence the Winchester quart."

"That such as either drinke drunke in their persons or suffer any to drinke drunke in their howses be enquired into amongst other misdemeanors and accordingly punished or fined or both by the descretion of the bench."

This regulation of the liquor traffic by confirming it to keepers or ordinaries or taverns sufficed for a number of years. In 1674 abuses having arisen, tavern keepers were prohibited from delivering liquor to the townspeople on the Lord's day and required to clear their houses of all people who were there "(on a drinking accoumpt)" except actual lodgers. Three years later, the traffic increasing rather than abating, this act was passed:—

"As an addition to former orders of the Court for prevention of the growing intolerable abuse of wine, strong liquors, etc., both amongst the Indians and English.

"It is enacted by the Court that Noe ordinary

keepers or other person or persons shall sell draw or suffer to be drawne any wine or stronge liquors to any but strangers except in case of manifest sickness or nessesitie in that kind; on paine of ten shillings fforfeite for every such default the one halfe to the country and the other halfe to the enformer.

"It is ordered by the Court and the authoritie thereof that none shall presume to deliver any wine stronge liquors or cyder to any person or persons whome they may suspect will abuse the same; or to any boyes or gerles or single persons tho pretanding to come in the name of any sicke person without a note under the hand of some sober person in whose Name they come; on paine of five shillings for every such transgression; the one half to the Country and the other halfe to the enformer."

So much importance was attached to the proper enforcement of this law that special agents were appointed to see to its observance in each town. John Bryant who had frequently done public service as a grand juryman and constable and Thomas Wade whose father was a tavern keeper on Brushy Hill in years before, were appointed for Scituate.

The keepers of these ordinaries or taverns were licensed by the General Court, during the pleasure of that body.

The provision for such a license appears first in 1646 when it was enacted:—

"That if any victualler or ordinary keeper do either drink drunck himself or suffer any person to be druncken in his house they shall pay a fine of five shillings a piece. And if the victualler or ordinary keeper do suffer any Townesmen to stay drinking in his house above an hour at one tyme the Victualler or ordinary keeper shall pay for every such default eleven shillings and the person so staying above the said hour three shillings.

The law also defined the state of drunkenness:

"And by drunkenesse is understood a person that either lisps or falters in his speech by reason of overmuch drink, or that staggers in his going or that vomits by reason of excessive drinking, or cannot follow his calling."

It may happily be recorded that none of the leading men and very few of the inhabitants of Scituate were haled into Court for this offence. On the contrary the licenses to keep public houses and to retail liquor were given to the best men in the community. Christopher Wadsworth of Duxbury, than whom none stand higher in the annals of the old colony was an ordinary keeper in Duxbury. Isaac Chittendon, Nicholas Wade, Edward Jenkins, Matthew Gannett and Joseph Barstow were all, at one time or another, tavern keepers at Scituate. There is no record that they either offended the proprieties or the laws, in the maintenance of their hostelries or that the licenses of either were ever revoked.

Tobacco also was taboo. The abuse sought to be remedied by law was "in takinge of Tobacco in uncivill manner in the streetes and dangerously in out houses, as barnes, stalls about hay stackes, corne stackes and other such places." Twelve pence fine was imposed for the first offence, two shillings for the second, and a repetition subjected the delinquent to be bound for his good behavior. Soldiers in training might use the weed however, but no person was allowed to smoke on the Lord's day going to or returning from church within two miles of the meeting house and no juror might smoke "whilst they are empannelled upon a Jurie x x x except they have given up their verdict or are not to give it up until the next day."

The only other minor offenses denounced and punished, were the making of seditious speeches against the government, failure to ring swine, and frauds by millers and tailors. The latter were not usual. George Pidcoke a tailor of Scituate was however indicted for withholding and detaining a part of a yard of "canvasse" from the owner. He was evidently one of the undesirables who had found his way across the ocean and into the Colony. In addition to his appearance in court for the fraud above named, he was presented for perjury, for persistent refusal to bear arms, and to "trayne" with the military company. It appears from the record that besides being a perjurer he was a successful malinger. At a Court of Assistants held on the second day of January 1643 "Upon certificates made to the Court by George Pidcock (then) of Duxburrow, Taylor, by reason of a cold palsy that his body is subject unto, is unable to bear armes or to exercise with a piece, is therefore by the Court freed from such service, and not to be fined for not trayneing hereafter, but to pay his fines for the tyme past, because the Court was not so informed formerly." Five years later however his ruse was discovered and this order was made:—

"George Pitcoke of Scituate being wholly defective in respecte of armes, is to provide arms compleat for one man, and constantly to pay his fines, for yt he beareth not armes."

He was still living in Scituate and presumably performing no military duty in 1670.

The millers of Scituate, Annable, Barstow, Stockbridge and the others were all honest. In 1637 "It is enacted by the Court, that the miller of Scituate shall not take above the twelfth part (of the bushel) for the tolle of grinding corne." There is no evidence appearing by the record that either this toll or good measure were violated.

Not so, however, in regard to seditious speeches against, and the upbraiding of the government. Scituate townsmen both before and after admission as freemen, were wont to speak their minds freely and the government was quite as ready to prosecute them therefor. John Stockbridge was a persistent offender in this particular. On June 5, 1638, "John Stockbridge of Scituate is presented for disgracefull speeches, tending to the contempt of the government, & for giving speeches to them that did reprove him for yt. Witnesse, Edward Foster & James Cudworth." "Fined for yt Again." In the same year he was presented for "receiv-

BOUND BROOK GLEN.
Morris's Sawmill and the mill-trail in November.
From a painting by Walter Sargent.

ing strangers & forreiners into his house & lands, without lycence of the Governor and Assistants, or Acquainting the towne of Scituate therewith." The next Court he took the oath of allegiance to the King and fidelity to the Colony but this did not stop his seditious speech. On the fourth of April 1642 he was put under bonds in the sum of £20 to be of good behaviour; but the following September found him again before the bench "for his contemptuous speeches against the government, proved by oath against him; is fyned £V," of which sum forty shillings were remitted. He was however elected a surveyor of highways in 1645, served as a grand-juryman in 1648 and propounded "to take up his Freedom" in 1650.

William Hatch was another to be prosecuted for his loose speech concerning the government, and his manifest contempt for its authority. The reason for this attitude is not readily apparent. As early as 1634, he had settled in Kent Street, was Elder of the church, frequently both a grand and petit juryman, and performed other important duties to the young colony. Even after the harsh treatment that was awarded against him for his seditious speeches he was twice elected a deputy and also placed at the head of the town's military company. He was apparently devoted to the welfare of the church, the colony and his neighbors; he was a man of some means and frequently became surety for the latter when any of them had fallen into trouble. One, however, William Holmes, was found to bear this testimony against him:—

"The deposition of William Holmes taken by and affirmed in the open Court. This deponent sayeth, William Hatch used these wordes, or to the like effect, viz: that the warrants sent from the governor were nothing but stincking commissary warrants or attachments and that the warrants sent in that kynd are no better than commissary court warrants; and that the warrant sent to the constable † to warne him the sd

---

† Samuel Fuller of Scituate.

Hatch to appeare at the Court of our Soveraigne lord the Kinge was but a commissary warrant."

The only explanation for his sneering comparison of the Governor's summons with the process of the Scottish divorce court which can be given, must be, that although four years had elapsed when this speech was uttered, he still smarted at having been required to appear before the Court in 1637, for an inconsequential trespass at Marshfield. After neighbor Holmes had testified, and without further ado, Hatch was "committed to goale for want of sureties for his good behavior." He did not stay long. On the same day, the devout and kindly Thomas Cushman of Plymouth, and John Coombs recognized with him in the sum of twenty pounds each for his appearance "at the next Generall Court of our said soveraigne lord the Kinge, etc., to be holden at Plymouth, etc., and in the mean tyme to be of good behavior towards our said soveraigne lord the King and all his leige people, and abide the further order of the Court, and not depart the same without lycence." Thereupon he was released. The next term of the General Court came and went but the record is silent as to any further action taken against him.

A third prominent citizen to be proceeded against, because of "unworthy carriages" and open disrespect to the Court and its orders, was Isaac Buck, blacksmith, clerk of the military company of Scituate, a brave officer in Phillips war, and for many years town clerk. It was before the war and while acting as clerk of the training band that he came under the disfavor of the Governor and Assistants. The incident is best told in the language of the accusation:—

"At the Generall Court held at Plymouth the 4th of October 1655.

    Before William Bradford, Gov., John Browne and
        Thomas Prence   John Alden
        Timothy Hatherley
                                    Asistants, etc

Whereas there is a complaint brought to us of the unworthy carriages of some persons in the traine band of Scituate in the choise of theire sargeants, which doth seem to us to be in contempt of the government in that they voted for divers unmeet persons for such a place, and alsoe in voting for the ensigne to bee a sargent that was formerly assigned to the place by us; now these are therefore to require you that in one time you come together and make choise of such as are fit for the place of sarjants and those men formerly chosen to attend the daies of training and bearing armes as before; and if you give us occation by a like complaint, we shall take further order as we shall see meet.

"And Whereas we are informed that Isaac Bucke, the now Clarke of the said band, in youer last daie of training, when he called the compaine together, did unworthily misdemean himselfe, we require him that hee make a publicke acknowledgement thereof att the head of the compaine, the next training day, or otherwise wee hereby require him to make his personall appearance att the Generall Court to bee held for this government the first Tuesday in March, next, to answare for his said misdemeanor.

    William Bradford
    Timothy Hatherly
    John Browne
    John Alden

Buck resented the interference by the court in the affairs of the "train band" with which he was justly popular. He refused to shoe the horses which were to be employed to carry one of the commissioners to New Haven on the country's business. A fine of twenty shillings was imposed upon him, but was later remitted.

The "Bench" was kept busy in the performance of a variety of duties. It visited its punishment alike upon male and female; upon old and young. It punished Lydia Rawlins of Scituate, the wife of Nathaniel "for lying, slandering and defaming her brother-in-law Thomas Rawlins of Boston." Mary, the wife of Walter Briggs of Scituate, "having bine presented for telling a lye, the Court, having examined particulars about it, have cleared the said Mary Briggs, but desired Mr. Hatherley for the Court to admonish her to bee wary of giving occation of offense to others, by unnecessary talkeing or the occationing of others to complaine or raise such aspersions."

It has been apparent that this tribunal was little inclined to severity of punishment in dealing with defendants brought before it. The women above-named might have been set in the stocks; Buck, Hatch and Stockbridge, if the full penalty of the law had been imposed, would have been banished, and Williams and Ellmes had they lived in Massachusetts Bay under Endicott would likewise have been condemned to exile. It was due in part to the wisdom and humanity of these Pilgrim magistrates that the craze against witchcraft which so obsessed Salem and Boston, found little or no foothold in the Old Colony. This is nowhere better evidenced than in the action of the Court in the matter of Elizabeth, the wife of William Holmes, of whom it had been currently reported in town that she had become bewitched and walked abroad in the semblance of a bear. Dinah, the eighteen year old daughter of Richard Sylvester and a sister of Lydia Rawlins, had given currency to this yarn. She was summoned before the Court for examination on March 5, 1660, when it appears that "Dinah Silvester, being examined, saith the beare she saw was about a stones throw from the highway when she saw it; and being examined and asked what manor of tayle the beare had, she said *shee* could not tell, for his head was towards her." Thereupon the "Clarke" of the court was ordered to make a record of the evidence "for the clearing of a report about William Holmes his wife being accused to bee a witch."

Two other cases will suffice to illustrate the way in which substantial justice was done, whether the court was sitting as a criminal or civil tribunal. One Isaac Gurney, a neerdo-well who was likely to become a public charge, being in Scituate, was complained of by the townsmen of Scituate for pilfering and disorderly living. He was "sentenced by the Court to be whipt, which accordingly was inflicted and thereupon an order of the Court was directed."

"To the Townsmen of Scituate

These may certify that Isaac Gurney, who was complained against by some of yours for pilfering and other disorderly living, hath for the same received such punishment as we judge he was capable of bearing; and not finding that he doth soe properly belonge to any other place as to youer towne, wee can doe noe less than send him back unto you with order that hee be provided for according to his condition, and that such as you shall place him with, doe so order and govern him, so that so far as he is able hee may bee made to worke for his living; and that whereas some extraordinary charge hath arisen by his imprisonment that it bee by you repayed."

"And accordingly the said Gurney was by warrant returned from constable back to constable backe to Scituate." Thus was justice satisfied and the designing "townsmen" hoist on their own petard.

But one case of homicide in Scituate occurred in the early years—that of Robert Doughty and Nathaniel Rawlings for the murder of three Indians. They were never tried, being successful in breaking jail and effecting their escape.

The record contains the complete story in itself:

"You Robert Doughty and Nathaniel Rawlings both of the Town of Scituate in the Colony of New Plimouth are hier Indicted ffor that you not having the fear of God before your eyes on the seventeenth day of April last past (1686) being Saturday near night at the house of Joseph Silvester in Scituate aforesaid; Did meet and then & there Did Consider and agree: And certain Indians vizt Mathias, Job & Will being then & there in the peace of our Lord the King you Did quarrell with, and them or some of them and especially the said Job in cruel and malicious manner Did beat and abuse and continued there in the sd quarrell with the said Indians, untill it was Darke and then & there near the sd house in violent maner (the said Will and Job having hold of a gun) you or one of you the sd Job did push soe as both the sd Will & Job were thereby thrown over a fence & soe the sd Will was murthered: All which you have feloniously wickedly wilfully and maliciously Done contrary to the Laws of God our soveraigne Lord the King and this Colony and contrary to the peace of your soverainge Lord the King his Crown and Dignity.

This above written Bill was also found by sd Grand Jury & Returned endorsed thereon (Billa Vera).

Plymouth, June 1686
At ye Court of Assists   Hinckley Govr.

Also at said Court the persons before in the other leaf mentioned vizt: Robert Doughty and Nathaniell Rawlings having been committed to Goal at plimouth for the offences & crimes before mentioned and Breaking out of said Goal before sd Court and haveing made their escape were Indicted as next followeth:

You Henry Neal, Robert Doughty and Nathaniel Rawlings are here Indicted for that you not having the fear of God before your eyes, after your commitment to his majesties Goal at New Plimouth for Divers wicked & felonious actions Did on the eleventh day of May 1686 in the evening ffeloniously break out of sd Goal and there made your escape and Did flee from Justice with Intent to evade a legall tryall; all which you have wickedly and feloniously Done against the peace of our soveraigne Lord the King his Crown and Dignity and contrary to the law in such cases made and provided.

This above written Bill being also found by the Grand Jury who returned their verdict endorsed thereon Billa Vera.

The sd persons having escaped as aforesaid hindered or prevented any further prosecution at that Court."

While the Court was thus dealing with murderers, miscreants and criminal offenders, it was also busy on the civil side.

Here marriages were performed and few, a very few, divorces granted. Wills were proved, estates of deceased persons settled, and disputes between the living tried by jury or before the Court. Besides the Court of Assistants a Selectman's Court empowered to try issues involving five pounds or under, was established in 1658.

It must be remembered that none of the men occupying these judicial positions were educated in the law or practised that profession. In the Puritan Colony of Massachusetts Bay lawyers were frowned upon. They were ineligible to sit as deputies in the General Court to enact the laws, and little heed was given to such of them as found places in the magistracy, in the interpretation of them. For this purpose the assistance of the clergy was invoked. In Plymouth Colony however, the members of the legal profession were better treated. While they were not discriminated against neither were they made the objects of favor or high place. There were three lawyers in Scituate from the early days of Plymouth Colony to the Union in 1692. They were Edward Foster, a first comer, and John Hoar and John Saffin, neighbors at little Musquashcut Pond. The latter evidently did not find the practice of law profitable. His legal abilities were recognized however when he removed to Boston and later took up his abode in Bristol.

Hoar †, although a man of breeding, intelligence and

---

† He was a son of Charles Hoar, who was for a time in the reigns of the earlier Stuarts, Sheriff of the city of Gloucester, England. His mother, Joanna, came to Massachusetts, a widow, with five sturdy sons in 1640. Three years later John settled in Scituate. Another brother Hezekiah was here for a time, Daniel

education was never called upon while he lived in Scituate to take an active part in public affairs, nor do the records disclose that he practiced his profession in the Courts.

Indeed, his sole appearance there was as a litigant over disputed titles with some of his fellow proprietors in the Conihasset partnership. He removed to Concord in 1660.

By far the greatest number of the cases tried before the early Pilgrim tribunal were actions concerning land titles and debt. Every man was his own lawyer,—for the Massachusetts Bay practice of engaging the services of "Patrons" to defend or aid parties in their suits, did not obtain to a great extent in the Plymouth Colony. This served to engender litigation and stir up strife. Nor was such engagement expensive. Here is a copy of the costs in the action of William Hatch of Marshfield against John Hoar "for sowing, reaping and carrying away wheat off the land that the said Hatch hired of Robert Hammond."

"The charge of the Court as it respects William Hatch about the above suite, comes to

---

was of Concord, Richard of Yarmouth and Leonard succeeded Rev. Charles Chauncey as President of Harvard College. Charles Francis Adams, in the "Three Episodes of Massachusetts History" says of this sterling woman: "About 1640, after the death of her husband, Joanna Hoar came to Massachusetts with her five children and died in Braintree in December in 1661; where she sleeps in the old burying ground in a common grave with her son, the third President of Harvard College, and Bridget, wife of that son, and daughter of John Lisle by his wife, Known in English History as the Lady Alice Lisle; whose tragic fate made familiar through the page of Macauley, furnishes one of the historic incidents deemed worthy to be immortalized by the artist's hand on the walls of the entrance to the chambers of Parliament. The threads of human destiny are apt to interlace in a way calculated to excite surprise; and it is interesting in the old burying ground of a New England town thus suddenly to come upon an inscription which tells him who stops to decipher it that the daughter of her whom Jeffreys caused to be put to death for succoring the fugitives of Sedgmuir. there lies buried." That President Leonard Hoar had a high opinion of the abilities of his brother John's children is evidenced by this extract from his will. "x x x" My medical writings to my wife's custody till some of my kindred addicted to those studies, shall desire them, and especially John Hoar's or any of my brothers' or sisters' sons or grandsons."

TOWN GOVERNMENT AND FREEMEN

		s.	d.
Videlecet, for the witnesses, the Clarke, the jury, and the Marshall, the sume of	....	17	:06
To the Clarke for making an execution	....	02	:06
To the Clarke for a suppena	....	00	:06
To Edward Tarte, a witness	....	01	:00

Slander, and "defamation of character" were favorite and frequent actions. These were presented with great zeal and much interest, not only by the litigants, but also among the witnesses. It was not an unusual occurrence after the verdict in one of these cases that an onlooker, a neighbor or friend of one of the parties would accuse a witness of perjury in the case; whereupon a new suit would be instituted. The damages recovered were usually not large,—a few shillings. The Marshal and constables were often plaintiffs in such actions. In the discharge of their official duties they distrained cattle, household furniture and all kinds of personal property and belongings. In one case a pewter basin was taken by a constable to satisfy an execution for seven shillings. Some friend of the owner of the basin proclaimed that the constable stole it—and was himself promptly sued. George Barlow the colony Marshal who collected fines and penalties imposed by the Court by way of distress, frequently was criticised for the heartless manner in which he served the Court's processes. In 1660 he was ordered to collect a fine of twenty-four pounds from one Goodman Gaunt. John Jenkins alleged that failing to receive payment of this amount the Marshal seized seven cows and heifers, two steers and seven and one-half bushels of peas in satisfaction; that while he had this property of Gaunt's in his possession under execution, one of the cows died, whereupon Barlow repaired again to Gaunt's home and seized another cow. For this statement, which was probably exaggerated, Jenkins was brought to court. The jury returned a verdict for the marshal and thereupon Jenkins was ordered to pay five pounds and costs, to the maligned Barlow or make such an acknowlegement in open court as should be satisfactory to him. He chose the latter.

James Doughty of Marshfield, a spinner, "complained against Peter Collymore (of Scituate), in an action of slander and defamation, to the damage of one hundred pounds, for reporting that Thomas Ingham tould him that the wife of said James Doughty did advise, or put the said Thomas Ingham in a way, how he might steale yearne, and make his cloth hold weight, and a pretty matter to spare." This slander cost Collamore five pounds, which he paid.

Even Mr. Chauncey caught the spirit. He sued William Barstow for slander and recovered "an hundred pound damage and the cost of the suite." Mr. Chauncey remitted the damages, satisfied with the moral effect of the verdict; he took only the costs taxed at eighteen shillings and sixpence. Deacon Joseph Tilden who had been slandered by William Randall was of a like forgiving mind. He brought two suits against Randall both of which he subsequently withdrew upon the making of this acknowledgement:—

"Whereas Mr. Joseph Tilden hath two actions depending against William Randall, for slandering and defaming of him now, that all men may see and know that it not William Randall's estate that he lookes at, but only to his credit, name and reputation, therefore the said Joseph Tilden is willing to lett fall his actions and rest satisfyed, if the said Randall should justify his witnesses, who witness that Randall should say that the said Tilden is a cheather, a divilish rogue; as cheating divill as ever went to hell and one that had cheated him of many a pound; and that he made nothing of takeing a false oath, and was noe more cleare of the false oath hee tooke than the divill was. In all which, I, the said William Randall, did sinfully and wickedfully speake, haveing no ground soe to say; and do declare the said Tilden, before all the world to be free from the guilt of the slanderous charges before mensioned; and this publickly to declare and acknowledge in the open Court, and at a publicke meeting at Scituate; and also give this acknowledgement of clearing under my hand and satisfy the said Tilden what just and due charges he hath been att in preparation of his actions.

The last day of October
Anno Dom. 1666

The marke of X
William Randall

In 1685, the colony was divided into the three counties of Plymouth, Bristol and Barnstable and County Courts "Kept by the magistrates (Assistants) living in the several counties or by and other magistrate that can attend the same or by such as the General Court shall appoint from time to time" were established. These had the same jurisdiction as had formerly been exercised by the General Court, in the probate of estates of deceased persons, and in civil and criminal proceedings, except in matters of divorce and "in cases extending to life or banishment." After the downfall of Andros and upon the annexation, in place of the courts as they had previously existed there was a Court held by a Justice of the Peace appointed by the Governor, in which civil actions involving forty shillings were tried; an Inferior Court of Common Pleas composed of four of the Justices of the Peace; a Court of Quarter Sessions of the Peace which tried criminal cases, and a Superior Court of Judicature composed of a Chief Justice and four other justices, which acted both as an appellate court, and one of original jurisdiction in all cases civil and criminal. This Court held one session yearly on the third Tuesday of February at Plymouth. These justices also "kept a court of assize and general goal delivery for the respective counties." The sittings of the common pleas, and the quarter sessions were likewise held at Plymouth, "on the third Tuesdayes in March, June, September and December." The Governor or a specially appointed chancellor sat with members of the council as "a high court of chancery." There was also a "judge for the probate of wills and granting of administrations" over whose decrees the Governor and Council had appellate jurisdiction. Scituate was represented upon the benches of both the Inferior and Superior courts from this time on until the close of the Revolution. John Cushing the son of the first comer, and his son, John; as well as Elijah, Nathan and William, of the same family, were learned and able members of the one or the other; Thomas Clap, a grandson of the Thomas who settled here in 1640 was another. John Turner, a descendant of Humphrey was appointed in 1780, Joseph Otis in 1703, and Barnabas Lothrop, a justice of the Inferior Court for Barnstable County, was a descendant of the worthy churchman who in 1640 left Scituate to set up his congregation at Barnstable. John Otis was born here. He was the grandfather of James Otis the patriot. Ezra Bourne also a member of the Barnstable Court was the brother of Rev. Shearjashub Bourne of Scituate, who married for his third wife Deborah, the daughter of Samuel Barker and preached and lived here for twenty years. John Saffin was a justice of the Superior Court from Bristol, now in Rhode Island, but then the shire town of Bristol County.

CHAPTER IX

TOWN GOVERNMENT AND FREEMEN

"All praise to others, early come or late—
For love and labor on our Ship of State;
But this must stand beyond all praise and zeal,
The Pilgrim Fathers laid the ribs and keel;
On their strong lines we base our nation's health—
The man, the home, the town, the Commonwealth." †

THE establishment of the town in 1636 meant little in the way of the management of its own affairs by the freemen. They were all managed by and from the seat of the General Court at Plymouth. No strictly town officer save that of constable was chosen until 1666. This office was an important one. The power and authority of the Court in dealing with the inhabitants of the colony were personified in it. None were elected to it but men of the highest standing in their respective communities and of proved integrity. The duties of the constable are best shown by the oath taken by him in qualifying for the duties of the office.

"The Oath of a Constable:

"You shall sweare to be truly loyal x x x x you shall faithfully serve in the office of Constable in the ward of Scituate for this present yeare according to that measure of wisdome understanding and discretion God hath given you. In which time you shall diligently see that his Majesties the peace commanded be not broken, but shall carrie the person or persons offending before the Governor of this Corporation or some one of his Assistants, and there attend the hear-

---

† John Boyle O'Reilly's poem written for and read at the dedication of the Pilgrim Monument, Plymouth.

ing of the Case and such order as shall be given you. You shall apprehend all suspitious persons and bring them before the said Governor or some one of his Assistants as aforesaid. You shall duly and truly serve such warrants and give such summons as shall be directed unto you from the Governor and Assistants before mentioned, and shall labour to advance the peace and happiness of this Corporation and oppose anything that shall seeme to annoy the same by all due means and courses."

Anthony Annable was chosen to this office in 1633, 1634 and 1637 and Humprhey Turner, James Cudworth, George Kennerick, Samuel Fuller, Josiah Checkett, John Stockbridge, Robert Stetson, William Reade, Thomas Clap, Ephraim Kempton, John Hollett, Edward Jenkins, George Sutton, George Russell, John Williams, Jr., Peter Collamer, John Whitcomb, William Parker, Joseph Coleman, William Randall, Thomas Robinson, William Hatch, Thomas Pynchon, John Turner Sr., Abraham Sutton, Joseph Wormell, Henry Ewell, Humphrey Johnson and Isaac Buck from thence during the next twenty-five years. It was one of the first duties of Annable in his office of constable to demand from his neighbors Nathaniel Tilden, Samuel Hinckley, George Kennerick, Samuel Fuller and John Lewis a penalty of half a shilling each imposed upon them by the Court for "keepeing" various "swine unringed."†. The constables collect the rates, or taxes that were from

---

† In order to protect the meadows (the only source of grass in the early days) a law was passed in 1633, "that no man keepe more swine than he can ordinarily keepe about his owne place, and that they be doubly wrung or at least sufficiently wrung that they root not up & destroy the meadows &c x x x x Also if in case any shall finde himselfe aggrieved & required the yoaking of any unruly swine, by reason of damage he is like to sustain, then to forefeit for every such default, per weeke, besides the damage, five shillings. Also that all piggs at or before ten weeks old shall be wrung. And upon sufficient notice to the next justice of the peace (assistant) he to grant warrant to the constable to straine any of these fines. x x x But if any lose their rings or yoakes, the first notice to be without fine." Plymouth Colony Records Vol XI Page 15.

time to time assessed for various purposes. In 1646 the proportion of the publicke charges (i. e. the expenses of the Governor and Assistants) to be borne by Scituate was £4.10s. This sum should have been collected by Ephraim Kempton and John Hollett the constables of that year. For some reason they were remiss about it and at the next Court:

> "It was ordered that the now constables of Scituate be by warrant required to appear at the next Generall Court, to give their account concerning ye officers wages."

Prior to 1630 there had been no highways regularly laid out and established in Scituate. Such ways as existed in the colony had been built under an order of the Court that "at such convenient time as shall seeme meet to the Governor and Counsell (Assistants), upon warning given, all men meet together for mending of the highwaies, with such tooles and instruments as shall be appointed." In December 1638 it was

> "ordered by the Court that the Governor and Assistants shall appoint some to view the heigh ways, and repair them where they are amisse, and to alter those that are not convenyently layde forth unto a moore convenient place. And that the (y,) constables shall require some speciall help for the present repairs of them in the unpassable places and that those that help now to be spared in summer."

The next year:

> "Edward Winslow and William Collyer, both of Marshfield, are requested to take a view of the highwayes toward Greenes Harbor and Scituate from Plymouth, and to cause them to be amended that are in decay, or to alter them to more conveniency, and either of them to call one or two with them to do yt" and "Forasmuch as great complaint is made that the highwayes about the colony are in decay, it is ordered by the Court, that some shall be joyned with the con-

stables to survey the wayes about eich towne, and cause men to repair them viz x x x x for Scituate William Hatch and Edward Foster, and to call men to laboure thereat, as they shall bee found fitt, and if any shall refuse to help about the same, that they be presented by the grand enquest."

For eight years the highways of Scituate were neglected. None had been laid out or built, notwithstanding two juries had been empanelled to lay them out and the constables by a general law † charged with the duty of constructing them. In 1642 Thomas Rawlins and Henry Merritt were chosen the first surveyors of the town. They were followed after two years of service by John Stockbridge and Walter Woodward who together served until 1648. In that year four men were chosen, namely, John Willis, Thomas Chambers, Humphrey Turner and Thomas Bird. This larger board, if we draw a correct conclusion from the record, was not particularly efficient. Its members in the very year of their election were presented by the grand jury "for not mending the hyewayes according to order" but "upon redress thereof are cleared of this presentment" and again the next year, the Grand Inquest reports "We present the serveyers of Seteat for not repairing the hieway over a marsh called Rotten Marsh." ‡

John Hewes, Sr., the Welshman, Ephraim Kempton, John Hollett, Peter Collamore, William Randall, Stephen

---

† *"1640. March 2. That the Constable see the high waies for man & beast to be made and kept in convenient repair & therefore be also appointed surveighor for the liberty he is chosen.. That two serveighors in every constablerick be chosen each year to see that the high waies be mended competently.* And if it fall out that a way be wanting upon due complaint That then the Governor panell a jury & upon oath charge them to lay out such a way as in conscience they finde most beneficiall for the Common weale & as little prejudice as may be to the particular." Plymouth Colony Records Vol XI (Laws) page 11. That part of the above law which is italicized was repealed in 1658 when the constables were relieved from this duty and "Surveyors of highwaies x x chosen and established at the Court in June annually."

‡ The road from Greenbush to Doggett's ferry over the North River.

Vinal, John Cushing, John Williams, Jr., William Barstow, Thomas Pincin and Cornet Robert Stetson were among the important men of the town to hold this office, during the time when the principal highways were being constructed.

The first roads were built early. These were Kent Street, Meeting House Lane, Greenfield Lane, and the Driftway. The latter is the road leading from the third cliff westerly, skirting the New Harbor marshes as far as Stockbridge's mill on the first Herring brook. Its name was later changed to Water Street but is now the Driftway again. There was also the road running parallel with Satuit Brook, now called First Parish Road and a way, not much more than a cartpath, from the "Gulph," through Farm Neck to the Harbor. It was this road which John Williams "impropriated" by fencing in 1664. Upon complaint against him for this action, Messrs. Hatherly, Cudworth, Lieutenant Torrey, Cornet Stetson and John Turner were appointed by the court "to throw up the above mentioned fence that the highway x x x bee not unjustly impropriated."

In 1646 Mr. Hatherly at the request of the Court impanelled a jury to lay out a road from Stockbridge's Milldam to "Belle house necke" which was the name given by Vassall to the locality where he built his "West Newlands." It is the present road from Greenbush to Norwell. In 1653 a road was laid out from what is now Hanover Four Corners to the Harbor. Another in the same year was built from the Stockbridge Mill or George Russell's Mill, or the old mill or Isaac Stedman's Mill, as it is interchangeably spoken of in the records, over Brushy Hill at Greenbush toward Cohasset. Next in order of time came a road from Buck's field at the Harbor † and the continuation of the highway toward the present Little's bridge over the North River. In 1654 Mr. Hatherly was "appointed and requested by the Court, with other inhabitants of Scituate, to

---

† This was within the limits of the Conihasset Grant, and was therefore probably laid out by the Partners.

provide two or three men to view and lay out the most convenientest way from Plymouth to Scituate and to see they bee appointed." The commissioners of the United Colonies were frequently meeting both at Boston and Plymouth and it was important that there should be a convenient and direct way between the northernmost town of the Plymouth Colony which adjoined the "Bay Colony," and the seat of government of the former. It is not known who Hatherly chose to act with him, but they soon set about the building of the "Old Boston turnpike" as it has been called for many years, which runs from Queen Anne's Corner to Plymouth. A contract was made with William Barstow of Scituate to build a bridge over the North River (now connecting Hanover and Pembroke,) and this being accomplished the most "convenientest" way between Scituate and Plymouth was established. In 1658 "On complaint of Robert Studson (Stetson), for want of a convenient way from his house to the meeting, this Court doth request and appoint Mr. Hatherly and Capt. Cudworth with any other whom they shall choose, to lay out a footway from the uper (second) Meeting house at the North River att Scituate, up said river, to the house of Robert Studson, soe as may bee most convenient & least prejudiciall to any." It has been called "The Up River road," following the course of the stream to Hanover Four Corners, ever since. In 1661 the Conihasset partners agreed "that there shall be a highway left † for both cart and cattle from the Little Pond ‡ into the way that goes to Hoopole Necke, upon the undivided land and from the Little pond to the sea side where the way did formerly lie between 2 slows." This was clearly intended for the accommodation of Mr. Hatherly, who had his farm about the Great Musquashcut pond at the foot of Mann Hill; John Saffin and John Hoar who lived south of it, and Walter Briggs whose farm was at the Glades. Men now living remember the remains of a "way from the Little Pond to

---

† Left out of the division of lands among the Partners.
‡ Little Musquashcut Pond.

the seaside where the way did formerly lie between 2 slows." Violent storms have since then driven back the beach and filled in the slough hole on the easterly side, but the road itself was there seventy-five years ago.

Up to the year 1639 all of the business of the towns comprising the Colony was done at Plymouth. The election of constables and highway surveyors was held there and the Governor and Assistants conducted municipal affairs either directly, or through the agency of a local Assistant and such freemen or townsmen as might be joined with him, in a particular service. In that year towns were authorized to make such by-laws as were requisite "for the herding of cattell and doing such other things as shall be needful for the mayntenance of good neighbourhood," and affix penalties not repugnant to, or infringing upon any public law. They were also allowed to "make levyes, rates & taxes for their townes charges & to distraine such as shall refuse to pay the same upon warrant from the Court or Governor." The purposes for which these town rates were levied were the support of the poor and of the ministry. This latter was in accord with the Pilgrim policy, although it was not crystallized into statute until June 1657. Then it was enacted:

"Whereas this General Court takeing into their seriouse consideration the great defect that either is or like to bee in ye several Townshipes in this Jurisdiction for want of an able Godly teaching Ministrey and the great prejudice to the soules of many like to ensue; and being desirouse according to our duties that such defects should not bee for want of due Incurragement to such as either are or shall bee Imployed in soe good a worke of the Lord for his honner and the good of soules And in consideration that inasmuch as the several Townshipes granted by the Government; was that such a Companie might be received as should maintaine the Publicke worshipe and service of God there, do therefore judge that the whole both Church and towne are mutually Ingaged to Support the same; And therefore Order and agree That in whatsoever Townships there is or shall bee an able Godly Teaching Minnister which is approved by this Government that then four men bee chosen by the Inhabitants, or In case of theire Neglect chosen by any three or more of the Majestrates, to make an equall and just proportion upon the estates of the Inhabitants according to their abilities to make up such a Convenient maintenance, for his Comfortable attendance on his worke as shall bee agreed upon by the Church in each township where any is, with the concurrence of the Rest of the Inhabitants if it may be had, or by the Majestrates aforesaid in case of the apparent Neglect; and that destresse, according as in other Just Cases provided, bee made upon such as refuse to pay such theire proportions which is in Justice due; But in Case there bee any other way whereby any townships doe or shall Agree that may effect the end aforesaid this law not to bee binding to them."

Other strictly local taxes were imposed for maintenance of the town military company, its stock of ammunition and the building and maintenance of a town pound and bilboes or stocks. Individual citizens were chosen to attend to these necessities the "raters" "made" the taxes and the constables as collectors of taxes paid them. For instance:—

"At a towne meeting held ye 12d of July 1665 Mr. Tilden was appointed by ye town to provide a barrell of powder for ye towne and what pay Mr. Tilden doth pay for ye powder the same sorte of pay ye towne doth engage to pay Mr. Tilden. If Mr. Tilden pay money for ye powder ye towne is to pay Mr. Tilden in money again, and satisfy him for his paynes."

And

"August 7, (1667)

The town agreed that the constables should pay the town's creditors before the thirtieth of January next in merchantable corn."

Other public expenditures for the payment of which rates were made appertained to the government of the colony. Among them were the "wages" of the Governor and Assistants; their board or the "magistrates table"; the fees of the court "clarke" and messenger; and for a bounty on wolves killed by Indians and others.

"1 June 1641 Bradford Govr.

The rates of the severall townes for the payment of the clark, & 30 bushells of corn for the messenger:—

	£	S	d		£	S	d
Plymouth	05	00	00	Taunton	02	10	00
Duxbarrow	03	10	00	Barnestable	02	10	00
Scituate	04	00	00	Yarmouth	02	10	00
Sandwich	03	00	00	Rexhame †	02		

Persons were rated or taxed "according to theire visible estates and faculties, that is according to theire faculties and personall abilities whether they are in lands, both meddow lands, Improved lands or dormant lands appropriated, or in cattle goods or stock Imployed in Trading in boates barques &c., mills or other visible estate." The rate of taxation was about one pound on a hundred but this seemed burdensome and additional revenues were obtained by "letting out the fisheries att the Cape" and the trade at the Kennebic." ‡ Excise and impost duties were levied on wines, beer, tobacco, "strong water," and whales, whale oil, iron, boards, tar, oysters and mackerel. In 1645 the tax on "every gallon of Spanish wine was eight pence; every gallon of ffrench wyne four pence; every gallon of strong water eighteen pence & every pound of tobacco one penny." The latter was not imposed upon home raised tobacco much of which was grown from time to time in Scituate. These taxes went for the ordinary charges as well as the occasionally extraordinary ones. When in 1663, while Prence was Governor, his vanity sought surroundings more nearly

---

† The name given to the territory of Marshfield before its incorporation.

‡ Fur trading on the Kennebec River in Maine.

commensurate with his pride and dignity it was "ordered by the Court, that a convenient, handsome rome bee added to the Governor's house; and that the charg of the building thereof bee defrayed out of the pay for Kenebecke, if that kind of pay will doe it; and if not, then a parte of those goods and the rest to be raised by rate."

Town clerks were chosen in 1646. Their duties were prescribed by law and they have not materially changed in two hundred and sixty-nine years. Assessors were not regularly chosen until 1676.

It has been apparent that although an efficient local self-government was the result aimed at by the Pilgrims, it was slow of accomplishment. A law passed in 1656 created the office of "Celectman for the better managing of the afaires of the respective Town Shipes." They were petty judicial officers at first, rather than administratives and executives. The law authorized them to hear and determine differences involving forty shillings in amount, and controversies between the settlers and the Indians over damage done to the latter's corn by the cattle and swine of the former. They could summon witnesses in these causes and were to determine them "according to legall evidence." They were originally five in number, empowered to hold four courts a year, required to prosecute intruders into their respective towns, compel persons to attend divine worship and to regulate familes. †

Although another advance had been made toward self-government in the town, the spirit of paternalism in the magistracy was still dominant; and freemen chosen to the position of Selectmen must be approved by the Court before they could act in that capacity. ‡ Scituate did not choose

† "July 6, 1669 Whereas a great Inconvenience hath arisen by single persons in this Collonie being of themselves and not betaking themselves to live in well governed families, It is enacted by the Court that henceforth no single person be suffered to live of himselfe or in any family but such as the Selectmen of the Towne shall approve of."

‡ It was not until the creation of the Province, when they were called Selectmen or Townsmen, that they began to be town fathers in a real sense.

them until 1666. Elder Thomas King, Cornet Robert Stetson and Isaac Chittenden were the first. The law provided that they should be able and discreet men. They were,—the best men were chosen. John Cushing, the American ancestor of the great family of jurists, served continuously from 1672 until the reign of Andros, fourteen years later, temporarily put an end to local and colonial self-government in Massachusetts. Jeremiah Hatch served for eleven years, Isaac Buck eight: Samuel Clapp six; Cornet Robert Stetson and Isaac Chittenden each five; Elder King three; Capt. Michael Peirce the Indian fighter two; and John Sutton, John Damon, John Bryant, Sr., Thomas King, Jr., James Briggs and Nathaniel Tilden, each one year. The frequency with which the names of these same men appear in other public capacities asserts both their prominence and worth. In addition to serving as Selectmen Isaac Buck was Town Clerk for twenty-eight years. Other clerks were Richard Garrett, afterwards Clerk of the Conihasset Partners, for seven years; James Torrey, who was town clerk and clerk of the Partners at the same time, during a part of his term of service, of nineteen years: Deacon James Torrey, son of the lieutenant was in the office thirteen years; James Cushing, son of the first John, served for seven years; John Cushing, 3rd., called junior, a grandson of the above, was town clerk at the time of his death. He served for fifty-seven years, twenty-two and thirty-two each consecutively, the whole term broken only by the choice of Thomas Clapp in 1745. James Briggs above-named as selectman kept the town records for fourteen years. He was in office at the end of the Revolution, when this municipal record closes.

The towns in the colony were early ordered by statute to care for their poor. Three months' residence in a place without being "excepted against," gave a lawful settlement. The authority to "except against them" lay with the selectmen. They were strict and severe in the performance of this duty, largely because of the fear that a newcomer might become an eventual charge. Here is an example of it: "Ruth Crage, widow of Robert Crage, a transient person, with her children Robert, Elizabeth, Lydia and Lois, who have lately come into this town for the purpose of abiding therein, not having obtained, the town consent therefore, was notified and warned to depart and did depart from the town."

Deane † says that Overseers of the Poor were chosen in 1667. He is probably led into this error by the vote of the town passed April eleventh of that year.

"At a town meeting 11 April 1667—Whereas some persons out of their own sinister ends and by requests have so aptly been harbourers and entertainers of such as are strangers, coming from other towns and places, by which means the town cometh to be burdened, and themselves many times be invited. Wherefore for the preventing for the future, such and the like inconveniences as were likely to accrue by such practice, the town being meet this day and taking the premises into their serious consideration, do by virtue (of) their power and authority given and granted to them by the Court concerning things of this nature agree, conclude, enact and order, that if any person or persons whatsoever, shall after the date of these presents receive unto their houses or shelter, or harbour, entertain or retain any person that is or shall come from any other town or place, which hath not the approbation of the town, or of such men as the town hath appointed for such an end—that such a person entertaining or retaining any such aforementioned person, shall within five days after he shall be required thereunto by someone of the townsmen deputed for to take securitie in such case, put in such securitie as they shall except (accept) for to discharge the town of such person or persons; and in case any person or persons shall presume notwithstanding, to harbor retain and entertain

---

† History of Scituate page 110.

any such person and neglect to give in such securitie as is before expressed, that then every such person for entertaining or retaining, shall for every week after, forfeit ten shillings per week; and the town doth authorize with full power, those men that are appointed by the town to see the town secured from such persons, to take security in the towns behalf and for to ask, demand and receive such penalties or fines as by the breach of this order shall appear to be due to the town; and in case of refusing to make satisfaction therefor, to prosecute such aforesaid by due course of law in the town's behalf until they bring it to effect, and the town is to bear their charges.

The town chose these men to prosecute this order and the order bearing date the eighth of December 1664 respecting timber.

The men chosen are:
Capt. Cudworth,
Cornet Stetson
Mr. Tilden

The men chosen under this vote were not overseers of the poor as such. They were appointed under the statute of 1658 which required towns to choose two or three men to look after children "that all such as are not able to provide necessary and convenient food and clothing for theire children and will not dispose of them themselves, soe as they may bee better provided for: and such children shalbee disposed of by said men soe appointed as they shall see meet, soe as they may bee comfortably provided for in the premises; and the townes shall return the names of such men as shalbee so deputed into the Court." It will be seen that there is no provision in this law for an annual election of these officers at Plymouth, when the electors repaired in June of each year to choose their town officers, and that the "two or three men" so selected were confined in their duties solely to children. The statute passed June 6, 1683 put the care of the poor in the hands of "the celect men in each towne (who) shall take care and see that the poor in their respective townes be provided for." For forty years before then the town in open meeting dealt with each individual necessity.

The case of George Moore is in point. As a young man he had come into the colony and lived as a servant with Edward Doty of Plymouth. He became a charge there in 1645, when the Court ordered that his goods, which had been attached by Thomas Rickard and John Rogers, who had furnished him sustenance "be sold to the best advantage and the money due them for his keepeing to be payed them as far as it will extend & if there be any over plus, it to be payd for his further maintenance." He later appeared in Scituate and was accepted. How his record at Plymouth came to be overlooked is not clear. He was granted a quantity of upland and salt marsh upon the First Herring Brook and extending thence toward the North River. The salt marsh which was laid out to him was on either side of the present road from Greenbush to Little's Bridge and was called Rotten Marsh, or George Moore's Swamp. He did not prosper in Scituate. His marsh was apparently well named and his upland perhaps not better. In 1664 the court ordered the sale of his farm and he was put in the care of Ensign John Williams at the Harbor by the town. Two years later he was still there. On May 9, 1666:—"the day above wrighten ye towne did agree that ye Selectmen should provide for George Moore if ye town Did not met together againe before his time was expired with Ensign Williams." Later on Ensign Williams "agrees with the town to keep George Moore ye next year for 3 pounds 16 shillings, to be paid in wheat and barley." He must have still been with the Ensign in 1668 for on June 26, Williams was appointed the agent of the town "to provide a blanket and sheet for George Moore's bed." Eventually he was again at the First Herring brook. The final record seems to justify his penurious condition after years of toil upon his decayed acres.—

"The jury being unpannelled and sworne to inquire of the death of George More, this 26th day of March 1677, given in this following for theire verdict:—

Wee, who according to our oath had the viewing of the body of George More, of Scituate, cannot find either by persons or things what was the cause of his death, but according to our best understanding, wee apprehend that it was some suddaine fainting fitt, or some stoping of his breath, was the whole and sole cause of his death." †

It is not the purpose of the writer to dwell in these pages, upon those unfortunates whom adverse circumstances forced to "go on the town." The sole reason for doing so, exists in the fact that no true picture of this colonial town can be drawn, and no just estimate of the pilgrim character be reached, without showing the latter as he was in the creation and maintenance of that civil body politic for the advancement of the Christian faith, which he had promised in the cabin of the Mayflower to uphold. No better opportunity is offered than the manner in which he treated the public poor. One more case will suffice:—Thomas Hickes had come to Scituate from Plymouth, where he had been for seventeen years, in 1640. Both he and his wife were well advanced in years. His farm here was at the east of Brushy Hill and about a mile southwest from the Harbor. It was small and unproductive. For twelve years both managed to subsist upon it and in 1652 when he died, the small estate remained to her intact. Old, sick and feeble, she was unable to maintain herself, and was compelled to seek assistance from the town. In town meeting it was:—

"agreed, and chose Walter Briggs and Robert Sprout to take ward of Widow Hickes and to maintain her upon her own estate as far as it will go, and then the town to make supply afterwards, and place her in the fittest place they can for her comfort and the towns profit; and the town is not willing to be charged with

---

† Plymouth Colony Records Vol. V Page 250.

above 2s. 6d. a week except in extraordinary cases, and the town hath ordered that there shall be 3 pounds put in the next rating to be in readiness to supply the widow's wants when necessity shall require."

There is the point—a prominent pilgrim characteristic—justice before generosity.

There was no thought of public schools in the early days of the colony. The leaders were mostly men of education. They had expected that their new commonwealth would attract to itself men of that class. In this they were partially disappointed. The words of Governor Bradford quoted in the preface to this volume, evidence the concern which he and others felt.

Rev. Charles Chauncey, the second minister, was an accomplished and well educated man. Cotton Mather in his *Magnalia, Christi Americana,* says of him that, "he was incomparably well skilled in all the learned languages, especially in the oriental, and eminently in the Hebrew." Rev. William Witherell, the first pastor of the second church, had been a grammar school teacher in the Bay Colony before his ordination to the ministry, and while he lived in Duxbury (1638) although nominally a "planter," clearing and tilling his fifty-five acre farm on the South River, undoubtedly continued his vocation among the families there. These men privately instructed the youth of the town and, upon the erection of the "college at Cambridge," fitted them for entrance to it. It is probable also that Henry Dunster, resigning his place as president of the college, to minister to the first parish of Scituate, found here opportunity for continuing his services as an educator while engaged in the work of the church. Capt. Cudworth too was a man of good education, something of a critical analyst and a writer of good, if quaint, English. As showing this an extract from letter hereafter alluded to † is given.

"You may remember a law once made, called Thomas Hinckley's law; that if any neglect the worship of

---

† Post page 264.

God in the place where he lives, and set up a worship contrary to God and the allowance of this Government to the publick profanation of God's Holy Day and ordinances, he shall pay 10 shillings. This law would not reach what then (early in the year 1658) was aimed at, because he must do all things therein express'd or else not break the law. In March last a Court of Deputies was called, and some acts touching Quakers were made: and then they contrived to make this law serviceable to them by putting out the word (*and*) and putting in the word (*or*) which is a disjunctive and makes every branch to become a law; yet they left it dated June 6, 1651. And so it stands as an act of the Gen. Court they to be the authors of it seven years before it was in being."

William Vassall who quarrelled so constantly with Mr. Chauncy was by no means ungifted in facility of expression. He must certainly have received a good education for the times in which he lived, to be able to indite his reverend antagonist in this manner.

"We did not renew our Covenant surreptitiously. We secreted nothing by fraud from you, for you had before sent messengers to tell us that we were not of your church; and if you have any just exceptions against some of our persons, you have broken Christ's rule which require 'If thou has aught against thy brother, to tell him between thee and him &c: But thy brother intreats thee to show him his offence and offers satisfaction; and yet you will cast evil reports abroad of him, who may not know the fault committed."

A brief relation of the trades and callings in which the early colonizers of Scituate were engaged at the time they left England, and some of their known characteristics, may shed an added light upon that view of their condition now under consideration.

William Gilson was a miller.

Anthony Annable, Henry Merritt, Peter Collamore, Thomas Pincin and Isaac Stedman, although all men of substance could not write their names.

Timothy Hatherley was a merchant and a man of means.
Edward Foster, John Hoar and John Saffin were lawyers.
Humphrey Turner was a tanner.
Joseph Coleman, a shoemaker.
John Bryant, a carpenter.
Isaac Buck, a blacksmith.
George Pedcock and Ephraim Kempton, tailors.
Edward Jenkins, an inn keeper.
George Lewis and James Torrey weavers.

John Stockbridge a mill wright; and Gowin White, Richard Mann, William Holmes and John Hollett were farmers.

All of necessity became planters when they began the foundation of the "New Freedom." They were outcasts, voluntary exiles, and their social condition was not to be compared with their compatriots of the Massachusetts Bay Colony who with royal charter and as colonizers for the Crown, settled in and about Boston. Roxbury and Charlestown had their grammar Schools in 1635, Braintree a Latin school a few years later and Cambridge the "College" for the education of "pious ministers" for them all.

It is not to be denied that for half a century the undesirables of whom Bradford wrote continued to come. In 1678 "Att the Generall Court of his Majestie held att Plymouth for the Jurisdiction of New Plymouth the fifth of June 1678. Ffor the preventing of prophanes † Increasing in the Collonies which is soe provoaking to God and threatening to bring Judgments upon us:

It is enacted as an addition to our printed order Chapter 9th folio 30th That none shall come to inhabite without leave &c; and if any have or shall att any time intrude themselfes to Inhabite anywhere within this Colonie, not attending the aforesaid order, shall forthwith be warned to be gon out of the Collonie, which if

---

† Profaneness-ridicule of the word of God and of His worship.

they shall not speedily doe, then every such offender shall pay five shillings per week for every weekes continuance in this Colonie after warning to be gon:

And if any of our inhabitants shall at any time sell or hier out accommodation in this Collonie to any that have not according to Court order bin accepted, into this Government, or otherwise entertaine any such inhabitant they shall be fined five or ten pound, or more according to the discretion of the Court; hoping the Court wilbe careful that whom they accept off are persons orthadox in their judgment."

Four years before this, the Deputies sitting in General Court "being informed that it is upon the harts of our Naighbours of the Massachusetts Colonie to support and incurrage that Nursery of Learning att Harvard College in Cambridge in New England" † concluded that they "would particularly and earnestly stirr up all such in their several townes as are able to contribute unto this worthy worke, be it in money or other goods."

There was a "Schoole" at Plymouth at about this time maintained in part from the revenues of "the ffishing att Cape Code;" but it was not until 1677, when, being cognizant of the profaneness of the times and bearing in mind that the undesirables who were amongst them, many originally indentured servants, having "come out of their time" and become fathers and mothers of families, had come to stay, that education was determined upon as the one and surest means of their redemption. It was therefore enacted that:—

> "Fforasmuch as the Maintenance of good literature doth much tend to the advancement of the wealth and florishing estate of societies and Republiques.

---

† "In 1669 the condition of the seminary was critical and apparently hopeless—when its buildings were pronounced ruinous and almost irreparable, and it was declared that without a new building its situation was desperate,—in this great Emergency, Braintree was one of the towns which responded most liberally to the loud groans of the sinking college." Adams' "Three Episodes" Vol. II Page 767.

This Court doth therefore order: That in whatsoever township in this Government consisting of fifty families or upwards any meet man shalbe obtained to teach a Gramer Schoole such township shall allow att least twelve pounds in currant marchantable pay to be raised by rate on all the inhabitants of such Towne and those that have the more emediate benefitt thereof, by theire childrens going to scoole, with what others may voluntarily give to promote soe good a work and generall good, shall make up the residue Nessasarie to maintaine the same and that the profitts ariseing of the Cape ffishing heretofore ordered to maintaine a Gramer Scoole in this Colonie be destributed to such townes as have such Gramer scooles, for the maintenance thereof, etc." There were not fifty freemen with families living in Scituate at the time this law was enacted, but the law clearly meant familes of inhabitants as well as freemen. No grammar school was established until 1700 when "The Town desired James Torrey to teach children and youth to read and write as the Law requireth, and said Torrey consented to make tryall thereof awhile, on these conditions, that he be paid 20s in money for each and every person sent to school, the parent or master engaging to pay fifteen shillings of the said twenty, the Town having agreed to pay the other five shillings for each, and that those that send any children or youth to the school, shall provide books, pen, ink and paper suitable for their learning as aforesaid." This school was kept at Deacon Torrey's own house, about a mile from the present Little's bridge. Whether its location was unsatisfactory or the trial had satisfied Mr. Torrey that the effort was not worth while, is not known. The school itself was a success but its master did not care to continue it.

The next year the town contracted with Capt. John Jacobs, a nephew of John Cushing, to teach the school for a year at a salary of £20 and also to build a school house at the same price. This, the first school house in Scituate, was erected near his own home. The locality was that of the second church, or the society at the North River, as it was called. It was not satisfactory. Manifestly the long controversy between the two church bodies had left its impression which had become engrafted into the school, and after three years "the Town directed the school to be kept one third of the year at each end of the Town, and one third in the middle." This arrangement held for seven years until 1711, when the Selectmen who also acted as a school committee were instructed by the town that they "should provide but one grammar school, and that to be kept in the middle of the Town and not to be removed." The next annual meeting reversed this vote. "The town ordered three schools, one in the middle and one at each end." In order to meet the expense of the increased attendance, the town the same year, appropriated sixty-four pounds for their maintenance. † Undoubtedly three schools were needed, but the evidence of geographical jealousy and local covetousness is too strong not to admit of the conclusion that these considerations were paramount. This lack of stability and permanency of action taken in town meetings, is often pointed to by critics as one if not the principal weakness of the town form of government. In this particular it does not differ from many higher deliberative representative assemblies whose membership is made up of the ablest selected from the whole. It is well also to bear in mind that the Scituate townsmen in developing the muncipal structure were pioneers. They

---

† The town was in difficulty over its grammar school as late as 1797. For a few years prior to the year it had failed entirely through disagreement as to locality or otherwise to provide one. For this failure some of the heads of families having children, caused it to be indicted. At the May Term of the Superior Court of Judicature for the province "Elijah Turner Agent for the town of Scituate has this indictment read to him—he says that the said inhabitants of the town of Scituate will not contend with the Commonwealth." A satisfactory grammar school was thereupon established.

had neither charter, counsellor, prophet, guide nor chief. Theirs was the entire responsibility and the consequences of error were visited alone upon their own devoted heads. While at the period of which we are writing, Scituate was no longer Colonial but Provincial, yet for sixty years the town meeting had been the forum in which everything closest to their own welfare except church affairs (and these sometimes crept in) was discussed and settled. The taxes, defense of their own homes from the Indians, their schools, the poor and insane, highways and the support of the church were all important matters for settlement. Undoubtedly they erred; yet in the process of solution of these questions they developed a sturdy self-reliance, mistaken by some for a stubborn individuality. All of which is written to the point that the town meeting as the truly democratic deliberative body, first begotten out of the womb of privation, want, heart burnings and suffering found in Plymouth, Scituate, Duxbury, Marshfield, Barnstable, Rehobeth and Bridgewater,—the plantations of the "Collonie" of New Plymouth in New England"—is the very foundation stone of American polity.

A Latin School, or one in which "youths were fitted for the College" was established in Scituate in 1765. Previous to this time young men had been prepared for college here by the ministers or some residents who had themselves received the advantages of a higher training. Mr. Chauncey had fitted his six sons for entrance into Harvard and all graduated there. Joseph Cushing a grandson of the first John who taught a grammar school here did likewise for his sons, Joseph, who graduated in 1752, Nathan in 1763 and Lemuel in 1767.

Richard Fitzgerald and Thomas Clapp, afterward President of Yale, also fitted for the college; and William Turner, a descendant of old Humphrey taught the Latin school in Scituate after his graduation from Harvard in 1767. Deane seems to think that the second and third generations, descended from the first comers, suffered to

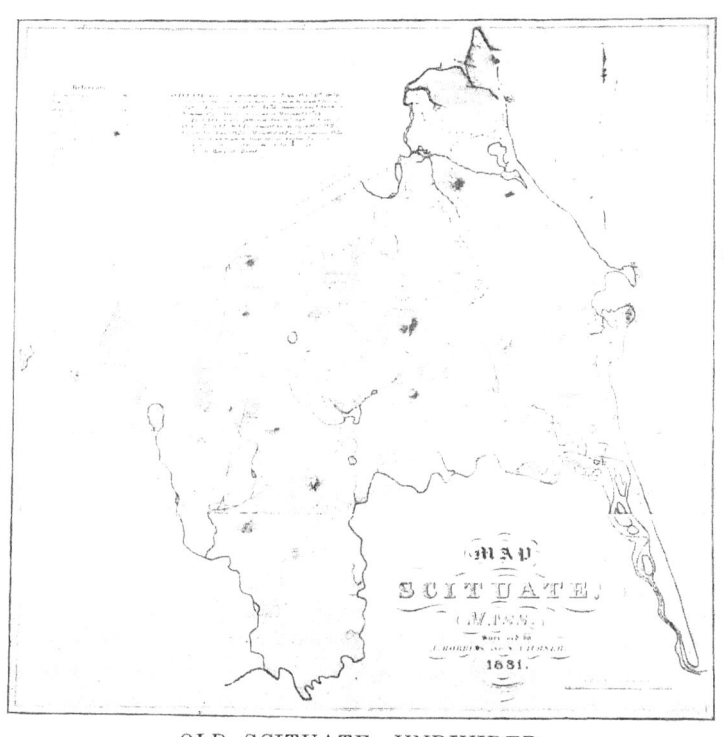

OLD SCITUATE, UNDIVIDED.
From map of 1831, surveyed by Robbins and Turner.

a considerable extent for lack of early education; but if heredity counts for aught, and we may judge by their deeds and accomplishments which are matters not only of local but of state and national history, that lack, as compared with the opportunities for learning of others of their time, is not apparent.

CHAPTER X

THE INDIANS

1. "That neither he nor any of his should injure or doe hurte to any of their people.
2. That if any of his did any hurte to any of theirs, he should send ye offender, that they might punish him.
3. That if anything were taken away from any of theirs, he should cause it to be restored; and they should doe ye like to his.
4. If any did unjustly warr against him, they would aide him, if any warr against them, he should aid them.
5. He should send to his neighbors confederats, to certifie them of this, that they might not wrong them, but might be likewise comprised in ye conditions of peace.
6. That when there men came to them, they should leave their bows & arrows behind them."

Treaty of amity and peace between Massasoit and the Englishmen March 21-22, 1620.

THE legitimate field of human interest to be covered by a town history is so limited, that the chronicler may well be tempted to depart from it into both realms of tradition and the current of events in the political division of which the given municipality forms a more or less important integral part. The writer of these pages has studiously refrained from the former and sedulously avoided trenching upon the later. The attempt is made here to bring into prominence those characteristics, either foibles or sterling merits, which made the early planters of Scituate prominent in their day and generation as part and parcel of the larger events which have proven the influence of the Pilgrim forefather upon succeeding generations in this great freedom of states. The history of these larger events has been well and fully written, and they are gone into now with such particularity as may be found, only because the part borne in them by Scituate men has not heretofore been entirely told, and in order that a background may be furnished to complete the picture of their bravery, their devotion, their sufferings and their patriotism. This by way of further preface, because in writing of their dealings with the Indians, the student is taken into the colonies of New Haven and Connecticut with the Pequots; from the Deerfield valley in Massachusetts to Rhode Island and the lower towns of the Old Colony itself, while the bloody war was raging with Phillip. The parts borne in these affairs by General Cudworth, Captain Michael Peirce, the Bucks, Cornet and Lieutenant, and the Stetsons, Ensign and Cornet, show them always at the front, resourceful, indomitable and filled with stubborn courage. This chapter in the history of the ancient town is its bright particular star. In it and the distress and anguish of the men and women who are of it, may be seen the constellation of one of God's far off purposes.

An English speaking Indian in 1620 was a rarity; yet there were a few like Hobomok, † the faithful friend and servant of Miles Standish and a member of his family; and Squanto, who had been taken to England by one of Sir Ferdinand Gorges' kidnaping captains, and afterwards returned to Plymouth by Dermer, who could make themselves understood in the English tongue. Both of these men had been well treated by the whites into whose company they had been thrown, and were kindly inclined. It was Squanto who brought Massasoit and the Pilgrim leaders together at the meeting which resulted in the peace pact which heads this chapter. The agreement thus made lasted for years. It was further cemented by the friendship for and justice shown to the aborigines, whose numbers along the south shore had been only two years before the landing of the Pilgrims, so seriously decimated by the scourge, in their trading with the forefathers and the lat-

---

† In the Indian language Hobomok means an imaginary evil spirit or "Devil." Why this inmate of Standish's household and friend of the Pilgrims was so called is not known. Hubbard's Indian Wars. Vol. 1. Page 176.

ter's purchase of their lands. Carver, Standish, Bradford, Cudworth, Hatherly and the other leaders realized that in this attitude of friendship they were laying the surest foundation of their own safety. While they bought from the red man the skins of such animals as he could trap, and paid him for his lands more than they were worth; while they whipped in his presence, the man who stole from him; and publicly hanged those who took his life, yet all were prohibited from inflaming him with liquor and no man could loan, sell or deliver to him either gunpowder or shot, except the Indian was such an one as first had the approval of the Court.

Various opinions have been expressed by local historians and others, concerning the purchase from the Indians, of the lands to the occupancy of which, the forefathers succeeded. Some have extolled the act; others have belittled it. Adams †, speaking of the Indian title taken by Richard Thayer to the Braintree lands says: "While the controversy with Boston was still dragging on, certain inhabitants of Braintree in behalf of the whole, secured as a muniment of title and out of mere superabundance of caution, a deed of the township from some of the Indian descendants of Chickatawbut. ‡ This deed duly signed and sealed, with delivery "by turf and twigge" conveyed to the grantees one of those Indian titles so frequently met with in the early records of New England,—titles the result of transactions which grave historians have not hesitated to defend and even to extol, but which in point of fact were a mockery of law and entitled to no more consideration than if those defrauded through them, had been infants or simpletons. Nevertheless the so-called Wampatuck deed of 1665 professed to convey a title to Braintree township from certain ignorant savages who never owned the soil."

---

† Adams' Three Episodes—Vol. II Page 653.
‡ This descendant was Josias Wampatuck, the same person who in 1640 conveyed to certain persons the land comprised within the limits of Scituate for the benefit of the whole and who prior to this had conveyed the Conihasset territory to the Partners.

Deane † a conservative chronicler with an advantage of observation earlier by eighty years than that of Adams—if such be an advantage—takes this view:—"It has been very common for people to lament over the fallen fortunes of the Natives of these shores, and to the forefathers for driving them from their wonted forests, and occupying their lands by force, or purchasing them for an inadequate trifle. As general remarks, we believe these to be the cant of very superficial readers and reasoners and certainly without the least truth or pertinency so far as respects Plymouth Colony. The lands were purchased whenever a tribe could be found to allege the slightest claim. The sums paid were small but they were a sufficient compensation to the few wandering natives whom the pestilence had spared, and who could make no use of their lands; nay they were often above the full value of the lands to the English. These lands were a dangerous and uncultivated wilderness, and had they been received without compensation, they would have been a perilous possession."

Whatever the truth may be, the weight of evidence deducible from the one thing open after the lapse of nearly three centuries—the written testimonies of the times—seems to be with the forefathers. The third article of the treaty with Massasoit: "If any thing were taken away from any of theirs (The English), he should cause it to be restored, and they should do the like to his" indicates a desire to do justice on both sides. There is abundant evidence which will be noted later in this chapter that the Pilgrim lived up to his part of this agreement. Again, it does not seem to have occurred to either Deane or Fiske or Adams in dealing with this question, to take into consideration the fact that the forefathers for a long time felt insecure in their patent and may have desired to obtain such an advantage in dealing with those others upon whom a fickle crown might bestow the lands colonized by them, as the Indian title, scoffed at by Adams, might give them. At

---

† Deane—History of Scituate page 145.

all events they proposed, that for what it was worth, it should belong to the Colony and not the individual. In 1643 this law was enacted:

"Whereas it is holden very unlawful and of dangerous consequence and it hath beene the constant custome from our first beginning That noe person or persons have or ever did purchase, rent or hire any lands, herbage, wood or timber of the Natives but by the Majestrates consent. It is therefore enacted by the Court that if any person or persons doe hereafter purchase rent or hyre any lands herbage, wood or tymber of any of the Natives in any place in this Government without the consent and assent of the Court every such person or persons shall forfeit five pounuds for every acre which shalbe so purchased, rented, hyred, and taken And for wood and tymber to pay five tymes the value thereof to be levyed to the Colonies use."

Fiske † corroborates Deane in these words:

"The policy pursued by the settlers was in the main well considered. While they had shown that they could strike with terrible force when blows were needed, their treatment of the natives in times of peace, seems to have been generally just and kind except in the single case of the conquered Pequot territory; they scrupulously paid for every rood of ground in which they settled, and so far as possible they extended to the Indians the protection of the law. On these points we have the explicit testimony of Josiah Winslow, the Governor of Plymouth, in his report to the Federal Commissioners in May 1676; and what he says about Plymouth seems to have been equally true of the other colonies. Says Winslow, 'I think I can clearly say that before these present troubles broke out, the English did not possess one foot of land in this colony but what was fairly obtained by honest purchase of the Indian proprietors. Nay, because some of our people

---

† Fiske, The Beginnings of New England page 198.

are of a covetous disposition, and the Indians are in their straits easily prevailed with to part with their lands, we first made a law that none should purchase or receive gift of any land of the Indians without the knowledge and allowance of the Court x x x And if at any time they have brought complaint before us, they have had justice impartial and speedy, so that our own people have frequently complained that we erred on the other hand in showing them overmuch favor."

In addition to all of the above we have the sale by Chickatawbut of Nantasket, to Thomas, Gray and Knight; by his descendants of Merrymount to Captain Wollaston; by Massasoit of the territory formerly occupied by the extinct tribe of Patuxets and comprising Plymouth, Duxbury, Kingston, Carver, Plympton, Halifax and Marshfield to the Pilgrims; and of Conihasset to Hatherly and his partners by Josias Wampatuck, Chickatabut's heir. † An analysis of this last transaction given in full in the note furnishes further evidence that the purchase of land titles from the Indians by the Pilgrims was genuine both as to certainty of the grantor's title and adequacy of price. It may be mere

† Pecumcke, Ahiumpum, Catscimah, Webacowett and Masbanomett doe all afferme that Chicatawbutt his bounds did extend from Neshamagoquanett near Duxbury Mill, to Teghtacutt (Middlebrough) neare Taunton, and to Nunckatatesett, (Pembroke) and from thence in a straight line to Wanamamprike, which is the head of Charles River; this they doe all sollemly afferme, saing, God knoweth it to be true, and knoweth their harts.
Dated the first of the Month 1650.
Witness: Encrease Nowell,
    John Elliott
    John Hoare
Josiah Wampatucke, Indian, Sagamore of the Massachusetts, and Nahatan the sonne of Jumpum came to Ply the 7th of June 1650 and there did testifye, that the land, according to a drauft in the keeping of Mr. Hatherley and others, and the particulars therein specifyed was the only proper lands of Chickatabut, father of Josiah Wampatuke aforesaid; and this he acknowledged before Captain Standish, Mr. William Thomas and Mr. John Alden.
Mr. Hatherley and others with him have bought so much of the land above mensioned of the said Josiah Wampatuke as concerned them to Buy."
Plymouth Colony Records Vol. II page 157.

coincidence that Increase Newell of Cambridge, Secretary to the Generall Court of Massachusetts, Reverend John Elliott of Roxbury, the friend and apostle to the Indians, and John Hoar, † the lawyer of Scituate, met at Plymouth on this spring day and chanced to witness the declaration of the five Indians as to the ancient ownership of Chickatawbut in the lands which the Conihasset Partners bought a week later. If the native witnesses were Plymouth Indians they were Patuxets and owed no faith to the Sagamore of Massachusetts. If they were his friends and their testimony was given to bolster up his title, it was the Englishmen and not the Indians who were being cheated. Three of the most important men of the colony, Standish and Alden of Duxbury and William Thomas of Marshfield were called upon to witness the acknowledgement of Wampatuck himself that he sold the land freely. If Hatherly and his associates were in a conspiracy to defraud the ignorant redmen they prepared an elaborate stage setting for the performance. Finally, we know that thirty-seven years later the grand-

---

† Hoar was trusted by the Indians. After he removed from Scituate to Concord, he was sent by the Council in 1675, to negotiate for the ransom of Mary Rowlandson, Goodwife Devens, Goodwife Kemble, John Moss of Groton and Lieut. Carter's daughter of Lancaster. Mrs. Rowlandson, who had been taken captive by the Indians in February gives this account of the arrival of Hoar and two friendly (praying) Indians among their captors.

"On a Sabbath Day, the sun being about an hour high in the afternoon, came Mr. John Hoar (the council permitting him, and his own forward spirit inclining him) together with the two forementioned (praying Indians) Tone and Peter, with the third Letter from the Council. When they came near, I was abroad. They (the Indian captors) presently called me in, and bid me sit down and not stir. Then they catched up their Guns and away they ran, as if an Enemy had been at Hand and the Guns went off apace. I manifested some great Trouble, and asked them what was the matter? I told them I thought they had killed the Englishman (For they had in the Meantime told me an Englishman was come.) They said, no, they shot over his horse, and under, and before his horse, and they pushed him this way and that way, at their Pleasure, shewing him what they could do. Then they let him come to their Wigwams. I begged of them to let me see the Englishman, but they would not. But there I was fain to sit their Pleasure. When they suffered me to go to him. As a result of Hoar's efforts all these captives were released.

Hubbard's Indian Wars. Vol. I, Pages 214-217 and notes.

son of Chickatawbut, himself a Josias Wampatuck, confirmed the title in Hatherly's grantees, the Conihasset Partners, and received an additional eighteen pounds to the consideration paid his father. †

The Indian title to the land of Scituate as the territory of the township stood in 1653, was extinguished by a deed given to Timothy Hatherly, James Cudworth, Joseph Tilden, Humphrey Turner, William Hatch, John Hoar and James Torrey for the proper use of the town. It is in full as follows:—

"1653. Bradford Govr.

I Josia Wampatuck do acknowledge and confess that I have sold two tracts of land unto Mr. Timothy Hatherly, Mr. James Cudworth, Mr. Joseph Tilden, Humphrey Turner, William Hatch, John Hoar and James Torrey, for the proper use and behoof of the inhabitants of the town of Scituate, to be enjoyed by them according to the true intents of the English grants; The one parcel of such land is bounded from the mouth of the North River as that River goeth unto the pond at the head of that River upon a straight line unto the middle of Accord Pond; from Accord Pond by the line set by the Commissioners as the bounds betwixt the two jurisdictions, until it met with the line of the land sold by me unto the sharers of Conihassett and as that line runs between the town and the shares, untill it cometh to the sea; and so along by the sea unto the mouth of the North River aforesaid. The other parcell of land ‡ lying on the easterly side of the North River, begins at a lot which was sometime the land of John Ford, and so to run two miles southerly as the River runs, and a mile in breadth toward the east, for which parcel of land I acknowl-

---

† Conihasset Records page 486.
‡ The "Two Miles" so-called, lying between the North and South Rivers, granted by the Court to Scituate in 1640. It was annexed to Marshfield in 1788.

edge to have received of the men whose names are before mentioned, fourteen pounds in full satisfaction in behalf of the inhabitants of the Town of Scituate as aforesaid; and I do hereby promise and engage to give further evidence before the Governor as the Town of Scituate shall think meet; when I am thereunto required; in witness whereof I have hereunto set my hand in presence of

Nathaniel Morton	Wampatuck
Edmund Hawes	Josias
Samuel Nash	marke

At the same time when Josias made the acknowledgement as above mentioned there was a deed brought into the Court which he owned "to bee the deed which he gave to them whose names are above specified for the same land and that hee had not given them another; which deed was burnt in the presence of the Court."

The league entered into between Massasoit and the Pilgrims was the instrument of peace for half a century. Trouble arose with the Pequots in 1637. This tribe, under its chief Sassacus, had been particularly aggressive toward the whites about Hartford where it also had its habitat. Members of it had kidnapped a Wethersfield man and burned him alive. They had sacked the town, murdered its people and taken children into captivity. Connecticut was wild with alarm and called upon Massachusetts and Plymouth to come to her aid. The former furnished twenty men. When the Plymouth magistrates called for volunteers, thirty responded. Of these, Henry Ewell, Hercules Hill and George Kennerick from among the score of able bodied men at Scituate, represented this town. Mr. Gilson and Edward Foster were "added to the Governor and Assistants to assesse men towards the charges of the souldiers that are to be sent forth for the ayde of the Mattachusetts Bay and Connectacutt." The cost of the expedition to Plymouth Colony was estimated to be two hundred pounds, of which the town of Plymouth was assessed one hundred, and Scituate and Duxbury fifty each. They sailed from Plymouth in the summer with a crew on board "sufficient to manage the barque;" but it is not known if they were in time to participate in the short and bloody war of extermination which Mason and Underhill waged "on the tribe which lorded it so fiercely over the New England forests." Whether they saw service or not, the three Scituate volunteers returned safely, Ewell to build a home which was burned thirty-nine years later by the Narragansetts, his allies in the Pequot campaign; Hill to his home in Kent street and Kennerick to remove to Boston. Following the complete annihilation of the Pequots as a tribe there was peace with the redmen for many years. The boldness and bloodiness of that slaughter and the terrible vengeance wreaked by the whites may have served to revive the feeling of superstitious awe with which, very early, the latter were regarded by the natives whose country was being usurped.

One beneficial result of the war was the treaty of amity and peace with the Narragansetts negotiated originally by Roger Williams and later ratified at Boston between Governor Vane and Miantonomo. It likewise furnished the immediate incentive for the confederation of the four colonies which followed. It was at a sitting of the Court at Plymouth on September twenty-seventh 1642 that

"The Court, being mett togethere, & haveing intelligence of a generall conspiracy intended by the natives to cutt off all the English in this land, tooke the same into serious consideracion, and duly waying such informacions which they have received, together with the circumstances concurring there withall, do adjudge it absolutely needful and requisite to make speedy preparation throughout the government for a defensive and offensive warr against them, as if they were presently to be sent forth.

2. It is agreed and concluded that Mr. Edward Winslow, Mr. Tymothy Hatherley, & Captaine Miles Standish shalbe sent into the Bay Co., & to have power

to agitate and conclude with them for a present combinacion with them in the present warrs, and to treat with them about a further combination or league but not to conclude that without the consent of the Court here.

Their commission is as followeth:—
Mr. Edward Winslow, Mr. Tymothy Hatherley, and Captaine Miles Standish are deputed and authorized by the Generall Court this day, to treat and conclude with such commissioners as the Governor & Court of Massachusetts shall appoint for that purpose, upon such heads and proposicions as the Lord shall direct them for our combineing together mutually in a defensive and offensive warr for our present defence against the intended surprisall of the natives; and also to treate & conferr with them about a further combination & League to be concluded betwixt us for future tymes, & to certify this Court of the heads thereof, that upon our approbation of the same they may be confirmed by a Generall Court. †

The war scare was genuine and thorough. Having taken the steps indicated in the foregoing excerpt from the record, the Court proceeded to name Captain Standish as the leader of "those forces that shalbe sent forth;" Mr. Thomas Prence "to be his counsell and adviser in the warrs," &d William Palmer to be lieutenant and Peregrine White "ancient bearer." A tax of £25 was immediately assessed for "the charges for & about ye souldiers which are to be sent forth" of which Plymouth was to pay five pounds, Scituate four, Duxbury and Sandwich each three and Barnstable, Yarmouth, Taunton and Marshfield each two, plus. A council of war consisting of the Governor and eleven of the foremost men of the colony was chosen. Timothy Hatherly and William Vassall represented Scituate upon this newly created board. Before the magistrates adjourned on this feverish occasion, "fynding the danger to be so great, and every man's life

---

† Plymouth Colony Records Vol. II Page 46.

THE INDIANS

in such hassard" and realizing that they were "Marvelously unprovided of lead and powder in the various townships," they let down the bars and authorized the partners in the trade at Kennebec, who under their agreement were restricted from selling furs and skins out of the colony, to sell "some moose skins and other skins out of the government." They further ordered that these partners should forthwith procure the necessary ammunition and sell it to the towns named taking their pay in corn.

The fear was groundless and the preparation unnecessary; but the fright had its good effects. Military service and training at once became and continued, (1642) active.

Although a military discipline was not regularly established in Scituate, probably as Deane † says because of the recent removal of so many of the freemen with Mr. Lothrop to Barnstable, William Hatch having been "elected by the townsmen to be their leiftennant for trayneing their men, was presented by their committee to the Court and allowed." The commissioners who had been chosen to treat with the Bay Colony upon the confederation, had agreed with the latter and in 1643 articles, having been read in court, were subscribed with Massachusetts, Connecticutt and New Haven. This same year the General Court framed and promulgated its orders for the organization and control of the militia. Each "band or company" was to have a "captain, leiftenant, clark" and one or more "serjeants." General orders were issued August 29, 1643 as follows:—

ORDERS

1. That the exercise be always begunn and ended with prayer.
2. That there be one procured to preach a sermon once a yeare viz: at the election of their officers, and the first to begin in September next.
3. That none shalbe received into this military company but such as are of honest and good report, & freemen, not servants, and shalbe well approved by

---

† History of Scituate page 118.

the officers & the whole company, or the major part.
4. That every person, after they have recorded their names in the military list, shall from tyme to tyme be subject to the commands and orders of the officers of this military company in their places respectively.
5. That every delinquent shalbe punished at the discretion of the officers and the military company, or the major part thereof, according to the order of military discipline and the nature of the offence.
6. That all talking, and not keeping sylence, during the tyme of the exercises, jereing, quarrelling, fighting, departing collers, without Lycence, or dismission &c or any other misdemeanor, so adjudged to be by the officers and the company or the major part thereof, to be accounted misdemeanors, to be punished as aforesaid.
7. That every man that shalbe absent, except he be sick or some extraordinary occation or hand of God upon him, shall pay for every such default 1js And if he refuse to pay it upon demand, or within a month after, then to appear before the Company, & be distrayned for it & put out of the list.
8. That if any man shall upon the dayes appoynted, come without his armes, or with defective armes, shall forfaite for every trayneing day as followeth:—

For want of a musket or a piece approved every time	vjd
For want of a sword	vjd
For want of a rest	vjd
For want of bandelires	vjd

Six months tyme given to provide in
9. That every man that hath entred himself upon the military list and hath not sufficient armes, & doth not or will not procure them within Six monthes next ensuing, his name to be put out of the list.
10. That there be but xvjteene pikes in the whole company, or at the most for the third part, viz: viij

for Plymouth, vj for Duxburrow, and two for Marshfield.

11.   That all that are or shall be elected cheefe officers in this military company shalbe so titled and forever afterwards be so reputed, except he obtayne a heigher place.

12.   That every man entred into the military list shall pay vjd the quarter to the use of the company.

13.   That when any of this military company shall dye or depart this life, the company, upon warneing, shall come together with their armes, and interr his corps as a souldier, and according to his place and quallytye.

14.   That all that shall be admitted into this millitary company shall first take the oath of fydellyty, if they have not taken it already, or else be not admitted.

15.   That all postures, of pike and muskett, motions, rankes, & files, &c., messengers, skirmishes, seiges, batteries, watches, sentinells, &c bee always performed according to true military discipline.

16.   That all that will enter themselves upon this company shalbe propounded one day, received the next day, if they be approved."

No sooner was this military establishment accomplished, than use for it became apparent.   The occasion arose through the meddling by the federal commissioners in the affairs of the Mohegans and Narragansetts, between whom the hatred was bloodthirsty and of long standing.   They were at war.   In a battle at what is now Norwich, Connecticut, Minantonomo, chief sachem of the Narragansetts, was captured by his enemy Uncas, and taken before the Governor and Assistants at Hartford.   These worthies advised that he be taken to Boston, that his ultimate disposition might be determined by the Commissioners for the United Colonies.   This was done, Uncas being summoned thither at the same time.   The Narragansetts were also represented.   They claimed that a ransom had been paid by them to Uncas for the life of their captive chief and his return. This Uncas denied. The tribunal was certainly not an unbiased one if we are to believe its own records. Extending in writing the proceedings of September seventh 1643, it says:—

"But understanding how peaceable Conoonacus, & Mascus the layte father of Myantenomo, governed that great people, we rather ascribe these late tumults outbreakings & Malitious plots to the rash and ambitious spirit of Myantenomo than any affected way of their owne x x x x And Whereas Uncas was advised to take away the life of Myantenomo whose lawful captive he was, They may well understand that this is without violation of any Covenant between them & us for Uncas being in confederation with us and one that hath diligently observed his covenants before mentioned for ought we know, & requiring advice from us upon serious consideration of the premises, viz: his treacherous and murtherous Disposition against Uncas &c and how great A Disturber hee hath biene of the Commonpeace of the whole countrey we could not in respect of the justice of the case, safety of the Country and faythfullness of our frend do otherwise than approve of the lawfullnes of his death, which agreeing so well with the Indians owne manners and concurring with the practise of other Nations with whom we are quainted, we persuade ourselves however his death may be greivous at present, yet the peaceable fruits of it will yield not only matter of safety to the Indians but profitt to all that inhabit his continent." †

Sentence of death was thereupon pronounced against the unfortunate Miantonomo:—that he be delivered to Uncas "so execution may be donn according to justice and prudence, Uncas carrying him into the next part of his owne government and there put him to death. Provided that some discreet & faythfull persons of ye English accompany

---

† Acts of the Commissioners of the United Colonies Vol. I Page 14.

and see the execution for our more full satisfaction and that the English meddle not with the head or body at all." It must not be supposed that the words "for our more full satisfaction" import any revengeful or bloodthirsty design on the part of the Englishmen toward Miantonomo in thus consigning him to death at the hands of his red brother. They mean that the English members of the death party should see to it that the execution should be performed properly, without torture. The whole text of the record indicates that they felt an ultimate benefit would result from the removal of Miantonomo even though it might "be greevous for the present;" and they soothed their consciences by recalling the mischievous character of the culprit, their treaty obligations to his captor and the fact that other nations concurred in such a "practise."

Uncas with his prisoner and the accompanying Englishmen started from Boston to the Mohegan territory for the execution; but they did not reach "the next part" of Uncas' government. On the way and to the surprise of the whites the Mohegans tomahawked the defenceless sachem, and Uncas is declared to have "cut a warm slice from the shoulder and greedily devoured it, declaring that the flesh of his enemy was the sweetest of meet and gave strength to his heart." †

It is not surprising that the tribesmen of this mighty sagamore who was thus foully murdered, saw in the manner of his taking, the most insidious treachery on the part of the English. They felt that they had been double-crossed and they showed it. Still fighting with the Mohegans their bearing toward the whites was surly, revengeful and pugnacious.

The forces from New Haven and Connecticut sent to the aid of Uncas, having been found insufficient, a "meetinge extraordinary" of the Commissioners was called by "speciall Order of the General Court of Massachusetts." The occasion was urgent. They sent Sergeant John Davis, Bene-

---

† Fiske—The Beginnings of New England page 171.

dict Arnold, the great grandfather of the traitor, and Francis Smith to bring the sagamores of the warring tribes before them. The messengers went, but returned unaccompanied by representatives of either party to the conflict. They brought however a letter from Roger Williams in Rhode Island which convinced the Commissioners that "warr would presently break forth." This was in July 1645. They wasted no time in convening the colonial legislature; but asserting that the articles of Confederation gave them power to declare war and prepare for it, they called out three hundred troops,—one hundred and ninety from Massachusetts, forty each from New Plymouth and Connecticut and thirty from New Haven. Plymouth's quota was made up of eight men each from Plymouth town and Scituate, six from Duxbury, five each from Sandwich and Yarmouth, and four each from Barnstable and Marshfield. The statement of Deane that Scituate was impoverished in men to make up her contingent, is verified by an inspection of the list of the men she furnished for this expedition; John Turner, George Russell, Jeremiah Burrowes, Hercules Hill, Edward Saunders, Nathaniel Moate, John Robinson, Richard Tart. Of these men only Turner, Russell and Robinson were freemen, lawfully entitled or required to bear arms. All the others were servants. There must certainly have been a paucity of material to include them in the town's quota. Opposed to this view is the list of non-commissioned officers and privates composing the Scituate Company (males between the ages of sixteen and sixty years, who are able to perform military duty) in August 1643, contained in Peirce Colonial Lists. [†] This list contains the names of Christopher Winter who was then in Plymouth; James Cudworth who is likewise therein accredited to Barnstable; Ephraim Kempton, Jr., then unborn; George Russell who did not come to Scituate until 1646; Richard Curtis who came in 1648 and Thomas Wyborne (or Weyborn) who was either of Plymouth or

---

[†] Peirce's Colonial Lists (Boston 1881) Page 74.

Boston. The latter did not appear in Scituate until 1660. It must be concluded that the list of the Scituate Company published by Peirce is not an accurate compilation of the freemen of Scituate liable to bear arms in 1643.

A month's provisions was sent with the little army. "For every souldier x x x 1 of biskett; xijl of pork; xxl of beefe, and a half bushel of pease or meale. Compare this ration with that taken out by the Puritan soldier of the Bay Colony in the same expedition, the total being for one hundred and ninety men, namely "Bread, tenn thousand; fish, ten kintalls; bief, six hogheads; strong water, one hogshead; wine at your pleasure; biere one tuun." † The Puritans were on a picnic; the Pilgrims prepared for fight. Or, it may have been that the item in the Plymouth Treasurer's account of the financing of the ,expedition, "James Coles Bill, £14 :0 :5" ‡ concealed expenditures for staples of this same kind.

The Plymouth Colony men were absent but seventeen days, getting no farther than the frontier towns of Rehoboth and Taunton, which by the way "were freed from sending forth men" because they were both new plantations and as well had "billited all the souldiers freely during all the tyme they stayed there." By this time the show of force represented by the three hundred men under the threatening Major (General Gibbons) not to mention Boston's "tunn of beere" and one hogshead of strong water, had overawed the Narragansetts. "Persecus, Mixanna and Witowash, three principal Sachems of the Narrohiggansett Indians and Awasequen, deputy for the Nyanticks with a large trayne of men, within a few dayes came to Boston." Peace was declared and a new treaty was "opened and cleared." Not however until they had imposed a war indemnity "of two thousand fathoms of good white wampom" upon the Narragansetts, and taken four of their children as hostages or pledges for its payment. It does not appear how much of

---

† Adams' Three Episodes Vol. II Page 828.
‡ Plymouth Colony Records Vol. II Page 91.

this tribute when received, was paid to the colony of New Plymouth as its share. One hundred fathoms were given to Uncas out of consideration of the great damage that he sustained, and four hundred to Connecticut and New Haven because "they have been out of purse a good value a considerable tyme before the other Colonies were at any charges about the same." Whatever the colony may have received by way of reimbursement, the immediate outlay for the war was sixty-six pounds, three shillings and three pence. Of the tax levy which followed Scituate paid the largest proportion—twelve pounds, seventeen shillings and six pence, with Plymouth, much larger in population, five shillings and three pence behind. Although deficient in numbers of its fighting men, Scituate made up in material wealth what it otherwise lacked.

The treaty of peace then made was an effectual agent to the end sought, for thirty years. During this time Rev. John Elliot, the Indian Apostle, was preaching to the natives and organizing his bands of praying Indians, segregating them into communities to live after the manner of the white men. There were seven hundred of these Christianized sons of the forest living in the Plymouth Colony at the time of the outbreak of the sanguinary conflict with King Phillip.

This struggle brought the horrors of war to the very hearthstones of the Stockbridges, the Turners, the Vinals, the Tildens, Merritts, and other Scituate families. It saw these devoted husbands and fathers not only defending their own homes, but going forth under General Cudworth, Captain Michael Peirce and Lieutenant Buck into the enemy's country. The cause of the war dates back to a few years after the death of Massasoit in 1660. The treaty which this chieftan made with the English was faithfully kept so long as he lived. Upon his death "the Court att the earnest request of Wamsitta, desiring that in regard his father is lately deceased, and he being desirous, according to the custome of the natives, to change his name, and that the

Court would confer an English name upon him, which accordingly they did, and therefore ordered, that for the future he shalbe called by the name of Allexander Pokanokett; and desireing the same in the behalfe of his brother, they have named him Phillip." † He also desired to be allowed to purchase a quantity of powder for himself and his brother. This request was denied but as a token of appreciation of this act of comity on his part "a smale gratuitee" of half a dozen pounds was bestowed upon him. Wamsutta's chieftancy of the Wampanoags was short. He died in 1662 and was succeeded by his brother Metacom or Phillip.

Some historians, as well as the early Indian chroniclers have claimed that his death followed his return from Plymouth, where he was summoned by the Governor and Assistants, placed upon the mat and accused of conspiring against the English. If he was so summoned there is no record of it. The only trouble at that meeting which appears, concerned the sale of some land at Rehoboth which he said belonged to him and was claimed by other Indians who sought to have it occupied by certain of the Narragansetts distasteful to both Alexander and Phillip. The Court diplomatically "engaged to doe what they could in convenient time for their reliefe in the premises." Before that "convenient time" arrived Wamsutta had died. The committee of the Court consisting of Governor Prence, John Alden and Josias Winslow, proceeded to arbitrate the differences and having given a lengthy hearing to the parties, finally dismissed them with this advice: "that all unkindness may be buried between them, and that the remembrance of this difference, ariseing from such small beginnings, may for future make them wise to live in peace and love." ‡

It is apparent that Governor Prence and his associates

---

† Plymouth Colony Records Vol. III Page 192.

‡ Plymouth Colony Records Vol. IV Page 24.

on this committee in agreeing upon the decree which accompanied this good advice, not perhaps improperly, favored Phillip. He seems at the time to have been regarded as a mischief maker but rather to be placated than treated harshly. Nevertheless the English did not propose that he should think them afraid of him, and at the same court (October eighth 1662) when the committee announced its decree concerning the land controversy, Phillip himself was summoned to appear before the Magistrates "to make answar unto such interrogatories as should be proposed unto him x x x x and to deliberate and congratulate with him about such matters as might tend to a further settlement of peace, and renewall of former covenants, as he seemed to desire, plighted between our predecessors and his ancestors."

When he appeared in answer to this order the magistrates plainly told him that rumors of his plotting against their government were rife; that they had some suspicion these stories were true; that they believed he was conspiring to "cut us off" and wanted to know what he had to say. After courtesy expressed upon both sides, and a larger and deliberate debate of particulars "hee absolutely deneyed that hee had any hand in any plott or conspiracy against the English." As a result of the conference and after a further interchange of gracious remarks and assurances of friendships, a continuance of the ancient covenant of peace was agreed upon and signed. In it Phillip agreed for himself and his successors, that he and they were lawful subjects of the King of England; he would neither provoke nor raise war with the other natives, nor sell his land without the consent of the English; and would in all respects carry himself peaceably and inoffensively toward them. This pact he subscribed with his uncle Uncompowett and four of the Sagamores of his tribe. He seems to have kept it for five years.

In 1667 he was again accused, this time of conspiracy with the French and Dutch; again he explained, offered up his arms to the custody of the English as an evidence of good faith, and naively pleaded "how erationall a thing it was that hee should desert his long experienced friends, the English, and comply with the French or Dutch, whoe had the last yeare kiled and carryed eighteen persons, both men and women of his, from Martin's Viniyard."

The wars with the Pequots and Narragansetts had taught the colonists a lesson. They saw by this time that the Indians were beginning to appreciate the effect of the continued colonization of their territory; that it meant extinction. The natives, docile in 1620 by reason of decimated ranks from the plague of four years previous, were now emboldened by the force of their increasing numbers, and Prence, Cudworth, Alden and the rest did not give Phillip's words and promises full faith and credit. As they themselves put it "though there was great probabilitie that his tongue had been running out, yett not having due proofe as was meet, judged it better to keep a watchful eye over him, and still continew tearmes of love and amitie with him, unless something further did manifestly appear." They were right in thus suspecting Phillip. In the light of subsequent happenings it is clear that the son of Massasoit was waiting for the appropriate time to strike the blow which he confidently believed would mean the extinction of the white man from the territory of his tribe.

For the next seven years frequent reports came to the Plymouth magistrates that Phillip was negotiating with the Narragansetts for their cooperation and an offensive alliance. On one occasion he acknowledged it and voluntarily surrendered his arms as security for his future good behavior. He posed to the officials of the Bay Colony as one being persecuted and seems to have won his way into their good graces so far that Major General Leverett, Captain William Davis and Thomas Danforth, Esq., came with Governor Winthrop of Connecticut to Plymouth to intercede and mediate for him. Phillip came too, but the case presented against him was so strong that the Massachusetts men were won over and his own weapon turned against him. As a result of this meeting a third peace agreement was signed in which he promised very much as before. It lasted for three years,—no longer. In 1674 John Sassamon, Indian, a loyal friend to the English, who had studied at Harvard, had acted as interpreter and in many friendly ways for them, while on a journey from Phillip's country to Plymouth, was murdered at Assawompsett Pond in Middleborough and his body concealed through a hole cut in the ice. There was no doubt but that this was done at the instigation of Phillip. He hated Sassamon, both because of this attachment to the English and of his belief that at the time the journey was taken, the latter was about to become the bearer to Plymouth of news of the former's active offensive operations. This murder was so flagrant and hostile an act that immediate action was necessary. Three Indians were arrested, a jury, to which were added six "of the most indifferentest, gravest and sage Indians x x to healp to consult and advice with," was empaneled and the men tried. Here is the verdict:—

"We of the jury, one and all, both English and Indians, doe joyntly and with one consent agree upon a verdict; that Tobias, and his son Wampapaquan, and Mattashimnamo, the Indians, whoe are the prisoners, are guilty of the blood of John Sassamon, and were the murderers of him according to the bill of inditemente."

Having hanged two of the murderers and shot the third, the colonists proceeded in October 1675 to gather together the various town councils of war which had organized about the time of the Pequot War, and to address the Commissioners of the United Colonies in support of offensive hostilities. Cornet Robert Stetson and Isaac Chittendon were the local members of the war board. Its first act was to unanimously choose James Cudworth, then seventy years of age, as a "generall or commander in cheiffe, to take charge off our forces that are or may be sent forth in the behalfe of the colonie against the enimie."

The Commissioners of the United Colonies authorized the

enlistment of a thousand men. The quota of Plymouth Colony was one hundred and fifty-eight and to this was added a force of twenty-five to garrison a fort at Mount Hope. Scituate furnished twenty-seven of this number, more than any other town in the colony. They rendezvoused at Rehoboth, Providence and Taunton. With Cudworth were his neighbors, Sergeant Theophilus Witherell, Joseph Turner, William Perry, John Wright, Job Randall and John Vinall. There is no complete list of those who went out with him or of the fatalities among them. They spent the summer with Henchman, Page and Mosely of the Massachusetts Bay contingent in endeavoring to engage and capture the wary Phillip in Rhode Island and the lower Plymouth Colony towns; and in supressing the uprising of the Indians at Brookfield. The Plymouth men were at Pocasset holding the fort which had just been built when the Commissioners of the United Colonies alarmed at the wide area covered by the Indian depredations, ordered a thousand fighting men to be gathered † under Governor Josiah Winslow as commander-in-chief. This force, augmented by General Cudworth's command and some "Voluntiers of Indian Friends" repaired to the country about Warwick, Rhode Island.

It was December. The highways between the Indian villages and English settlements were little more than bridle paths. Most of the white troops were on foot and carrying their own rations. Their sufferings were great, yet they plodded ahead. On the day set apart for the outward observance of the worship of God, Sunday, December nineteenth 1675, they came upon the crude fortress into which Canonchet had crowded and herded his sagamores and their squaws and children, to the number in all, of several thousand. It was built upon rising ground, of about six acres in area, surrounded by the thick tangled timber and roots of a virgin swamp. Armed with powder and bullets,

---

† Massachusetts Bay furnished 527: Plymouth Colony, from which a large number were already under arms and at the front, 158 and Connecticut 325.

in the use of which the Indians were now as proficient as their adversaries, the former had a distinct advantage. They no longer feared the English. They had forgotten the slaughter of the Pequots forty years before, and were prepared to face death with the stolidity capable only by the fatalists that they were. The fight commenced in the afternoon, but was over ere the sun of the short winter day had gone down. With it went the sachem of the Naragansetts and his two thousand men. Were it not that Hubbard and Church and all the rest of the chroniclers of the Indian troubles agree upon the length of time of the engagement and the extent of the human havoc wrought, it would seem next to impossible that a thousand white men poorly sustained, fatigued and worn by an exhausting journey of many miles, could in two short hours meet, fight and vanquish more than twice their number, well, if rudely intrenched and battling on their own ground. The Connecticut men lost most heavily.

Cudworth with his little army, came limping back into Plymouth. There was need for his immediate return home. Phillip with his allies the Nipmucks was raiding all about Scituate; at Weymouth, Middleborough and Bridgewater. Watch and ward was being kept by youths and old men accoutred with "fixed armes and suitable ammunition." The council of war ordered a garrison to be kept at the house of Joseph Barstow at Hanover Four Corners "both in respect to the towne of Scituate and the country" and a guard of ten or twelve men was furnished. The principal garrison was near the present Little's bridge on the North River and the third was at the home of John Williams, the present Barker farm, at the harbor. It also ordered Captain Michael Peirce of Scituate in command of a small company of whites and thirty friendly Indians to proceed against the enemy in Rhode Island. †

---

† Hutchinson's History of Massachusetts (London Ed. 1768) Vol I Page 304.

In March 1676 Captain Peirce marched to Patuxet where, he was given to understand, the Indians were gathered in a large force. Hubbard † says of him:—"he being a Man of Resolute Courage, was willing to engage them, though upon never so great Disadvantage." It was this very resolute, not to say reckless, courage which was his undoing. Being apprehensive of the danger he confronted he dispatched a messenger to Providence to Capt. Edmunds for reinforcements. Aid from this quarter was not forthcoming however ‡ and with his own meagre command he found the enemy and gave them battel. No sooner was the engagement commenced than he discovered that they largely out-numbered his own force. The Indians dissembled by crossing the river and Peirce followed in hot pursuit. This was as the enemy had planned; they led him into ambush. Once on the opposite bank, he was assailed from all around and all were slain.

Captain John Williams with thirty others was doing good service at Plymouth and Middleborough. With this command were Lieut. Israel Buck, Zachariah Damon, John Damon, Richard Prouty, Cornet John Buck, Jonathan Jackson, Thomas Clarke, William Hatch, Walter Briggs, Joseph Gannett, Richard Dwelley, Benjamin Woodworth, Benjamin Chittenden, John Lothrop, Joseph Wade, Jeremiah Barstow, Joseph Cowan, John Ensign, Joseph Perry, John Perry and John Rose, all Scituate men.

This was the situation when, on the twenty-first day of April an attack was made upon the town. It was repulsed by the townsmen led by Isaac Chittenden and Cornet Robert Stetson, an Indian fighter of no mean abilities and then sixty-four years old. It is evident that few males save youths under sixteen and old men over sixty who were do-

† Hubbard's Indian Wars (Drake's Ed. 1865) Vol I Page 173.
‡ Hubbard says:—"he sent a Messenger, timely enough to Providence for Relief: but (as Solomon saith, 'a *faithful Messenger is as Snow in Harvests: another is as Smoak to the Eyes and Vinegar to the Teeth*') whether through Sloth or Cowardice, is not much material, this Message was not delivered to them to whom it was immediately sent." Hubbard's Indian War. Drake's Edition 1865 Vol I Page 175.

ing watch and ward, and those in the three garrisons were at this time in the town. A new requisition for troops had just been promulgated, and Scituate was called upon to furnish fifty, as against thirty for Plymouth, a like number from Taunton, Barnstable and Rehoboth, twenty-six from Marshfield and sixteen from Duxbury. There were not fifty able bodied men left in the whole town. The bodies of Samuel Russell, Gershom Dodson, Samuel Pratt, Thomas Savery, William Wilcomb and ten others, were then lying where they had fallen with Peirce on the bank of the Pawtuxet River. Captain John Williams was along the frontier and those of the valiant twenty-seven who went forth with Cudworth, engaged Canonchet in the "swamp fight," and who had returned, were crippled and worn. This fact is attested by the proportion (£12) given to Scituate out of the generous contribution which came from Ireland a year later, for distribution "for the relieffe of such as are impoverished, detressed and in neccesities by the late Indian warr." When the council of war met at Plymouth on the eleventh day of April 1675, this town's quota of fifty men was not full. Both Governor Winslow and the Council criticised the town for its failure to make good the number of men required of it. They were unjust and the citicism was apparently made in ignorance of the real facts. The following letter to Governor Winslow from Col. Nathaniel Thomas of Marshfield throws light upon the former's error.

Swanzey, June 25, 1675.

Right Honored Sir:

A particular account of our arrival here, and the said providence that, yesterday, fell out at Mattapoiset, of the loss of six men, without doubt you have from our General (Cudworth) which may, I desire, be an inducement to you to strengthen our towns that are weakened by our departure, since the Indians do their exploits on outhouses and straggled persons. It is reported credibly, that Uncas sent Phillip twenty men last Saturday. Sennight and Nameo sent him word that if he sent him six English head, then all the Indians in the country were engaged against the English. Sir, our men are well and cheerful, through God's mercy. Send not your southward men to us, but secure yourselves with them. Send us help from the Massachusetts, which is our General's and Consul's advice. The forces here are dispersed to several places of the town and some to Rehobeth, which this day we intend to draw into a narrower compass; in which when we have done, we intend to lay ambushment in the Indian's walks to cut off their men as they do cut off our men; for their present motion is to send forth scouts to lie in our walks, to make discovery and cut off our men. I pray, sir, remember me to my wife, and bid her be of good cheer; the Lord is our keeper. Our soldiers here desire to be remembered to their wives and friends. Will Ford is well of his ague. Thus desiring your honor's and all God's peoples prayers for us,

 I remain,
  Your honor's servant
   Nathaniel Thomas"

The Indians themselves knew better than Governor Winslow the lack of capable defenders within the town limits. Hence they selected it for attack. Coming by the old Boston turnpike from Hingham where they had burned five dwellings, on the twentieth day of May, they appeared at what is now Hanover Four Corners, burned the house of Joseph Sylvester and the "Cornets Mill" on the Third Herring Brook. They avoided the Garrison at Barstow's and came burning, pillaging and murdering, attacking, but not carrying the blockhouse near Union Bridge, to the fort by Stockbridge's Mill at Greenbush. The stockade faced the highway and was protected from attack on the rear by what is now known as Old Oaken Bucket pond. Here they fought all day. The Englishmen, against a largely superior force, encouraged by the venerable Stetson and Isaac Chittenden who was later killed in the fight, held the red terrors at a distance while the latter burned their dwellings, destroyed their cattle and newly planted fields, and then returned to the fight. It was onslaught and rebuff; assault with burning brands, to fire the garrison and a return of well directed lead. All the afternoon it continued, until the twilight of the May day saw the besiegers, lessened in numbers and satiated with arson, repulsed and beaten. Coming out of their stockade in the morning the freemen found ashes and devastation where but a few hours before had been the homes and hearthstones erected through their labors and the fastness of their purposes. Their courage is manifest in the way they fought and foiled the red devils who attacked them. It is better seen in the resolution and patience with which they set about to restore that which had been destroyed.

Another call for troops came close on the heels of this calamity. This time it was for twenty-five men from Scituate, and as usual this town like Abou Ben Adhem "led all the rest." They were to be "sent forth towards the frontiere partes of this collonie, to be upon motion to scout to and frow for the safety of the Colonie." The quota must have been furnished; but where it came from, is not at this day readily apparent. There were less than fifty freemen in the whole town and this meant that the total population was perhaps not more than three hundred. Of the men who had been with General Cudworth in the Warwick expedition, Sergeant Witherell, Jonathan Jackson, John Barker and William Perry and been wounded or disabled in the fight at Greenbush in May. Jeremiah Barstow was in captivity. Timothy White had "received damages in his head by a shott" and Joseph Thorne, "shot through the arme" was "lame for a time." General Cudworth himself again took the field. He was with Captain Benjamin Church in the "frontiere partes" chasing Phillip who was now scuttling away from the English. They followed the son of Massasoit who had called himself King, to his old home at Mount Hope, and there on the twelfth day of August 1676 in a daybreak attack upon his camp, he met his death,—it is said, shot in the back by one of his own tribesmen. The death of Phillip ended the war. It had been costly to Scituate in many ways. Some of her most promising and valued men had been killed, twenty-three buildings had been levelled by the redskin torch; mothers had been widowed and to crown it all the town itself was struggling under a debt of nearly eight hundred pounds. Truly the second generation suffered equally with the forefathers, in their determination to preserve and maintain what the latter had founded.

CHAPTER XI

CUSTOMS PREVIOUS TO REVOLUTION

"Was that country rightly dependent and inferior where law and custom were most in accord with the philosopher's ideal society? In that transvaluation of old values effected by the intellectual revolution of the century, it was the fortune of America to emerge as a mind of concrete example of the imagined State of Nature. In contrast with Europe, so 'artificial,' so oppressed with defenseless tyrannies and useless inequalities, so encumbered with decayed superstitions, and the debris of worn-out institutions, how superior was this new land of promise where the citizen was a free man, where the necessities of life were the sure reward of industry, where manners were simple, where vice was less prevalent than virtue and native incapacity the only effective barrier to ambition! In those years when British statesmen were endeavoring to reduce the 'plantations' to a stricter obedience, some quickening influence from this ideal of Old World philosophers came to reinforce the determination of Americans to be masters of their own destiny."
"*The Beginnings of the American People.*"—*Becker.*

IN the first century which elapsed after the establishment of the town Scituate prospered. The evolution from the pioneer to the comfortable householder was gradual and at the same time healthy and strong. The character of the citizenship of Scituate, and indeed, of the whole colony of Plymouth in the years from 1725 to the Revolution, indicates that the progenitors who came in the Mayflower, the Ann and the Fortune, were men and women of a superior type, capable of governing and controlling not only themselves, but of successfully and happily assimilating the less determined and weaker, not to say grosser, members of the pilgrim communities, who sought homes among them.

In these fifty years the descendants of the first comers were found in Scituate occupying the homesteads and farms built and tilled by the fathers; and also upon those of their own rearing. Hatherly was gone, leaving no issue to perpetuate his name.

CUSTOMS PREVIOUS TO REVOLUTION

John Cudworth was living at Hooppole Neck on a part of the farm of his great grandfather.

Ebenezer Bailey had his homestead at Farm Neck,— the same acres which were given to the original John Bailey by his friend Capt. John Williams.

Zachary Damon, whose forbears came to Scituate with their uncle Anthony Annable, was at Assinippi.

Thomas Webb was on Brushy Hill at Greenbush and his nearest neighbor, Nathaniel Wade, tilled the same acres that had been broken out and cultivated by his ancestor Nicholas in 1638.

Anna Vinal's devotion had reared a sturdy family. Her great grandchildren were living on Kent street.

Captain Samuel Barker from the old garrison house at Cedar Point, now comfortably framed and enlarged, watched the fleet of schooners, scows, sloops and ketches go out over the bar on their coasting and fishing trips. His neighbors at the Harbor were the Briggses, who occasionally built a schooner at the "Will James" yard next the tavern; the Merritts; Israel Chittenden; John Manson, Ensign Otis and John Stetson, the descendant of Cornet Robert, who owned and operated the tide mill.

Deacon Stephen Clap lived in "Samuel Clap's new house" at White Oak Plain, built before the two colonies joined their fortunes. Here he was proud to receive the infrequent visits of his son Thomas, the President of Yale College, and to accompany him to church to listen to the sermon of Mr. Eells from Deuteronomy XXXII 47, a text upon which that venerable gentleman delighted to discourse.

Capt. Enoch Collamore kept the public house at Valley Swamp, on the Plymouth road, and the Jacobs, David, Joshua and Joseph, ran the saw-mill on Third Herring brook a short distance away. Zebulon Sylvester and the Stodder family were also at Assinippi. On the way thence toward Greenbush at No Pork Hill, Capt. Caleb Torrey kept a tavern and over its bar dispensed the crude New England rum which the Boston distillers in Essex Street sold him at two shillings a gallon. Further on, near Union Bridge overlooking the sinuous river on its way to the sea, lived the great grandchildren of Humphrey Turner, the first tanner in the colony. Their near neighbor was Deacon John James, who lived on the site of the Block House of King Phillip's War. Just before reaching Greenbush the Cushings, John and William, father and son, had their homes, the former at Belle House Neck and the latter at Walnut Tree Hill. This was in the days of their service to the Massachusetts judiciary. When not riding the circuit in discharge of their duties, each dispensed a charming hospitality among a wide circle of the eminent men of the time. Benjamin Woodworth lived at Greenbush just beyond Judge John Cushing's. At that time his bibulous descendant had not written the inspired lines which have made "the wide spreading pond and the mill which stood by it" famous. Then the little village was noted only as the home of Dr. Benjamin Stockbridge and his son Charles also a physician. These men, celebrated in their profession the colony over, rode their saddle bagged mares among a large number of widely separated patients and the former found time also to educate his son-in-law and other young men in the science which he successfully practised. His not infrequent prescription, which he dispensed himself, for mild forms of fever was:

"First, as soon as taken ill, take a vomit of the infusion of *crocus metallorum.* When it hath done working, some hours later, take a small dose of *pil rufi,* two or three, more or less according as they work. Take once in twenty-four hours, to keep the body soluble throughout the whole sickness. Three hours after the pills first given, or the first dose of pills, take two full and large spoonfuls of treacle water to a man or woman, and proportionably to a child. Let the treacle water be thoroughly tinged or colored with saffron; and after this, take only one spoonful of treacle water every eight hours throughout the sickness. This is

THE OLD OAKEN BUCKET PLACE, GREENBUSH.   From a crayon drawing.

to drive out the malignity by sweat; to keep the sick in a breathing sweat; which is the most hopeful sign of recovery. If they be distempered in their heads, then, instead of one dose of pills, give the following glister, viz: one handful of common barley, washed and boiled in water. To the barley-water add a good spoonful of butter, as much of sugar and as much of small salt as will lie upon a sixpence. When it is almost cold enough to be given, add the yolks of two eggs beaten and give it. If the disease continue strong, and much afflict the head, apply blister-plasters to the ankles, a little above the ankle-bone, on the inside; sometimes, in case of strong deliriums, or distraction, to the neck; sometimes to the wrists. Drink barley-water, in which boil anise seed, liquorice, figs sliced, raisins stoned, a good quantity of maidenhair and pimpernel or as many of these things as may be had. Of this they may drink always their fill. Beer or cider are not good. For change of drinks sometimes, take posset-drink, in which boil feather-few. If the pain of the side be very grievous, we apply stone horse dung outwardly, and steep some in white wine or cider, and give inwardly, and administer a salt water glister. For the mouth we take strawberry leaves, five finger, violet, columbine, black-briar leaves, sorrel, of each a like quantity boiled in spring water; sweeten it with sirup of violets, or honey. With this both wash and spray the mouth and throat often, night and day. It availeth much to the comfort of the sick to keep the mouth clean. Stew prunes, together with a little quantity of senna, tied up in a rag. Take it sometime, instead of the pills."

Charles Stockbridge was no less renowned as a physician than his father. When the latter's death occurred the son was already engrossed in a large practice over a wide territory.

The mill which his ancestor had built in 1650 was still

in the possession of the family, and formed the industrial nucleus around which centered the homes of Robert and Abraham Northey, Isaac Stetson, Benjamin Woodworth and Peleg Ford.

Thomas Curtis and David Little's son Barnabas lived at Egypt. William Collier owned and occupied the Walter Briggs farm near the Glades and John Tilden cultivated the Conihasset farm which Timothy Hatherly gave to his great grandfather.

These were the prominent families in Scituate during the fifty years preceding the war of the Revolution. They were well-to-do and industrious. They owned the ships that were built at the Wanton, Chittenden, Block House and other shipyards on the North River and financed the fishing and coasting in which the vessels were themselves engaged. They also owned the ferry at Littles Bridge kept by John Doggett and that by his son at the upper ferry at Union Bridge. Deacon Stephen Otis and Anthony Waterman operated tanneries; there were grist mills at the Harbor, on the three Herring brooks and at Hugh's Cross brook.

Once a week the mail was sent over the road from Boston in the custody of the messenger to Plymouth. He brought the *Boston News-Letter, the New England Weekly Journal, the Boston Gazette or Country Journal, the Massachusetts Spy and the Boston Post Boy and Advertiser.*

Thomas Clap, before becoming the head of Yale College, Richard Fitzgerald, Timothy Symmes, William Turner and Joseph Cushing were the schoolmasters. Symmes taught the grammar school and others privately or at the "Latin School," preparing the young Litchfields, Turners, Cushings, Otises, Stockbridges and Vinals for entrance to "the College at Cambridge."

Besides the doctors Stockbridge at Greenbush there were Dr. James Otis at the Harbor, Dr. Ephraim Otis, Dr. Jacobs at Assinppi and for a few years prior to his death in the Revolutionary army, Dr. Lemuel Cushing,—all ministering

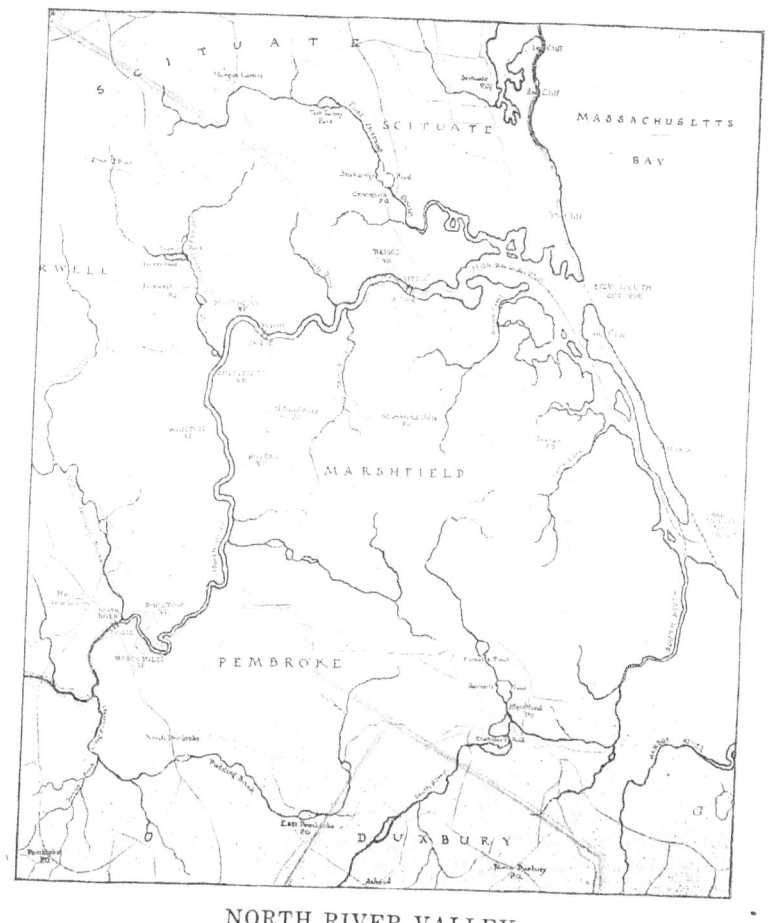

NORTH RIVER VALLEY.
With location of Colonial Shipyards. From a sketch map by Henry T. Bailey.

to the ills of a rapidly growing community. Dr. Cushing was a grandson of Joseph, the eleventh and youngest child of the original John Cushing, and was a famous surgeon of his day.

The Cushing family likewise furnished the lawyers who attended to the not infrequent litigation in which the Scituate people were engaged during this period. Judge John, the third of that name, while most of his life was spent upon the bench, practised in town until 1738, when he was made Judge of Probate for Plymouth County. Nathan, the son of his cousin Joseph, kept a law office for ten years until the beginning of the Revolution, when he too was elevated to the bench and made a judge of the admiralty. Thomas Turner, who lived at the Harbor, on Kent Street, was declining in his years and practice in 1725, and his clients were gradually turned over to David Little, who although living in Marshfield, had an office here.

The dwelling which housed the average family was a story and a half structure built of wood, cut near by, and covered on the outside with cedar shingles. The more pretentious had an upper story, sometimes overhanging the lower by a foot and a half. Of whichever style of construction, they were all reared about a generous chimney, containing enough bricks to erect a small jail. The men of the time were no mean builders. Sills were of oak and plates and studding usually of walnut. The size and weight of the latter made it necessary to gather a good number from among the neighbors for each house raising. Upon such occasions what beef and brawn lacked in strength and force, large quantities of hard cider and the product of the New England still, in due measure, supplied. The house was usually placed so that the living room should face the south, and this without much reference to the highway on which it was located. Immediately upon entering the front door, the visitor was confronted by a solid face of the immense chimney about which wound the stairs to the best room, the spare room, the parlor chamber, the guest room or the attic as the case might be. In both the living room and front room or parlor, the great fireplace was the principal feature. Built to accommodate a cord-wood length of oak, it nevertheless failed to afford a uniform and sufficient heat for the whole room, and while the sitter by the hearth had his or her face subjected to the heat of the equator, the spine was subjected to the discomforts of an arctic night, Beside the sitting-room fireplace hung the brass bedwarmer which, filled with live coals, warmed the winter beds of the children. In the best parlor of the Turners, Fords, Tildens, Cushings, Vinals, Wades, Barkers and others of the more wealthy families, were stiff slat-backed chairs with rush seats, standing squarely against the wall. There were, during the period of which this is being written, no such dust gathering abominations as sofas. In the center of the room was a claw-and-ball foot table, and in the corner a tea-table the top of which threw back upon its hinges against the wall. These were made of solid St. Domingo mahogany in true puritanical contrast to the veneers and inlayings of Chippendale, Hepplewhite and Sheraton which succeeded them in the early part of the nineteenth century.

There were a few books, among which, of course, was the family Bible bound in sheep or red Turkey leather, "Translated out of the original tongues" x x x and "diligently compared and revised by His Majesty's Special Command. Printed by T. Wright and W. Gill, and sold *cum privilegio* by S. Crowder, Paternoster Row, London, and by W. Jackson at the University in Oxford."

On the mantel stood two whale oil lamps (other parts of the house were lighted solely by candles) and above, hanging against the wall, was a looking glass framed in mahogany and gilt. Its outline was fancifully sawed, and surmounted by a circular opening partially filled by three feathers, a conventional shell or a flower in gilt. †

Beside the "best parlor" fireplace a rude cupboard was

---

† Frances Clarey Morse—"Furniture of the Olden Time" page 349.

built into the wall. It contained conch shells from the South Seas, bits of red coral from the Indian Ocean, china from Nagaski and Hong Kong, all carefully kept from sight except on occasion when the dark, stuffy and illy-ventilated room was opened for the entertainment of some distinguished visitor.

In the kitchen, which also served as the family meeting place at meals, was the great brick oven and again the open fire place, cluttered with pot hooks and kettles and on its jamb bellows and candle moulds. Standing in a corner, beside the long straight handled ash shovel, was a bowl shaped iron utensil, in which father and the boys melted lead for the bullet mould and in the winter time reduced the tallow to liquid, which they smeared upon their rough boots to make them water proof. Above the fireplace, just underneath the "mantel-shelf" hung the flint lock and on its butt a copious horn. In this room also was likely to be found the flax and spinning wheels. Rows of dried apples covered with corn husks to prevent them from becoming flyblown, were drawn across the ceiling. There were also, perhaps, freak ears of corn, a suggestively shaped gourd or an Indian stone hatchet hobnobbing with the candlesticks and the candle snuffer upon the mantel. A portion of the kitchen was invariably partitioned off for a pantry, from which access was conveniently had to the well. Here the thrifty housewife "set" the milk and with a quahog shell skimmed the thick cream for the churn in the corner. This was also the storage room for pan dowdy, bang-belly vengeance, pumpkin pies, marmalades of wild grape and beach plums, all the products of her culinary skill. There were also the two containers marked "blackberry brandy" and "cherry rhum" each of home concoction and for invalid consumption.

In the more ordinary houses the kitchen occupied a lean to—pronounced "leanter"—built on the back of the house, its roof extending from the eaves, to within five or six feet of the ground. In one end of this was the side door leading to the barn and corn crib or the well.

Is the picture attractive? Does the severe provincial life of the middle of the eighteenth century appear to be more desirable than that of the greater material enjoyments of the twentieth? John Adams, the second President of the United States, who had enjoyed the best that his time afforded in the way of creature comforts, said towards the end of his life that he "used to wish he could go to sleep in the autumn like a dormouse, and not wake until spring." †

And yet the people of those days were not without substantial household comforts. They expressed a taste for, and appreciation of, handsome silver and brass, mahogany highboys, four posted canopied beds and fine glass ware and napery. The appraisers of the estate of John Barker who died in 1729 were shown a silver tankard which they valued at £26; a silver colander and silver spoons and plate worth as much more. There were napkins, table cloths, "pillow coats" and sheets, all of fine texture and appraised at £12. In his library were works on law, divinity, history; and books in Latin, Greek and Hebrew. His estate was not large as the fortunes of Scituate planters then went, yet the whole of his household furniture and plate reached a value of £374.

The inventory of Benjamin Turner who died in 1734 discloses, napkins, pillow coats, table cloths, towels and sheets valued at "£18:02s;" his pewter, "lanthorn" and warming pan were worth three pounds and fifteen shillings more. In his cellar was found fifty gallons of rum and wine, cherry rum, "cyder" and brandy, while in the larder were "Biskit and Ginger bread £2."

The probate records amply warrant the belief that the average Scituate townsman filled his home with things which were substantial if not elegant, but comfortable and pleasant to look upon. Carpets are frequently mentioned. Now and then "an oval table of black walnut and another

---

† Three Episodes of Mass. History. Adams Vol. II Page 682.

small ditto" appear. There were always feather beds, "coverlids," woolen blankets, underbeds, chests of drawers, looking glasses; now and then a "multiplying glass" and invariably pails, washing tubs, trays, milk pans and the steelyard and mortar.

The larder contained sausages, salt pork, and other soused and smoked meats in large quantity. Very little fresh meat was used. Fish of course was plentiful and liberally eaten. The barn yard furnished fowl and the garden produced pumpkins, corn, beans, peas, parsnips, turnips and carrots. Potatoes did not become general until after the Revolution. Eight bushels was considered a large crop in 1763. † There was much pickling and preserving of samphire, fennel, purple cabbage, bay berries, beech plums, huckleberries and quinces; besides the manifold uses to which the apple was put.

Sweetening was supplied by molasses, maple sugar and honey. In the homes of the more wealthy a loaf sugar which was purchased in lumps of nine or ten pounds apiece, was carefully cut into small cubes with the assistance of a pair of sugar shears, an implement designed for the especial purpose.

Indian corn, that Pilgrim staple, which the aborigines had taught the forefathers to grow, was still the chief bread ingredient. Corn meal was not infrequently used with rye in the making of "rye-an-injun" bread, a nourishing and hearty food.

The dairy furnished milk, butter and cheese in abundance. The house-wife was no mean artist in the palatable preparation of all the food stuffs which the farm and woods provided and the family table was a gathering place for good appetites. It is not to be ascertained that dyspepsia was either common or prevalent.

The pilgrim maiden is invariably pictured as a person of serious and demure mien, clothed in plain garments of the severest cut. Not so her sister of a century later. Silks,

† "Home Life in Colonial Days"—Alice Morse Earle page 144.

crinoline and velvets were materials in general use. Laces were worn by the women of the wealthier families and hoop-petticoats, heavy corsets or "stays" as they were called, pandered to their vanity. The head gear was a ponderous contrivance of black or colored silk attached to wire hoops, usually seven in number, the whole being readily collapsed or expanded like an accordion. This was called a calash, and was especially in fashion for twenty years preceding the close of the Revolutionary War. In Abington in 1775 this headcovering became such an abomination that the church of which Rev. Samuel Niles was pastor, openly condemned in parish meeting the "indecent way that the female sex do sit with their bonnets on to worship God."

Nor were the men far behind their wives and sisters in the gaiety of their apparel. Waistcoats of fancy colors, small clothes, silk hosiery, and silver buckles were among their personal adornments. After the death of Samuel Turner, the inventory of his estate disclosed "hats, shirts, waistcoat, gold buttons, trousers, breeches, stockings, gloves, wig, great coat and jacket of the value of £31:00:08d." His contemporary Deacon Joseph Bailey, a sober pillar of the church, arrayed himself in a wardrobe that was appraised at "£22:09s." They wore wigs of all sorts of grotesque shapes and fashions, and when ridicule had accomplished the discard of this unsanitary head covering, the gentleman of the day let his hair grow long behind, greased it with pomatum, powdered it and tied it at the nape of his neck with a bow of silk or satin ribbon.

This outward display of frivolity did not affect the constant attendance upon divine worship and the strict observance of religious forms. The Dutch in New York were not more exact. The Sabbath commenced at sunset on Saturday and no work save the milking of the cows, the feeding of the "critters," and the essential duties of the household was performed. Washington Irving's quip that the "sponge" was not set on Saturday night, lest the yeast should work on Sunday, is undoubtedly true to the letter.

On Sunday morning the whole family went to the meeting house. The elders either rode in chaises or on horseback with the women folk mounted behind upon pilions. The children walked. All remained the entire day listening to sermons of tedious length, and at intermission eating the luncheon of buttered bread, doughnuts, cheese and gingerbread which had been brought along in the family splint basket. The singing accompanied by a bass-viol, clarionet and flute was confined wholly to the Psalms. A pitch-pipe set the key. Psalms of praise or thanksgiving were sung to St. David's tune and the Martyrs' tune. The accomplishment often occupied half an hour. As the supply of psalms books was frequently limited, line after line was sung after first being read by the deacon. Prayers were usually as long as the sermons, the exhortations of the minister as fervent as the singing of his congregation, and thus the day passed, whether the participants in the ceremonies sweltered on the hard board seats and straight backed pews in the heat of the stiff and uncomfortable Sunday dress, or shivered in the frigid atmosphere of the unwarmed temple.

In the middle of the week the same meeting place was sought for the Thursday lecture at which, contrary to Sunday practice, young men and women were permitted to sit together and from which the youth who was courting his damsel might "beau" her home.

If dancing were permitted it was indulged in only at taverns or huskings and raising. The Scituate churchgoer deemed it unseemly and frivolous and it was generally frowned upon.

As a holiday, training day of the "train band" or military company outshone either Thanksgiving or Christmas. It was the occasion in all the year when freedom of action was unshackled. While the militia men were put through the manual of arms, the townsmen who gathered to look on, drank rum and cider, ate cakes and cheese, swapped horses and stories and generally behaved in a manner far from bearing any resemblance to the deportment of their forbears. There were two training fields, one at Herring Brook hill, near the south meeting house, and the other opposite the end of Meeting House lane, directly across the street from the present Union Cemetery.

The members of this train band were active in the French War. Captain John Clap, afterward a colonel in the Revolutionary army, Captain Benjamin Briggs, Lieutenants Elisha Turner, Viney Turner and Job Tirrell and Sergeant Barnabas Barker, were all active in the expeditions against Crown Point, Ticonderoga and Lake George. Captain Clap's Company got as far as Quebec and Reuben Bates and David Dunbar participated in the second taking of Louisberg. The two Doctors Otis, Ephraim and James, did surgeon's duty with the troops, the one at Fort William Henry; and the other at Crown Point.

It is greatly to be doubted if this one training day of the year performed a definitely useful purpose in preparing the men of that day for military duty. Naturally hardy, always courageous, and accustomed to follow obediently where brilliantly led, the excellence of the work which they performed as soldiers, is more correctly ascribed to their sturdiness of purpose and readiness to take up arms in support of a conviction. The training field was after all, a play ground.

CHAPTER XII

TOWN ACTS AGAINST TORIES

"We, therefore, apprehending such a subjection utterly inconsistent with the just rights and blessings of society, unanimously instruct you to endeavor that our delegates in Congress be informed in case that representative body of the continent should think fit to declare the Colonies independent of Great Britain, of our readiness and determination to assist with our lives and fortunes."

Vote of the town June 7, 1776, instructing Nathan Cushing, Representative to the Great and General Court.

FOLLOWING the close of King Phillip's war a substantial peace settled upon the town, colony and province. Scituate men played a small part in the northern expedition under Andros and that commanded by Benjamin Church against the eastern tribes. In the Canadian Invasion and the French and Indian War a considerable body of troops from this town served under Captains John Clapp and Benjamin Briggs in the regiment led by Col. John Winslow of Marshfield. The Scituate companies were with the New England troops which took Louisberg in 1744. They were at Crown Point, Ticonderoga and before Quebec fifteen years later, where most of the fatalities were from small pox and other natural causes, rather than from the enemy's attack.

The first generation of settlers had been gathered to its fathers. The sons and daughters were of none less stern stuff, and the beginning of the eighteenth century saw Benjamin Stetson, the son of the cornet, Samuel Clapp, son of Deacon Thomas, Joseph Otis, the third male heir of the founder of this distinguished family of patriots, John Cushing, Jr., Thomas Turner, Nicholas Litchfield, Deacon James Torrey and Ann Vinal's grandson, the younger Stephen, upholding the family names and spirit in town and governmental affairs. Most unhappily the Hatherly name was not perpetuated, and the three sons of General Cudworth showed none of their father's aptitude for leadership in public affairs.

The descendants of the Pilgrims in the fourth generation who fought the Revolution were quite as devoted to principle and ready to make personal sacrifice for it, as were the forefathers themselves.

For nine years previous to 1774 the revenue laws enacted by the British Parliament had been especially vexatious to the people of Scituate. The town in those years was not the farming community that it is to-day. Shipyards dotted the banks of the North River. Two were at the Harbor. The iron mills or forges on Indian Head River and the three "Herring brooks" were turning out anchors, chains, nails and at "Kings forge," cannon. It was not alone "taxation without representation" that they denounced. They feared for their industries and commerce, which would be crippled, perhaps destroyed, and the consequences of the "importation of European commodities, which threaten the country with poverty and ruin." When the time for action came, they met it calmly and deliberately. There was no boisterousness, no rioting, no violence. There were a considerable number of known tories living in town. In the neighboring town of Braintree two hundred patriots seized the deputy sheriff, one Vinton †, took from him two processes bearing the royal seal, and burned them. In Scituate they treated the crown sympathizers differently. At a town meeting held:

"January 18, 1775.

At the aforesaid meeting said town accepted & past the following Vote Respecting Two Refractory Shopkeepers in town viz:—

Scituate, January ye 18th, 1775.

PUBLIC INFORMATION

That the Obstinancy of Two Refractory shopkeepers

---

† Vinton Memorial, Pages 57-61.

in this town may be justly cencered (if they be not too obscure) The Publick are hereby Informed, that on the ninth Instant the Committee of Inspection by Request of the Town waited on Charles Curtis & Frederic Henderson, shopkeepers, to know whether they Determined to adhear to the continental Association, the former of whom rendered the following peremptory Answer: I shall not adhear to it!!! The latter as ye former, adding I don't know any Congress!!! whose ignorance is the more to be wondered at seeing he has been an Inhabitant of this Continent and Town since quitting his marine vocation.

Therefore the Inhabitants of this town do hereby Resolve to break of all dealings whatsoever with said Refractory Shopkeepers until they shall give publick and absolute satisfaction to the aforesaid Committee & Town touching their present open Refractoriness relative to said Salutary Association, trusting in the meanwhile the Publick will condescend to trouble their memories with their names and characters.

Per Order of ye Committee of Inspection
& vote of ye Town
JOHN CUSHING, Jr.
Chairman of sd Committee and Clarck of sd Town"

Thus early had the Irish Capt. Boycott implanted the moral weapon which bears his name on the shores of New England. Thus also did conservative, yet none the less earnest, Scituate use sarcasm and ostracism where Boston and Braintree took recourse to violence and threats. But to go back for a year. The first official action taken by the town was at an annual meeting held on the twenty-first day of March 1774. †

"The town chose Nathan Cushing, Esq., Dr. Ephraim Otis, Nath'l Clap, Esq., Dea. William Turner, Jas. Otis, Israel Vinal, Jr., Galen Clap, Joseph Tolman, Barnabas Little, Anthony Waterman and John Clap,

---

† Scituate Records Vol. VIII page 46.

Jr., a committee to draw up something if they thought proper for the town to come into, touching the difficulties of the present times and to present the same to the town at the next May meeting."

The report of this committee drafted by Nathan Cushing, its Chairman, who with Gideon Vinal, was also the Representative to the General Court was unanimously adopted:—

"That although we join with most of our brethren in this and ye other Colonies sentimentally, that those acts of ye British Parliament which have a tendency to control our internal commerce and manufactures, and more especially to extort our monies from us, are not only disconsonant with good and lawful government; but entirely subservise of those precious rights and privileges our fathers purchased with blood, and handed down to their children by ye sword; and although doubtless our brethren and neighbors rationally expect that we join them in common form, in this common cause:—Nevertheless, as this is the truly alarming crisis, when the shackles of slavery and oppression (long preparing) are already fixed on the ankles of some of our neighbors in particular and fixing in the ankles of all in general—

Therefore, we think it meet not to color so much of the proceedings relative to the establishing of a late Act, as rashly and precipitously to determine, without deliberate inquiry and calmness.

And therefore, advise and move that a committee be appointed to make all suitable inquiry into our public disturbances and difficulties and lay their counsels, determinations and results before the town when and so often as they shall think necessary by applying to the Selectmen to warn a meeting for the purpose."

In the above, the characteristic caution of the early settler, a prominent and valuable hereditament in his progeny, is prominent. Nathan Cushing, who was its author and one of the leading spirits in its adoption, was no less patriotic

"THE TWO STACK," NORTH SCITUATE, MASS.
From a pencil drawing by Henry T. Bailey.
Built by Barnabas Little.

because of that caution than was John Adams, the second President, who on like occasion prepared the following and reported it to his townsmen of Braintree who "accepted (it) without a dissenting voice."

"We further Recommend the most clear and explicit assertion and vindication of your Rights and Liberties to be entered on the public records, that the world may know in the present and all future generations, that we have a clear knowledge and just sense of those Rights and Liberties and that with submission to Divine Providence we never can be slaves."

There are interesting coincidences in the lives of these two men at this period. Both were graduates of Harvard College and both lawyers. They were of about the same age when they promulgated the revolutionary resolutions to their respective towns, each was a patriot of the purest type, and both performed distinguished service when the result of their labors was reached in the formation of the Union.

In this year Barnabas Little was sent as a delegate to the Provincial Congress at Concord and was likewise returned the next year with Nathan Cushing to the same body when it convened at Cambridge on the first of February 1775.

Although the town, heeding the advice of Nathan Cushing and his associates, did not act rashly and precipitately, when it did move, the action was comprehensive and thorough. Early in 1775 it saw both need and occasion for some form of protection against the Tories who were within its limits. They did not so much fear physical violence from these pro-British sympathizers, as that information might be sent to Boston of the vulnerability of the town. The coast line was unprotected save for the guard at three "watch boxes," one each at the Glades, Mann Hill and the Third Cliff. These were in charge of Paul Bailey and Barnabas Little at the Glades, Eleazer Litchfield at Mann Hill and James Briggs, Jr., at the Third Cliff. Of course such slender protection against landing a force from the

British fleet which was then at anchor before Boston and from which expeditions had already been sent up the Fore River, alarming Weymouth, and threatening the north precinct of Braintree, was grossly inadequate. It was time therefore for committees of inspection and correspondence. Most of the towns hereabouts had already organized similar bodies following the removal of the sessions of the General Court from Boston to Salem by order of General Gage. In making up these important committees the town engaged its best citizens. John Cushing, Jr., grandson of the first settler, and father of William, who was then a member of the Superior Court of the Province; his cousin, Nathan, Joseph's son, who was already at the forefront fomenting revolution: Barnabas Little, the Representative to the General Court who had gone into secret caucus with his fellow legislators, planning for the Continental Congress which was soon to meet at Philadelphia: Israel Vinal, Jr., who had married into the Cushing family; Joseph Tolman, then but twenty-five years of age, and his father-in-law Abiel Turner; William Turner, later an officer in the Revolutionary army; the two brothers, Anthony and Nathaniel Waterman, who had but recently come from Marshfield; the two Clapps, Galen and Increase; John Palmer from Church Hill; Noah Otis, related by blood and in the cause of freedom to that provincial Advocate General who resigned his office rather than support an application for the Writs of Assistance; Deacon Joseph Bailey and Eli Curtis. These gentlemen with Charles Turner, Joseph Stetson, Samuel Clapp, Barnabas Barker, James Otis, George Morton, Ignatius Otis, Deacon Thomas Mann, Samuel Jenkins, Paul Bailey, Calvin Peirce, Amasa Bailey, Constant Clapp, John Jacobs and James Briggs, Jr., constituted the Committee of Inspection. At the time of its appointment the town provided for its organization and that "any seven of ye above Committee to be a Coram." It was two years after its appointment that a "coram" of the whole committee became active in the performance of the duty for which it had been created. Here again is evidence of the caution, not to say tardiness, with which the town acted in important affairs. Considering that in 1775 everybody in Scituate knew everybody else, two years seems to have been sufficient time in which to learn the names of those who were "inimicall to the interests of the colony." Yet it was not until June 3, 1777 that the committee reported that action should be taken, and "the town chose Capt. Israel Vinal to prosecute and lay before the court," the evidence of the hostile disposition toward this or any of the United States, of any of the inhabitants of the town of Scituate, who stand charged with being persons whose residence in the state is dangerous to publick peace and safety." Twenty-four persons were so charged. Frederick Henderson, who two years before had been boycotted, was still under suspicion and he with Elijah Curtis, Benjamin James, Job Otis, James Curtis, David Little, Jr., Benjamin Jacobs, Ebenezer Stetson, Benjamin James, Jr., Elisha Turner, David Otis, Prince Otis, Joseph Turner, Jonathan Fish, the two doctors Stockbridge, Benjamin and Charles, father and son, William Hoskins, John Stetson, William Cole, Samuel Stetson, Elisha and Joseph Jacobs, Joseph Hayden and young Jonathan Fish were given "liberty to be heard at this present town meeting or at any other day, that their names may be erased on giving satisfaction." Henderson, who was a retired officer of the British navy, living here upon a small pension, soon satisfied the authorities that his physical condition would not permit his going into active service, and upon his promise to take no part and behave himself, his name was erased from the list. Others, it subsequently appeared, had been erroneously suspected, so that in a fortnight only Job Otis, Benjamin and Joseph Jacobs, Elisha Turner, John Stetson, Elijah and James Curtis and Joseph Hayden remained. The two last named with Charles Curtis, the refractory shopkeeper had, it was believed, joined with the tories of Marshfield of whom there were many, in petitioning Gen. Gage to send the Queen's guards to that town for the protection of its loyal inhabitants. This action had been firmly protested by the Selectmen of Plymouth, Scituate, Duxbury, Kingston, Hanson and Pembroke in a letter to that British officer "assuring him that there was no truth in the statements of those of Marshfield and Scituate, who declared that this was necessary to protect them from the exasperated fury of the whigs." † The troops were sent however and the Provincial Congress then in session at Cambridge, taking recognition of this protest, voted "that these towns are highly approved of in finding out the malicious designs of their enemies in requesting Gen. Gage to station there a body of troops; and that they do steadily persevere in the same line of conduct, which has in this instance so justly entitled them to the esteem of their fellow-countrymen; and to keep a watchful eye upon the behavior of those who are aiming at the destruction of our liberties."

Public spirit and loyalty ran high and in brilliant contrast to the attitude toward the war, later on, when Scituate in common with many other towns in Massachusetts, was forced to offer larger bounties to fill its quota for even short terms of enlistment. At a town meeting on January eighteenth 1775 it was voted to refuse a bounty proposed by the Provincial Congress. At another held in May, the Committee of safety suggested that Capt. Noah Otis be paid for keeping guard day and night at the watch boxes. This was very promptly voted down when the men who have been hereinbefore mentioned, immediately volunteered for that service without charge. The Selectmen were instructed to see that the town was provided with "warlike stores." The inhabitants were "recommended" to bring "their firearms and accoutrements to meeting with them on the Sabbath" as the forefathers had done before them. Hawkes Cushing, Nathan Cushing, John, Increase and Galen Clapp, Nathaniel Turner and Isaac Stetson were appointed a committee for "drafting and enlisting minnit

---

† Winsor, History of Duxbury page 127.

men." There was no necessity for the draft however, if the town in making this appointment, meant by the use of the word, to force service in the Continental cause. That the ranks of the Minute Men were soon full is evidenced by entries like this:—"March 6, 1775, James Cudworth and Daniel Litchfield excused from serving as warden because he was a Minuteman."

Thus matters continued with an interest very active and alive. It was not confined to the men. The wives and mothers, beside the necessity of guarding the family economy, were now called upon to assist in making thirteen thousand coats—one for each officer and soldier in the Massachusetts forces called out by the third Provincial Congress which assembled at Watertown. Of this number Scituate furnished one hundred and twenty-five.

It is not, of course, the purpose of this history to follow the course of the Revolution. Only as it bears the familiar names of those by whom this town is peopled, and records some act of worthy bravery or devotion by one of them, has the record an appropriate place in these pages.

The battles of Lexington and Bunker Hill had been fought. The Scituate companies were in camp near the Second Meeting house awaiting the call to join General Sullivan in the campaign in Rhode Island. The Continental Congress in session at Philadelphia was deliberating upon the affairs of the thirteen struggling colonies and time was ripe for independence. Nathan Cushing was Representative of the town in the "General Assembly." Determination and action had now succeeded caution and the town on June seventh 1776 in meeting assembled gave the following instructions to its representative in the legislature upon the declaration of that independence which all now prayerfully sought. The draft was that of William Cushing then a judge of the Superior Court.

"The inhabitants of the town being called together on the recommendation of our General Assembly to signify our minds on the great point of Independence of

Great Britain think fit to instruct you on that head. The ministry of that kingdom having formed a design of subjecting the colonies to a distant, external and absolute power in all cases whatsoever wherein the colonies have not, nor in the nature of things can have, any share by representation, have for a course of years past exerted their utmost act and endeavors to put the same plan,—so destructive to both countries—into execution. But finding it, through the noble and virtuous opposition of the sons of freedom, impracticable by means of mere political artifice and corruption, they have at length had a final recourse to a standing army, so repugnant to the nature of a free government, to fire and sword, to bloodshed and devastation, calling in the aid of foreign troops, being determined, as well as endeavoring, to stir up ye savages of the wilderness to exercise their barbarities upon us and by all appearances, if practical, to extirpate the American from the face of the earth, (unless they tamely resign the rights of humanity) and repeople this once happy country with the ready sons of vassalage if such can be found.

We, therefore, apprehending such a subjection utterly inconsistent with the just rights and blessings of society, unanimously instruct you to endeavor that our delegates in Congress be informed, in case that representative body of the continent, should think fit, to declare the colonies independent of Great Britain, of our readiness and determination to assist with our lives and fortunes in support of that—we apprehend—necessary measure.

Touching other matters, we trust in your fidelity, discretion and zeal for the public welfare, to propose and forward all such measures as you shall apprehend may tend to our necessary defence in the present threatening aspect of affairs, or to the promoting of the internal peace, order and good government of this colony."

Following promulgation of this, its own declaration of independence, on October fourteenth the town voted as follows, upon the question of adopting a state constitution:

"Agreeable to a Resolve of the General Court, said town voted that they give their consent that the present House of Representatives of the state of ye Massachusetts Bay, together with the Council, if they consent in one body with the House and by equal voice, should propose and agree on such a constitution and form of government for this state, as the House and Council aforesaid, on the fullest and most mature deliberations shall judge will most conduce to the safety, peace and happiness of this state; and then be submitted to the people at large for their ratification and promulgation or disapprobation."

The committee which drafted and proposed this vote to the town consisted of Elisha Tolman, Nathaniel Waterman, Increase Clapp, Barnabas Little, Israel Sylvester, Daniel Damon, Israel Litchfield, Elisha James and Deacon Joseph Bailey. This committee was a most important one; it had to deal with a weighty and serious occasion. That the towns of Massachusetts were by no means unanimous in their opinions upon the advisability of the proposed move is evident from the great variety of returns made to the Secretary of State in response to the request in the Resolve for that action.† The Scituate attitude was thoroughly and characteristically cautious. While the neighboring towns of Duxbury and Weymouth voted unanimously against the action proposed; Middleborough for a caucas or convention; Hingham for publication first; Bridgewater and Pembroke for the resolve as it stood, it remained for Scituate to suggest that the people alone and not their representatives should ratify or disapprove it, once it had been enacted by the legislative department. It is not claimed for the members of the Scituate committee that the procedure outlined in the above vote originated in its entirety with them.

---

† Mass. Archives Vol. 156. The vote from many towns including Plymouth, Braintree, Abington and others in the old colony is missing. That of Scituate is found only in the Town Records Vol. VIII.

Attention is now called to it for the purpose of again accentuating the deliberation and wisdom, inherited from the forefathers, shown by subsequent generations in Scituate, in dealing with public questions of grave concern, in which the rights of the individual were at stake. Braintree, its neighbor, the home of John Adams, through its committee, composed of one general, two colonels, two majors, one captain, one lieutenant, two deacons and a judge †, did not approve of the proposed constitution drafted by their own great townsman, without "some alteration and amendment." Scituate, not only sanctioned it, save as to the first and eleventh articles ‡ but pointed out a method for its adoption which was followed. The satisfaction properly derivable from this commendable achievement by a committee of men of limited education is great. It gives an analytical retrospection of their work, an appropriate place in these pages.

Meantime the town was doing its duty toward the provincial government and its own troops in the field. In 1776 and 1777 it economically refused to appropriate any money for the highways, granted a bounty of "40s per month to a man, as additional encouragement to the Continental pay" and gave "20s. each as ½ month advance pay." Benjamin Hatch, Sr., and Benjamin Hatch, Jr., were added to the Committee of correspondence from the "Two Miles" in order that that neighborhood might be represented. William Turner had resigned his position on the Committee of Correspondence, had taken command of the troops which during the first winter had been quartered at the Harbor, and later had come out of the service a colonel. The Jacobs family at Assinippi, among whose members in the year 1774 had been found some tories, had furnished its son John, whose services were rewarded with the title of Colonel and Joshua, a Captain. Major John Clapp, a veteran of the French and Indian war, was also a colonel in the Revolution. Nathaniel Winslow of Scituate, unlike his namesake and relative, Edward, who was warming his tory shins

---

† Adams—Three Episodes of Mass. History Vol. II page 891.
‡ On the Judiciary and House of Representatives.

before the open fire in the family hearthstone at Marshfield, went heartily and cheerfully into the toils and dangers of the southern expedition, leaving his wife, four small boys and little Anna, just born, to be watched over by the willing women folks at home. He returned a major. If old Humphrey Turner could have arisen from his grave on Meeting House Hill, he would have seen two of his name and family, Jonathan and Amos, both captains, leading commands in the fight for freedom and the right, as he himself had done one hundred and forty years before. Captain Williams Barker too, the successor of fighting John Williams in the ownership of the farm at Cedar Point, was early in the field with thirty-eight of Scituate's citizen soldiery, under Sullivan in the Rhode Island campaign. Capt. Peter Sears, who had recently come from Halifax, Lieut. Edward Damon and Deacon Elisha James, the latter approaching seventy years of age, were in the engineering corps, or "Mechanicks" as they were called, and Dr. Lemuel Cushing, the brother of Nathan, was surgeon in the third regiment. Nor were the private soldiers less representative of the fair name and good fame of the ancient town. There were John Whitcomb, the great-great grandson of brave Mary Cudworth; Stephen Vinal, the fourth of his name; William and Amasa Hyland, whose ancestor Samuel died fighting in Phillip's bloody war; Jesse Dunbar, a boy in his teens, Elisha Briggs and Daniel Merritt. To single out any of these for particular and meritorious comment is unworthy. Each served the Commonwealth and confederation earnestly and well in the place assigned to him. His best monument is the position which his name bears on the rolls of combatants in that successful but disheartening struggle. The pages of this volume have been written to some purpose if for no other, than to assist in perpetuating this list in full.

Colonels: William Turner, John Clapp, John Jacobson, and John Cushing. Major, Nathaniel Winslow. Captains, Elijah Crocker, Samuel Stockbridge, Hayward Peirce, Edward Sparrow, Joseph Stetson. Lieutenants, Edward Mott,

Joseph Barstow, Calvin Peirce, Jacob Turner and Elisha Curtis. Ensigns, Jonathan Turner, Caleb Nichols, Nathaniel Chittenden and Francis Cushing.

Sergeants—Enoch Collamore, Lazarus Bowker, Stephen Palmer, Joseph Benson, James Nash, Lawrence Litchfield, Benjamin Vassall, Benjamin Hatch, Thomas Webb, Benjamin Peakes, Isaac Stetson, Ira Bryant, Jacobs Turner, Ephraim Palmer, Colburn Burrill, Benjamin Vinal, John Sutton, Benjamin Bailey, Micah Mott, Benjamin Holmes and Elisha Foster.

Corporals—Thomas Totman, James Lincoln, James Stockbridge, Benjamin Holmes, Noah Litchfield, Samuel Curtis, Consider Merritt, Gethelus Cowing, Samuel Peirce, Joseph Brown, Samuel Young, Samuel Gray, Eleazer Peakes, Zadoc Damon, William Brooks.

Fifers—Bela Clapp, Reuben Damon, Abner Sutton, Sylvanus Peirce and Nathaniel Barstow.

Drummers—Nathaniel Cushing, Christopher Stetson, William Studley and John Doherty.

Joshua Clapp was Clerk to Captain William Turner's company during its four days' service on the march to Lexington and return on April 19, 1775 and James Jenkins acted in a like capacity for Captain Hayward Peirce's company when it joined the regiment of which John Cushing was colonel, and participated in the Rhode Island campaign.

The privates were: Samuel Clapp, Barnabas Barker, Edward Bowker, Daniel Damon, Ebenezer Eddy, Samuel Damon, Gershom Bowker, Bartlett Bowker, Stephen Damon, Isaac Sylvester, David Jordan, Elisha Jacobs, Ebenezer Copeland, Ephraim Stetson, Noah Barrell, Joseph Brown, James Gray, James Barrell, Benjamin Collamore, John Damon, Eells Damon, Daniel Edwards, William Hyland, Charles Otis, Simeon Prouty, Joshua Prouty, James Prouty, John Wright, George Torrey, Micah Hinds, Matthew Stetson, Stephen Totman, Nehemiah House, Consider Turner, Samuel Curtis, Gideon Jenkins, James Jenkins, David Bowker, Thomas Holmes, Calvin Jenkins, Nathaniel Eells, Luke

Bowker, Nehemiah Merritt, Sylvanus Damon, Jabez Standley, John King, John Ellms, Joseph Briggs, David Merritt, Charles Curtis, Simeon Pincin, Anthony Collamore, Isaac Stetson, Daniel Merritt, Stephen Wade, John Merritt, Caleb Nichols, Joseph Nash, Gamaliel Curtis, Abdenego Wade, Geva Jenkins, Zaccheus Lambert, Noah Nichols, Lothrop Litchfield, David Dunbar, William Pincin, James Litchfield, Joseph Ellms, Zaccheus Merritt, Benjamin Curtis, Dearing Jones, Calogus Vinal, Anthony Collamore, Henry Sutton, Guy Bates, David Bowker, George Cole, William Damon, James Cushing, Benjamin Collamore, Stephen Fish, Michael Frazier, John Henley, William Henley, Ezekiel Jones.

Ephraim Litchfield, Nathaniel Lapham, Lemuel Lapham, John Mitchell, Eliphalet Northey, Theopilus Southworth, Laban Sprague, Samuel Brown, Abner Briggs, Zenas Bryant, Elijah Bryant, Luther Chittenden, Charles Curtis, Isaac Collier, Abner Dwelley, Amos Dunbar, Ezekiel Dunbar, David Dunbar, William Dwelley, Charles Fish, Elisha Grose, Joshua Grose, Benjamin Gannett, Bela Hayden, William Hayden, Josiah Holbrook, David Hammond, Nathaniel Hollowell, Thomas Holmes, Joseph Hayden, Benjamin Hyland, Benjamin Hammond, Edward Jenkins, Nathaniel Jenkins, Charles Litchfield, Nathan Litchfield, Elisha Litchfield, Samuel Litchfield, Josiah Mann, Lemuel Mayhew, John Manson, Job Neal, Samuel Nichols, Noah Nash, Augustus Peirce, Edward Ramsdell, Lemuel Sylvester, Asa Turner, Benjamin Wade, John Wade, Benjamin Woodworth, William Barrell, John Bowker, Joshua Bowker, Benjamin Collamore, David Clapp, Nathaniel Cushing, D. Costo, Stephen Damon, Edward Dunbar, Hosea Dunbar.

Daniel Edwards, Nathaniel House, Elisha Joy, William Jones, James Jeffreys, John King, John Lincoln, William Mayhew, Joshua Merritt, Daniel Merritt, Noah Nicholson, Charles Otis, Simeon Prouty, James Prouty, Stephen Vinal, John Prouty, John Wright, Laban Rose, Samuel Stetson, Peter Sears, Samuel Simmons, Barnabas Simmons, Amos Stetson, Thomas Totman, Benjamin Tower, Ebenezer Totman, Abner House, Nathan Thomas, Nathan Tower, Ebenezer Wing, Elijah Delano, Abijah Clapp, E. Dingley, Abner Curtis, Joel Sylvester, Israel Turner, Elisha Stetson, Barnabas Webb, Joshua Merritt, Adam Cushing, Stephen Tower, Lemuel Lapham, James Lapham, Peleg House, Charles Litchfield, Joshua Sprague, Josiah Litchfield, Ezra Hayden, Ezekiel Jones, Daniel Dunbar, Noah Stoddard, Laban Sprague, Calvin Bowker, Ebenezer Bates, Seth Bates, Warren Torrey, Nathaniel Tower, Josiah Hatch, David Ford, Nathan Stetson, Bejamin Studley, Elijah Sylvester, Samuel Ramsdell, Issacher Wade, Elisha Hayden, Abner Litchfield.

Reuben Curtis, Thomas Curtis, Paul Bailey, Abner Bailey, Elisha Litchfield, Thomas Litchfield, Daniel Litchfield, Barnabas Litchfield, John Litchfield, Eleazer Litchfield, Amos Litchfield, Lot Litchfield, Jonathan Collier, Joseph Vinal, Jr., Joseph Damon, Levi Newell, Seth Merritt, Matthew Peirce, Elisha Hyland, Melzar Merritt,, Robert Vinal, John Studley, Daniel Briggs, John Cushing, Oliver Delano, Isaac Lapham, Asa Lapham, Daniel Hayden, Jesse Sutton, Prince Witherell, Richard Witherell, Thomas Church, William Lincoln, Asher Freeman, Samuel Stoddard, Nathaniel Jones Nehemiah Manson, George Merritt, Nehemiah Sampson, Ezra Hayden, Noah Nichols, Isaac Torrey, Samuel Simmons, John Whitcomb, David Barnes, Thomas Ruggles, James Stockbridge, Elijah Stoddard, Benjamin Delano, James Clapp, Peleg Curtis, Sylvanus Clapp, Richard Ford, Charles Totman, George Torrey, Simon Damon, Nathaniel Turner, Nathaniel Brooks, Levi Wade, Elijah Clapp, Stephen Wade, Jonathan Brown, Ensign Brown, Josias Wade, Thomas Grose, Levi Nash, Theophilus Corthell, Thomas Farrar, Eleazer Peakes, Jonathan Mann, Daniel Hayden, Israel Cowen, Knight Brown, Luther Brooks, Abial Studley, Israel Nash, Thomas Lapham, Charles Turner, Thomas Church, Caleb Litchfield, John Gibbs, Gamaliel Curtis, Michael Clapp, Benjamin Briggs, H. Stoddard, Abijah Turner, Frederick Hammond, Isaiah Stoddard, John

Brown, Isaac Brown, Robert Erskine, Thomas Grose, Abijah Clapp, Ezra Hayden, Samuel Stoddard, Nathaniel Jordan, Nehemiah Sampson, Nehemiah Manson, Gideon Stetson, William Mayhew, John Wright, William Mann, Abiel Turner, Joshua Gannett, Daniel Corlew, William Nicholson, Winsor Baker, Asaph Jacobs, Peleg Hayden.

John Gibbs, Seth Orcutt, Frederick Hammond, Elisha Grose, Amasa Hyland, Josiah Leonard, Elisha Dunbar, Josiah Compsett, (an Indian) William McNevin, William Perry, John Russell, James Barrell, Jr., Nathaniel Cook, Simeon Stoddard, Asher Freeman, James Barrell, Isaac Woodworth, Warren Little, Samuel Sprague, Levi Bowker, Roger Clapp, Nathaniel Jordan, James Cushing, Jonathan Brown, Bela Brown, Charles Church, Israel Mayhew, Elisha Hayden, James Stetson, Bejamin Jones, Ezra Hayden, Matthew Peirce, Amos Perry, Zeba Sutton, Calla Brown, John M. Gill, Eli Litchfield, George Mann, Ezekiel Merritt, Nehemiah Manson, Thomas Nichols, William Lincoln, and Signor Layonne, said to be a Frenchman who came to America with Lafayette. The thirty-four last named were the quota furnished by the town under the resolve of the General Assembly December 2, 1780, for three years' service. They saw the end of the war.

CHAPTER XIII

BIOGRAPHICAL SKETCHES

THE men who made Scituate prominent, not to say foremost, in the settlement of Plymouth Colony, came, like Myles Standish, from comfortable homes and surroundings in the old country. Nothing short of an almost fanatic ardor toward, and devotion to, religious principles, impelled them. Theirs was to labor and to fight, to hope and to pray, while being sustained in their struggle and privations by a firm faith in divine guidance, to lay down and follow such rules of action for their own conduct and for those whom fortune commingled with them, that their dreams of a great state should be realized and come true. Those who followed them in the century succeeding the first planting of "New Plymouth" were not the less actuated by the same high ideals and aspirations.

The succeeding pages deal with the lives and accomplishments of those who were particularly conspicuous in bringing and keeping Scituate to the forefront. While it may appear that many of the incidents and happenings which have found place in these pages, are of trifling and insignificant importance, they collectively afford such a true presentation of the Pilgrim character, his energy and patience in unpropitious surroundings, as to enhance their value far beyond what at first appears.

JAMES CUDWORTH

James Cudworth was born in London and came to Scituate, † probably with Mr. Hatherly in 1632. In 1634 he was admitted a freeman and had his house and five acres

† Deane—History of Scituate page 245.

OLD CUDWORTH HOUSE, 1723, SCITUATE CENTER.
Home of the Scituate Historical Society.

of land near Coleman Hills, south of Mr. Lathrop's. He was a constable of Scituate in 1637. He sold his farm to Thomas Ensign in 1642 or before. The deed was recorded on the eighth day of June 1642:—

"Memorand. That James Cudworth of Barnstable gent doth acknowledge that for and consideracon of the sume of Eighteen pounds to him in hand fully payd by Thomas Ensigne of Scittuate plant'r Hath freelly and absolutely bargained and sold unto Thomas Ensigne All that his dwelling house wherein said Thomas now dwelleth in Scituate aforesaid and an out-house with five acres of upland thereunto adjoyneing lying to the lands late Mr. Lathrop's to the north and to the lands of Mr. Timothy Hatherly East and South and to the Comon lane West with all and singular thappurtenances thereunto belonging with all the Right title and interest of and into the same and every part and pcell thereof." †

When the trouble occured in Mr. Lathrop's congregation, Cudworth was one of his supporters. On January twenty-second, 1638, he with Anthony Annable, Thomas Besbeech (Bisby), William Gilson, Henry Cobb, Henry Rowley, Edward Foster and Robert Linnell obtained a grant of land at Sippecan for the "seating of a town and congregation." This was not accepted,—instead they went to Barnstable in 1639-40. Cudworth took with him from Scituate the son of his neighbor Thomas Byrd, as his servant or apprentice. The manner in which the young men of this period thus bound out, were treated, is strikingly shown in the official account of the trouble which was had with this boy. On "January 4, 1641, Thomas Byrd, servant to Mr. James Cudworth, of Barnstable, for running away from his sd master, and breaking a house or two in Barnstable, and taking some apparell and victualls is censured to be once whipt at Plym and once whipt at Barnstable, before the next Court of Assistants; and when his sd mast'r comes,

---

† Plymouth Colony Records Vol XII (Deeds) page 84.

then order to be taken for the payment of his fees; and at the next Court of Assistants following the sd Byrd, remaining in the messengers hands upon letters from Mr. Freeman that the sd Thomas Byrds father had agreed with the sd Mr. Cudworth for the tyme he was to serve the sd Cudworth, the sd Thomas Byrd was released paying the messengers fees and for tother part of his censure which should have been executed upon him in Barnestable, in regard to the coldnesse of the present season it is to be inflicted upon him at Scituate whether he goes to dwell, when it shall be convenyent season." †

Shortly after his marriage and before going to Barnstable, Cudworth wrote a letter to Rev. John Stoughton ‡ which has most happily been preserved through the fidelity of Samuel G. Drake, who found it in the British State Paper Office and became possessed of it. §

Letter from James Cudworth to John Stoughton D. D.

"Citewat the of December 1634.

Deare & Worthey Sur:—my Bownded duty & ernest affections in the bowells of love to you Remembered, & also to my most deare Mother. The Lord who is the sercher of the heart & treyer of the Raynes, knowes that I do unfainedly desire the pease prosperity & wellfare both of youre soules & bodyes as of mine owne. These are to let you understand. That I have Received youre godley & peyous letter full of grave & holsume exortations which argues youre unfained desieres & continuall indevores for the good of my soule, & indeed, I have cause if every eny had to blesse the Lord that ever I saw you, for under God you have bine the gretest Instrument of good to mee in the world, & since my absence from you the care you had of mee with youre paynes in laboringe with mee is frequent in my mind & dus take a depe impretion in my soule, & has

---

† Plymouth Colony Records Vol. II Page 30.
‡ His step-father.
§ New England Hist. and Gen. Reg. Vol. XIX pages 101-104.

bine an instrumentall cause of workinge mee nerer unto & walkinge Closer with the Lord, & more & more to see the vanity of all these outward things & that fullness that is Christ-Jesus. I desire that you will be as frequent in youre letters as you may, for I finde a greate deale of sweetnes in them; for they put a great dele of quickoninge life & edge unto my Affections & you know that the best in this life are subject to grow cold in oure p'fetion; that wee Dayley neade sum exortation & consolation both to provoke to the practice of holy things & to spport us in the time of temptation or Afiliction; that wee may wade thorow all the Difficulteyes of this short life with Cherfulness of hearte. Laboringe to make sum benefit to our soules of all the Lords Dealinges with us, whether they be merseyes that they may alare us or chastisements that they may Corect & amend us; or Judgmentes that may terefy or Afflictiones that they may Refine us so that at length we may bee more than Conquerereres over all oure Corruptions so that wee may serve the Lord with the hole man & worshipinge him according as he has Reveled in his holy word, walkinge the way & order of the gospell *standing fore the purity of his ordinances* and as Moses wold not part with one of the *ordinances but to bee Redye to lay downe oure lives for them for With those wee might serve our God.* I am very sorry to hear youre sickness my prayeres shall & have bin continualy to the Lord for yours, I shall intreate you to beare with pasience what the Lord shall lay upon you. Laboringe to make a sanctifiede use of all his dealinges & in all things submitinge youre willes unto his, & there all thinges shall worke together for the best unto those that love him.

Allso I understand that there is *like to bee* 20 li. lost by Walter Gamblinge, if it bee so. I know it is the Lords doinge & if I consider what have I, that I have not Received the Lord, nay, what have I deserved-

shurly nothinge but eternall wrath & condemnation therefor. Let him doe with his owne as seemeth good in his eyes. I thanke the Lord it is no trouble but rather cause of rejoycinge when I way a temporall loss with a sperituall gayne when the Lord is pleased even to befole me theare that I could not manadge my affayeres with comfort even as if the Lord should say it is but a foly to a tempe any thinge afote heare I will take away they abiliteyes thou shalt not be able to go thorow such with any thinge heare but thou must go far from thine owne Land & fatheres howse & theare I will reveall myselfe to thee; & theare shalt thow honer, worship & serve mee as I shall reveale my selfe to thee out of my sacred word. I doe ingeniously freely confess to you now the Lord has brought mee heither & in a small mesure made me acquainted with his wayes, & *how & in what maner he will be worshipped in. All though heare bee many difficulteyes to be under gone, yet I account it an excellent mersey that the Lord has brought me to see that which my forefathers desired to see but could not; to see so many Churches walkinge in the way and order of the gospell. Injoyinge that Christian liberty that Christ has purchased for us.*

And to relate to you that which yett I have not, concerning the estate of New England, heare, are these Churches. 1, Plymouth, wheare Mr. Smith is Pastor, No Techer. 2. Boston, Mr. Wilson, Pastor, Mr. Cotton, teacher, 3. Dorchester, Mr. Wareham, P. Mr. Mavoricke, T: 4, at Rockes Burey, Mr. Weeldes, P; Mr. Elyot T; 5, at Charles Towne, Mr. Jeames, P. & my Cosson Simes is now gone thether to bee there Teacher. 6, at Newtowne, Mr. Hoocker P. Mr. Stone Teacher. 7, at Watertowne, Mr. Phillipes P. 8, at Saugus where Mr. Somphereyes (Humphrey) lives, Mr. Bachelor, P; 9 at Salem theare Pastor, old Mr. Skelton is dead. Thear is Mr. Williams who dos exersies his giftes but is in no office. 10, at Ipsidge a plantation made upe this yeare Mr. Ward, P. Mr. Parker, T.

Now these plantations that are not yet settled & are newly begun are three; Duckes burey where Mr. Colyer dwelles. No Pastor nor Teacher Oures Cittewate, to whom the Lord has bine very gracious, & his providence has bine Admorably sene, our beyenge to bringe us oure Pastor whom wee so long expected—Mr. Lathrop, who the Lord has brought to us in safety, whom wee finde to be a holy Reverat & hevenly minded man. And the other is Beare Cove † wheare is no Pastor nor Teacher.

Now one thinge I will intreate youe, that if you doe know eny of youre frendes & acquaintances that come over hither, that youe would direct them to our Plantation. The nature of the place being as in my former letters you shall finde, & is still, though now I have seene more of the plantations than then I had, & yet it findes place in my affections before any. And with all such as you sall advise to sit downe with us wee wold intreate you they may bee such as you judge to bee fite to bee Received unto Church fellowshipe.

Allso, if it should please God to bringe you into this land amongst us, I would intreate you for youre owne good, not to come ingaidged to eney people till you come heare youre selfe, & see the nature of the plase wheare you are to site downe, together with the condition of the People.

One thing I canot but relate, & that not only with grefe, for & with feare of what will bee the event of a strange thinge put in practice by sum in the Churuch of Salem; but by whom I heare not. And that is they have cut out the Crosse in the flage, Or Ansient that they carie before them when they trayne. Indeed it is contrary to the mindes & willes of all that I cann heare

---

† Hingham.

of. Captaine Indicat there Captaine is a holy honest man & dus utterly abandone it & who are the Aegeentes in it I cannot heare.

Now, as concerning my owne pertickular, I thanke the Lord I have wanted no thinge since I came into the Land. I have, I blese God, as yet, the best howse in the plantation, thowgh but a meane one it contentes us well. I planted corne, contrary to Mr. Hatherly's mind, which I know not how I adune. † I bless the Lord I have, I thinke, at least 50 bushels of corne, which is worth 12 li. So that I think I shall not neade but shall have anaught till next harvest. My howse is the meeting howse because it is the biggest, but we are but few, as yet, in number—not passinge 60 persons.

As concerning my unkills, ‡ blessed be God they are both in good health and my unkill Thomas is to be maried shortly to a widow that has good meanes & has 5 children. Thus much I make bold to trouble yow with all, being all for the present, only desiring to be remembered to all my brothers & sisters and all my friends, & my wife likewise desires her duty to you both her love to the rest & I would pray whereas I wrote for stufe for 2 cotes it was rashly dun, that you would refrayne till you have of mine to pay youreselves with all. x x x x So for the present, I commende you to the protection of the Allmighty & ever rest yowre dutyfull sunn till death.

James Cudworth

To his very Lovinge &
Kinde ffather Dr.
Stoughton at his howse
In Alldermanbury

(Endorsement) James Cudworth to Doctor Stoughton shewing his privat correspondency with ye irregular,

---

† Have done.
‡ Probably Israel & Thomas Stoughton of Dorchester.

incomformable † fugitive ministers beyond ye Seas in New England."

Cudworth was a deputy to the General Court at Plymouth from Barnstable in 1640 and 1642, but was back in Scituate in 1648 ‡ and obtained a one-thirtieth share in the Conihasset grant made by his friend Hatherly to Charles Chauncey and the others. With this as a nucleus he bought, about 1659, the home and farm buildings of John Hoar near Mann Hill. The remaining portion of the latter's farm when he removed to Concord in that year, was sold to John Saffin. This is the farm upon which the heirs of Ward Litchfield now live and was the home of Deacon Marshall Litchfield at the time of the trial of the famous "beach cases" (Litchfield vs Scituate). In July 1673, there having arisen some dispute between Cudworth and Hoar the latter sued him:—

"John Hoare of Concord, complained against Captain James Cudworth of Scituate, in an action on the case, for unjustly detaining of the said Hoares lands, which said lands, together with housing, orchard, and fencing hath biene in the occupation of the said Cudworth now about twelve yeares past, being part of the land the said Cudworth now lives att, as more fully appear by a deed and writings, and all due damages sustained thereby.

This action was withdrawn.§"

He was a modest, sincere man, of good education for the time and was devotedly attached to both church and colony. It is something of a shock to the belief in this devotion and his amiable qualities, that we find him punished in 1638 with Humphrey Turner and three others, for not attending a session of the General Court at Plymouth when the colony was governed by all of the freemen in a

---

† Dr. Stoughton was prosecuted by Laud in the High Commission.
‡ He was enrolled upon both the Scituate and Barnstable Military companies in 1643.
§ Plymouth Colony Records Vol. VII Page 178.

body; and in 1640 just before he left Scituate to go to Barnstable to learn of his being fined for "selling and retayleing wine contrary to order."

He sat upon both the grand and traverse juries and also at inquests. He was frequently chosen by his neighbors to arbitrate between them or appointed by the Court to settle boundary and fence disputes. He was selected to determine the line of the grant to Hatherly and the Merchant Adventures, and was one of a committee in 1650 to decide between the English and the Indians as to the title to lands at Showamet and Pautuxet. In 1652 he was captain of the military company at Scituate and in 1653 and 1654 one of the Council of War when an expedition was contemplated against the Dutch.

He was a deputy to the General Court from Scituate during the years from 1649 to 1654. He performed these services while in office conscientiously and well. On October 7, 1650, the General Court, perhaps recalling the punishment it had meted out to him and to Humphrey Turner for non-attendance upon one of its sessions ordered:

"Mr. James Cudworth and Humphrey Turner are allowed 25S, for charges of attendance at June Court last past. Item, for five daies, videlecet from Fryday until Tuesday following 25, 6d p day."

No other deputies were so singled out for preferment. Evidently it did not deter Cudworth from absenting himself again when occasion occurred. During his last year of membership in the Court he was again fined, this time £5 "for departing the Court, being required to stay on Special occation." It took a suit by the Treasurer to collect this fine, which was eventually paid. While a member of this body he acted on committees for letting the trade at Kennebec, to take the account of the Treasurer of the Colony, and in the latter year he, with "William Collyare and Lieut. Southworth together with some of the majestrates are appointed to view the writing lately sent out by the Bay, and compare it with the articles of confederacon, and give in their thoughts about ut unto the Court they are to meet the first Tuesday in July next." Later he twice served on a committee to revise the colony ordinances. He was appointed to solemnize marriages and on occasion was the guardian of the children of his deceased neighbors whose estates he likewise frequently administered. Following his retirement from the General Court he was, the next year, surveyor of highways of his town.

In 1656, 1657 and 1658 he was an Assistant to the Colony Court. He was returned in 1659 but Governor Prence, who had been his persistent enemy, caused his rejection on account of his pre-Quaker leanings.

During these years, 1655 and 1657, Cudworth was also one of the Plymouth Commissioners of the United Colonies. In the former John Brown of Plymouth, a quiet, resourceful man not unlike Cudworth himself, and his very warm friend, was his associate on the Commission. In the latter year it was Governor Prence. In September 1657 the Commissioners had been informed "that divers Quakers are arrived this summer att Road Island and entertained there, which may prove dangerous to the Collonies." They wrote a letter to their Rhode Island neighbors containing an illy concealed threat couched in language which embraced them with the most affectionate greetings, but roundly denounced the Quakers. It sought that the Colony of Rhode Island should prohibit the coming of this sect to that plantation under severe penalties and ended :—

"and we further declare that wee apprehend that it will be our Duty seriously to consider what further provision God may call us to make to prevent the aforesaid mischiefs; and for our further guidance and direction heerin wee desire you to Imparte youer mind and Resolution to the General Court of Massachusetts which Assembleth the 14th of October next." †

---

† Acts of the Commissioners of the United Colonies Vol. II Page 180.

All the Commissioners except Cudworth signed this letter. He refused; and later, among his colleagues in the magistracy at Plymouth he not only fought the enactment of the law † for the banishment and punishment of the Quakers but delivered himself concerning the Quakers, their beliefs and actions, as a most tolerant lawgiver. In 1657 the trouble which had been threatening came to the surface. Cudworth charged that certain of the magistrates conspired with some unfriendly neighbors in Scituate, nineteen in number, to oust him from his position as the head of the town's military company.

---

† At a meeting of the Commissioners of the United Colonies of New England held at Boston on the second day of September 1658 the following ordinance against the Quakers was proposed by the Commissioners for adpotion and enactment by the four colonies of Massachusetts, Plymouth, Rhode Island, Connecticut and New Haven.

"Whereas there is an accursed and pernicious seett of heritiques lately Risen up in the world whoe are comonly called Quakers whoe take upon them to bee ymediately sent of God and Infallably assisted; who soe speake and writ blasphemos thinges dispising Government and the order of God in Church and Comonwealth the speaking of dignities Reproching and Reviling Majestrates and minnesters of the Gospell seeking to turne the people from the faith and to gain proselites to their pernicious wayes; and whereas the severall Jurisdictions have made divers lawes to prohibite and Restraine the aforesaid cursed heretiques from coming amongst them; yet notwithstanding they are not detered thereby; But arrogantly and presumptuously doe presse into severall of the jurisdictions and there vent their pernicious and divellish oppinions which being permitted tends manifestly to the Disturbance of our peace; the withdrawing of the harts of the people from theire subjection to Government and soe in Issue to cause division and Reuin if not timely prevented it is therefore propounded and seriously comended to the severall general Courts upon the considerations aforesaid to make a law.

That all such Quakers formerly convicted and punished as such (if they Returne againe) bee Imprisoned and forthwith banished or expelled out of the said Jurisdiction under paine of Death and if afterwards they presume to come again into that Jurisdiction then to bee put to death as presumtuously Incorragable unlesse they shall plainly and publickly Renounce their cursed opinions; and for such Quakers as shall come into any Jurisdiction from any forraigne partes of such as shall arise within the same after due. conviction, that either hee or shee is of that cursed sect of heritiques they bee banished under paine of severe Corporall punishment and if they Returne againe then to bee punished accordingly and banished under paine of death and if afterwards they shall

Undoubtedly he was correct in his ascertion.† At a session of the court held on the second day of March, 1657, the following action was taken:—

"Whereas this Court received a petition from sundry persons of the town of Scituate, both the millitary companie and others, therein expressing sundry grievances relating unto some late carriages of Capt. James Cudworth a comission officer of the milletary companie of Scituate, in reference to entertaining of such persons as are comonly called Quakers, by suffering them to meet in his house, and others with them, which said Quakers have rendered themselves in theire doctrines, speeches and carriages destructive of the peace of this jurisdiction, the Court having seriously weyed and considered the premises, together with other concurrent expressions which have come from him, the said Capt. Cudworth, which in their nature, as wee apprehend, tendeth to the desturbance of the peace of this present government, doe order as followeth, viz: that the said Captaine James Cudworth, by the Court is discharged of his place as Capt. of the milletary company of the towne of Scittuate; the said Capt. James Cudworth also desired the same."

---

yett presume to come againe then to bee putt to death as aforesaid except they doe then and theire plainly and publickly Renounce theire said cursed opinions and Devillish tenetts.

These foregoing Conclusions were agreed and subscribed by the Commissioners on the 23rd day of September.

	JOHN ENDICOTT, Presedent
	SIMON BRADSTREET,
FRANCIS NEWMAN	THOMAS PRENCE
WILLIAM LEETE	JOSIAAS WINSLOW
	JOHN WINTHROP, looking att the last as a query and not an Act,
	I subscribe JOHN TALCOTT

---

† Contained in a letter to Mr. John Browne who was then temporarily in England. "A seditious letter sent for England, the copy whereof has come over in print." Plymouth Colony Records Vol. III Page 188.

This order was thereupon issued to Lieut. Torrey and Ensign Williams.

"The Court, seeing cause to discharge Capt. James Cudworth of his place as captaine of the milletary companie of Scituate, do by these presents order and require you, Lieutenant James Torrey and Ensigne John Williams, to dissipline the said companie as occation shall require untill you shall have further order from the Court; and that you signify and declare in the head of youer company that they are to obey you, in all lawfull milletary comands as theire milletary comanders in cheife, and to carry peaceably and quietly respecting the premises."

Although the deposed officer was willing to be deprived of his command, not so the members of the company itself. Cudworth was popular with them; but for his cooler counsels they would have laid down their muskets, disbanded, and refused to further bear arms in defense of the colony. This action, had it been permitted by him, would have entailed serious consequences, for in 1657 military duty was compulsory upon every man both freeman and foreigner, between the ages of sixteen and sixty.

The loyalty to Cudworth of a large majority of his townsmen was shown at the next general election when he was returned as an Assistant to the Colony Court, and again in 1659 when he was chosen a Deputy. Under the law as it then existed, the Governor and Assistants might exercise the veto power upon the action of any town in choosing a given person as deputy. They might reject him. When Cudworth was so chosen, Governor Prence and Alden, Winslow, Bradford, Thomas Southworth of Plymouth and Thomas Hinckley of Barnstable together constituted the court, and he was not approved. At this same court, fifty-four of his neighbors presented a petition asking for the reinstatement of their captain to his military command.

The Court would not accede to their request and sent them this answer:—

"An Answare to a Petition prefered to the Court by
divers of the Towne of Scittuate

Youer petition presented to the Court they have seriously weighed, and being affectionately desirouse to gratify youer desires to youer full satisfaction soe farr as they may, yett considering the dissatisfaction of the countrey yett remaining concerning youer former Capt. as appears by their dismising of him from that place of trust to which hee was by youer town chosen, and in reason would bee ill resented by them, if att such a time as this wee should confeirme him in such a place of trust as you desire; and therefore hope you will not account it any disrespect unto youerselves that he is not confirmed in statu quo prius according to youer request.

  By order of the Court.
   per me   Nathaniel Morton, Clarke." †

Meantime the letter referred to above had reached Mr. Browne in London, been printed there, and copies of it sent to Plymouth. The last paragraph of it which held the Court and its members up to ridicule was especially displeasing. Cudworth wrote:—

"As to the state and condition of things amongst us, it is sad, and so like to continue. The antichristian, persecuting spirit is very active, and that in the powers of this world. He that will not lash, persecute and punish men that differ in matters of religion, must not sit on the bench, nor sustain any office in the Commonwealth. Last election Mr. Hatherly and myself were left off of the bench, and myself discharged of my Captainship, because I had entertained some of the Quakers at my house, thereby that I might be the better acquainted with their principles. I thought it better to do so, than with the blind world to censure, condemn, rail at, and revile them, when they neither saw their

---
† Plymouth Colony Records, Vol. III, Page 168.

persons nor knew any of their principles. But the Quakers and myself cannot close in diverse things, and so I signified to the Court; but told them withal, that as I was no Quaker, so I would be no persecutor.

This spirit did work those two years that I was of the Magistracy, during which time, I was, on sundry occasions, forced to declare my dissent in sundry actings of that nature; which altho' done with all moderation of expression, together with due respect unto the rest, yet it wrought great disaffection and prejudice in them against me; so that they themselves set others to frame a petition against me, so that they may have a seeming ground (though first moved by themselves) to lay me under reproach. The petition was with nineteen hands; it will be too long to make rehearsal. It wrought such a disturbance in our town, and in our military Company, that when the act of Court was read at the head of the Company, had I not been present and made a speech to them, I fear there would have been such actings as would have been of sad consequence. The Court was again followed with another petition (counter) of fifty-four hands; and the Court returned the petitioners an answer, with much plausibleness of speech, carrying with it great show of respect to them, readily acknowledging with the petitioners my parts and gifts, and how useful I had been in my place professing that they had nothing against me, only in that thing of my giving entertainment to the Quakers." (Here follow extracts of the laws against the Quakers, &c) "All these carnal and anti-christian ways, being not of God's appointment, effect nothing to the hindering of them in their course. It is only the word and the Spirit of the Lord that is able to convince gainsayers. They have many meetings and many adherents; almost the whole town of Sandwich. And give me leave to acquaint you a little with their sufferings, which is grievous, and saddens the hearts of most of the precious saints of God; it lies down and rises up with them, and they cannot put it out of their minds, when they see poor families deprived of their comforts and brought into penury and want. As for the means by which they are impoverished—they were in the first place, scrupulous of an oath; why then we must put in force an old law; they must all take the oath of fidelity—this being tendered they will not take it—then they must pay five pounds, or depart the Colony in such a time; when the time comes, the Marshall goes and fetcheth away their cows, and other cattle; another court comes, they are required again to take the oath—they cannot—then five pounds more. A poor weaver than had 7 or 8 small children, had but two cows, and both were taken from him. The Marshall asked him what he would do—and the man said, that "God who gave him them, he doubted not would still provide for him." The last Court of Assistants was pleased to determine fines on Sandwich men for meetings, one hundred and fifty pounds, whereof W. Newland is twenty-four pounds, for himself and wife, at ten shillings a meeting—W. Allen forty-six pounds—the poor weaver before spoken of twenty pounds. Brother Cook told me, one of the brethren of Barnstable was in the weaver's house, when cruel Barloe (Sandwich Marshall) came to demand the sum, and said he was fully informed of all the poor man had, and thought it not worth ten pounds. What will be the end of such courses and practises the Lord only knows. x x x x x x I am informed of three or four score, last Court presented, for not coming to publick meetings; and let me tell you how they brought this about. You may remember a law once made called Thomas Hinckley's law, 'that if any neglect the worship of God in the place where he lives, and set up a worship contrary to God, and the allowance of this Government, to the publick profanation of God's Holy Day, and ordinances, he shall pay 10 shillings.' This law would not reach what then was aimed at, because he must do all things therein express'd, or else break not the law. In March last a Court of Deputies was called and some acts touching Quakers were made, and then they contrived to make this law serviceable to them, by putting out the word (*and*) and putting in the word (*or*), which is a disjunctive, and makes every branch to become a law; yet they left it dated June 6, 1651; and so it stands as an act of the Gen. Court, they to be the authors of it seven years before it was in being; and so yourselves have a share in it, if the Record lie not.

"We are wrapped up in a labyrinth of confused laws, that the freeman's power is quite gone, and it was said last June Court by one that he knew nothing the freemen had there to do. Sandwich men may not go to the Bay lest they be taken up for Quakers—warrants lie in ambush, to apprehend and bring them before a Magistrate, to give an account of their business. Some of the Quakers in R. I. came to bring them goods, and that on far more reasonable terms than the professing and oppressing Merchants of the County—but that will not be suffered. And truly it moves bowels of compassion in all sorts, except those in place, who carry it with a high hand towards them. Through mercy, we have yet among us, the worthy Mr. Dunster, whom the Lord hath made boldly to bear testimony against the spirit of persecution.

"Our bench now is Thomas Prence, Gov., Mr. Collier, Capt. Willet, Capt. Winslow, Mr. Alden, Lieut. Southworth, W. Bradford, Thomas Hinckley. Mr. Collier, last June, would not sit on the bench if I sat there, and will not sit the next year, unless he may have thirty pounds to sit by him. † Our Court and Deputies last June, made Capt. Winslow, Major. Surely we are all mercenary soldiers, that must have a Major imposed upon us. Doubtless, the next Court, they may choose us a Governor, and Assistants also; a freeman shall need to do nothing but bear such burdens as are laid upon him. Mr. Alden hath deceived the expectations of many, and indeed lost the affections of such as I judge were his cordial Christian friends, who is very active in such ways as I pray God may not be charged upon him to be oppressions of a high nature."

What would naturally follow such an attack happened. On the seventh of March 1659, this order was entered:—

"Att the Generall Court held att Plymouth, the seaventh day of March, 1659.

Before Thomas Prence, Gov'r.   Josias Winslow
William Collyare   Thomas Southworth
John Alden   William Bradford &
Thomas Willett   Thomas Hinckley
            Assistants &c.

In reference to Capt. James Cudworth, the Court takeing notice of his great disaffection to this government and manifest abetting and incurragement of those called Quakers, expressed partly in a letter, owned by himselfe in the manor of sending it, and in many other carriages of his knowne to us, and alsoe in a letter strongly conjectured and suspected to bee by him sent unto England, the which himselfe hath not yett deneyed:—

The premises considered, the Court see cause to bind him over to make a further answare heerunto att the next General Court, to bee holden in June next; and doe therefore require that hee put in good security to

---

† Plymouth Colony Records Vol. III, Page 166.

the value of five hundred pounds, for the end above said." †

Although the pound sterling did not then represent the value which now attaches to it, the bail thus required was nevertheless oppressively large. The Bill of rights, as it had then been adopted, did not contain the provision of our present day Constitution, that excessive bail shall not be required.

The sum in which Cudworth was forced to recognize gives a very clear idea of the importance of this prosecution, to the entire colony. The names of his sureties do not appear. It may fairly be inferred however, that his friend Timothy Hatherly was one of them. When June arrived, the case was continued, probably because of the inability to obtain the presence of Mr. Browne to whom the letter had been written. The same bond was continued. This entry appears:—

"In reference unto a seditious letter sent for England a copy whereof is come over in print, Captaine Cudworth, being groundedly suspected to bee the author thereof, the Court have ordered that hee shall put in sufficient securitie, to the value of five hundred pounds for his appearance att the next October Court, and soe from one General Court unto another untill June next if the Court shall see reason; and the Court doe use their best endeavours forthwith to procure further testimony from Mr. Browne, or any other for the clearing of the case." ‡

But the indignant magistrates led by the vengeful Prence were not to be stayed from taking some action against their critic because of the absence of Mr. Brown. Another letter, which Cudworth had addressed to his enemy the Governor, was produced. It was not deemed wise to go to trial upon this communication alone and on the second day

---

† Plymouth Colony Records, Vol. III, Page 183.
‡ Plymouth Colony Records, Vol. III, Page 189.

of October the trial was again postponed to await the arrival of Mr. Brown to whom the most incriminating letter had been written from London. The case was of such consequence to the Court that Major Winslow and Thomas Southwort, both members of it, were "Appointed and deputed by the Court to implead the case, and it is left to their libertie to make choise of whome they please out of the deputies or freemen to be assistant to them therein." This appointment, seemingly unfair, loses somewhat its aspect of injustice, when it is remembered that in those days there was neither Attorney General nor Public Prosecutor, and the offence for which Cudworth was to be tried was against the court itself. Brown having finally returned and being present, was interrogated. The record † says:—

"Mr. Browne, being deposed, testifyed in Court having heard a printed letter read, that is supposed to bee sent from Capt. James Cudworth to himselfe; hee testifyed that hee did receive a letter subscribed James Cudworth, of Scituate, which was the substance of what hee had now heard, but to all particulars his memory would not reach; and further saith that when he received the said letter hee did not question but it was his hand.

The said Capt. Cudworth being required to answare whether it was pened by him or not, refused to answare directly, saying, if any thinge could be produced under his hand, hee would take to it, or to the like effect; on which the Court prepared for a further tryall of the case for the clearing of theire innossensy concerning the premises, according to the manor before expressed, and the said Capt. Cudworth was for the present released." ‡

---

† Plymouth Colony Records Vol. III, Page 199.
‡ A note on the margin of the record in the handwriting of Nathaniel Morton the "clarke" says, "Att this Court Capt. Cudworth appeared, being bound, and others with him, in the sume of five hundred pounds, and the bonds were cancelled and the said Capt. Cudworth for the present released."

This ended the abortive attempt of the magistrates to punish Cudworth for the criticism of them and their methods. The records of the Court to which the case was adjourned contain no reference to it. Whether the matter was dropped because of the failure of Browne to produce the original letter or whether the proclamation of Charles II, who had just been restored to the throne of England, was the controlling cause, the trial never proceeded further. Prence's persecution however did not cease. On June 6, 1660 Cudworth was disfranchised by the following order:

"Captaine Cudworth being found a manifest opposer of the lawes of the government in a letter directed by him to the Governor and otherwise, is sentenced, according to the law to bee disfranchised of his freedome of this corporation."

For twelve years thereafter Cudworth lived on his Mann Hill farm with no public duties to harrass him. He was still busied as arbitrator or umpire in the land disputes of his neighbors and indeed, was appointed by the Magistrates themselves, to settle some of the quarrels which arose. He laid out William Randall's land at the North River, acted with Joseph Tilden, Lieut. Torrey and Cornet Stetson in making division of the undivided lands between John Williams, father and his son, and appraised the property of the latter in his alimony difficulty with his wife Elizabeth. He also found time to settle his own bounds with that litigious individual. He served on committees to settle the division of the Scituate common land; to lay out lands to "the old or first comers" and was requested by the Bench to act as its immediate and personal representative in rebuking his neighbor Richard Man for this freeman's breach of the Sabbath. During all this time he bore himself quietly, modestly and with a dignity out of which he never could be surprised or cajoled into complaining. The day came when he was to be publicly restored to his right and station.

Prence having been succeeded by Governor Josiah Winslow, on July fourth 1673 the Magistrates :—

"Voted Captaine James Cudworth, upon his owne desire and the request of sundry others in his behalfe, to be reestablished into the right and priviledge of a freeman of this jurisdiction; and hee did openly declare before the Court that he is and remaines bound by the oath of a freeman, which hee formerly tooke, unto all fealty and duty therein required unto his Majestie, &c and unto this government. †.

In the following year another expedition,—one of those sporadic uprisings of sentiment against the Dutch at New York—was in contemplation and Governor Winslow offered to Major Cudworth the position of General and Commander-in-Chief of all the Plymouth forces. This he declined, urging his own "unsufficiency" and the age and illness of his wife. His magnanimity of spirit is shown in a paragraph of his letter ‡ to the Governor in which he refers to his persecution under Prence. He says:—

"Sir, I can truly say that I do not in the least waive the business out of any discontent in my spirit arising from any former difference; for the thought of all which, is and shall be forever buried, so as not to come in remembrance."

It was with different feelings however that he accepted the same position tendered him at the opening of Phillip's War. He now justified his expression on the above letter wherein he said "It" (the declination) is "neither out of any effeminate or dastardly spirit; but I am as freely willing to serve my King and Country as any man, in what I am capable and fitted for." He was disinclined to lead his troops against the neighboring colonists of New York in warfare for the conquest of additional territory; but when called upon to engage in conflict with the treacherous enemy at home, it was without hesitation that he sought the thick

---

† Plymouth Colony Records.
‡ Mass. Hist. Soc. Coll. Vol VI Page 81.

of the trouble in the Narragansett country. † Here he remained until peace was secured, only now and then visiting home to encourage new enlistments by his own example, voice and presence. After the close of hostilities he was appointed to distribute Ireland's bounty to the sufferers in that war, and was one of a committee to make sale of the Indian conquest lands, and the division of those at Showamett, Assonet, Agawam, and Sippecan, which were awarded to the individual soldiers for their services. He was again made an Assistant, serving from 1674 to 1680, and was a Commissioner of the United Colonies in 1678 and 1681.

In 1680 he was appointed with Governor Winslow and Thomas Hinckley, then Deputy-Governor, to prepare an address to Charles II in regard to the enlargement of the civil and religious liberties of the Colonists. On September twenty-eighth of that year; the draft of this committee was adopted and this vote passed:—

"The Generall Court, taking into their consideration, the many favors wee have received from the Lord the year past, in the continuance of our peace, a considerable measure of health in our tabernacles, and the great blessing we have had upon the labours of our hands and the fruits of the earth, with the injoyment of our liberties both sacred and civil, through the mercy of our God and the favor of our prince, do propound the twentieth day of October next ensuing to be cellibrated as a sollemne day of thanksgiving, by all the congregations in this collonie, wherein we may present our joynt praises to our good God for these and whatever other mercyes wee doe injoy, requesting grace at his hands to walke in a holy improvement of them, to his glory and our eternall good.

Thought meet to allow unto our honored Governor and Deputy Governor, to each of them the sume of six

---

† Hutchinson's History of Massachusetts. (London Ed. 1768) Vol. I, Page 287.

pounds, in compensation of their charges expended, and care and paines taken, in the collonies behalfe, in and about the late addresse of our collonie to his majestie, our dread sov'n. &c.

And unto the honored Major Cudworth the sume of three pounds, in such like respects." †

On June 7, 1681 Cudworth was chosen Deputy Governor. Yet a still greater honor was in store for him. In September of that year, while holding this office, he was made agent of the colony and dispatched to London to cooperate with William Blathwayt in obtaining from the Crown a new charter patterned after that of Connecticut. In this Charles had repeatedly encouraged them. Its accomplishment was very near to their hearts. Only a man in whose diplomatic ability and honesty they had the utmost confidence would be chosen for such a mission. Cudworth was selected not alone because he possessed these qualities, nor because the Court sought still further to make amends, but because the embassy required a man who was at the same time patiently persistent and untiring. On September 15, 1681, before he sailed, he made his will ‡ which was proved and allowed July 7, 1682, as follows:—

"In the name of God, Amen.

The 15th day of September 1681, I, James Cudworth of Scituate in the Jurisdiction of New Plymouth in New England, being of sound and perfect memory, praise be Given to God for the same, and Knowing the uncertainty of this Life here on earth, and being Desirous to settle things in order, Doe make this my Last Will and Testament in Maner and form following: That is to say, first and principally I commend my soul unto Almighty God my Creator and my body to the earth from whence it was taken; To be buried in such Decent manner as to my executors hereafter

---

† Plymouth Colony Records Vol. VI, Page 52.
‡ Plymouth Colony Records (Wills) Vol. IV Part 2, Page 8.

named shall be thought meet & convenient; and as touching my worldly estate as the Lord in Mercye hath put me; my will and meaning is, the same shalbe employed and bestowed as hereafter by this my will is expressed. And first I doe Revoak, Denounce, Disclaim and make void all wills and testaments by me formerly made; and declare and appoint this My Last will and Testament and Noe other. First of all I will that all those Debts and Dutyes as I owe in Right and Conscience to any maner of person or persons whatsoever, shalbe well and duly contented and payed or ordained to be payed within Convenient time after my decease by my Executors hereafter Named; my mind and will is that after severall expenses and debts being payed I give and bequeath all the rest of my estate reall and personall to be equally divided amongst my children into six parts or shares; my oldest son James Cudworth he to have a double share with what he hath already received; my son Israell to have one-sixth part with what he hath already Received; my son Jonathan he is to have one-sixth part or share. My daughter Maryes four children Israell Whitcomb, Robert, James and Mary I give to them one sixth part or share of my estate to be equally divided betwixt them; I give to my daughter Hannah Jones one-sixth of my estate and my mind and will is that Israel Whitcomb and Robert Whitcomb and James have their portions payd them in Current Country pay when each of them shall attaine the full age of twenty-one years and Mary Whitcomb at the age aforesaid or day of marriage. And my mind and will is that my sonnes enjoy and possess all my lands; my eldest son James two thirds; Israel and Jonathan both of then one third; and my mind and will is that what the Moveables fall short of making good, Joannah's portion and the four grandchildren's portions, then that my sonnes Make it Good out of their estate, and I do ordaine and appoint my three sonnes James, Israel and Jonathan the joynt executors of this my last will and testament."

In presence of

JAMES CUDWORTH

Thomas Hiland
Richard Curtis

Arriving in London, he sought out the colony's friend and agent at Court, William Blathwayt, and delivered a letter from Governor Hinckley. It is probable that Cudworth himself did not appear at Court. He had time only to pen a letter to Governor Hinckley at Barnstable when he was stricken with the small pox and died. †

---

† Deane says: page 250. "It appears that General Cudworth did not proceed to England on his mission until the summer of 1682." This error is refuted by a number of well authenticated facts. Governor Hinckley writing to Blathwayt May 26, 1682, refers to a letter sent the latter "per hand of Major James Cudworth" (Mass. Hist. Coll. Hinckley Papers)—Fourth Series, Vol. V. page 65; and in another dated November 18, of the same year he writes:—"Since mine of the 26th of May last unto you per Mr. Dudley, I received a letter by way of Barbadoes, from Major James Cudworth, our then Deputy-Governor, (of which I had only then heard, as I then signified to you) wherein he acquainted me of his safe arrival, in London; and being writ immediately on his arrival, had not then opportunity to inform me what progress was made in the business of our patent committed to your trust, hoping that per first ship hither bound, he should be enabled to give us some good account thereof; But, so it pleased God, that (to our grief) the next news we heard was of his death; which, being so sudden, we doubt he had not fit opportunity to present himself before the King and Council in our behalf, by your help and advice nor to render to yourself some small testimony of our grateful respects for your trouble, and pains about our concern."

(Ibidem page 74.)

Again, the records of the General Court fail to disclose the attendance of Deputy-Governor Cudworth at any meeting of that body save one, the first.

Finally, the will itself is conclusive. At the time when Deane states that he was on his way to England in the summer of 1682, his children were dividing his estate among themselves as he himself had directed in that instrument.

JOHN SAFFIN

John Saffin was born † at Woolverston in the County of Somerset, England. The exact date is uncertain nor is that of his coming to Scituate known. Deane, (page 335) says that he was a Selectman here in 1653. This office, however, was not created until 1666 and Saffin at no time held it in Scituate. Abner C. Goodell, Esq., in an article read at a meeting of the Colonial Society of Massachusetts held in March 1893 places him here 1645-7, which is probably correct. His farm adjoined that of John Hoar near Little Musquashcut ‡ Pond. He was a remarkable man in many ways. Although most of his acts which obtained notoriety and his service in public office were after he had left Scituate, no history of the town during the colonial and provincial periods is complete without an extended notice of him. He always owned land here, was a Conihasset partner in 1673 and even after his removal from Scituate to Boston, the General Court of Plymouth granted that he and his partner Mr. Richard Wharton, should "have a peculiar libertie to themselves and other ptenors to improve such pyne, spruce, and cedar timber as groweth on our country commons, for the producing of rosen, turpentine and mastick x x x for the tearme of ten years from June 15, 1671."

His first marriage was to Martha, the daughter of Capt. Willett of Plymouth. It was solemnized at Plymouth, December 2, 1658 and Saffin brought his bride to the farm near Mann Hill, just after the ceremony. Here five of his eight sons were born. Thomas, the second son, born in 1664, was sent as a youth to England, presumably for an

---

† A deposition recorded in Suffolk Probate Records Vol VI Page 356, taken in an action to which Saffin was a party states that he was born in 1634. This is manifestly an error. In 1646 he was one of the witnesses to the deed from Timothy Hatherly to Rev. Charles Chauncey and the Conihasset partners, a service which a boy of twelve would not have been called upon to perform.

‡ Written also Musquashteck, meaning in the Indian tongue, "the place of red wood."

education. He was stricken with small pox while living in London in 1687, and died. The epitaph † carved upon his head-stone in the churchyard of Saint Stepney, has attracted much attention in later years;

> "Here Thomas Saffin lies interred: Why?
> Born in New England, did in London die;
> Was the third ‡ son of eight, begat upon
> His mother Martha by his father John:
> Much favor'd by his Prince, he 'gan to be
> But nipt by death at the age of twenty-three;
> Fatal to him was that we small-pox name;
> By which his mother and two brethren came
> Also to breath their last, nine years before,
> And now have left their father to deplore
> The loss of all his children with his wife
> Who was the joy and comfort of his life.
> Deceased June 18, 1687."

Saffin was not much in the public eye during his residence in Scituate. He was evidently intent upon clearing his farm (he bought that of his neighbor, John Hoar, in 1660), and rearing his sturdy sons. His knowledge of the law § was infrequently called into use by his neighbors and there are to be found but three instruments, evidences of transactions in Scituate, which he probably drew ¶. To a limited extent also, he litigated on his own account. One John Lewis, a servant of Mr. William Vassall, became indebted to him. When he sought to collect, the servant had departed. As on such occasions, Saffin had "recourse to Plymouth." He brought his cause of action to the attention of the General Court at Plymouth and on the sixth day of March 1654 it was ordered that "Whereas John Lewis,

---
† See the "Spectator" for October 24, 1712.
‡ Second.
§ It has been said that he had been educated for the bar.
¶ Hatherly to Chauncey et als. Plymouth Colony Records, Vol. XII Page 158. John Hanmore to Joseph Tilden Ib. Page 168. John Williams to Humphrey Johnson Ib. Page 202.

sometimes servant to Mr. William Vassall of Scituate, is departed the government indebted to John Saffin and others, and hath left some goods in the hand of William Parker of Taunton, the Court doth order, that the said goods shalbee for the satisfying the debts he owed to the said John Saffin att his departure." In 1653 he was a defendant with Rev. Charles Chauncey, Anthony Eames of Marshfield and Samuel Jackson of Scituate in a suit brought by Thomas Hyland and his son against all of the above-named. Jackson and Hyland had entered into a written agreement, probably drawn by Saffin, the nature of which does not appear, and Rev. Mr. Chauncey, Anthony Eames and Saffin had subscribed to it as witnesses. Viewed from the standpoint of the plaintiffs it must have been an important agreement and its breach fraught with most dire consequences, for they say in their complaint to the Court: "By subscribing to and publishing the same. x x x x the said Hielands are both damnified and the said Thomas Hieland Junier, his life is endangered." The damage was set at two hundred pounds and a trial was had before a jury composed of the Elder and younger Winslow, Philip Delano and George Partridge of Duxbury, Ephraim Morton and James Browne of Plymouth and other men of consequence and prominence in the Colony. The jury found for the defendants. It is not however, to be learned that because thereof, the life of son Hyland was thereafter jeopardized. He and his father were mulcted in costs "which came to 14s, the clarkes, marshalls, and juries encluded." At the same sitting Jackson brought his action against the Elder Hyland alleging his damage to be five pounds for the refusal to perform the same agreement. The same jury tried this case and also found for the defendant— the plaintiff in the former case. Thus were the defendants in each action cleared and justice satisfied; but the end was not yet. It remained for the "charges" to be determined and the costs taxes. Here is the way in which the damnified Hyland bettered his adversary.

"the charges came to,	s d
Item, to the jurye	06:06
Item, the clarke	02:00
Item, to the marshall	00:06
Item, 3 witnesses, 4 daies a piece	18:00
	27:00

In 1660 Saffin went to Virginia and for a short time engaged in trade there. This is shown by:—"A writing of protestation appointed to bee recorded as followeth:—" †

"The occation of our coming into this harbour of Plymouth is this: that by crosnes of wind and weather, we haveing beat so long to gett into Verginnia, till all our victualls were soe neare spent that we had not bin able to subsist, had not wee mett with a shipp which spared us a little victualls; soe after that wee beat so longe till that victualls and our water was very near spent and still the winds kept contrary; and finding ourselves soe fare to the eastward, and no hope of giting into Verginnia, were in hope to get to Monhatoes, but could not and soe were forced to come to this place to recruite, the wind still hanging westerly; and soe doe intend, after wee have taken in such necessaries as wee want, to sett sayle, God willing, the first opportunite of wind and weather, for our intended port in Verginnia, according to the orders of Mr. John Saffin."

His sojourn in Virginia may have been for the purpose of engaging in the tar and resin trade which he afterward conducted in Boston. He removed from Scituate to the latter town in 1670-71 and it is said, while successfully conducting a respectable mercantile business, he engaged

---

† Plymouth Colony Records Vol III Page 212.

with other Boston merchants in importing negroes from Guinea. † ‡

---

† New England Hist. and Gen. Reg. (1877) Vol. XXXI. Pages 75 and 76.

‡ He was not opposed to slavery. When, upon the death of his father-in-law Capt. Willett, he became his administrator, there came into his possession a negro slave named Jethro, who was captured by the Narragansetts during Phillip's War. The Indians were planning an attack upon Taunton on July 11, 1676, when Jethro understanding the Indian tongue and discovering their purpose, escaped to give such timely warning of the plot, that the enemy was driven off and the town saved.

Hubbard's Indian Wars, Vol. 1, page 256 note.

Judge Sewall gives a different account of the happening.. Writing in his diary under date of July 1, 1676, he says "Mr. Hezekiah Willet slain by Narragansets, a little more *than* Gunshot off from his house, his head taken off, body stript, Jethro, his niger, was then taken; retaken by Capt. Bradford, the Thursday following. He saw the English and ran to them. He related Phillip to be sound and well, about a 1000 Indians (all sorts) with him, but sickly; three died while he was there. Related That the Mount Hope Indians that knew Mr. Willet, were sorry for his death, mourned, kombed his head, and hung peag in his hair.

Mass. Hist. Soc. Coll. (Fifth Series) Vol. V Page 14.

It is probable that Hubbard's version is the correct one, inasmuch as Judge Sewall was entering in his Journal only the reports and rumors which reached Boston, (Ibidem, note page 15.) and in view of what followed at the Plymouth Colony Court in November following, when Jethro's ultimate freedom was provided for:—

At a General Court held before Governor Josiah Winslow, John Alden, Thomas Hinckley, William Bradford, Constant Southworth, James Browne and James Cudworth on Nov. 1, 1676.

"In reference unto a negro named Jethro, taken a prisoner by the Indians and retaken againe by our army, which said negro appertained to the estate of the successor of Capt. Willet, deceased, our General Court have agreed with Mr. John Saffin, administrator of the said estate, mutually, that the said negro doe forthwith betake himself to his former service, and to remain a servant unto the successors of the said Captain Willett, untill two years be expired from the date hereof, and then to be freed from and sett at libertie from his said service, provided also, that during the said terme of two years, they doe find him meat, drink and apparell fitting for one in his degree and calling, and at the end of his said service, that he goe forth competently provided for in reference to apparell." Plymouth Colony Records Vol. V Page 216.

This agreement between the Court and Saffin concerning the

It was some years after taking up his domicile in Boston that Saffin's § abilities began to be publicly noticed. On March 13, 1682 he was appointed with the Selectmen of the town, Anthony Chackley and Samuel Sewall, a committee to draw up instructions for the deputies of the town to the General Court. This was an important trust. It was a practise that had been originally adopted in the Massachusetts Bay Colony and was followed in Plymouth for a century. To this duty the best men of the locality were always called. Judge Cushing, Ephraim Otis, Deacon William Turner, Nathaniel Clap, Israel Vinal, Jr., and Anthony Waterman frequently performed a like service in Scituate during the trying years from 1770 to 1776.

In 1684-5 Saffin was made a deputy to the General Court from Boston, second in choice to Isaac Addington who afterward sat with him as Chief Justice in the Superior Court of Judicature. In 1686 he failed of the nomination, but was successful at the polls and elected speaker, the last person to hold that office in the Colonial House of Representatives. There is no better evidence of the esteem in which he was held and the implicit confidence that was placed in his honesty and courage, than the action which was taken by the General Court upon the arrival of Sir Edmund Andros in that year. The coming of this royal Governor was attended with deep apprehension and dread upon the part of the people of the Bay Colony in particular. They feared for their land titles, their liberties and their cherished institutions. Just before the House was proroqued that they might save such vestige of their rights as would possibly be serviceable after the charter of the colony had been vacated through the agency of Andros, this order was passed:—

---

freedom of Jethro can mean nothing else than that it was given as a reward for the service in warning the inhabitants of Taunton, which Hubbard says Jethro performed.

§ Records of the General Court of the Colony of Mass. Bay (1854) Vol V Page 516.

"May 20, 1686. Ordered by this Court, that Samuel Nowell, Esq., Mr. John Saffin, and Capt. Timothy Prout be a comitee for a repository of such papers on file with the Secretary, as referr to our Charter and negotiations from time to time, for the security thereof. with such as referr to our title of our land, by purchase of Indians or otherwise; and the Secretary is ordered accordingly to deliver the same to them." †

While he was living in Boston Saffin was buying lands in the vicinity of Swansea being one of the purchasers of Mount Hope (Bristol). While attending to his business there he was arrested by Increase Robinson a constable upon a warrant dated August 19, 1682, which ordered the constable to collect a rate of ten pounds alleged to be due from Saffin to the Colony, but said by him to be excessive. The latter refused to pay, and the constable imprisoned him. Saffin brought his complaint to Governor Hinckley and the Assistants the next year. Upon the jury sat his old Scituate neighbors Nathaniel Turner and John Barker; but both Court and jury were against him. The verdict was for the constable with the costs of suit. ‡ This action of the Colony Court in justifying and upholding this imprisonment of a man of Saffin's standing for the nonpayment of a tax aroused the people of both colonies. Edward Randolph, who was about to visit England, was so disturbed lest knowledge of this action, coming to the attention of the King and Parliament, should serve to further the purpose of the Crown to curb the Colonies, (which crystallized three years later in the appointment of Andros as Royal Governor), addressed Governor Hinckley most seriously in the letter which follows:

"Nober. 24th, 1683

Sir,—I am not a little concerned to find that not only the complaint that the Quakers in your Colony are whipped and fined for not marrying according to your

---

† Records of the General Court of the Colony of Mass. Bay (1854) Vol V Page 516.
‡ Plymouth Colony Records Vol VII Pages 263 and 264.

law, but that you have countenanced the late arbitrary, and till now unheard-of, proceedings against Mr. Saffin, by imprisoning him, with other illegal practices; all which will fall very heavy upon you particularly; for unless you had assented, no man durst venture upon such methods; and assure you nothing could so much impede the getting-out of your patent as this. For thus will the Lords of his Majesty's Council argue, that if you have no grant or power to govern (for all you can pretend to by your grant from the Earl of Warwick, is only the soil in your Colony, and no color for government) : so that you have very much exposed yourself. I am now going for England; and would be very glad to be instructed what answer to make when these matters are laid before the lords, and backed with undeniable proofs which will be here made and taken.

Sir, I write not this out of friendship to Mr. Saffin, —I am sorry that you have given him such advantage against you,—but to assure you that I cannot omit to show my respect to that Colony whereof I am a member; and therefore, in great friendship, advise that you send me down your narrative of the matter, and also empower me, by the seal of the Colony, to appear on your behalf. I would gladly have this matter accommodated; and, for the future, let me entreat you not to appear to gratify one party to wrong your own judgment, and to give occasion of such reflections as must be made by all impartial men upon your government. You may send your papers to Mr. Shrimpton, who will take care to convey them to me, if gone for England; but, if you had rather engaged Mr. Jesson, you have your liberty.

I am, sir, your assured loving friend and countryman,

ED. RANDOLPH

Saffin himself did not take his arrest as seriously as Randolph and some of the others. He continued to quarrel with the raters over the large valuations which they put upon his property at New Bristol and Swansey, though he was much interested in both those municipalities. He was apparently friendly with Governor Hinckley, who sat in judgment upon him when suits over the collection of these assessments were brought before the Court. The following letter shows both this friendliness toward and respect for the Governor, as well as his interest in Swansey.

"Boston, 29th, May, 1685

Sir:—

I was in some hope to have seen your honor at our election at Boston; but Providence having ordered otherwise, I presume upon your favor, by these, to certify your honor, that matters at Swansey, relating to the settlement of the Rev. Mr. Tho. Barnett, are in sore travail (and though nigh unto the birth); yet, if not furthered by the inhabitants (called the Town) are in great conflict with those called the Church, who by their restless and indefatigable industry increase their party, and, notwithstanding their specious pretensions of respect to Mr. Barnett, do all that possible they can to oppose the town in their proceedings towards his settlement; so that, by the strenuous endeavors of the one party, and the supineness and indefference of some of the other, Mr. Barnett is discouraged, and the Anabaptists get ahead; being confident (and that not without ground), that, if they can now put by Mr. Barnett, they shall never be troubled with any such encounter again, but go on in their heady high-mindedness without control.

The sum is this, sir; The town are just now about weathering the point; and, if a fresh gale of the favor and justice of the court do but fill their sails, they will soon bear away large; otherwise they will run to leeward, and be exposed to unavoidable shipwreck.

I understand the town are making their address to the Honored Court, by which your Honor will understand the matter more particularly; and your wisdom will be sufficient to direct as the matter doth require, which is humbly implored by—

Your honor's most humble servant, and a well-wisher to the interest of Christ, as in all places, so now more especially in the town of Swansey.

JOHN SAFFIN

Soon after the death of his second wife in 1687 he married Rebecca, the daughter of Rev. Samuel Lee, who had come to Boston with Andros, and thereupon he moved to Bristol. Here he was once again in the Old Colony and became immediately identified with its progress. He was chosen a deputy to the General Court in 1689 and 1691. At the sitting of that body in the former year he, with nine others, was fined twenty shillings apiece for not appearing thereat or disorderly departing therefrom. At a later day the fines were remitted, "it being the first offence in that kind."

When in 1685, the Plymouth Colony was divided into counties, Bristol was made the shire town of the county bearing that name. The county officers were appointed under the charter of William and Mary and Saffin was made the first Judge of Probate. † He served in this office until his appointment as a judge of the Superior Court in 1701. After the amalgamation of the two colonies, he was chosen a member of the Council, and held both offices, until he was negatived by Governor Dudley to the latter, in 1703. He held his position upon the Superior Bench but for a short time. Governor Washburn ‡ says of him:

"From some memoranda left by Judge Sewall, Mr. Saffin's qualifications were not the best suited to the place which he was called to fill, and intimations

---

†. Washburn, Judicial History of Mass. page 269.
‡ Ibidem.

are pretty distinctly given that he was guilty of tampering with Jurors, using influence to obtain improper testimony upon the trial of causes, and equivocating, when charged with dishonorable conduct in which he had been detected. How much of this was true need not now be determined."

It is hardly fair to Judge Saffin to condemn him thus harshly upon loose memoranda left by Judge Sewall. † That diarrhoetic diarist was wont to record in his journal, not only the gossip, rumors and happenings of the time but his own petty and daily annoyances and troubles as well. His relations with Saffin had always been amicable up to the time when he attacked the latter for his pro-slavery beliefs and practices, in the pamphlet entitled "The Selling of Joseph." Saffin's spirited reply may have had something to do with the animadversions of which Governor Washburn speaks. It is well known that Sewall did not hesitate to speak harshly of those who thwarted his desires, aspirations or purposes. That Saffin was determined, disputatious and in the declining years of his life, sometimes fierce and violent, is true. He quarrelled with the amiable lady who was his third wife and refused to live with her. This brought down upon his head a scathing letter from his brother-in-law Cotton Mather; but in all the reproachful sentences of that communication no charge is made that he was dishonest. It is not readily to be believed

---

† Sewall had always heretofore been friendly with Saffin and when at Bristol was his guest. On September 12, 1698, he enters in his diary "In a case of Saffin vers. Curtis, which Capt. Byfield was concerned for Curtis, Jury brought in for Curtis—Capt. Byfield with a remarkable Air, thank'd the Jury for their Justice and sentence. For their Justice, and with a voice a little lower said, He had none before. I told him he deserved to be sent to prison. He disown'd the words, and alleged; He said he had none to thank anybody for. Mr. Cook seconded me. Mr. Danforth heard not. Capt. Byefield declin'd. Rain hindr'd our sitting out that day. So after dinner at Mr. Saffin's, not knowing better how to bestow my time. Look'd on Mr. Saffin's Books &c" and "Sept. 21, 1699, Governor invites me to dine with him at Mr. Clark's. Mr. Saffin lodges with me."

that the man who had been chosen in time of stress as the keeper of the most cherished possessions of the Colony, became at a later period a pettifogger and jury fixer.

Among the men of consequence at Bristol when Saffin moved to that part of the Plymouth Colony, were Capt. John Walley and Nathaniel Byfield. They were large land owners there; each had been a deputy to the General Court and prominent in the public service. Together they sought to sell lands to prospective settlers to create a "town of trade" at Bristol; and had made many promises of public improvements. Saffin was equally well known and prominent when he took up his abode there. It was not long before these men clashed. Some of the land owned by Walley and Byfield had been purchased by Saffin. In 1683 he erected a fence along the west side of Mount Hope Neck and Swansey River. Walley and Byfield requested its removal, which was denied. They thereupon, with Steven Burton and Nathaniel Oliver, sued Saffin

> "for his setting up, or causing to be sett up, or refusing to remove or take away, a certain fence, or soe much thereoff as stands upon land of the said Walley, Byfield, Burton and Oliver which fence is between the gate that is towards the west side of the necke and Swansey River, and takes in the bounds sett between the land of Mount Hope and the town of Swansey by a committee formerly appointed for that end; notwithstanding wee in our sales to said Saffin, reserved two rod in width, having reserved the like bredth acrose the necke, to be improved for an hieway, if wee see need thereof, which fence goes crose the said two rodd and takes in severall rodds in length, preventing us for laying out a way towards the river and taking in the said fence the bounds sett between Swansey and us, which is a defamation to our title to said land &c &c.†"

The plaintiffs prevailed and thus began a feud which

---

† Plymouth Colony Records Vol VII Page 270.

lasted for seventeen years. Other suits were brought and other acts done by Walley and his associates which not only angered Saffin personally but prompted him to take up the cause of the townspeople of Bristol whose interests were likewise jeopardized by the sharp practices of these land owners. Saffin inveighed vigorously against the proprietors. Finally he published a manuscript monograph entitled, "The Original of the Town of Bristol or a True Narrative of the First Settlement of Mount Hope Neck." In it he told many truths. It was perhaps more the manner of the telling than the truth itself, which so angered Walley and Byfield that they went to the Courts with it. The matter was heard by William Stoughton, Lieut. Governor Isaac Addington afterward judge, and John Leverett, son of the Governor of that name, as arbitrators. The award was against Saffin †. By it he was required to sign and publish a retraction. This recantation is worthy of a place in any chronicles of the time, as showing not only the author's pertinacity, but the boldness with which he still flouted his accusations against the objects of his first attack:—

"Whereas I, who have heretofore subscribed, am enjoyned by an award of arbitration dated 7th of July, 1696, given under the hands and seals of the Hon. William Stoughton, lieutenant governor, Isaac Addington, Esq., and John Leverett, M. A. Fellow of Harvard College, to make a retraction and acknowledgement in writing under my hand of supposed ill treatment wrong and injury offered to Major John Walley and Captain Nathaniel Byfield, two of the first purchasers of Mount Hope Neck, by sundry reflections in a manuscript entitled "the Original of the Town of Bristol, or a true narrative of the first settlement of

---

† Bailey, in his Memoir of Plymouth Colony says that the allegations in Saffin's pamphlet "probably had some foundation in fact: but were much exaggerated through the spleen of the accuser." Vol II Page 62.

Mount Hope Neck &c.", which was made in behalf of the inhabitants of said town, who for divers years have complained and groaned under the grievances therein mentioned.

Now in order thereunto, I do hereby own and declare unto all mankind, that if breach of promise to a person or people, in a matter of great concernment, be no evil; if the chopping and changing of the town commons to the great prejudice of the town; obstructing and stopping up several ways leading to men's lands (some of them that have been enjoyed above thirty years without molestation or disturbance) to be tolerable, and not a nuisance strictly prohibited by the laws of our nation, then I am exceedingly to blame in charging with evil so doing. If the granting of land upon good consideration, and upon the same, promising to give a deed for the confirmation thereof, but delaying it, and after eight or nine years quiet possession by the grantee, these grantors give a deed of the sale of the same lands unto others; if this, I say, be just and righteous dealing, then &c; if the taking up and dividing amongst themselves, and converting to their own private use in farms and great pastures, the most of a considerable number of one hundred and twenty-eight house lots and ten acre lots, which were by the four first purchasers † in their grand articles under their hands and seals proposed, designed and accordingly laid out, and declared to be for the encouragement, use, benefit, and accommodation, of so many families to build upon and settle on Mount Hope Neck, (besides farms and bigger parcels of land) to make a town of trade as they were enjoyned by the Court at Plymouth; I say if these actions of theirs be not prejudicial and injurious to the inhabitants of the town of Bristol, then I have done them wrong in saying or writing so.

† Walley, Byefield, Burton and Oliver.

If the wilful suffering a certain water mill, (built for the town's use) to fall and go to decay and utter ruin for by ends and sinister respects, not repairing it themselves nor suffering others to do it, who have also some rights in it, be not a wrong and abuse to the town, said purchasers making it first a great argument of encouragement for our men to come and buy land of them to settle, in order to a town of trade as aforesaid, which is at large set forth in their said articles, and backed with many specious pretences and verbal promises never fulfilled; now if these things are right and just, then &c.

Again, if it be not an unrighteous thing in Major Walley, to take and receive £10 of the town of Bristol, and also many days work of them, promising and engaging himself for the same, to make a bridge over a certain creek in a way that should lead to said mill, but never performed it, nor returned the money again, but instead thereof hath stopped the way as aforesaid; I say if such doing and actions be just and right, then I have done them wrong in saying or writing to the contrary.

And further, if the making a deed by three of the first purchasers for the dividing of sixteen of the remainder of the one hundred and twenty-eight house-lots amongst four of them pretending that Captain Nathan Hayman was then and there acting with them, as if he were alive, and did act and do as they did in all respects, (excepting subscribing his name) for which he left blank or space giving under their hands and seals that on the twenty-seventh day of June, 1690, if the said Nathan Hayman did with them personally oblige himself, his heirs &c., in the same manner as they did, three or four times mentioned in the said deed, whereas the man was dead and in his grave eleven months before, I say if these and such like, strange actions and doings before mentioned, (all which they have either owned, or have proven to be done by them,) be warrantable legal, just and right in the sight of God, or according to the laws of the nation, then do I hereby own and humbly acknowledge that I have done the said Major John Walley and Captain Nathaniel Byefield much wrong and injury in rendering their said actions in my said narrative to be illegal, unjust, and injurious to the town of Bristol in general, and to myself in particular, for which I am sorry.

I confess, I might have spared some poetical notions and satyrical expressions which I have used by way of argument, inference or comparison, yet the sharpest of them are abundantly short of those villifying terms and scurrilous language which they themselves have frequently given each other, both in publique and private, generally known in Bristol.

But above all I am heartily sorry that it is my unhappiness to differ so much in my apprehensions from the honorable gentlemen, the arbitrators, for whom I have always conceived and retained an honorable esteem and veneration, that I would even put my life into their hands; the truth whereof may appear by this late submission of mine, otherwise I should not have exposed myself as I have done.

JOHN SAFFIN"

During the time the hearings were being had before the arbitrators Saffin was sitting in the General Court at Plymouth with Byefield himself also a co-deputy from Bristol. From 1693 to 1699 he also sat in the Council. He was again elected to that body in 1703, but the Governor having the veto power over the choice of the electorate, and Dudley,† the Chief Executive at the time being an ardent opponent of Saffin, he was negatived. The controversy which gave Saffin his greatest prominence was that of Rex. v Adam mentioned in the note. It was the occasion of the publication by Judge Sewall of a memorial entitled "The Selling of Joseph." Sewall says of the feelings which prompted its publication:—

"Having been long and much dissatisfied with the Trade of Fetching Negroes from Guinez; at least I had a strong inclination to write something about it; but it wore off. At last, reading Bayne, Ephes. (Paul Baynes "Commentary on the First Chapter of the Ephesians") about servants, who mentiones Blackamoors; I began to be uneasy that I had so long neglected doing anything. When I was thus thinking, in came Bro'r Belknap to show me a petition he intended to present to the General Court for the freeing a Negro and his wife, who were unjustly held in Bondage. And there is a Motion by a Boston Committee to get a Law that all Importers of Negros shall pay 40s pr head, to discourage bringing of them. And Mr. C. Mather resolves to publish a sheet to exhort Masters to labour their Conversion. Which makes me hope that I was called to God to Write this Apology for them; Let his Blessing accompany the same." ‡

An examination of the text of the pamphlet, as well as the fact that Saffin answered it in a "Brief and Candid

---

† Dudley pretended to be very much shocked and incensed over the fact that in 1701, Saffin, then a Judge of the Superior Court of Judicature, sat in the case of Rex. v. Adam, the defendant being a negro slave of Saffin's whom he sought to press into the service of one Thomas Shepherd a tenant of one of his farms at Bristol. Such a course, while justly censurable, was not regarded at that time as tainted with the least impropriety. Lynde, Sewall and the other judges of the day, themselves not infrequent litigants did likewise without criticism. At the time of the affront to Gov. Dudley in the so-called Carter's case his son Paul then attorney General acted on behalf of his father and the latter addressed private communications to all the judges concerning it.

‡ Mass. Hist. Soc. Coll. (Fourth Series) Vol. VI Page 16.

Answer to the late Printed Sheet, entitled 'The Selling of Joseph' " attest the fact that Judge Sewall had Adam's case in mind when he publicly expressed his views upon slavery. On September 11, 1701, this entry occurs in his diary.

"Mr. Saffin tampered with Mr. Kent, the Foreman, at Capt. Reynold's, which he denyed at Osburn's. Conived at his Tenant Smith's being on the Jury, in the case between himself and Adam (a negro) about his Freedom."

While he is thus condemning Saffin, even after that gentleman's denial, he is unmindful that he himself had already published, in the neighborhood from which jurors for that trial were to be drawn, and at which he would sit, a brief for the defendant.

The action itself was of comparative insignificance. The attention which it attracted was great. At the foundation of it was the following agreement signed by Saffin June 26, 1694.

"Bee it known unto all men by these presents That I, John Saffin of Bristol in the Province of Massachusetts Bay in New England, out of meer kindness to and for the encouragement of my negro man Adam, to go on cheerfully in his Business and Imployment by me now put into the Custody, Service and command of Thomas Shepherd my Tenant, on Boundfield Farm in Bristol aforesaid, for and During the Terme of Seaven years from the Twenty-fifth day of March last past 1694—fully to be compleat and ended or as I may otherwise see cause to imploy him. I say I doe by these presents of my own free & voluntary Will and pleasure, from and after the full end & expiration of seven years beginning on the Twenty-fifth day of March last past, and from thence forth fully to be compleat and ended, Enfranchise clear and make free my sd negro man Adam, to be fully at his own Dispose and Liberty as other free men are or ought to be, according to all true Intents & Purposes whatsoever. Always provided that the sd Adam my servant do in the meantime go on cheerfully, quietly and Industriously in the Lawfull Business that either myself or my assigns shall from time to time reasonably sett him about, or imploy him in, and doe behave and bear himself as an Honest true and faithfull servant ought to doe, during the Tearm of Seven years as aforesaid. In Witness Whereof I the sd John Saffin have hereunto sett my hand and seal this twenty-sixth day of June 1694. In the sixth year of their Majestic Reign.

JOHN SAFFIN   (*Seal*).

Signed, Sealed &
Delivered in the presence of
Rachel Brown X her marke
Rich'd Smith
Samuel Gallop

This instrument above written was Entered in the First book of Wills and Inventoryes page the last November 15th 1694—by John Cary Recor. †

Saffin claimed, and afterward offered evidence tending to prove, that during the term of his service with Shepherd, Adam had been "very disobedient, turbulent, outrageous and unruly" toward Shepherd; that he had attacked him at different times with a knife, an axe and a pitchfork, had beaten his children and so violently carried himself, that he was forced to get rid of him. He was put to work upon the fortification of Castle Island in Boston Harbor, then in progress, under Capt. Clark but proved as refractory there as on the farm at Bristol. He attacked that functionary with a shovel, and, in the language of the deponents who witnessed the assault, Capt. Clark "might have been grievously mischiefed thereto; butt the Deponents with some others ran into the rescue of the Capt. but the sd negro was so furious and outragious and putt forth so great strength that it was so much as Six or Seven of us could do to hold and

---

† Suffolk Probate Files.

restrain him." Saffin, thereupon ordered Adam back to Bristol. He refused to go, saying that he was free. He appealed to Judge Sewall. The latter sent for Saffin, who appeared before him and Judge Addington. Sewall, whose anti-slavery pamphlet had already been published, severely criticised his judicial associate, Saffin, and producing the release, signed by the latter, advised him to give the negro his liberty. Addington concurred in this; but Saffin insisted that the terms of the release had not been complied with by Adam, and caused the negro to be arrested. He was convicted; but, because there was some doubt in the minds of the members of the Court as to the form the judgment should take, and also some disagreement or misunderstanding between Saffin and themselves as to whether or not Saffin should promise to keep the negro in the country, the judgment was suspended. At the same term Adam presented a petition for his enfranchisement. Upon this the Superior Court provided him with two Attorneys, Thomas Newton and Joseph Hearne, ruled that the petition should be heard by the Inferior Court and "that the Petitioner in the mean time be in peace until the Coming of the Justices" (of that Court). Adam thereupon brought suit against Saffin in the Court of Common Pleas for Suffolk County, but upon the return of the writ therein it was abated for the reason that both parties being domiciled in Bristol, it should have been brought in that County. Adam endeavored to appeal but failed. Thereupon Saffin renewed his threat to send his unruly servant out of the province and Newton, one of his attorneys, filed the following petition.

"To the Honorable the Justices of her Majesties Superior Court of Judicature held at Boston for the County of Suffolk being ye 8th day of May 1703.

Thomas Newton of sd Boston humbly showeth That Whereas your honors at the Superior Court of Judicature, held at Boston for the said County on the first Tuesday of November now last past, upon the petition of Adam a negro, late slave of John Saffin,

Esq., for his freedom appointed the sd Thomas Newton and Mr. Joseph Hearne, attorneys for the sd Adam, and that in order thereunto the sd attorneys should commence an accon for him agt the sd John Saffin at the then next Inferior Court of Comon Pleas to be held at Boston for sd County, for the Tryall of his liberty; and the sd Thomas Newton and Joseph Hearne accordingly brought an accon for the sd Adam agt the said John Saffin at the inferior Court of Comon pleas held at Boston on the first Tuesday of January last, where the said accon was dismissed and an appeal to this Court thereupon denyed And forasmuch as the sd Adam dayly pursues your subscriber for the Tryall of his said liberty the sd Adam being dayly threatened by the said Mr. Saffin to be sent out of this province into forreigne parts to remaine a slave during life.

Your subscriber humbly prays your honors will be pleased to take the premises into your consideration, and give such further directions therein as to your honors shall seem meet.

And your subscriber will ever pray &c

(Signed)

THO. NEWTON"

Now note the remarkable decree entered by the court of which Judge Sewall was a member upon this petition which sought merely "directions." It does not appear that Saffin ever had notice of it and the decree fails to recite that there was a hearing.

Upon Reading the Petition of Mr. Thomas Newton relating to Adam negro, late Slave to John Saffin, Esq., That notwithstanding the former Order of this Court † he is pursued by Mr. Saffin as his slave and has endeavored to support him beyond sea. ‡ Its therefore

---

† There was no former or other order. The judges claimed and Saffin denied that he had made a promise not to remove Adam from the province.

‡ There was no evidence of this. It was the mere statement of the attorney.

considered by the Court That Adam negro be in peace untill by due process of Law he be found a Slave." †

It is hardly to be expected that Saffin would rest content with this judgment. He appealed to the Legislature. That body on June 3rd 1703 ordered "That the matter be heard before the next Court of General Sessions of the Peace for Suffolk." A trial in this Court was had, and Adam again convicted. Once more he appealed, this time to the Court whereon sat Judge Sewall who had roundly berated Saffin ‡ in chambers for his action toward his servant, and Major John Walley, his enemy of Bristol, since then elevated to the bench. The jury found for Adam and the court accepted the verdict. Apparently not disheartened or defeated, Saffin again appealed to the Legislature § and was again "Referred to the law." He did not do so. For three years he had been before the courts in an endeavor to obtain what he honestly believed to be his rights.

In the trials before the Inferior Court his servant had been convicted. He had been justly criticised for sitting in judgment upon the negro upon the latter's appeal, although Saffin himself would not admit the righteousness of the censure. He had been accused of tampering with the jury and had quarrelled with his associates upon the bench over the entry of judgment on that jury's verdict. He had repeated the trial before a court in which sat two of his violent opponents, and had failed. The lower branch of the

---

† Records of the Superior Court of Judicature (Suffolk County) A. D. 1700-1714, page 100.

‡ Judge Sewall's feeling of Hostility toward Saffin at the time is shown by the following lines penned in his diary June 1703 when the General Assembly had ordered a trial in the Courts. The judge was known to have a special aversion to periwigs. He himself always appeared with his long hanging loosely down his back and surmounted by a close fitting, black, papal skull cap.

"Superanunated Squier, wigg'd and powder's with pretence,
Much beguiles the just Assembly by his lying Impudence.
None being by, his bold attorneys push it on with might and main.
By which means poor simple Adam sinks to slavery again.

§ Massachusetts Archives Vol IX Page 153.

General Assembly had favored him † but the Council presided over by his enemy Gov. Dudley, negatived it. He was growing old and perhaps more irascible, and he quit. Deane says that he died at Bristol July 29, 1710. Governor Washburn in his Judicial History does likewise. Baylies in his Memoir of Plymouth Colony without mentioning the place gives the date as of May twenty-ninth of the same year. Each is wrong. His executors in their account to the Probate Court ‡ name the date of his death as July 28, 1710, and the place Boston. Judge Sewall, not to let him pass out of this life without notice, records in his diary "Satterday, July 29th. last night, John Saffin, esqu'r died. He expressed to Mr. Pemberton § an Assurance of his good estate 2 or 3 hours before his death."

In his will he remembers his Sciutate relatives—"Item. I give and bequeath unto my kinsman Joseph Garrett of Scituate two tenth parts of that one thousand acres of land granted to me in the Narrhagensett Country by the Committee for the Mortgage land there; and to his Two Brethren (Garret's) each of them one tenth part of sd thousand acres."

---

† House Journal June 1, 1703. "Ordered—That the Petitioner have a Hearing before this Court on the 2nd Wednesday of the next session."
‡ Suffolk Probate Records Number 3264.
§ Pastor of the (Old) South Church.

JUDGE WILLIAM CUSHING MEMORIAL AT GREENBUSH.
From a photograph by Alden S. Cook.

THE CUSHINGS

The progenitors of the New England branch of this brilliant family were Matthew Cushing and his wife Nazreth (Pitcher). They came to Boston in August 1638 and later with their children, Daniel, Jeremiah, Matthew, Deborah and John settled in Hingham.

John, the youngest, was then a lad of nine years. He spent his boyhood and young manhood in that town. In 1656 he married Sarah, a daughter of Nicholas Hawkes and six years later came to Scituate. He was then thirty-five years old and of sufficient financial ability to purchase from the son of William Vassall, the farm at Belle House Neck which the latter had quitted, with more or less disappointment, ten years before, to go to Barbadoes. The first ten years of Cushing's residence in Scituate do not find him performing much public service. He served on the grand jury and was a receiver of excise. Seven of his eleven children, John, Thomas, Matthew, James, Joshua, Sarah and Caleb, were born during this time. In 1672 he was a selectman. This office he held many years. In 1673 and again in 1683 he was appointed to solemnize marriages and administer oaths, though not then of the magistracy. In 1676 he was made a deputy from Scituate to the Colony Court and in this capacity served his constituency continuously until 1685. In that year the colony having been divided into the three counties of Plymouth, Bristol and Barnstable, he was chosen an Associate for the former. In 1689 he was made an Assistant and was annually returned to that office until the amalgamation of the two colonies in 1692.

He was the founder of a family of statesmen, patriots, judges, teachers, lawyers and physicians, who in their respective generations have been prominent in widely settled communities especially in New England. His descendants have contributed to the best public thought and action of their times to a greater degree than probably any other Old Colony family, Standish, Alden, Winslow and Bradford not excepted.

His eldest son, bearing the same name, was born at Scituate in 1662, and at the age of forty was appointed Chief Justice of the Superior Court of Common Pleas for Plymouth County, a tribunal of limited civil jurisdiction, which sat once a year at Plymouth. In his day, and for many years thereafter, it was not deemed inconsistent, that the same individual should be at the same time, a judge of one of the courts and a member of the provincial council, a body commissioned to act with and advise the President (Governor), in matters of government. Judge Cushing was chosen to this body in 1710 and continued a member of it until 1728. He was then commissioned to be a judge of the Superior Court, the court of general jurisdiction in the province, and occupied a place upon this bench until 1733 when "his name was omitted in the commission which was then issued to other members of the court." For many years the Commonwealth of Massachusetts has perpetrated the libel in its Manuel for the General Court that Judge Cushing was removed. Although this publication has, in all probability, not injured the good repute which the venerable gentleman left behind him, in the interest of truth it should be written here that the occasion of his failure to be recommissioned was his advanced age—seventy-one—and not his removal. In these days we accomplish the same result with a pension. Governor Washburn says, speaking of Judge Cushing's attainments while a member of the Superior Court, "I do not find that he was educated beyond what was requisite for the duties of a highly respectable walk in private life, and of course he could not have held high rank for learning in comparison with some of his Associates upon the bench" †. On the other hand, Reverend Josiah Cotton, his contemporary, says of him at

---

† Benjamin Lynde, the elder, Addington Davenport, Edmund Quincy and Paul Dudley.

this time "He was a gentleman well versed in law; the life and soul of our court while he continued in it, a man in the main, of justice and integrity" †.

He was twice married. From him descended James Savage, the antiquarian and historian. He deceased in 1737.

John Cushing, the third to bear that name, and son of Judge John above named, was born July 17, 1695, on the ancestral farm at Belle-House Neck. At the age of twenty-six he was a member of the provincial legislature from Scituate, and later Judge of Probate for the County of Plymouth. Like his father he was a judge of the Superior Court of Common Pleas, holding this office at the same time that he was a judge of the Probate Court. In addition, he was a member of the Council and still in emulation of the example set by his father, occupied these two positions simultaneously. He was appointed to the Superior Court in 1747 by Governor Shirley and continued to sit upon this bench until his resignation in 1771.

The historian ‡ of his son says of him that "He was bred to the bar; and with abilities, learning and genial manners, rapidly achieved the honors of his profession." His contemporaries upon the Superior bench were the younger Benjamin Lynde, Stephen Sewall, Chambers Russell, Peter Oliver, Thomas Hutchinson (afterward colonial Governor for three years) and, for a portion of the time, Edmund Trowbridge. Most of these men incurred for themselves in the discharge of their judicial duties, the enmity of the revolutionary leaders and the provincial populace over the Stamp Act and the issuance of Writs of Assistance to the port collectors, for the seizure of uncustomed goods. Otis, Sam Adams and their followers were impatient at the attitude of the court. They were ready by whatever means, to break down any barrier that stood as an obstacle to their great object, and wont to ascribe disloyal and unworthy

---

† New England Hist. and Gen. Reg. for Jaunary 1854 P. 42.
‡ Flanders—Lives and Times of the Chief Justices Vol II P. 12.

motives to those who disagreed with them. Thus John Adams, whose political virulency was always acid, wrote in his diary ten years later, when, on his way to attend court at Ipswich, he overtook Judge Cushing:—

"Overtook Judge Cushing, in his old curricle, and two lean horses, and Dick, his negro, at his right hand, driving the curricle. This is the way of travelling in 1771:—a Judge of the Circuits, a Judge of the Superior Court, a Judge of the King's Bench, Common Pleas and Exchequer for the Province, travels with a pair of wretched old jades of horses, in a wretched old dung cart of a curricle, and a negro, on the same seat with him, driving. But we shall have more glorious times anon, when the sterling salaries are ordered out of the revenue to the judges, &c., as many most ardently wish, and the judges themselves, among the rest, I suppose. † Stopped at Martin's, in Lynn, with Judge Cushing; oated, and drank a glass of wine, and heard him sigh and groan the sighs and groans of seventy-seven, though he kept active. He conversed in his usual, smiling, insinuating, scrupling strain." ‡

It was said that the judges through party bias, failed to pronounce impartial judgments. Especially was this criticism advanced in the matter of the issuance of the Writs of Assistance. Historians of the Revolutionary times have left nothing untold of the brilliancy of Otis and Thacher when this question was argued by them in 1761, before the Superior Court of which this third John Cushing was a member. Whatever may be said of Chief Justice Hutchinson and the others, Judge Cushing, like his son William, was no Tory. He occupied a delicate position, however. As a judge of the highest court of the province he was sworn to uphold the law. Writs of Assistance, before 1761, had

---

† It had been suggested, that the judges appointed by the Crown would be less subject to its influence, if their salaries were paid out of the local revenue. The Legislature later crystalized this suggestion into law.

‡ John Adams' Works Vol II P. 279.

frequently been issued by it. They were authorized by the Statutes of 14 Charles 11, Chapter 2; and 7 George III Chapter 46. The Court of which he was a member had the same jurisdiction as that which the courts of "the Kings Bench, Common Pleas and Exchequer united," exercised in England. English laws, so far as was consistent with the state of the country, were made its guide" †. When Charles Paxton, Surveyor of the Port of Boston, applied to the Court for the Writ of Assistance, that tribunal, already sensing the popular feeling, "desired the Opinion of the Bar, whether they had a Right and ought to grant it." ‡

James Otis, Jr., then Advocate General, resigned his commission to argue against the issuance of the writ. With him was Oxenbridge Thacher, astute, learned and resourceful. Against these two were pitted the dean of the bar, Jeremy Gridley, and Robert Auchmuty, soon to take the place resigned by Otis, and later to be made judge of the Admiralty.

Thacher opened the arguments against the writ. He contended that although the statute of Charles II provided for and authorized it, yet in the sixty years of the life of that statute up to the time of argument, it neither was applied for or granted until 1756. Therefore that *non user* was a great presumption against it. He urged also that the Massachusetts Court had not in this particular the powers of the English Court of Exchequer, and that in the case of McNeal vs Brideoak previously decided by the provincial tribunal, it had expressly disclaimed the authority of the Exchequer. Josiah Quincy, Jr., the reporter, does not give Otis' argument in full. Enough is published however to show that it partook largely of an historical character. Replying to it Gridley said: (The writ) "is properly a Writ of Assistants, not Assistance: not to give the Officers a greater Power, but as a check upon them. For by this they cannot enter into any House without the

---

† Washburn—Judicial History of Massachusetts Page 97.
‡ Quincy,—Mass. Reg. Page 51.

presence of the Sheriff or other civil officer, who will be always supposed to have an eye over and be a check upon them. Quoting History is not speaking like a Lawyer. If it is Law in England, it is Law here; it is extended to this Country by Act of Parliament. By Act of Parliament they are entitled to like Assistants; now how can they have like Assistants, if the Court cannot grant them it; and how can the Court grant them like Assistance if they cannot grant this writ. Pity it would be, they should have like Right, and not like Remedy. But the General Court has given this Court authority to grant it, and so has every other Plantation Court given their Superior Court." † These arguments occurred at the August term, and on December second the Court unanimously granted the writ. This action did not, of course, increase the popularity of the judges, although they had declared the law as they saw it.

On the other side of the water, Sir William Blackstone in the debate on the repeal of the Stamp Act, is said to have "declared Tory as he was, that Parliament had no right to impose internal taxes" but Coke, and Charles Pratt, Earl of Camden, later Lord Chief Justice, each asserting a different reason, disagreed with him." ‡

It must be undoubted that Judge Cushing, in agreeing to the issuance of the writ, did so purely because his reasoning, or his regard for precedent led him in that direction. If the latter, he has since been well supported. Many an eminent jurist has shown an equal devotion to the doctrine of *stare decisis.*

When the time came however, for Judge Cushing to show his mettle, he was not slow in making the exhibition. The occasion arose in December 1765. At that time the Superior Court, in the several circuits, for the want of "stamp-papers" had done no business, "except opening the court, and continuing all matters to the next term, ever since the Stamp Act was to have taken place in the Colonies."

† Quincy,—Mass. Rep. Page 57.
‡ Ibidem Page 516.

In this situation the town of Boston, at a meeting on the eighteenth day of December, memorialized the Governor and Council to the effect that "The Courts of law within the Province, in which alone justice can be distributed among the people, so far as respects civil matters, are to all intents and purposes shut up; for which your memorialists apprehend no just and legal reason can be assigned." The memorial asked that directions be given to the several courts and their officers, that they might be opened to litigants. The Governor and Council called before them, the three leaders of the Suffolk bar, two of whom had five years previous appeared before the Superior Court and argued on opposite sides, on the question of issuing the writs of Assistance. On this occasion Otis and Gridley were joined by John Adams. All were in accord that the courts should be opened and business conducted in them. The Governor and his advisers trimmed however. They declared that the memorial raised a question of law; and that the tribunal to pass upon it was the court itself. This was reported to the town. After holding three meetings, it unanimously disapproved the action of the Council. It resolved that the courts ought to be open and instructed its representatives in the General Court to use their utmost endeavors to bring this about. The last of these meetings was held on the sixteenth day of January 1766, and the following March was the date for the regular sitting of the court. When the time arrived Hutchinson did not appear. It was charged that he purposely made the flimsy pretext of going on a journey to explain his absence. † Cushing, Lynde and Oliver attended. The latter timidly suggested that he was there under duress; that if forced to proceed in defiance of the Stamp Act, he would do so only as an act of self preservation, as he knew that he was in the hands of the populace and his judicial acts, if so performed under duress,

---

† It was a few short months before (August 1765) that his house had been beset by a mob and property valued at £3000 destroyed. Quincy—Mass. Rep. Page 168.

would be void. Cushing on the contrary, apparently taking the ground which had been urged by Gridley, Otis and Adams the December previous, that the passage of the Stamp Act neither deprived his court of jurisdiction, nor excused him from exercising his judicial duties, announced himself as ready to proceed. Lynde followed him. Again Cushing pursued the dictates of duty as he saw it. Had he been of Tory leaning, he could have run away as did Hutchinson; or protested, with Oliver. His conduct was admirable. It was dignified and courageous. It merited and received the commendation of his critic John Adams, who gives this account of the first day of March term 1766:—

"11 Tuesday. Went to Boston. The Chief Justice not there; a piece of political finesse to make the people believe he was under the necessity of going a journey this week, but would be here by the next, was put about, while care was taken to secure an agreement to an adjournment for three or four weeks; so that Hutchinson is to trim and shift and luff up and bear away; and elude all blame of the ministry and the people. Cushing spoke out boldly and said he was ready to go on; he had no difficulty about going on."

Judge Cushing sat in the trial of Capt. Preston who was indicted for the murder of Crispus Attucks and others, in the "Boston Massacre." The trial took place in October. It was the last important case in which he sat. John Adams and Josiah Quincy, Jr., each, moved by a fine spirit and a desire that the accused captain should have his full rights accorded him, appeared in his defense. Before agreeing to the employment Quincy sought the advice of Judge Cushing, John Hancock and Joseph Warren. Each counselled him to undertake it. This action of the young patriot barrister in resorting to Judge Cushing for counsel, speaks decisively for the high place which the latter held in the hearts of the leaders of public opinion, in the hour of his retirement.

He resigned the next year, came back to his farm in Scituate, and died in 1786.

His son William immediately succeeded him upon the Superior Court of Judicature. He was for a time as much the object of distrust, so fickle is the public mind, as his father had been in the days of writs of Assistance and the Stamp Act.

William Cushing was born at Scituate, March 1, 1732. He was prepared for college by Mr. Richard Fitzgerald the Latin School Master in Scituate and graduated from Harvard at the age of nineteen. This does not denote any precocity upon his part. They matriculated younger at Cambridge in 1751, than they do to-day. Having received his degree he taught a grammar school at Roxbury for a year and then entered upon the study of the law in the office of Jeremy Gridley, Esqr., in Boston. Flanders † says that he remained in Mr. Gridley's office until he was "called to the bar, in 1755." This is an error. Under the then rule of the Superior Court of Judicature for the Province, the lawyer must practice for three years in the inferior courts ‡ before being "called by the Court to be a Barrister at Law." This did not take place until the August term 1762. § The same rule required that the judges and lawyers be clothed in robes. While sitting in the trial of civil and ordinary criminal cases, the gowns worn by the judges were of black silk with white bands; when capital cases were on, the robe was of scarlet with black velvet collar, cuffs and facings. ¶ The head of the judge was covered with the large judicial peruke, while the barristers wore a tie-wig. Cushing at the time of his admission did not appear clad in this apparel. When later, he was a judge of the same court which promulgated this requirement, he

---

† Flanders—Lives and Times of the Chief Justices Page 16.
‡ John Adams' Works II Page 133.
§ Quincy, Massachusetts Reports, page 35.
¶ Memoirs of Increase Sumner. Genealogical Register for Apr. 1854, page 116.

became strongly addicted to the wig wearing habit. This story is told of him, that:—

> "making his appearance in the streets of New York whence he had gone for the purpose of being present at the first term of the Supreme Court of the United States held there in February 1790, his head was covered with the large English wig which he had worn in Massachusetts. He noticed that he was attracting considerable attention and being a modest man, rather marvelled at it. He was at a loss how to account for it, until, turning a corner he came abrutply upon a sailor, who, surprised into astonished expression, exclaimed "My eyes! what a wig!" Cushing was now let into the secret, and returning to his lodgings, sent for a peruke-maker, and obtained a more fashionable covering for his head." †

Admitted to the bar, William Cushing began the practise of his profession in Scituate but soon removed to Pownalborough (now Dresden) in Maine. His father owned lands in that region, and this, it is supposed, was the cause of his going there." ‡ In 1760, the new county of Lincoln having been created, and Maine then being territorially a part of the province of Massachusetts, Sir Francis Bernard the Royal Governor made him Judge of Probate for that county. He was back in Boston, however, in two years to be called as a barrister to the bar of the Superior Court as already told. §

At the close of the year 1771 "Lynde, Chief Justice (of

---

† Address of J. D. Hopkins, Esquire, before the Cumberland County (Maine) Bar Association, 1833.
‡ Flanders Lives and Times of the Chief Justices page 16.
§ Cushing says that Cushing remained Judge of Probate for Lincoln County for twelve years. If this is correct it occasions the inquiry, as to why he should have been admitted as a barrister in Boston in 1762. The statement seems to be supported however, by the fact that his name does not once appear as counsel in any of the cases argued in the Superior Court and reported by Quincy, although those of his contemporaries, Otis, Adams, Dana, Fitch, Sewall, Paine and Samuel Quincy are mentioned with repeated frequency.

the Superior Court) and Cushing Justice, resigned and the Honourable Peter Oliver, Esq., was made Chief Justice, and the Honourable Nath'l Ropes and William Cushing Esquire, were made Justices and all took their seats accordingly in Suffolk February Term 1772." † When this occurrence took place the public mind was much inflamed. In the same court to which this new blood was thus added, only the year before, Captain Prescott and six of his company who were engaged in the Boston massacre, had been acquitted; and the two who had been convicted of manslaughter for the death of Attucks had been ordered to be punished merely by branding the palms of their hands. Whatever may have been the righteousness of either verdict or punishment, the court, which imposed the latter, was not in favor with the commonalty.

Cushing had been less than six months upon the bench before the question respecting the payment of the judges' salaries arose. On August seventh 1772 the ministry provided that they should be paid by the Crown. The Legislature, when it met the following January, equally determined, ordered an appropriation out of the provincial revenue for the purpose. Governor Hutchinson, in whose time as Chief Justice of the Superior Court, the same question had been exploited, withheld his assent and John Adams thereupon proposed the impeachment of those who should refuse to accept the salaries provided by the Assembly. The state of affairs cannot be better described than in his own words, written later:—

"At this period the universal cry among the friends of their country was, what shall we do to be saved? It was by all agreed, as the Governor was entirely dependent upon the Crown, and the Council in danger of becoming so, if the judges were to be made so too, the liberties of the country would be totally lost, and every man at the mercy of a few slaves of the Governor, but no man presumed to say what ought to be done,

---

† Quincy, Massachusetts Reports page 330.

and what could be done. Intimations were frequently given, that this arrangement should not be submitted to. I understood very well what was meant and I fully expected that if no expedient could be suggested, the judges would be obliged to go where secretary Oliver had gone, to the Liberty Tree, and compelled to take an oath to renounce royal salaries. Some of these judges are men of resolution; and the Chief Justice in particular, piqued himself so much upon it, and had so often gloried in it on the bench, that I shuddered at the expectation that the mob might put on him a coat of tar and feathers, if not put him to death. I had a real respect for the judges; three of them, Trowbridge, Cushing and Brown, I could call my friends. Oliver and Ropes, abstracted from the politics, were amiable men, and all of them were very respectable and virtuous characters." †

Under the threat of impeachment, and perhaps fearing the more debasing, not to say possibly fatal action by the mob, suggested in the fear of Adams, Judge Trowbridge at the opening of the January session of the court in 1774, announced his intention of receiving his salary in the manner laid down by the Assembly. Cushing did not act with haste. By some this was ascribed to timidity; by others, to royal leanings; and there are also those who claim that his inaction was due to a desire to please both factions. Neither of these critics are probably correct, and all are unfair. Judge Cushing is described by those who knew him well as a man of great "caution and reserve;" of "unshaken integrity and deliberate judgment" and whose "excellence consisted in his cool, logical and lucid argumentation, which convinced if it did not move his hearers." ‡

---

† John Adams' Works Vol II Pages 328-330.
‡ The quoted opinions are gathered from three different writers: Washburn's Judicial History, page 316. Flander's

He took his time to deliberate upon the question and finally acquiesced in the proposal of the Legislature, taking Judges Ropes and Foster Hutchinson, a brother of the Governor, with him. This left Chief Justice Peter Oliver to stand alone the threatened impeachment which never eventuated.

Subsequent events demonstrated that Judge Cushing's course during these trying occurrences met with the popular approval. When the court was reorganized by the Provincial Congress in November 1775, and John Adams was made Chief Justice, Cushing was the only one of the judges commissioned by the Crown, whose services were retained upon the new tribunal. Adams did not sit; and upon his resignation in 1776, Judge Cushing was appointed Chief Justice. This position he not only accepted, but in doing so, showed a moral courage, the possession of which had been openly doubted. Had the cause of liberty been unsuccessful, he would have been in the same class for punishment with those who had incited rebellious opposition to the mother country, and had taken up arms against the exercise of her authority. Usurpation of the judicial function was a most serious undertaking, and had the Revolution been crushed he would have been severely dealt with.

Lives of the Chief Justices page 19 and Warren's American Revolution Vol I page 117. Perhaps the last embodies in effect the feeling of all:- "Two of the judges, Trowbridge and Ropes, readily complied with the demand and relinquished the offensive stipend. A third was William Cushing, Esq. a gentleman rendered respectable in the eyes of all parties by his professional abilities and general integrity. He was a sensible, modest man, well acquainted with law, but remarkable for the secrecy of his opinions. This kept up his reputation through all the ebullitions of discordant parties. He readily resigned the royal stipend, without any observations of his own; yet it was thought at the time that it was with a reluctance that his taciturnity could not conceal. By this silent address he retained the confidence of the Court faction, nor was he less a favorite among the Republicans".

Should further doubt remain as to his devotion to the cause of freedom, one has but to read his draft of the instructions † of the town to its representatives offered at a town meeting held in Scituate on the fourth day of June 1776. The man who in that resolution charged Great Britain with "being determined to exercise their (its) barbarities upon us, and, to all appearances, to extirpate, if practable, the Americans from the face of the earth, unless they will tamely resign the rights of humanity, and to re-people this once happy country with the ready sons of vassalage," could not, a short three years before, have seriously considered becoming such a vassal himself by the acceptance of a salary from that government, when the propriety of such action was called in question. Happily his place upon this bench was saved to him and his services to the people preserved by the result of the Revolution.

Of his work during this time, little has become a matter of record, except unimportant memoranda or judgments found among the papers, in the clerk's offices.

One charge to a Worcester County jury involving his views upon slavery, is vouched for by Flanders.

"At the April term of the Superior Court, held at Worcester, in 1783, Nathaniel Jennison ‡ was tried for assault and battery on one Quorks (or Quork Walker). 'The justification is' said the Chief Justice, 'that Quorks is his slave; and to prove it, it is said that Quorks, when a child about nine months old, with his father and mother, was sold, by bill of sale, in 1754, about twenty-nine years ago, to Mr. Caldwell now deceased; that

---

† Ante page. 239.

‡ Governor Washburn in a paper read before the Massachusetts Historical Society, (Fourth Series Vol IV. Pages 333 et seq.) on the "Extinction of Slavery in Massachusetts" maintained not only, that Judge Cushing did not charge the jury in the Jennison case, but that he did *not sit at all.*

This statement will create a mild surprise when the occasion, the auditors before whom it was made, and the person promulgating it, are taken into account. The facts are obtained through the medium of the docket of the Supreme Judicial Court for the

when he died Quorks was appraised as a part of his personal estate, and set off to the widow in her share of the same; that Dr. Jennison, marrying her, was entitled to Quorks as his property; and, therefore, that he had a right to bring him home when he ran away, and that the defendant took only proper measure for that purpose. And the defendant's counsel also rely on some former laws of the Province, which give countenance

---

County of Worcester. This docket, together with those from the various counties of the Commonwealth and the province of Maine, were after great diligence, gathered together by John Noble, Esquire, for many years clerk of the same court for the County of Suffolk and deposited in the archives of this court at Boston. They contradict Governor Washburn flatly, though, of course, they do not disclose that Judge Cushing charged the jury. This copy of the entry is from the criminal docket for the year 1783:-

Before
WILLIAM CUSHING, Esq., Chief Justice.
NATHANIEL PEASLEE, Sargent
DAVID SEWALL
INCREASE SUMNER
Esquires Justices.
"No. 8 Commonwealth vs Nathaniel Jennison.

Upon an indictment for assault. This indictment was found September Term A. D. 1781 and now in this present Term, the said Nathaniel Jennison comes into Court & has this indictment read to him, he says that thereof he is not guilty & thereof for Trial puts &c. a Jury thereupon is impannelled & sworn to Try the issue viz., Jonas How, Foreman & fellows namely, Wm. McFarland, Isaac Choate, Joseph Bigelow, John White, Daniel Bullard, Ebenezer Lovell, Phillip Goodridge, John Lyon, Jona Woodbury, Thomas White and John Town, who after hearing all matters and things concerning the same, return their verdict, and upon their oath do say, that the said Nathaniel Jennison is guilty: It is therefore considered by the Court that the said Nathaniel Jennison pay a fine of Forty shillings, pay costs & stand committed "till sentence be performed, costs taxed at £." The reason for the failure to carry out the taxation of costs is probably found in the fact that Jennison had brought proceedings in the Inferior Court of Common Pleas for the County of Worcester through which in the civil side he sought to get the custody and possession of Quork Walker as his chattel. The decision was against Jennison. He appealed to the Supreme Judicial Court, but failed to file therein "attested copies of the writ judgment or evidence filed in the Superior Court as the law directs" and was defaulted. Thereupon Walker sought and obtained affirmation of this judgment and collected damages and costs in the sum of "£50 gold or silver, or bills of public credit of the new emission equivalent to $1\frac{7}{8}$ for one silver dollar" and "costs taxed at £1:10:07"

to slavery. As to the doctrine of slavery and the right of Christians to hold Africans in perpetual servitude, and sell and treat them as we do our horses and cattle, that (it is true) has been heretofore countenanced by the Province laws; but nowhere is it expressly enacted or established. It has been a usage; a usage which took its origin from the practice of some of the European nations, and the regulation of the British government respecting the then colonies for the benefit of trade and wealth. But whatever sentiments have formerly prevailed in this particular, or slid in upon us by the example of others, a different idea has taken place with the people of America, more favorable to the natural rights of mankind, and to that innate desire of liberty, with which Heaven, without regard to color, complexion, or shape of feature has inspired all the human race. And upon this ground, our Constitution of Government, by which the people of this Commonwealth have solemnly bound themselves, sets out with declaring that all men are born free and equal, and that every subject is entitled to liberty and to have it guarded by the laws, as well as life and property; and, in short, is totally repugnant to the idea of being born slaves. This being the case, I think the idea of slavery is inconsistent with our own conduct and Constitution, and there can be no such thing as perpetual servitude of a rational creature, unless his liberty is forfeited by some criminal conduct, or given up by personal consent or contract." After this charge Dr. Jennison was found guilty.

Twice during his term of service on this bench Cushing was importuned to become a candidate for Governor. When Governor Hancock declined a re-election in 1785, both parties wanted to nominate him. Each time he declined, saying, "but many weighty reasons prompted me to decline the too high and arduous task." He did however, accept from his Scituate neighbors in 1787, an election to the Massachusetts Convention which met in January of the following year, for the adoption of the Federal Constitution.

He was chosen Vice-President of that body and, because of the ill health of John Hancock, the President, he presided during a greater part of the session, over its debates and proceedings. While as presiding officer, Judge Cushing could not largely participate in the serious discussions which marked the sessions of the convention, his tact was at all times apparent. It was due doubtless, in some measure, to the high esteem in which he was held, and the known fact of his own approval of it, that the Constitution was finally ratified. Out of a total membership in this convention of three hundred and sixty, it obtained a majority of only nineteen votes.

After it became operative, upon its ratification and adoption by Massachusetts, Maryland, South Carolina, New Hampshire and Virginia, all of which followed their sister states in this final act of devotion to the federal cause, Judge Cushing again consented to run for elective office. He was chosen an Elector of President and Vice-President and helped to cast the ten votes of his Commonwealth for George Washington of Virginia and John Adams of Massachusetts to those offices.

When that great constitutional tribunal — the Supreme Court of the United States—was organized, Judge Cushing was called upon by Washington to bring his learning, sagacity and well equipped judicial mind to its membership. The President later on, after the resignation of John Jay, determined upon the appointment of Cushing to be Chief Justice, apparently without consulting the person upon whom the great honor was to be bestowed. It is told that Cushing first heard of it at a dinner party given by the President, when he was accosted as Chief Justice and told by Washington to take the place at table at his right hand. Although unanimously confirmed to the position, he declined it, pleading that his health would not permit it. He presided however, during the absence of Chief Justice Jay upon his diplomatic mission to the Court of St. James, negotiating the first treaty with the defeated mother country.

Judge Cushing's health at this period of his life was poor. We have his own statement for that fact. The reports of the activities of his court from 1789 to 1810 when death removed him, show that he took his full part, however, in the transaction of its business. This was no easy task. While there was in the beginning, comparatively little to occupy the attention of the judges upon the appellate side of the court, under the Judiciary Act they sat in the Circuit Courts from Massachusetts to Georgia. In his travel over this big circuit Judge Cushing was invariably accompanied by his wife, a woman twenty-two years his junior, highly accomplished, much devoted to, and very proud of her husband. They travelled in what has been described, both as coach and phaeton, drawn by a pair of horses driven by the judge himself. A collateral relative, Charles Cushing Paine, Esq., in an unpublished sketch of Judge Cushing says that the conveyance which ever it may have been, "was remarkable for its many ingenious arrangements (all of his contrivance) for carrying books, choice groceries, and other comforts. Mrs. Cushing always accompanied him, and generally read aloud, while riding. His faithful servant, Prince, a jet black Negro, whose parents had been slaves in the family, and who loved his master with unbounded affection, followed behind, in a one horse vehicle with the baggage."

While thus riding the circuit, the cases which he decided were infrequently of more than local importance. The most noteworthy was that of McDonough vs. Dannery and the ship Mary Ford. † In the war between England and France which followed the former's disastrous conflict with her colonies in America, a French privateer had captured the English ship Mary Ford. After taking her, her captors abandoned her, through stress of weather, and she was salvaged by Americans, who claimed thereby to become

† 3 Dallas, Page 188.

the true owners. Judge Cushing denied them this title. He held that a ship of a belligerent nation, taken by an enemy ship as a prize of war, and afterward abandoned, was still the property of the original owners; that after payment of salvage from the proceeds of the sale of ship and cargo, the balance of the avails of the sale belonged to these owners. The case was taken to the full court of which Judge Cushing was a member. There he was sustained.

Judge Cushing's greatest decision was given in the case of Chisholm, Exor. vs. Georgia †, a case thus early involving states' rights. The plaintiff, a resident of South Carolina, instituted an action against the State of Georgia. The state did not appear, refusing thus to recognize the jurisdiction of a federal court over it as a sovereign commonwealth; but Ingersoll and Dallas, two leading members of the bar of the Supreme Court, "presented a written remonstrance and protestation on behalf of the state, against the exercise of jurisdiction in the cause." Edmund Randolph, then Attorney General, had moved that the state be defaulted for its non-appearance. Addressing the Court upon this motion he said:—

"I do not want the remonstrance of Georgia to satisfy me that the motion which I have made is unpopular. Before that remonstrance was read, I had learned from the acts of another state, whose will must always be dear to me, that she too, condemned it. On ordinary occasions, these dignified opinions might influence me greatly; but on this, which brings into question a constitutional right, supported by my own conviction, to surrender it, would in me, be official perfidy."

Thus, is partly shown the public interest in, and intense feeling which surrounded the case. The Court itself was divided. Judge Iredell led those of the judges who argued for state sovereignty. Chief Justice Jay and Judge Cushing, led those against it. It devolved upon Cushing to

---

† 2 Dallas Page 419.

write the opinion. Speaking for a majority of the Court, he held:

"The grand and principal question in this case is, whether a state can, by the Federal Constitution be sued by an individual citizen of another state. x x x x As controversies between state and state and between a state and citizens of another state, might tend gradually to involve states in war and bloodshed, a disinterested civil tribunal was intended to be instituted to decide such controversies, and preserve peace and friendship. Further: if a state is entitled to justice in the Federal Court against a citizen of another state, why not such citizen against the state, when the same language equally comprehends both? The rights of individuals and justice due to them, are as dear and precious as those of states. Indeed, the latter are founded upon the former; and the great end and object of them must be to secure and support the rights of individuals, or else vain is Government. But still, it may be insisted, that this will reduce states to mere corporations and take away all sovereignty. As to corporations all states whatever are corporations or bodies politic. The only question is what are their powers? As to individual states and the United States, the Constitution marks the boundaries of powers. Whatever power is deposited with the Union by the people for their own necessary security, is so far a curtailing of the power and prerogatives of states. This is, as it were, a self-evident proposition; at least, it cannot be contested. Thus the power of declaring war, making peace, raising and supporting armies for public defence, levying duties, excises and taxes, if necessary, with many other powers are lodged in Congress; and are a most essential abridgment of state sovereignty. Again, the restrictions upon states "No state shall enter into any treaty, alliance, or confederations, coin money, emit bills of credit, make anything but gold and silver a tender in payment of debts, or pass any law impairing the obligation of contracts;" these, with a number of others, are important restrictions of the power of states, and were thought necessary to maintain the Union; and to establish some fundamental, uniform principles of public justice, throughout the whole Union. So that, I think no argument of force can be taken from the sovereignty of states. Where it has been abridged, it was thought necessary for the greater, indispensable good of the whole. If the Constitution is found inconvenient in practice in this or any other particular, it is well that a regular mode is pointed out for amendment. But, while it remains, all officers, Legislative, Executive and Judicial, both of the State and the Union, are bound by oath to support it."

Nothing less could have been expected of a descendant from two other judges who had adhered closely to the voice of judicial conscience when its promptings dictated a course adverse to the popular will. The general feeling was against the opinion. It is certain that it was responsible for Article XI of the Amendments of and in addition to the Constitution of the United States, proposed in the same year that the opinion was handed down (1793); and adopted on January 8, 1798. †

One other case, ‡ of equal importance at the time, presents the opportunity for observation of the courageous bearing, profound learning, keen logic, force and clearness of expression possessed by this most distinguished son of Scituate.

During the war (in 1777) the Assembly of Virginia passed an act sequestering all British debts within her limits. The treaty negotiated by Jay in 1783, provided that credi-

---

† "Article XI. The judicial power of the United States shall not be construed to extend to any suit in law or equity commenced or prosecuted against one of the United States by citizens of another state, or by citizens or subjects of any foreign state".

‡ Ware vs Hylton, 3 Dallas at page 281.

tors on either side should meet with no lawful impediment to the recovery of all *bona fide* debts theretofore contracted. Judge Cushing held, and in this he was again supported by a majority of the Court, that the treaty revived the debts in favor of creditors, and removed the bar to recovery which the act of the Virginia Assembly had interposed. His opinion, in part, follows:—

"I shall not question the right of a state to confiscate debts. Here is an act of the Assembly of Virginia, passed in 1777, respecting debts which, contemplating to prevent the enemy deriving strength by the receipt of them during the war, provides that if any British debtor will pay his debt into the Loan Office, obtain a certificate and receipt as directed, he shall be discharged from so much of the debt. But an intent is expressed in the act not to confiscate, unless Great Britain should set the example. This act, it is said, works a discharge and a bar to the payer. If such payment is to be considered as a discharge or a bar, so long as the act had force, the question occurs,—Was there a power, by the treaty, supposing it contained proper words, entirely to remove this law and this bar, out of the creditor's way?

This power seems not to have been contended against, by the Defendant's counsel. And indeed, it cannot be denied; the treaty having been sanctioned in all its parts, by the Constitution of the United States, is, as the supreme law of the land. Then arises the great question, upon the import of the fourth article of the treaty. And to me the plain, obvious meaning of it goes to nullify, *ab initio,* all laws, or the impediments of any law, as far as they might have been designed to impair or impede the creditor's rights or remedy against his original debtor   x   x   x   x   What has some force to confirm this construction, is the sense of all Europe, that such debts could not be touched by States, without a breach of public faith. And for that, and other reasons, no doubt, this provision was insisted upon in full latitude, by the British negotiators. If the sense of the article be, as stated, it obviates, at once, all the ingenious metaphysical reasoning and refinement upon the words, *debt, discharge, extinguishment*, and affords an answer to the decision made in the time of the interregnum—that payment to sequestors, was payment to the creditor.

A State may make what rules it pleases; and those rules must necessarily have place within itself. But here is a treaty, the supreme law, which overrules all state laws, upon the subject, to all intents and purposes; and that makes the difference."

During the argument of this case at the bar, many objections were made to this construction of the law and the treaty by Judge Cushing. He answered them all however, spoke for the Court in writing the opinion, and was sustained by a majority of his brethren.

During his service upon the Supreme bench Cushing was the close friend of Washington. They were much in each other's company; sat for their portraits to the same artist; hunted and fished the woods and streams of Virginia together, and were altogether intimate and cordial.

William Cushing had no children. He always retained in his possession while he lived, the family acres at Walnut Tree Hill, Scituate. Here was his home, though infrequently visited by him in the last twenty years of his life. Rev. Dr. Kendall, his friend, says of it, "his mansion was a place of resort not only by his fellow townsmen but also by citizens of the neighboring cities." His contemporary Josiah Quincy sums up his character thus:

"His virtues were of the pilgrim cast; pure in morals and inflexible in principle. x x x x The friend of such men as John Adams, Francis Dana, and Oliver Ellsworth, all of whom entertained for him the highest respect, could not be otherwise than of an elevated cast of intellect and moral power."

He died in 1810. He was buried in the family burial ground, overlooking the new mouth of the North River, where a modest shaft of granite over his grave, points to the heavens—the source of his inspiration—and through and far beyond the heavens, to the source of all truth.

Another son of John Cushing, the third of that name, was Elijah, who lived in Pembroke and was a judge of the Court of Common Pleas for Plymouth County. He had all of the shy and retiring traits of his brother William but none of the latter's great abilities.

The second son of the original John Cushing of Scituate was Thomas, born in 1663, an ensign of the Ancient and Honourable Artillery Company and a member of the Provincial Council. He settled in Boston and was the sire and grandsire of those two other Thomas Cushings who as legislators, presiding officers and patriots, continued to uphold the family name and make history during the progress of those events in which their relatives were bearing so prominent a judicial part. Caleb, another son of the first John, born at Scituate in 1672, graduated from Harvard twenty years later and was settled in the ministry at Salisbury. His son Caleb, though born to the cloth, adopted the judicial wig and gown, became a judge of the Common Pleas Court for Essex County and after its reorganization, its Chief Justice. In a more obscure but none the less sincere way than his cousins, he lent his aid as a judge, patriot and member of the first Provincial Congress, to the cause of American liberty.

The youngest of the eight sons of John Cushing and his wife Sarah, was Joseph, born in 1677. His farm was near Henchmans Corner. He seems to have had no other ambitions than to be a good husband and a devoted father to his only son, who was also named Joseph. The latter was a deacon, and devout worshipper under Mr. Eels, at the Second Church. He was educated at Harvard from whence he graduated in 1721. Eleven years later this "Deacon Joseph, Jr.," as he was called, married Lydia King a descendant of Elder Thomas King, Vassal's friend. By her he had fifteen children. He was the grammar school master in Scituate for many years and fitted three of his own and many of the neighbors' sons for college. Five of his children died in childhood or early youth. Joseph, Nathan and Lemuel each graduated from Harvard. Nathan occupied the pupit for a short time and afterward being admitted to the bar, practiced law in Boston. In 1776 he was made Judge of the admiralty and his zeal in this office won for him a place upon the Supreme Court thirteen years later.

His brother, Lemuel, was that young surgeon attached to the third Massachusetts regiment, who abandoned a promising opportunity for private practice in Scituate, and devoted himself to the health of the continental troops so faithfully that he sacrificed his own, and died in the army at the age of only thirty-two.

Another descendant of Joseph Cushing the School Master was Caleb Cushing of Newburyport, who in 1852 was appointed a judge of the Supreme Court of Massachusetts and later became Attorney General in the cabinet of Franklin Peirce.

In every field of action and endeavor, where a descendant of John Cushing of Scituate has been placed, each has maintained a lofty standard; has been actuated by high ideals and has measured up well.

TIMOTHY HATHERLY

When Timothy Hatherly came to New Plymouth in the Anne in August 1623, he brought with him a letter to the people at Plymouth from some of his fellow Merchant Adventurers, in which they said:

"Let it not be grievous to you, that you have been instruments to break the ice for others who come after with less difficulty; the honor shall be yours to the world's end; we bear you always in our breasts and our hearty affection is towards you all, as are the hearts of hundreds more which never saw your faces, who doubtless pray for your safety as their own, that the same God which hath so marvellously preserved you from seas, foes, and famine, will still preserve you from all future dangers, and make you honorable among men, and glorious in bliss to the last day."

He had already been a generous subscriber to the fund with which the Pilgrims were fitted out. In addition, and beyond the pecuniary interest which he had in the colonization venture and his approval of the non-conformist views of the forefathers, he was their constant friend in the disputes which occurred among the Merchant Adventurers themselves, when that partnership would have enacted further and more onerous interests and penalties from them. Likewise he stood with Winslow and Bradford when those of the Adventurers who were attached to the regular church, imposed the obnoxious Lyford upon them.

Hatherly tarried in Plymouth until the winter of 1624 †. During that stay, which was not intended to be permanent, he built a house that later was burned. In 1625 he is found again in London, subscribing a small sum in addition to the already large amount invested by him, at the urgent solicitation of Miles Standish who visited England in that year, as the agent of the Colony, to raise more funds.

---

† Young's Chronicle of the Pilgrims page 352 note.

THE TIMOTHY HATHERLY MEMORIAL
AT NORTH SCITUATE BEACH.
From a photograph by Alden S. Cook.

Hatherly remained six years in London before coming again to this side of the water. The dealings between the colonists and the Adventurers in these years, were in a state far from satisfactory. The interests of the selfishly designing Pierce had been purchased by his associates, leaving Hatherly and forty-one other Merchant Adventurers † in Old England interested in the happenings over seas. Of these Sherley, Beauchamp, Joseph Tilden and Hatherly himself, were most interested in the success of the colony from a purely religious standpoint. The former was constantly, so far as the opportunities permitted, in correspondence with Governor Bradford and the latter early sent his son Nathaniel to join the Mayflower's Company in their endeavors and hardships on this side. So far as the records show this son was one of the first owners of land in Scituate. ‡ Richard Andrews was largely interested financially, but from the fact that he was afterward Lord Mayor of London § it must be assumed that he was of the regular church and out of sympathy with the Separatist views of the forefathers. In 1624 twenty-eight of the Adventurers withdrew entirely from the partnership after having attached the cargo of a vessel returning to England. They were bought out by the rest. Hatherly, Sherley, Beauchamp, Tilden, Andrews, William Collier, Thomas Fletcher and Robert Holland were among those to purchase the shares of the malcontents. Of this defection they wrote to the Plymouth settlers:—

---

† John White, John Pocock, Robert Kean, Edward Bass, William Hobson, William Pennington, William Quarles, Daniel Poynton, Richard Andrews, Newman Rookes, Henry Browning, Richard Wright, John Ling, Thomas Goffe, Samuel Sharpe, Robert Holland, James Sherley, Thomas Mott, Thomas Fletcher, Thomas Brewer, John Thorned, Myles Knowles, William Collier, John Revell, Peter Gudburn, Emanuel Alltham, John Beauchamp, Thomas Hudson, Thomas Andrews, Thomas Ward, Fria. Newbald, Thomas Heath, Joseph Tilden, William Perrin, Eliza Knight, Thomas Coventry, Robert Allden, Lawrence Anthony, John Knight, Matthew Thornhill, Thomas Millsop. Bradford's History 256 note.
‡ On the First Cliff.
§ This statement is made upon the authority of Baylies Memoirs of Plymouth Colony Vol I Page 279. Other writers state that he was an Alderman.

"To our loving friends &c

Though the thing we feared be come upon us, and ye evill we strove against have overtaken us, yet we cannot forgett you, nor our friendship and fellowship which togeather we have had some years; wherein though our expressions have been small, yet our harty affections towards you (unknown by face) have been no less then to our nearest freinds, yea to our owne selves. And though this your friend Mr. Winslow can tell you ye state of things hear, yet least we should seeme to neglecte you, to whom, by a wonderful providence of God, we are so nearly united, we have thought good once more to write unto you, to let you know what is here befallen, and ye resons of it; as also our purposes & desirs toward you for hereafter.

The former course for the generalitie here is wholy dissolved from what it was; and whereas you & we were formerly sharers and partners, in all viages & deallings, this way is now no more, but you and we are left to bethinke ourselves what course to take in ye future, that your lives & our monies be not lost.

The reasons and causes of this allteration have been these. First and mainly, ye many losses and crosses at sea, and abuses of sea-men, wch have caused us to rune into so much charge, debts, & ingagements, as our estats & means were not able to goe on without impoverishing our selves, except our estats had been greater, and our associats cloven beter unto us. 2ly as here hath been a faction and siding amongst us now more then 2 years, so now there is an uter breach and sequestration amongst us, and in too parts of us a full dissertion and forsaking of you, without any intente or purpose of medling more with you. And though we are perswaded the maine cause of this their doing is wante of money (for neede whereof men use to make many excuses,) yet other things are pretended, as that you are Brownists, &c. Now what use you or we ought to make of these things, it remaineth to be considered for we know ye hand of God to be in all these things, and no doubt he would admonish some thing thereby, and to looke what is amise. And allthough it be now too late for us or you to prevent & stay these things, yet it is not too late to exercise patience, wisdom and conscience in bearing them, and in caring ourselves in & under them for ye time to come.

And as we ourselves stand ready to imbrace all occasions that may tend to ye furthrance of so hopefull a work, rather admiring of what is, than grudging for what is not; so it must rest in you to make all good againe. And if in nothing else you can be approved, yet let your honestie & conscience be still approved & lose not one jote of your innocencie amidst your crosses & afflictions. And surly if you upon this allteration behave yourselves wisly, and goe on fairly, as men whose hope is not in this life, you shall need no other weapon to wound your adversaries; for when your righteousness is revealed as ye light, they shall cover their faces with shame, that causlesly have sought your overthrow.

Now we think it but reason, that all such things as ther apertaine to the generall, be kept & preserved togeather, and rather increased dayly, then any way be dispersed or imbeseled away for any private ends or intents whatsoever. And after your necessities are served, you gather togeather such comodities as ye cuntrie yeelds, & send them over to pay debts & clear ingagements hear, which are not less than 1400 li. And we hope you will doe your best to free our ingagements, &c. Let us indeavor to keep a faire & honest course, and see what time will bring forth, and how God in his providence will worke for us. We are still perswaded you are ye people that must make a plantation in these remoate places when all other faile and returned. And your experience of Gods providence and preservation of you is such as we hope your harts will not faile you, though your friends should forsake you (which we ourselves shall not doe whilst we live, so long as your honestie so well appereth). Yet surly help would arise from some other place whilst you waite on God, with uprightnes, though we should leave you also.

And lastly be you all intreated to walke circumspectly, and carry yourselves so uprightly in all your ways, as yt no man may make just exceptions against you. And more especially that ye favour and countenance of God may be so toward you, as yt you may find abundante joye & peace even amids tribulations, that you may say with David, Though my father & mother should forsake me, yet ye Lord would take me up.

We have sent you hear some catle, cloath, hose, shoes, leather, &c., but in another nature then formerly as it stood us in hand to do; we have committed them to ye charge & custody of Mr. Allerton and Mr. Winslow, as our factours, at whose discretion they are to be sould, and comodities to be taken for them, as is fitting. And by how much ye more they will be chargable unto you, the better they had need to be husbanded, &c. Goe on, good friends, comfortably, pluck up your spirits, and quitte yourselves like men in all your difficulties that notwithstanding all displeasure and threats of men, yet ye work may goe on you are aboute, and not be neglected. Which is so much for ye glorie of God, and the furthrance of our countrie-men, as that a man may with more comforte spend his life in it, then live ye life of Mathusala, in wasting ye plentie of a tilled land, or eating ye fruite of a growne tree. Thus with harty salutations to you all, and harty prayers for you all, we lovingly take our leaves, this 18. of Des: 1624.

Your assured freinds to our powers,

J. S.　W. C.　T. F.　R. H. &c †"

† Probably James Shirley, William Collier, Thomas Fletcher and Robert Holland.

By 1630 all of the remaining interests of the London partners had been acquired by Hatherly, Beauchamp, Sherley and Andrews. The colonists during this time had been represented by Edward Winslow and Isaac Allerton, each of whom had made frequent voyages to the old country. In that year the latter had, while in London, aroused the suspicion of these four, that he was diverting his dealings with them for his own account, rather than for the people of Plymouth whose factor he was. The suspicion was well grounded. Allerton had purchased the ship "White Angel" with funds provided by Hatherly and the others who believed it to be for the joint account. † With this ship and another, the "Friendship," he had started from Bristol to engage upon a fishing trip. Tempests and high seas had driven both vessels back to port. They were then laden with general cargoes designed by Allerton, and suspected by Sherley, to be for trade with the newly settled colony of Massachusetts Bay, at Boston. When therefore Allerton set sail in the White Angel, Hatherly was sent by the London partners to accompany him in the Friendship. They were not sure of Allerton's faithlessness to his principals, and moreover if it were true, they had no wish that it should be known in Bristol and London. Hatherly arrived first at Boston ‡ and came directly to Plymouth bearing this letter:

"Gentlemen, Partners, and Loving Friends, etc.

Briefly thus: we have this year set forth a fishing ship, and a trading ship, which later we have bought; and so have disbursed a great deale of money, as may and will appear by the accounts. And because this ship (called the White Angel) is to acte 2. parts, (as I

---

† "The coming of ye White Angele on your occounte could not be more strange to you, than ye buying of her was to us; for you gave him commission that what he did you would stand to; we gave him none, and yet for his credite and your saks, payed what bills he charged on us, &c" A letter from Sherley to Governor Bradford dated November 19, 1631.—Bradford's History, page 337.

‡ July 14, 1630. Allerton in the White Angel, came eight days later.

may say,) fishing for bass, and trading; and that while Mr. Allerton was imployed aboute the trading, the fishing might suffer by carlesnes or neglecte of the sailors, we have entreated your and our loving friend, Mr. Hatherley, to goe over with him, knowing he will be a comforte to Mr. Allerton, a joye to you to see a carfull and loving friend, and a great stay to the business; and so great contente to us, that if it should please God the one should faile, (as God forbid) yet the other would keepe both recconings, and things uprighte. For we are now out great sumes of money, as they will acquainte you withall, etc. When we were out but 4. or 5. hundred pounds a peece, we looked not much after it, but left it to you, and your agente, (who, without flaterie, deserveth infinite thanks and comendations, both of you and us, for his pains, etc.); but now we are out double, nay, treble a peece, some of us, etc.; which makes us both write, and send over our friend, Mr. Hatherley, whom we pray you to entertaine kindly, of all which we doubt not of. The main end of sending him is to see the state and accountes of all the bussines, of all which we pray you informe him fully, though the ship and bussines wayte for it and him. For we should take it very unkindly that we should intreat him to take such a journey, and that, when it pleaseth God he returned, he could not give us contente and satisfaction in this perticuler, through defaulte of any of you. But we hope you will so order bussines, as neither he nor we shall have cause to complaine, but to doe as we ever have done, thinke well of you all, etc. I will not promise, but shall indeavor and hope to effecte the full desire, and grant of your patente, and that ere it be longe. I would not have you take anything unkindly. I have not write out of jeoloucie of any unjuste dealing. Be all you kindly saluted in the Lord, so I rest,   Yours in what I may,

March 25, 1630 (-31)   JAMES SHIRLEY"

Bradford expressed the feelings of the Pilgrims upon the receipt of this letter in the following words:—

"It needs not to be thought strange, that these things should amase and trouble them; first, that this fishing trip should be set out, and fraight with other mens goods, and scarce any of theirs; seeing their maine end was (as is rembered) to bring them a full supply, and their speatiall order not to sett out any excepte this was done. And now a ship to come on their accounte clear contrary to their both end and order, was a misterie they could not understand; and so much the worse, seeing she had such ill success as to lose both her voiage and provisions. The 2. thing, that another ship should be bought and sente out on new designes, a thing not so much as once thought on by any here, much less, not a word intimated or spoaken of by any here, either by word or leter, neither could they imagine why this should be. Bass fishing was never lookt at by them, but as soon as ever they heard on it, they looked at it as a vaine thing, that would certainly turne to loss. And for Mr. Allerton to follow any trade for them, it was never in their thoughts. And 3ly, that their friends should complaine of disbursements, and yet rune into shuch things, and charge of shiping and new projects of their owne heads, not only without, but against, all order and advice, was to them very strange. And 4ly, that all these matters of so great charg and imployments should be thus wrapped up in a breefe and obscure letter, they know not what to make of it."

Nor was the mystery cleared in the conference which was had between the Plymouth people and Hatherly and Allerton. The latter boldly told them that the "White Angel" did not belong to them nor to their account. Hatherly confirmed this saying that "Mr. Allerton laid downe this course, and put them (namely, Andrews, Beauchamp, Shirley and himself), on this projecte."

And herein Hatherly showed his very substantial interest in the Colony and its members, by announcing that the losses which the White Angel had sustained should be in no part borne by the Colony. On the other hand the voyage of the Friendship had been profitable. He

"tould them they need not be so much troubled, for he had her accounts here, and showed them that her first setting out came not much to exceed £600 as they might see by the accounte, which he showed them; and for this later viage, it would arrise to profite by ye fraight of ye goods, and ye salle of some katle which he shiped and had allready sould, & was to be paid for partly here & partly by bills into England, so as they should not have this put on their accounte at all, except they would. And for ye former, he had sould so much goods out of her in England, and imployed ye money in this 2 viage, as it together with such goods & implements as Mr. Allerton must neede aboute his fishing, would rise to a good parte of ye money; for he must have ye sallt and nets, allso spiks, nails, &c.; all of which would rise to nere 400 li.; so, with ye bearing of their parts of ye rest of the loses (which would not be much above 200 li) they would clear them of this whole accounte. Of which notion they were glad, not being willing to have any accounts lye upon them; but aboute their trade, which made them willing to harken thereunto, and demand of Mr. Hatherley how he could make this good, if they should agree their unto, he told them he was sent over as their agente, and had this order from them, that whatsoever he and Mr. Allerton did togeather, they stand to it; but they would not alow of what Mr. Alerton did alone, except they liked it; but if he did it alone, they would not gaine say it. Upon which they sould to him & Mr. Allerton all ye rest of ye goods, and gave them present possession of them; and a writing was made, and confirmed under both Mr. Hatherleys and Mr. Allertons hands, to ye effecte afforsaide. And Mr. Allerton, being best acquainted with ye people, sould away presently all shuch goods as he had no need of for fishing, as 9. shallop sails, made of good new canvas, and ye roads for them being all new, with sundry such usefull goods, for ready beaver, by Mr. Hatherley's allowance. And thus they thought they had well provided for themselves. Yet they rebuked Mr. Allerton very much for runing into these courses, fearing ye success of them"†.

The cargo of the Friendship did not turn out as profitable as Hatherly and the Plymouth people had expected. On the contrary, this particular venture proved a losing one and was, with the White Angel controversy, long a matter of dispute between them. While the Merchant Adventurers charged the forefathers thirty, forty and sometimes fifty per cent. interest on the money advanced upon their joint venture or "generall," as it was called, the latter were quite ready to make the most extravagant claims upon questionable grounds, when by so doing, their own financial interests would be benefited. Yet Governor Bradford, probably voicing the sentiment of all the others, writes in the highest terms of appreciation of "Mr. Hatherley's honest word;" and of Mr. Sherley, "I believe he never would side in any perticuler trade which he conceived would wrong ye plantation and eate up & destroy ye generall."

Hatherly remained in New England for a little more than a year. He returned to London in the White Angel, accompanying Mr. Allerton ‡ and arriving in November 1631. Undoubtedly he had now made up his mind to take up his permanent abode in the Plymouth Colony. He came finally for this purpose in the Charles of Barnstable, England arriving here on June 5, 1632 §. Bradford records his arrival and says:—

"Mr. Hatherley came over again this year, but upon

---

† Bradford's History page 324.
‡ Bradford History page 335.
§ From "A booke of Entrie for Passengers &c., passing beyond the seas, begun at Christmas 1631 and ending at Christmas 1632".

his owne occasions, and begune to make preparation to plant & dwell in ye countrie. He with his former dealings had wound in what money he had in ye partnership into his owne hands, and so gave off all partnership (except in name), as was found in ye issue of things; neither did he medle or take any care aboute ye same; only he was troubled about his ingagements aboute ye Friendship. x x x And now partly about yt accounte, in some reconings betweene Mr. Allerton and him, and some debts yt Mr. Allerton otherwise owed him, upon dealing between them in perticuler, he drue up an accounte of above £2000, and would faine have ingaged ye partners here with it, because Mr. Allerton had been their agent. But they (the Plymouth people) tould him they had been fool'd longe enough with such things, and showed him yt it no way belonged to them; but tould him he must looke to make good his ingagement for ye Friendship, which caused some trouble betweene Mr. Allterton and him.†"

Hatherly already had in Plymouth some live stock which he had brought in the Friendship two years before and part of which he had sold there. He brought with him in the Charles two men servants ‡ and staid at Plymouth upwards of a year §. In 1633 he had "made choice" for himself and Beauchamp, Shirley and Andrews of the land lying north of Satuit Brook, between that stream and the Gulph, and had taken out of it for cultivation by and for himself a farm near Musquashcut Pond.

---

† Bradford History page 360. Two years before, when the Friendship adventure had apparently shown a profit, the Plymouth colonists had evinced a willingness to ratify Allerton's action in chartering the vessel. Now that it was certain that a loss had been sustained they repudiated it.

‡ "Mr. Hatherlies two men" were "rated for publick use
  I : S : d
  00 18 00   March 25, 1633. Plymouth Colony
                              Records Vol I Page 10.

§ Ibidem page 14.

None of the New England historians † speak of but one marriage by Hatherly,—that to the widow of his friend Nathaniel Tilden. Rev. John Lothrop, the first pastor, in giving a list of the members of his congregation in 1634, includes "Mr. Hatherley and wife," Jan. 11, 1634. On the fourteenth day of January 1640 when he conveyed the whole of the first cliff to Thomas Ensign for twenty-eight pounds, Susan Hatherly, though not mentioned in the body of the deed, signed it with him. In addition to the two sons mentioned by William T. Davis there was surely one daughter born of this first marriage,—Susanna who married a Dunham at Plymouth and upon his death, William Brooks of Scituate.

Of course, a man of Hatherly's activity and abilities could not long remain in the new and struggling community without public recognition. In 1635 he was chosen an Assistant and continued in that important office until 1658, with the exception of one year. For some reason, which has never appeared, he refused to accept his election in 1638. On the fifth day of June of that year, when the others gathered at Plymouth to be sworn into office, Hatherly declined and the Court entered upon its record:—

"Because Mr. Tymothy Hatherley was elected to the office of an Assistant the last Court & will not take the said place upon him, Mr. John Browne, being next in the number of votes, was by the generall consent elected to the office of an Assistant in his stead; and for the fyne ‡ Mr. Hatherley is thereby lyable unto, the Court will further consider whether the same shalbe esteated or noe."

It was not "esteated" and soon forgotten. The next

---

† William T. Davis in his "Ancient Landmarks of Plymouth" says (Page 131);— "He m. a 2nd wife, Lydia, wid. of Nathaniel Tilden" 1642, and had no children. He may have had by 1st wife, a son Arthur, who was in Plymouth in 1660, and a son, Thomas, of Boston.

‡ "That if any elected to the office of Assistant refuse to hold according to the election, that then he be amerced in ten pounds starling fyne." Plymouth Colony Records (Laws) Vol XI page 10.

year he was willing to serve, and in addition, was chosen Treasurer of the Colony. He was authorized to solemnize marriages; to "Issue warrants for actions and administer oaths" and to empanel juries to lay out highways in Scituate. He was one of the committee to let the colony fishing trade at Kennebec; a member of the Council of War; and was requested to see that the military company at Scituate "exercise in arms" and engage in regular and sufficient training. These were among the more serious duties which he performed. He was often called upon to do other things of a trifling importance, less dignified in their execution, but of a substantial and real value to both town and colony. For instance, Mary, the wife of Walter Briggs of Scituate, having been indicted for telling a lie, "the Court having examined particulars about it, have cleared the said Mary Briggs, but desired Mr. Hatherly from the Court to admonish her to be more wary of giving occasion of offence to others, by unnecessary talking to the occasion of others to complaine or raise such aspersions." Again, he was requested by the Court "to make inquiry concerning a stray stier which is at Thomas Tilden's near North River in Marshfield, which stier Mistress Richards layeth claim to." He was also "ordered to set at right such things as concern Thomas Rawlins & John Damman by reason of costs and charges" by the former upon land of the latter's uncle, William Gilson. And again, James Till of Plymouth a servant of Mr. Hanbury, being sent to Scituate with two hides to be delivered to Humphrey Turner, the tanner, he sold them to Joseph Tilden "for sixteen shillings, less than half their worth." Thereupon the Court ordered that "James Till shall dwell two years now next ensuing with Mr. Tymothy Hatherley," who was to see six pounds a year "bestowed upon him for his necessary apparell and to give an account thereof to the Court; that if anything remayne it may be payed to the country towards the satisfaction of his (Till's) bonds for breach of his good behavior."

In June 1650, Hatherly was licensed by the Court to set

up an iron mill on land "lying between the path and the ponds betwixt Namassakeeset † and Indian Head Rivers, "within three years." Davis in his Ancient Landmarks of Plymouth ‡ says that it was accomplished, but the earlier chronicler bearing the same surname, states that:—"It did not however take place at that period, but a smelting furnace was erected upon the precise grant, by Mark Despard and the family of Barker about 1702" §. He was one of the committee "to review the lawes and reduce them to such order as they may conduce to the benefit of the government." On September 27, 1642, he with Edward Winslow and Miles Standish "are deputed and authorized by the Generall Court, this day to treate and conclude with such Commissioners as the Governor and Court of Massachusetts shall appoynt for that purpose, upon such heads and propositions as the Lord shall direct them for our combineing together mutually in a defensive and offensive warr for our present defence against the intended surprisall of the natives;

---

† The Mattakeeset River in Pembroke. The "Path" referred to crossed Indian Head River at "Ludden's" or Luddam's ford. Governor Winthrop in his journal (Vol I Page 92) records his return trip to Boston after a visit to Plymouth in 1632. "About five in the morning the Governor (Winthrop) and his company came out of Plymouth; the Governor of Plimouth, with the pastor and elder &c. accompanying them near half a mile out of town in the dark. The Lieut. Holmes with two others and the governor's mare came along with them to the great swamp about ten miles. When they came to the great river, they were carried over by one Luddam their guide, (as they had been when they came, the stream being very strong, and up to the crotch) so the governor called that passage Luddam's Ford. Thence they came to a place called Hue's Cross. The Governor being displeased at the name, in respect that such things might hereafter give the Papists occasion to say, that their religion was first planted in these parts, changed the name and called it Hue's Folly". Winthrop's editor Savage calls this a "slight usurpation" or jurisdiction for the reason that the Governor was in another colony. Governor Winthrop in doing so was under the mistaken idea that the name had reference to the papal insignia. It did not. The place was called Hewes' Cross Brook from the crossing of the First Herring Brook and a small stream. John Hewes lived there. He was both a Welchman and a freeman, but never a Papist. Savage in making his mild criticism probably overlooked this.
‡ Page 147.
§ History and Description of Scituate, 1815, by Samuel Davis.

and also to treate & conferr with them about a further combination & league to be concluded betwixt us for future tymes, & to certyfy this Court of the heads thereof, that upon our approbation of the same they may be confirmed by a Generall Court".† Thus was Hatherly a pioneer in the negotiations which finally crystalized into the Commissioners of the United Colonies, a body with which he was later prominently indentified. On June 4, 1645, "Mr. Tymothy Hatherley is chosen to supply Mr. Princes roome in the comission for the United Collonies, if Mr. Prence be not able, who is now very sick. He was again chosen in 1646 and 1651.

Hatherly was a man of great generosity. He was liberal in thought and with his gifts. Like his near neighbor and warm friend Cudworth, while failing to agree with the Quakers, he was nevertheless tolerant of their presence in both the town and colony, and being ready and outspoken, this stand lost to him much of the public confidence at the time. He was no longer made an Assistant and during the last ten years of his life, with the one notable service on the committee to revise the laws of the colony, he performed no important public function. He died in 1666, his estate impoverished through his own generosity. He had given the parsonage house and land to the church, and his farm at Musquashcut to that body and the society; he had offered a comfortable home and farm to Reverend Mr. Chauncey, whose faithful friend and loyal supporter he had been, when the latter contemplated returning to England, if he would remain at Scituate; to the Conihasset partners he gave the major part of his tract nine miles square lying southerly of Accord Pond and many a worthy friend and neighbor profited in other ways by his unostentatious kindness. His will, ‡ made on the twentieth day of December 1664 was probated on October 30, 1666. It follows:—

"I, Timothy Hatherley of Scituate, being weake and

† Plymouth Colony Records Vol II Page 88
‡ Plymouth Colony Records. Wills Vol. II (part 2) Page 34.

sicke in body but of sound and stedfast memory, blessed be God, doe make This as my last Will and Testament, in manner and form as followeth:—

Imprimis, I commend my soul to God that gave it and my body to the earth from whence it came. As for my worldly goods with which the Lord hath blessed me I do dispose of the same as follows:—

Item. I give unto my wife Lydia Hatherley my house I now dwell in with the rest of the housing thereto belonging, with all the land I die possessed of during her natural life. Also I give to her my silver plate and all my pewter and brass that I do not otherwise dispose of by will; also what moveables there are and my linen. Furthermore I give unto my wife my gray mare, two cows and two oxen and my coat with all my wearing clothes.

Item. I give to Edward Jenkins, his wife and children twelve pounds to be paid within one year after my decease in current New England pay.

Item. I give to Nicholas Wade his wife and children twelve pounds to be paid within one year after my decease in current New England pay as also one great brass kittle.

Item. I give to Susanna, the wife of William Brooks and her children twelve pounds and I acquit her of her first husband's debt to me. And also one copper kettle with three eares, to be payed within one year after my death.

Item. I give to Timothy Foster five pounds and to Elizabeth Foster three pounds in current New England pay within one year from my decease.

I give to Thomas Hanford ten pounds to be payed within one year after my decease in current New England pay.

Item. I give to Joan Robinson, the wife of Samuel Baker forty shillings, and to the other three children of Nath'l Robinson, John, Nathaniel and Christopher forty shillings apeice to be payed within one year after my decease in current New England pay.

Item. I give to Lydia Garrett my wife's daughter, three acres of land part of which her house stands on, unto her and her heirs forever. And five pounds in current pay of New England within one year after my decease and likewise acquit all former accounts and reckonings between she and I, from the beginning of the world to this day.

I give to the four children of the said Lydia Garrett forty shillings apeice to be payed to them by my Executors when they come to the age of twenty-one years in current pay of New England.

Item. I give to George Sutton his wife and children five pounds to be payed in current New England pay.

Item. I give to the widow Prebble my wife's daughter fifty shillings to be paid within one year after my decease in current New England pay. I give to Lydia Lapham one heiffer worth fifty shillings or fifty shillings in good goods, to be payed within one year after my decease.

Item. I give to Thomas Lapham thirty shillings to be paid within one year after my decease in current New England pay.

Item. I give to Christopher Tilden five pounds to be paid within one year after my decease in current New England pay.

Item. I give to Nicholas Baker eight pounds to be payed in six month after my decease.

Item. I give to my man Thomas Savery fifty shillings to be payed when his service expires in current New England pay.

Item. I give to Lydia Hatch the daughter of William Hatch eight pounds to be payed by my Executors when she comes to the age of twenty-one years in current New England pay or when she marries.

All the rest of my goods and lands not given and

bequeathed, my debts and legacies payed and funerall charges discharged, I give and bequeath unto my highly and well beloved friend Joseph Tilden whom I doe constitute and appoint to be the whole and alone Executor of this my last will and testament.

In witness whereof, I the said Timothy Hatherley have hereunto set my hand and seal this twentieth day of December Anno Dom. 1664.

TIMOTHY HATHERLY and a (seal).

Signed and sealed
in sight and presence
of Nicholas Baker
Nath'l Chittenden."

When this will was offered for probate Joseph Tilden the Executor declined to serve, and thereby was revealed a situation which for a time portended a contest over that document. Standing alone the Court record made at the time is inexplicable. It says:—

"Whereas Mr. Timothy Hatherly by his last will and testament, hath made, ordained, and appointed Mr. Joseph Tilden to be his sole exequitor; and the said Joseph Tilden doth refuse to accept of the said exequitorship according to the said will; wherefore the Court have appointed him to be administrator on the estate of the said Mr. Hatherly, to pay all debts and legacies due and owing from the estate so farr and by equall proportions as it will amount unto;" and at the sitting held June fifth 1667:— "Letters of adminestration were likewise granted unto Mr. Joseph Tilden to adminnester upon the estate of Mr. Timothy Hatherly deceased; and the said Mr. Tilden is hereby ordered and impowered to receive and dispose of the said estate in reference unto payment of debts and legacies due from the estate soe farr as there is estate to discharge, and in all points to act and do whatever may be requisite for preserving and disposing as an adminnestrator according to the will of the deceased." † The personal estate was appraised at £224; 12 S: 08d., not to mention £116 due him from John Hollett, James Cudworth and Rodolphus Elmes. The legacies were but £107. These were made to various friends; to all of his wife's children, and to his own relatives—Thomas Hanford a nephew, Susanna Brooks, who called herself a niece, Timothy Foster and John Robinson grand nephews, and Joan Robinson and Elizabeth Foster, grand nieces." ‡ To certain of them specific devises of land were made. When the will was offered for Probate, on the thirty-first day of October, 1666, they did not know, and Tilden did not inform them, that only a few days before, on October thirteenth, Hatherly had conveyed to his wife's son, the same Joseph Tilden who is named as Executor of his will, for a "valuable and sufficient consideration," his farm on the southerly side of Satuit Brook and one hundred and thirty acres which remained of the four hundred acres "layed out to" it. Included in the deed were Hatherly's remaining Conihasset shares. In fact all the real estate which he possessed. Tilden had simultaneously executed and delivered to Hatherly a bond § in the sum of "£100 good and current silver money," conditioned to "suffer Timothy Hatherley and Lydia Hatherley ¶ to severally and jointly possess and enjoy the use, benefit and profits of the housings and lands made mention of in the above deed, during the full term of their natural lives, without any disturbance or molestation."

Why such a transaction should have taken place so near to the time of Hatherly's death, when it may fairly be presumed that he knew his own days were few, is not at all clear. The will provided the same life tenancy for his widow as did Tilden's bond. Under the will the latter, being the residuary legatee and devisee, would have taken

---

† Plymouth Colony Records Vol IV Pages 138 and 155.
‡ Plymouth Colony Records (Deeds) Vol III pages 92 to 97 and 315.
§ Plymouth Colony Records (Deeds) Vol. III pages 103 and 104.
¶ Tilden's mother.

by far the greater portion of the estate. Perhaps Tilden sought to take the whole of the real property and a larger residuum of the personal. If so he was disappointed. Nephew Hanford, upon learning the situation immediately raised objection and threatened a contest. For six years the matter was in controversy. Meantime Tilden had conveyed all of the Hatherly real estate which he obtained through the above deed, to his sons Nathaniel and John, and had deceased. Finally, a settlement was made by which Hanford received twice what was given him under the will, and the relatives and all other legatees were paid the same sums which that instrument provided. The whole story is best told in the language of the release which Hanford gave in June 1673:—

"To all men to whom these present shall come, I Thomas Hanford of Norwalk in the jurisdiction of Connecticut, Pastour, being the alone son of Eglin Seallis † deceased, who was the natural sister of my unkle Mr. Timothy Hatherly deceased, and so by virtue of the near relation by blood, I the said Thomas Hanford do lay claim as heir unto the lands of my unkle Mr. Timothy Hatherly deceased, and the said Mr. Timothy Hatherly having made some conveyance of his land unto Mr. Joseph Tilden deceased as appears by a deed bearing date the thirteenth day of October 1666, one thousand six hundred and sixty-six. The said Joseph Tilden has conveyed the same alsoe to his two sonnes Nathaniel and John Tilden and so there is a difference and contest like to arise between the said Tildens and me the said Thomas Hanford. Wherefore Know You, that I, the said Thomas Hanford for and in consideration of twenty pounds to me in hand paid, before the sealing and delivery of these presents, by the said Nathaniel and John Tilden, twelve pounds thereof in current silver money and eight pounds

---

† Hatherly had already given this sister land in Scituate. Her first husband was Hanford's father. Upon his death she married Edward Foster and for her third husband Deacon Richard Sealis.

thereof in current English goods at Marchants prices at Boston; and also that there may be a composed and settled peace and quiet between me the said Thomas Hanford and Nathaniel Tilden and John Tilden, in, about, concerning and respecting the premises aforesaid; with which said sum and in consideration that peace and amity may be continued betwixt us if well & fully satisfied, contented and paid, and do exonerate, acquit and discharge the said Nathaniel Tilden and John Tilden, they and either of them, their and every of their heirs, Executors and administrators forever, do by this present writing, sealed with my seal and subscribed with my name in the presence of Richard Collicut and Edward Jenkins and James Cudworth, three credible witnesses whose names are subscribed to allow, ratify and confirm from me and my heirs, unto them, the said Nathaniel and John, them and their heirs and assigns forever, all the housing and lands, both upland and meadow expressed in the aforesaid deed from Timothy Hatherly, together with all the . . estate that doth or may belong to the heirs of the said Timothy Hatherly, for them the said Nathaniel Tilden and John Tilden, their heirs and assigns forever.   x x x x Dated this seventh day of June in the year of our Lord God one thousand six hundred seventy and three." †

Hatherly's place in the foundation of the Pilgrim Republic has usually, historically, been circumscribed by the bounds of the town which he founded, and of which he is described as the "father." Baylies who gives him this title says of the leaders who came in the Mayflower:

"It was only by the consummate prudence of Bradford the matchless valor of Standish, the incessant enterprise of Winslow that the colony was saved from destruction. The submissive piety of Brewster, indeed, produced a

---

† Plymouth Colony Records (Deeds) Vol III P. 315.

moral effect as important in its consequences as the active virtues of the others."

But what of the generous and able assistance which Hatherly gave to the little colony and its agent Winslow, in his own "incessant enterprise" to save it from "destruction." The latter made frequent necessary trips from Plymouth to the old country when disputes arose between the colonists and their financial sponsors, the Merchant Adventurers. Hatherly's purse was always open, his voice ever raised in support of the Pilgrims, and his activities directed to their welfare. Neither was he averse to share with them the physical hardships and dangers of the wilderness. In the ten years before permanently settling in Scituate, he lived at Plymouth more than half the time. Through him, the selfish and traitorous Peirce was exposed, and eliminated from the Adventurers. When dissatisfaction and disagreements in this partnership arrived at the dissolving point, it was Hatherly with Shirley, Beauchamp and Andrews who bought out the interests of the disaffected ones and became voluntarily liable for bringing out of Leyden many of the friends and brethren who had lingered there, awaiting an opportunity to join the voyagers of the Mayflower in their new home.

It was Hatherly who helped out the trusting Bradford and his neighbors when they had become involved with the no-longer-to-be-trusted Allerton. His generosity enabled them to square accounts with the successors to their original sponsors. His wisdom foresaw the benefits to be derived in a confederation of the struggling colonies. His diplomacy was invoked in many a trying situation. Yet, to the discredit of those whom he thus served—he was driven out of their counsels when his broad humanity led him to differ with them in the treatment of the Quakers.

By his example he taught tolerance, thrift, courage and devotion. None of the forefathers did more.

THE CLAPPS

The Clapps (or Clap as they spelled it) came from Dorchester in old England to the locality to which they gave the same name in New England. Thomas, the Scituate ancestor, came first to Hingham and then to Scituate in 1640.

In 1645 he purchased from Timothy Hatherly a farm of twenty-four acres at Greenbush adjoining that of Samuel Hinckley, the father of the governor. On these acres and in their vicinity his descendants have ever since had their abode. His children were Thomas, who went to Dedham, Eleazer, afterwards a resident of Barnstable; John, who died in youth; three daughters, Elizabeth, Prudence and Abigail, and Samuel who set the pace for prominence and public spirit in Scituate for those of his name who succeeded him. He married Hannah Gill of Hingham and lived on the farm at Greenbush, which his father bought of Hatherly.

With Thomas King and Theophilus Witherell, two of his neighbors living near the North River, and Ephraim Little and John Rogers of Marshfield, he was engaged in trade with the West Indies, the owner of the "good barque called the Adventure, of burden about forty tun," and thus early did much to give impetus to the shipbuilding which later developed upon that estuary.

He was a selectman of Scituate in the decade which followed the year 1682 and at the same time acted continuously as a deputy to the General Court at Plymouth. For sixteen years he served in a like capacity in the legislature of the Province. He was as popular with and respected by his fellow legislators as his townspeople. He served upon the most important committees and especially in matters of finance. In 1695, with the Treasurer of the Province and the famous John Walley he was appointed to report to the Privy Council in London "what quantities of Pitch, Tar, Rozin, Planke, Knee Timber and other Naval Stores for the use of his Majesty's Royal Navy &c the Government here may undertake to send yearly to England," and thereafter for a long time the export of these stores was based upon the recommendation of this committee. He had a large part in framing the legislation which was enacted in 1705 to prevent the debasing of the colonial currency. During the latter years of his legislative service he was annually chosen one of the "committee to view the work at the Castle," when the reconstruction of that fortification in the inner harbor of Boston, was put in charge of the engineer William Wolfgang Romer. He laid out the first turnpike from Middleborough and Bridgewater to Boston and acted as one of the two commissioners appointed by the General Court to levy and assess the tax for the French and Indian War. In the performance of these duties he found time to serve upon juries and to act as an inspector and viewer of whales and to be a town constable.

Two grandsons of Samuel Clapp, each named Thomas, have brought fair fame to the family. Col. Thomas Clapp, son of Samuel's fourth son John, born in 1705, was graduated at Harvard and educated for the ministry. Ordained and settled over the first church at Taunton, he soon tired of his pastorate and returned to Scituate. Here he was elected to the legislature for eight years, not however consecutively. Less prominent in that body than his grandfather had been, he was however a member of the first committee of the General Court to farm out the excise when that duty, having theretofore been rather scandalously performed by a commission, was intrusted to the law making body. As early as 1697, the practice of selling the revenue arising from licensing traffic in intoxicating liquors, or "farming out the excise" as it was called, had been in vogue. The law † provided:—

> "and that the said commissioners may lett or farme the excise, or any part thereof, to any person or persons, in any county, town or place within this province, for

---

† Acts of 1697 Chap. 3 Section 13.

the best profit and advantage of the publick that they can for the year ensuing."

During the years which ensued up to 1755, when the personnel was changed, the "profit and advantage" may have been all that the public could desire. In that year, for all sufficient reasons a change was decreed, the commissioners were deposed and the House with such as the Honorable Council should join appointed its own committee. To this duty Thomas Clapp, having discarded his vestments and put on the uniform of a militia colonel was chosen, with Elisha Barrow of Rochester. John Cushing was added by the Council. They sold the revenue in Plymouth County to Seth Bryant for £320 and that in Suffolk was knocked off to the patriot Samuel Adams for £2013: 063 :08d.

In 1743, he was made a judge of the Court of Common Pleas for Plymouth County and held this office acceptably for thirty-seven years.

The other Thomas was a son of Deacon Stephen Clapp born in 1703 and graduated from "the College at Cambridge" at the age of nineteen. Four years later he was ordained at Windham, Connecticut and preached to that congregation for fourteen years. In 1740 he was chosen "Rector of the College at New Haven."

He came to the college at a time when the revivalist Whitefield and the Evangelist Jonathan Edward were seeking to create a general religious awakening and restore the church to the real place of respect and power which it formerly held and from which they maintained that it had fallen. Clapp and the Rev. Joseph Noyes, a representative New Haven clergyman of the time, with others violently disagreed with Whitefield and Edwards. They sturdily maintained that neither the church nor religion had fallen into decay and decried the work in which the revivalist and his assistant were engaged, as calculated to work a distinct disadvantage to both. A war of pamphlets between them ensued. The clergy and the laity each became aroused and separated into two political parties— the evangelists calling themselves the "New Lights" and those of the clergy held responsible for the alleged decline in the power and position of the church the "Old Lights."

Clapp, under whose ministrations it was claimed that religious fervor had languished, was of the latter. It was said of him and the other ministers, that:—"their preaching lacked point and earnestness, and application; their devotional services were without warmth and unction; that their labors were not blessed by the Holy Spirit; their people slumbered; the tone of religious life and sentiment, was sinking; and true godliness seemed fast retiring from the land." †

He naturally resented this outspoken criticism and being in a position of power manifested his displeasure by expelling three of the college students who had attended meetings of the revivalists. This was one of his first acts as Rector. It brought him particularly and prominently to the notice of the Old Light party which was then in the political ascendency in Connecticut. It at once adopted and made much of him. The advantage thus obtained, he shrewdly made use of—but for the benefit of the college. In May 1745 he obtained for it from the legislature of Connecticut a broader and more appropriate charter. By this charter the trustees were incorporated under the name of "the President and Fellows of Yale College in New Haven." From this date the name of Yale, which had therefore strictly belonged only to the College Hall, became the name of the College itself. It was Thomas Clapp who gave legal permanency to that which, under Dr. Woolsey had been the name of the "spiritual body" only.

He did more. He obtained from the legislature, grants of public monies and permission to set up a lottery to reap additional funds. With both of these he built the dormitory called Connecticut Hall and the Chapel.

---

† Yale College, edited by William L. Kingsley. New York, Henry Holt & Co., 1879. Vol I Page 68.

In another year it became apparent to him that the New Lights had fully shot their denunciatory bolts. Always honest with himself, a little introspection persuaded him that he had really fallen to a low plane in his religious enthusiasm and fervor. The awakening was characteristic of the man. At the commencement of the revival, under the idea of repressing the fanaticism of the followers and imitators of Whitefield and the disorganizing tendency of their proceedings, he had thrown himself and had been received into the party of the Old Lights. He now saw his mistake—that notwithstanding the disorders which had accompanied the great religious awakenings the good had preponderated over the evil. The members of the Old Lights seemed really to have lost their earnestness and to have become indifferent to religion.

Always a great friend of the college, and anxiously seeking its welfare, he was fearful lest the supremacy of his faction should work to the detriment of that institution. This primarily, and his own honesty and openness of mind, led him gradually to reach a conclusion which eventually allied him with his former opponents.

Having once taken this position he began to reconstruct upon a sure and firm basis. He persuaded the corporation to appropriate £28:10S sterling to procure a public Professor of Divinity in the college and was later installed in the position himself. He did much for the spiritual life of the college from this vantage point and continued his practical interest in the educational side as well.

These activities, his bold change of front and his arbitrary action upon occasion, of course made him enemies which grew in numbers as the members of the Old Light party began to realize that he was not only deserting them but was gaining and enjoying the same popularity among his new friends that he had formerly held with them.

They began the attack. They alleged that he was arbitrary in governing the college, which was probably true, and in his treatement of the students,—which was quite as probably untrue. They said, without the slightest semblance of truth, that he fixed the annual expenses of the undergraduates at a grossly exorbitant figure, in order that he might thereby carry forward the ambitious plans which he had for the enlargement and advancement of the college.

Finally in 1763 they had made such progress toward undermining him, that a numerously signed memorial was presented to the Legislature in which that body was asked to enact a law providing for:—

"an appeal from any and every sentence given by the authority of the College (President Clapp), to the Governor and Council of the colony for the time being, and that the said Legislature would immediately issue forth a Committee of Visitation, enabling some suitable persons to inquire into all the affairs of said College and either of themselves rectify all abuses which they may discover, or make report of what they shall find, with their opinions thereon to the Assembly at their next session."

In the fight which followed the presentation of this memorial, the ablest jurists of the colony were arrayed upon its side. Clapp was alone but undismayed. He denied that the Legislature was either the founder of the college or that it had in any sense authority of visitation over it. He was blazing the way for Webster's tremendous argument fifty-five years later in the Dartmouth College case. He tactfully told the Assembly, "that our especial respect and gratitude is due to it as the great benefactors of the college," "but", he thundered back "the ministers who made the first donations in 1700 were its founders. They were its lawful visitors and that right of visitation passed to the trustees under the charter and now resides in the President and Fellows."

He successfully impressed this view upon his auditors. The Assembly supported him. As he himself naively put it:—

"When these arguments were considered by the honorable the General Assembly, but very few appeared to be of the opinion that the Assembly were the founders of the College, and so they acted nothing upon the memorial; and it is generally supposed that this question will never be publicly moved again."

It never was. The Scituate clergyman had saved to its patrons and the country the foundation stones of a great university. He had upheld the enunciation of Lord Mansfield "that the corporations of the universities are lay corporations, and that the crown cannot take away from them any rights that have been formerly subsisting in them under old charters or prescriptive usage." He had won for himself the encomiums of the matchless Webster and the great English Chancellor Kent who said of his argument seventy years later, "He grounded himself upon English authorities in the true style of a well read lawyer."

He had saved Yale College; but he did not live to see it benefit by his labor. The enemies which he had made continued to attack both him and the institution—not openly but insidiously, until his health was broken and at the end of three years he resigned.

He died at New Haven, January 7, 1767. As his enemies also passed away a true appreciation of his great devotion, his honesty and loyalty became uppermost and fixed.

The stone placed by a succeeding and appreciative generation to his memory bears this inscription:—

"Here lyeth interred the body of the revered and learned Mr. Thomas Clap, the late President of Yale College in New Haven; a truly great man, a gentleman of superior natural genious, most assiduous application and indefatigable industry. In the various branches of learning he greatly excelled; an accomplished instructor; a patron of the College; a great divine, bold for the truth; a zealous promoter and defender of the doctrines of grace; of unaffected piety, and a pattern of every virtue; the tenderest of fathers and best of friends; the glory of learning and ornament of religion;

for thirteen years the faithful and much respected pastor of the Church in Windham; and near twenty-seven years, the laborious and principal President of the College and served his own generation by the will of God. With serenity and calmness he fell on sleep the 8th day of January 1767 in his sixty-fourth year.

> "Death, great proprietor of all,
> 'Tis thine to tread our empires,
> And to quench the stars."

THE TURNERS

The progenitors of the family of Turner whose members have found so many important places in the life of the town, the colony, the province and of the Commonwealth was Humphrey, a tanner who came out of Devonshire in 1628 to New Plymouth. He built a house there and remained for five years. In 1633 he sold it to Josias Winslow for eight pounds. The price paid ($26.662-3) affords very accurate evidence of the crudity of the structure which he and his family called home. The one in Scituate to which he brought them the same year was of the same type and not much better. It was on the Driftway. He also had the fourth lot on Kent Street. Three years later he had a grant of eighty acres from the Colony Court on the North River near the present Union Bridge in Norwell. Here he erected the first tannery in the Colony † and for years received the hides from all the Pilgrim farmers until a "leather mill" was erected upon Town brook in Plymouth by Nathaniel Thomas. ‡

When he left Plymouth for Scituate he was amicably "dismissed" from the church body of the former place, in case he, Annable, Gilson, Foster, Rowley and Cobb who came with, or had immediately preceded him, "join in a body at Scituate." He was one of the seventeen organizers of the church here under the pastorate of Mr. Lothrop.

His family consisted of eight children. No mention is made of his wife in the enumeration of the members of the First Church by its minister, although those of the others who were married appear in the list. Neither is there any record of her death to be found. Winsor says that she was Lydia Gainer and deceased before her husband. The children were John, Senior, so-called, Joseph, John call-

---

† Plymouth Colony Records Vol II Page 68.
‡ Davis,—Ancient Landmarks of Plymouth Page 144.

THE HUMPHREY TURNER MONUMENT,
Meetinghouse Lane Cemetery, Scituate.

ed by his father "young John" † and by others John Junior, Daniel, Nathaniel, Thomas, Mary, the second wife of William Barker and Lydia, the wife of James Doughty.

When the town was incorporated, the father of this family at once was called into public affairs. He was a constable, a surveyor of highways, a grand and a traverse juryman. In the latter capacity he sat upon the first jury impannelled in the colony to try a white man for the murder of an Indian. John Billington of Plymouth had been hanged after a jury trial, eight years before (1630) for the murder of his neighbor Newcome or New-Comin, but the indictment of Thomas Jackson, Richard Stinnings, Arthur Peach and Daniel Crosse for the robbery and murder of the Indian Penowanyanquis on the trial of which Humphrey Turner sat, was the first opportunity offered the forefathers to show Massasoit their ability and willingness to scrupulously keep their treaty faith with him. The trial took place before Governor Prence, William Bradford, Edward Winslow, Miles Standish and John Alden and John Jenney ‡, John Browne and John Atwood, Assistants. Upon the jury with Turner sat Edward Foster, the lawyer, Elder William Hatch and Richard Sealis, his neighbors, John Peabody, a first citizen of Duxbury, John Winslow, the son of the Governor, and Samuel Hinckley, whose son Thomas was afterward the colony's chief executive. Cross broke jail and escaped, but the others had sentence of death pronounced; "vizt, to be taken from the place where they were to the place from whence they came, and thence to the place of execution, and there to be hanged by the neck

---

† The historians of Scituate, Duxbury and Hanover have referred to this son as "young son John" and allege that he was so named at the request of a godfather. Savage has it that this is mere tradition and says "but such folly should not have been allowed" (Gen. Reg. Vol IV Page 346). His father referred to him as "my son young John Turner". (Plymouth Colony Records (Wills) Vol III P 71.)

‡ The American ancestry of Judge Charles H. Jenney of the Superior Court of Massachusetts.

untill their bodyes were dead, which was executed accordingly."

From 1640 for fourteen years consecutively, save for the year 1643, Humphrey Turner was a deputy from Scituate to the Colony Court and meantime was commissioned by that body and the town to perform important public duties. He assisted in fixing the bounds of the Hatherly grant made by Prence and Collier; was on the committee to dispose of the land on the "Two Miles" to the residents thereon; designated with two others to settle the uncertain bounds of the land of William Randall and active in protecting the "common lands" of the town against trespassers.

The provisions of his will give an excellent insight into his chararter, and contradict as well the very prevalent impression, that the pilgrim parent was a stern and unforgiving one. Humphrey Turner's second son Joseph was a scape-goat and ne'er-do-well. He had been "found guilty of many abominable crimes;" had been arrested and escaped from the custody of the under marshal thereby causing the dismissal of that functionary from office; had participated in riotous trespasses and with an unbridled tongue had traduced the wives and sisters of his neighbors. He had frequently been in the turbulence which ensued from these actions, before the death of his father; and that parent well knew his propensity for trouble. Like so many affectionate fathers since, and lacking the same good judgment, he gave to this son the greatest portion out of his personal estate, more than four times that given to his eldest son. It did him no good. Just before his father died he was sued for slander by Charles Stockbridge and his wife, and a judgment of one hundred pounds recovered against him. The record does not recite that the execution which issued thereon was satisfied. He was also sued by John Jacob for a similar cause of action. He married Bathsheba, the daughter of Peter Hobart of Hingham †and perhaps the influence of this lady produced a change for the better.

---

† Savage, Gen. Reg. Vol IV Page 347.

He certainly, through this or other means, had established himself in the confidence of his neighbors in 1673 and had entered Phillip's War in the capacity of ensign. He joined the expedition against the Narragansetts and being severely wounded was invalided home. The town then "chose Serj. John Damon to go with Joseph Turner and procure a cure for him; also to support him at the Town's expense so long as he liveth." He refused thus to be made a pauper; but recovering sufficiently from his wounds through the "cure" which his neighbor Damon had obtained for him, rejoined the troops now led by Governor Josias Winslow in person, and with him was in the battle at Narragansett Fort December 19, 1675. In 1681 he was "freed from training" by the Colony Court on account of his first service. †

The eldest son of Humphrey Turner, John, married Mary, the granddaughter of Elder Brewster, on the twelfth day of November 1645. He succeeded to the tannery of his father with his brother Thomas. Like his father he held numerous town offices and was in the Narragansett campaign with his brother Joseph. His great affection was for his brother of the same name. These two were much attached to one another. They lived and worked in a complete harmony. If a committee was to be chosen to carry forward some action for the town, the name of both appeared upon it; if an inquest was to be held to inquire the cause of death of a Scituate freeman, both would be named for it, if one. They served together upon juries in the Court at Plymouth and they made division of lands between their neighbors. In 1647 the Colony Court permitted the purchasers and freemen of Scituate to dispose of the common lands. Soon thereafter these gave it over to the municipality and in the town meetings which followed for a decade, John Turner, Senior, and John Turner, Junior, were more frequently assigned to the performance of this duty than any other persons.

† Plymouth Colony Records Vol VI Page 64.

They did not actively participate in the acrimonious squabble that for a long time was kept up between the north and south religious societies although each was attached to a rival church gathering. Indeed, so amiable was the elder John that he was influential and forceful in an attempt to bring the two together, which nearly succeeded.

The younger John, while active, was not physically strong. On this account he was freed from bearing arms and training. He was one of the local Council of War however; and a colonial collector of the excise upon "tarr, boards and oysters." He married Ann James, the sister of the shipbuilder at the Harbor, and from them descended John Bryant Turner, Squire Bry., born in 1786, the intimate of John Quincy Adams. A genuinely strong fondness for each other existed between these two men. It led Turner to refuse an election to Congress in 1830 in order that his friend might occupy a seat in the lower branch of the National Legislature. Indeed it is highly probable that Turner himself suggested it and is the person referred to by Morse †, as remarking "that in his opinion the acceptance of this position by an Ex-President instead of degrading the individual would elevate the representative character." Mr. Adams replied that he, "had in that respect no scruple whatever. No person could be degraded by serving the people as a Representative in Congress. Nor in my opinion would an ex-President of the United States be degraded by serving as a Selectman of his town, if elected thereto by the people." Squire Turner's maternal grandfather was also the grandsire of that remarkable and able civil engineer, Gridley Bryant of Scituate, who built the first railroad ‡ in Massachusetts—the railroad over which was

---

† John Quincy Adams. By John T. Morse, Jr. (Am. Statesman Series) page 226.

‡ Charles Francis Adams says of him:—"Bryant was of that Scituate family which seventy-five years before had furnished Braintree its active minded minister. x x x x This famous structure (the railroad) marked an epoch not only in the history of Quincy but in that of the United States; and in every school

conveyed the huge granite blocks now composing the shaft on Bunker's hill, to the sea.

The eldest son of young John Turner was David, born in 1694 and graduated from Harvard College at the age of twenty-four. He was ordained to the ministry and settled over the parish in Rehoboth as its second pastor, in 1721. "He studied medicine some," says a descendant; "was styled Dr. and practised among his parishioners." He, like so many of the Turner family, was a very ready wit and apt at repartee. His pastorate was a long one, concluded only by his death in 1757.

The youngest son of Humphrey Turner, Thomas, had a son of the same name who practised law in Scituate from 1690 until the time of his death in 1721. He was a representative in the provincial legislature in 1711 and served with Nathaniel Byfield, Benjamin Lynde and Addington Davenport † upon numerous committees. These were all

---

history, it is mentioned as the most notable event during the administration of the younger Adams. Its projector Gridley Bryant has given this account of how he came to construct it, and of the obstacles he had to overcome. His story of private apathy and legislative obstruction reads like a repetition of the similar experience of George Stephenson at nearly the same time in England; and, while his project was looked upon as "visionary and chimerical" on the exchange, at the State House, it was solemnly argued that corporations in abundance already existed, and that it was wrong to take people's land under eminent domain, for purposes of more than questionable utility. Finally the success of the enterprise was altogether due to the munificence and public spirit of one of the most eminent and energetic of Boston merchants at a period when Boston still boasted of a race of merchants foremost in trade.—Col. Thomas Handasyd Perkins. He supplied all the funds needed to build the railway, over which, on the 7th of October 1826, Bryant passed his first train of cars. (Three Episodes of Massachusetts History Vol II Page 926). See also Memorial History of Boston Vol IV pages 116-120.

---

† A son of this Judge Davenport, Addington Davenport, Jr., being defeated for Attorney General of the province, went to England in 1732, obtained a master's degree at Oxford and having been ordained, came to Hanover and established the first church of England in Plymouth County—St. Andrews at Hanover. He was its first rector.

(Washburn's Judicial History of Mass.) page 207.

able men of their time and Turner's selection to act with them speaks highly for his abilities and legal qualifications. He was also on the committees for promoting the trade of the province; to take account with the treasurer and destroy some thirty-five thousand dollars' worth of torn and defaced bills of colonial currency which by reason of this condition had become no longer serviceable. † He was returned in 1717 and again the following year.

Still another member of the Turner family to be honored with place in the Massachusetts legislative assembly of the provincial period was Major Amos, who served as represntative from Scituate in the years 1726, 1727, 1728 and 1732. He did not attract much attention. In those years there existed a Province fund of £50,000 held by Trustees and created for the purpose of being loaned upon "good security" or first mortgages of real property to such as should be approved in the various towns, according to their population. Major Turner had, some years before, being chosen as representative, availed himself of this fund to obtain a mortgage upon his farm. He was three years in arrears of the payment of interest. It may be that he had a purpose in mind when he was first elected; or it may have been a mere happening that his fellow members in 1726 remitted this interest "because he sustained great loss in the burning of his barn." ‡ This was his only legislative accomplishment in the four years of his service. At this day it looks of doubtful propriety—the security having been diminished, the interest should therefore be rebated.

A great, great grandson of the first Thomas was Reverend Charles Turner, born September 3, 1732, and graduated from Harvard in 1752. He was educated for the ministry and on July 23, 1755, was called to the church at Duxbury. His pastorate here continued through twenty years of happiness and prosperity to the parish but in the latter, of ill health and physical infirmity to himself. On

† Province Laws Vol. IX (1711) page 525.
‡ Province Laws Vol. XI (1726) page 107.

this account he asked for and received his dismission. His congregation, grieved at his going, wrote a letter expressive of their great appreciation of him, to the Second Church in Scituate. "We lament" they said "that the righteous Governor of the world has in his Holy Providence deprived us of the ministerial labors of a man so universally esteemed by us as a friend, a minister and a Christian, and with whom we have lived in peace and happiness for this almost twenty years. But while we deplore our important loss, we heartily wish him the restoration of health, that he may yet be extensively useful in the world, and largely contribute to the happiness of mankind, as God in his wisdom may see fit."

The hope of his parishioners was to a degree realized. He spent the next five years living quietly with his family in Scituate, restoring his broken health. In 1780, with Daniel Damon, he was sent as a delegate from Scituate to convention at Cambridge to ratify the State Constitution, and eight years later with Judge William Cushing and Nathan Cushing to perform a like service upon the proposed Federal Constitution.

His son Charles served eight terms each in the state legislature and the national congress, and was a member of the convention of 1820 to revise the state constitution.

More than any other Scituate family, excepting possibly the Clapps, the Turners have served their town as its representative in deliberative and legislative bodies. In addition to the members of it already named, William Turner who graduated from Harvard in 1767 and was the Latin schoolmaster here, was elected to the Massachusetts House in the years 1777, 1779 and 1786. He sat in the convention which prepared the state constitution and during the entire period of the Revolution was efficient in public affairs. Elijah Turner served in the lower branch for fifteen years and John B. Turner for four.

All of these men have with but one or two exceptions taken a high place in the membership of the assemblies to which they have been chosen.

THE TORREYS

It is always a pity to spoil a good story, especially one that has been traditional in an old Colony family for over two centuries. A cherished anecdote of Josiah, the second son of Lieut. James Torrey, for which the amicable historian Dean has become sponsor, must in this instance be shattered, iconoclastic though such destruction may appear. On page 359 of his history Dean relates of Josiah Torrey that:—"He unfortunately lost his life A. D. 1693. He was in the act of drying the Town's stock of powder on the roof of his house, when a spark from the chimney falling, his life was instantly lost, and his house laid in ruins." The story is improbable— first, because the town's stock of powder, rarely over a barrel, could not have been "dried out" on the extremely sharp pitched roof of the dwelling of those days; second, because four of his children, Ruth, Caleb, Jemima and Keziah were all born after 1693 and as late as 1702, and finally because the law requiring each town in the colony to "provide a barrel of powder and lead or bulletts answerable to be kept by some trusty man or men," which had been passed in the Plymouth Colony fifty years before, was in 1693 of no effect by reason of the union of two colonies into the Province of Massachusetts Bay. Powder was then kept in magazines erected for the purpose. If the estimable gentleman was blown up it was not by the town's powder in 1693.

James Torrey and Ann Hatch were married on the second day of November 1643. He had already purchased land south of the first Herring Brook from John Stockbridge and six months later the dwelling was erected on what is now the Norwell road near the junction with Neal Gate Street. In 1653 he built a "clothing mill" on the first Herring Brook above that of Stockbridge and was at once propounded for the freedom of the colony. Two years later he was admitted. The high opinion in which he was justly held was first shown when the Cudworth trouble in the military company had become acute. A suitable person to command the company could not readily be found. This situation was a grave one not alone to Scituate but to all the towns in the colony, as the spirit of insurrection manifested by the Scituate train band might spread to the militiamen of Marshfield, Duxbury, and Plymouth. In this critical state of things, "according to the request of the several towns," Lieut. James Torrey was appointed to "dissipline the company, Capt. Cudworth being removed." He filled this position admirably but saw no actual service as death intervened before the Dutch invaded "Manhatoes" or Indian uprisings called the Pilgrim soldiers to the defense of their homes. It was Lieut. James Torrey who drew up the form for commissions to military officers and he was a member of the Council of War. He was town clerk for ten years and went to the General Court at Plymouth as deputy from Scituate for eight years, seven of them consecutively. In 1665 he was appointed as a magistrate to solemnize marriages and administer oaths but died before receiving his commission.

Shortly after his death, probably in recognition of his public services, but upon "a petition preferred to the Court to that purpose," there was granted to his four younger sons William, Joseph, Jonathan and Josiah, two hundred acres of land, which probably adjoined Hatherly's, 'three miles sqare,' on the west, "lying above Weymouth near unto the line of Massachusetts."

To the eldest son, named for his father and being distinguished from the latter, called Deacon James, descended the homestead and mill. He was an active member of the south parish, a clerk of the Conihasset Partners and the only man in Scituate in 1700, willing and able to teach the public school. He was three times married and the father of twelve children all of whom and their progeny had disappeared from Scituate eighty-four years ago. The family name is perpetuated here through Capt. Caleb Torrey, the son of that Josiah, who was *not* blown up by the town's powder.

MICHAEL PEIRCE

Capt. Michael Peirce the ancestor of this old Scituate family is generally credited with being here in 1647 when he bought land on the "Country Road" from the Conihasset partners.

He was originally of Little Hingham (Cohasset) and certainly did not erect the home on his Scituate farm until after 1663 as is evidenced by the following receipt recorded † by him in 1665.

"November 5th 1663.
Received by us Cornett Robert Stetson
and James Torrey of Scituate
of Micail Peirse of Hingham
the full and just sume of twenty
pounds for the use of Josiah Leich—
field of Scituate aforesaid;
which twenty pounds the said
Micaell Peirse was appointed
to pay unto us for the use of
Josias Leichfield aforesaid by
the Court holden at N. Plymouth
in New England in the month
of June last past. In witness
wee have hereunto sett our
hands this day and yeare
first above written.
    The marke of x   Cornett Robert Stetson
                          James Torrey

If there remains any doubt of the correctness of the assumption that Peirce did not come to Scituate to dwell until this time, it would seem to be set at rest by the entry

---

† Plymouth Colony Records Vol IV page 89.

which the "Bench" at Plymouth caused to be entered upon the records on June 5, 1666 † when it cashiered Captain Cudworth and the latter suggested "Mr. Peirse" for the place at the head of the Scituate train band from which he had been deposed. The Court replied—

"and alsoe concerning Mr. Peirse we have not to object to him but that hee is a stranger to us."

Such a state of ignorance on the part of the Court to which Cornet Stetson and Isaac Chittenden were deputies could not have existed had Peirce been then of Scituate. It is readily understood however if he was a resident of Hingham in the colony of Massachusetts Bay.

All of his nine children were born in Hingham. His wife died (1662) in bearing him the youngest Elizabeth and between this date and 1666 he had erected his home on the Egypt farm purchased from the Conihasset partners. Nine generations of his descendants have dwelt upon and tilled these same acres. Silas, the third of that name, occupying it at this writing. There is an element of devotion in this, frequently found in Pilgrim and Puritan families, but seldom in so marked a degree as the Peirce family. It began with Benjamin Peirce, son of Michael, who by the will of his father, made just before the latter started for Rhode Island in Phillip's War where he was soon to meet his death, came into possession of the homestead.

In that will, of which Benjamin was made Executor, very generous legacies were given so that the Court "not knowing whether there will remain so much cleare estate, when debts and the widdowes maintenance are discharged out of the same, as will amount to salve the executor's portion intended by his father," made an appropriate order with the consent of the rest of the children by which the homestead was "salved" to the eldest son and to his descendants for two hundred and forty years.

---

† Plymouth Colony Records Vol IV Page 127.

Before coming to Scituate Michael Peirce had upland assigned to him at White Head at Cohasset and a correspondingly appropriate acreage of meadow in the first division. He also bought from William James Conihasset marshlands which had originally been aloted to John Woodfield. Besides the homestead at Egypt he built a second house which was given in his will to his widow, a second wife whom he had married but a few years before.

His first public office was that of constable to which he was elected in 1667. By 1669 he had apparently become sufficiently well known to the colony court to be approved as captain of the Scituate military company. It was in this kind of public service that his abilities were especially conspicuous. His courage and constancy were brilliant in a company of brave and religious men. No greater tribute to his memory can be paid than the simple story of his death already told in these pages. He had demonstrated his willingness to surrender his individual interests to those of the public long before he sacrificed his life at Rehoboth for the safety of his colony. The occasion first arose in a contemplated expedition against the Dutch in 1673 when Peirce having married a second time was living comfortably on his farm surrounded by a family of growing children.

In August, a fleet of vessels which had been set fourth by the United Netherlands and "his sirene Highness the Lord Prince of Orange to do all manner of damages unto their enemies both by water and land," appeared in the Hudson River and threatened the eastern end of Long Island which was then English populated. The Governor and Council of Connecticut relying upon the assistance of the Confederation (although the Commissioners from the other colonies were not at the time consulted) sent two of their number to the "commander-in-chief" bearing a letter in which they sought to know "your further actions." The communication stated:—

"And we must let you know that we and our confederates the United Colonies of New England are by our Royal Sovereign Charles the 2nd, made keepers of his subject's liberties in these parts, and do hope to acquit ourselves in that trust through the assistance of Almighty God, for the preservation of his Colonies in New England."

This was on August seventh. As soon as the Commissioners could be called together they met at Hartford and ratified the action of the Connecticut authorities. It took until December to obtain action by the other colonies. Plymouth responded with one hundred men. † Captain Cudworth was placed at the head of the expedition but declined. Peirce was next in command as ensign at four shillings a day.

Although the commander of the fleet responded to the note of the Connecticut governor confirming his beliefs and fears as to his intentions, and stated:—

"We do well believe that those that are set for keepers of his Majesty's of England's subjects will quit themselves as they ought to do for the preservation of the Colonies in New England; however we shall not for that depart from our further resolutions."

The Plymouth men never left on the expedition, despite elaborate preparations had been made for it. Events had demonstrated that there was no occasion for Peirce's services or for the departure of his command. The recital of the incident is of value as showing the readiness of this primitive militiaman to answer with his services when the

---

† Said the Court:- "Altho not according to what wee are proportioned by our confederates, wherein wee are apparently overrated, yett to the utmost of our abilities." Plymouth Colony Records Vol. V page 135 et seq. See also Records of the Commissioners (Plymouth) Vol. X page 386.

call came, whether from his neighbors or the King's liege subjects in a distant colony, in the common defense. His prompt disposition on this occasion stands out the more attractively when compared with the refusal of Cudworth "to serve his country with the inevitable ruin and destruction of his own famly." †

Captain Peirce was not enrolled as a freeman until 1670. His civil activities were confined to serving on the grand and coroner's inquests, as surveyor of highways and as selectman in the years 1672 and 1673.

Like so many of the contemporaries of Capt. John Williams he did not escape embroilment with that ready litigant. In 1673 he with John Cushing and Jeremiah Hatch were sued by the former because as selectmen they had entertained an action brought by Captain Cudworth against him. Again when William Rogers and the owner of the Cedar Point farm were litigating over damages alleged to have been done to Williams' property by his servant, William's brother-in-law Anthony Dodson, had appeared as a witness. Capt. Peirce was present at the trial and heard Dodson's testimony. He said that the latter had "either lyed horribly or notoriously or forsworne himself." Thereupon he himself was promptly sued; but an amicable adjustment was reached without a trial. It may have been that this settlement was effective in another respect, for when John, the second son of Captain Peirce became of age, he married Patience, the amiable daughter of Anthony Dodson.

---

† The words are from Cudworth's letter to Governor Winslow, declining the command of the expedition ante page 272.

THE STOCKBRIDGES

John Stockbridge came to Scituate from London in the "Blessing" in 1635, bringing with him his son Charles then a child. His exodus from England was not prompted by a desire for greater religious freedom. It is more likely that his purpose was in the main, to embrace the better opportunity which New England offered for amassing a larger and speedier wealth. He was a wheelwright by trade and upon reaching Scituate built a house north of Satuit Brook on land that is at the northwest corner of Front and Brook streets. This was in the Conihasset territory and he was one of Hatherly's grantees of that tract in 1646. He had arable lands on the Third Cliff south of the five acres which John Emerson sold to Nathaniel Tilden in 1636. He also had a house on the Driftway and lands on the Fourth Cliff and at Brushy Hill.

He did not lend himself readily to the condition of the new community in which he had chosen his home. Nor did he prominently identify himself with the church, being content that his wife Anna, who joined Elder King and William Vassall, in the controversy with Chauncey, should represent the family in religious affairs. The civil code that had been adopted for the government of the town and colony was likewise not to his liking. He held it in open contempt and jeered and railed at it whenever public occasion offered. These odius public utterances did not of course commend him to neighbors who were promoting that which he ridiculed. Two of them, Edward Foster and James Cudworth, hailed him before the Court and caused him to be punished. The process was repeated when he again offended and he escaped penalty only upon taking the oath of allegiance to the King and fidelity to the colony. It would logically have happened, after this action, that he should have been admitted as a freeman, but this status was never permitted him, or perhaps he disdained it.

THE OLD STOCKBRIDGE MILL, GREENBUSH.
Built 1640. From a crayon drawing.

Meanwhile he continued to prosper. In 1650 he built the first water grist mill in the colony near where Isaac Stedman in 1640 had erected a saw mill, on the First Herring brook. When the latter sold to George Russell, Stockbridge purchased from him a half interest. Although he was getting what he sought in coming to Scituate—wealth—he was discontented with his surroundings, and in 1657 he removed to Boston. Here a young son, John, was born of a third wife, the same year. Neither survived long. The father deceased in 1658 and the son did not reach man's estate. Stockbridge left a large property. The house which he had built near his mill, on the road to Little's bridge and which was later the garrison about which waged the Indian onslaught at the time of Phillip's War, he left by will to his eldest son, Charles. The grist mill and half interest in the Russell mill also went to Charles.

In 1665 Charles purchased his partner's interest in the latter and became the sole owner. To these mills was brought the grist and lumber from all over the colony. In 1674 he built another on the Third Herring brook and in eleven years had so widely demonstrated his abilities as a miller that the town of Plymouth sought his aid and co-operation in building a water grist mill on Town brook, in that town. Strangely enough, although the Pilgrims and their children had been augmenting in numbers for over half a century but one grist mill had been operated in the town during that time. When advances were made to Charles Stockbridge this mill was about to be abandoned by the son of John Jenny, a Norwich (England) brewer, who had operated it, upon his removal to Dartmouth. No one was found in Plymouth capable of or willing to run it. Liberal terms which he accepted were offered to Stockbridge and under the contract † which he made for himself and

---

† Articles of Agreement made between the Town of Plymouth on the one party and Charles Stockbridge of Scituate, ,in the aforesaid Plymouth Colonie on the other party, concerning a Corn Mill, as followeth:
Whereas the towne of Plymouth have bin many years much

his successors, with the town, the mill was operated until 1838. During a portion of this time another son of Scituate, Haviland Torrey, was the owner. Stockbridge also owned an eighth interest in grist and saw mills at "Straits Pond in Hingham."

For a few years after the death of his father he lived in Boston and Charlestown, but unlike that parent he found contentment at Scituate and many friends among her people. In 1663 he was living at the homestead at Greenbush, carrying on the business of his mills and engaged then and in later years in the execution of the duties of constable, highway surveyor and other offices as were filled by the more important men in every township.

In 1671 a "great abuse by the excessive drinking of liquors at ordinaryes" had grown up in the colony. A law was passed that year which provided that:—

---

damnifyed for want of the right management of there corne mill, and having by theire agents made suite to the said Charles Stockbridge the whole use of theire brooke or streame, comonly called the towne brooke whereon the old mill now standeth; to him, the said Charles Stockbridge, his heirs and assignes, for the use of a corne mill or mills, as he or they shall see meet, and for no other use, nor more than any other townesman; which said brooke and priviledges said Charles Stockbridge, his heires or assignes shall have soe long as hee or they shall maintain a sufficient corn mill and miller, to grind the townes corn well and honestly for one-sixteenth parte of a bushell of corne or graine which shalbe brought unto the said mill in a fitt capassetie to grind; and for the further incurragemet of said Charles Stockbridge herin, the said town have paied unto him, said Stockbridge, eleven pounds in silver towards the raising of said mill dame, and makeing a wast water course for the herrings to pass over the dam into the pond; and the said town by their agent whose names are hereunto subscribed, doe heerby engage to and with the said Charles Stockbridge, and his heires and assignes to be att halfe the charge of maintaining the said water course successively; namely, all that part of it that is below the said mill dam. In confeirmation of which articles of agreement abovesaid, the agents for the said towne of Plymouth, and the said Charles Stockbridge, have put to theire hands this first day of May 1683.

Signed in   Ephraim Morton Sen'r.
presence of   Joseph Warren
Isacke Little   Joseph Bartlett
John Hathaway   Charles Stockbridge
    Plymouth Colony Records Vol VI Page 111.

"every ordinary keeper in this government shalbe hereby empowered and required, that in case any person or persons doe not attend order, but carry themselves uncivilly, by being importunately desirous of drink when deneyed, and doe not leave the house when required, such ordinary keeper shall return theire names to the next Court x x x x It is further ordered by this Court, that some two or three men be appointed in every towne x x to have the inspection of the ordinaries, or in any other place suspected, to take notice of such abuses as may arise in reference to the premises or otherwise, and make report thereof to the Court."

Charles Stockbridge, Cornet Stetson and Edward Jenkins were appointed to this duty from Scituate. Isaac Chittenden at the Harbor, Nicholas Wade at Brushy Hill on the "Country Road," Matthew Gannett at Booth's Hill and Joseph Barstow at the North River were the taverners at that time. Whatever action may have been taken by these inspectors it resulted in the entire abandonment of the business of innkeeping in Scituate for a time. In 1677, this condition still existing, the Court ordered "the towne of Scituate to appoint a fitt person to keep an ordinary at Scituate, betwixt this (3 July) and the next October Court, and then to propose him to the Court, and Edward Jenkins is allowed by the Court to keep entertainment for strangers, viz: provide victuall and draw bier (before) that Court. In October Jenkins was permanently licensed.

Unlike his father Charles was a good churchman and attended at the south parish which his mother had labored so long and zealously to establish. Again, unlike his father he was admitted a freeman. This was in 1682 when in his fiftieth year. He died two years later, intestate.

At the time of his death his sons Joseph, Benjamin and Samuel had not attained their majority. His large estate was divided under an agreement † between the widow and

---

† Plymouth Colony Records Vol VI Page 156.

the older children approved by the court. The sixth paragraph of this agreement was as follows:—

> "6. And further, we doe agree & conclude that Abigail Stockbridge the widdow of Charles Stockbridge, lately deceased, shall injoy all the housing, & lands & meadow corne mill & saw mill, by & standing upon the first herring brooke in Scituate, for her the said Abigail's use, untill Samuell Stockbridge, the youngest son of said Charles Stockbridge, comes to the age of twenty-one years, & then Benjamin Stockbridge & said Samuell Stockbridge shall have & injoy for there own proper estate all the said housing, lands and meadow, corne mill and saw mill, near or upon the said first herring brooke, (excepting the parlour for their mother to live in) to be equally divided betwixt them."

When Benjamin married Mary, the grand-daughter of Elder Nathaniel Tilden, in 1701, he bought out the interest of his brother Samuel in what their father had left them jointly, and took up his residence in the block house, which had now been transformed into a "mansion." Here his son Benjamin, destined to become one of the famous physicians of the province, was born in 1704. His great activity in the practice of his profession and his labors in teaching his art to younger men have already been told in these pages. There remains however to relate the true story of the erroneous accusations of toryism made against him and his son Charles in 1774 when the action of the Marshfield royalists in requesting the presence of troops from Gage's command in Boston in the former town, so aroused her neighbors in Scituate, Duxbury and Plymouth. The names of these two busy men had been exhibited to the Selectmen of Scituate by the "committie of Inspection and Safety" among a list of those inimical to the cause of liberty. Winsor †, erroneously says that "Dr. Stockbridge, Paul White and Elisha Ford, three of the leading tories in Marshfield, were

---

† History of Duxbury page 138.

seized and carted under the liberty pole in Duxbury and forced to sign recantations." Deane † says that the elder doctor "had been called to Ipswich, and on his return he was unfortunately detained many days by General Gage in Boston. This was known to the authorities of the town and as soon as he returned to his home, they conducted him to Plymouth with the design of securing him in prison; but they were soon softened by the intercession of the people of Plymouth and dismissed him. In the meantime his son Dr. Charles with several others, was conducted under guard to headquarters at Cambridge; but he was soon released. It was a suspicious circumstance that he had been found, with a few others, walking on the beach, between the third and fourth cliffs, apparently waiting for some communications from Boston by water." These statements are likewise error. Deane's mistake is comparable to that of Winsor. That most accurate of colonial historians, William T. Davis of Plymouth, in telling the story— "of the liberty pole recantations of Elisha Ford and Paul White leaves Dr. Stockbridge's name out entirely. The town records speak the denial of the assertion that Dr. Benjamin was first detained many days by General Gage and upon his release taken to Plymouth, and that his son was "conducted under guard to headquarters at Cambridge and soon released." On June 3, 1777 the town was assembled in meeting touching the uncertain and dangerous state of the country. At that meeting

"The Town chose Capt. Israil Vinal to prosecute and lay before the Court, the evidence of the hostile disposition toward this or any of the United States, of any of the inhabitants of the Town of Scituate, who stand charged with being persons whose residence in the State is dangerous to publick peace and safety."

Among the names in the list exhibited by the Selectmen

---

† History of Scituate page 139.

at this meeting were those of Dr. Benjamin Stockbridge and his son Charles. It was

"Voted that any of these persons might have liberty to be heard in this present Town meeting or at any other day, that their names may be erased upon giving satisfaction."

In sixteen days the town held another meeting. The list then presented contained but eight of the names that had been considered on June third and the names of the Greenbush physicians, were not upon it. They had satisfied their townsmen that they were not of "hostile disposition." In the short time which intervened between the two meetings there was not sufficient opportunity for all the happenings alleged by the two historians above quoted to have taken place. It is both doubtful that if these descendants of stubborn old John Stockbridge had been loyalists, they would have recanted or that the Scituate patriots would have easily forgiven them. The latter made a mistake in the case of the doctors, as they did in others and the "satisfaction" which the former gave must have been adequate and complete. The connection of the names of these worthy men with disloyalty must have come from their membership in the church of England. Both were worshippers under Reverend William Willard Wheeler, Rector of St. Andrews at Hanover.

THE DAMONS

John Damon, the forefather of all the Damons hereabouts, came to Plymouth with his sister Hannah in the company and under the care of their mother's brother William Gilson, before 1633. Their uncle was a man fairly well-to-do for the times, a good churchman and of very excellent abilities. Not long after Gilson's arrival he was made an Assistant to the Colony Court—counsellors they were called in those days—and in 1634 he is found at Scituate a member of Mr. Lothrop's congregation. His house was next to Edward Foster's, just south of Satuit Brook. He had land on the north side of the Second Cliff and in 1637, erected the first wind-mill in the colony; on the Third Cliff. Beside the nephew and niece Gilson and Goodwife Frances had for a time as an inmate of their household Priscilla, the daughter of Peter Brown of Plymouth, who had left his widow with a large family of children. Both Gilson and his wife were devoted to their young kinspeople. That he might "leave them something after his dayes was ended" the former applied for and received from the Court an allotment of more land than he personally could conveniently cultivate because "although he had no children of his owne, yet that he had two of his sisters children, which he looked upon as his own." † When he died in 1649 John and Hannah were awarded all of his possessions save one small legacy to another nephew and another of five pounds "to my Pastor Mr. John Lothrop."

Young Damon lived in the house on Kent Street which his uncle had left him and tilled the eighty acres which had been awarded to Gilson on his own (Damon's) and his sister's account.

He was warm-hearted, generous and ever ready to be of

---

† Plymouth Colony Records Vol II Page 143.

such measure of assistance as he was able, to a friend or neighbor who stood in need. This characteristic brought him collaterally into a pretty romance in which Governor Prence, his daughter Elizabeth and Damon's friend Arthur Howland, Jr., of Duxbury were involved. This was in 1666. At that time this provision concerning courtship was the law of the colony:—

> "Whereas divers persons unfitt for marriage both in regard to their yeoung years as also in regard of their weake estate, some practiseing the enveigleing of men's daughters and maids under guardians (contrary to their parents and guardians liking), and of mayde servants without leave and liking of their masters. It it therefore enacted by the Court that if any shall make any motion of marriage to any man's daughter or mayde servant not having first obtained leave and consent of the parents or master so to doe, shalbe punished either by fine or corporall punishment or both, at the discretion of the bench and according to the nature of the offence."

Young Howland and Mistress Prence were enamoured of each other. They were not "unfitt for marriage" within the meaning of this statute, both being of age and the former possessed of fifty acres of land in Duxbury which had been granted him by the colony court. There was however one grave and insuperable objection. Howland was a Quaker. His father, at first a sympathizer, had been frequently prosecuted before Prence, who was then Governor, for the entertainment of Quakers and assisting in the promulgation of their faith, and had finally embraced it. The Governor was rabid in his opposition to the sect and the marriage of his daughter to one of them was intolerable. The young woman was the third child of his second marriage. Her mother was a sister of William Collier, as prominent and persistent in his persecution of the Quakers as was the Governor himself. Both parents forbade the courtship which in spite of their joint efforts continued. No other means availing, recourse was finally had to a criminal prosecution against Howland under the law which has been above quoted. On March 5, 1666-7 Howland was brought before the Bench on which his accuser sat as the presiding magistrate and charged with:—

"inveigling Mistris Elizabeth Prence and makeing motion of marriage to her, and prosecuting the same contrary to her parents liking, and without theire consent, and directly contrary to their mind and will."

He was sentenced to pay a fine of five pounds, to find sureties for his good behavior:—

"and in special that he desist from the use of any meanes to obtaine or retaine her affections as aforesaid." †

Here John Damon came to the assistance of his friend. He became surety for that good behavior which the Court required. He also apparently counselled the action which was taken four months later when Howland "did sollemnly and seriously engage before this Court, (Governor Prence still presiding) that hee will wholly desist and never apply himself for the future, as formerly hee hath done, to Mistris Elizabeth Prence, in reference unto marriage." However solemn this agreement may have been, it was not serious on the part of young Howland; nor did Mistress Prence agree that the action either of the Court or her lover was final. The courtship continued and was consummated in a marriage later. The daughter was never forgiven. The bitterness which Prence showed toward General Cudworth for the latter's leniency toward the Quakers was greatly increased in the case of his daughter because of her successful rebellion to his stubborn will. Although he disinherited her, he lived to see her surrounded by a contented brood and the Scituate planter who had become the surety for the good behavior of the parent the Godfather of his children.

---

† Plymouth Colony Records Vol. III Page 140, 141.

John Damon's unselfishness and genuine interest in the welfare of others is also shown in his advocacy of the cause of Elder William Hatch who claimed a share in the town's common land. It has been told elsewhere in these pages that the Colony Court had permitted the freemen of Scituate to make division of these lands among the freeholders. In doing this there had been trouble. Two factions had sprung up, and the town had delegated the privilege to a committee. While the magistrates did not approve of this, they sanctioned it for a time and then re-established the bench in the performance of the duty by appointing a committee of its own choice from the townsmen made up however of the leaders of each faction. † These men were Capt. James Cudworth, Cornet Stetson, Isaac Chittenden and Lieut. Buck, on one side, and John Damon, John Turner, Senior, John Turner, Junior, and John Bryant, Senior, on the other. It is readily seen that they easily deadlocked. This was true upon the application of Elder Hatch for his allotment. In the argument which ensued Damon being deserted by John Bryant, won over Buck and Chittenden from the opposition and reported a layout for Hatch to the Court. It was not the fault of this majority of the committee that the magistrates acted unfavorably upon this report. It served Elder Hatch to no purpose but to make Damon himself the target for retribution at the hands of his opponents on the committee. When his turn came for a layout of fifty acres a majority of his fellows refused his request, weakly alleging "that hee had land on that accoumpt before." ‡ He appealed to the Court which returned this advice:—"therefore wee request and think hee ought to be considered, and desire you would soe doe." He was thereupon "accomodated."

He was a deputy to the Colony Court, one of the council

---

† Plymouth Colony Laws Vol V Pages 69 and 70.

‡ This could only have meant the eighty acres allotted to William Gilson and which Damon had inherited from his uncle.

of war, a Selectman and performed his full part in those other public services to which he was from time to time assigned.

He was twice married, his second wife being Martha Howland, a relative of his friend Arthur. He was the father of twelve children evenly divided as to the sexes. Of those which survived adolescence John and Zachary each did exemplary services in Phillip's War. Another son Experience was the pioneer at Pincin Hill and the daughters Silence, Martha, Hannah and Margaret through marriages with Scituate neighbors have established the Damon strain in the families of Chittenden, Merritt, Stetson, Eells, Woodworth and others.

THE BARSTOWS

William Barstow was the pioneer settler in that part of Scituate which in 1727 was set off from territory of the mother town and became Hanover. He was here before 1649, having been propounded freeman he had gone through the probationary period and was admitted in that year. He built his house near the present site of the Second Congregational Church in Hanover on the "country road" which was the means of communication between the principal towns of the Bay and Plymouth colonies.

His trade was that of a ship-builder and he and his descendants launched many a ship from the "Two Oaks" and "Old Barstow" yards on North River.

His name has gone down through the generations however, because of the bridge which he built and maintained over the North River near the present structure, and the tavern which was kept by him and his descendants near it.

On the fifth day of October 1656 the Colony Court entered into a contract with Barstow, evidenced by this record:—

> "William Barstow, of Scituate, covenanteth and ingageth to make a good and sufficient bridge over the North River, a little above the third herring brook, at a place called Stoney Beach, being the place wher now passengers goe frequently over, the said bridge to bee made sufficient for horse and foot; and he is to lay out, and clear, and marke a way from the said bridge towards the bay as far as Hughes Crosse, and to open and clear and marke a way along beyond Hughes Crosse towards the bay so as to avoid a certaine rocky hill and swamp; and for the true performance of all the said particulars, the said William Barstow is to bee paid by the Treasurer in the behalfe of the countrey the summe of twelve pounds in current country pay."

The bridge was completed and the way marked and cleared within a year and October 6, 1657:

> "It is ordered by the Court that Mr. Timothy Hatherly, and Capt. James Cudworth and Capt. Josias Winslow take convenient time to take notice of the horse bridge over the North River, that it bee sufficiently don and alsoe of the way unto it, and accordingly to judge what William Barstow is worthy to have for his worke and paines thereabout, and then to returne what they have don in the premises unto the Treasurer, that accordingly he may bee satisfyed." †

In 1660 the bridge was out of repair and the Major and Treasurer were appointed to agree with Barstow concerning its yearly upkeep, "the charge thereof to bee levied by vote upon the several townshipes of this government." An agreement was reached under which Barstow was to repair and maintain the bridge for a period of twenty years for one pound annually.

This arrangement was especially advantageous to Barstow notwithstanding the seeming inadequacy of price, in view of the fact that travel between the Bay towns and Plymouth was constantly increasing and it all went over this bridge. He probably agreed to the small annual stipend because at the same time he was:—

> "allowed by the Court to draw and sell wine, beer, and stronge waters for passengers, that come and goe over the bridge hee hath lately made, or others that shall have occation, unless any just exception shall come in against him."

and he opened a public bar for dispensing these refreshments. He apparently had no thought to do more than this but in 1666 complaint was made that there was "great neglect on his part in not keeping an ordinary for the entertaining of strangers" and he was ordered to "make competent provision for strangers for theire entertainment

---

† Plymouth Colony Records Vol III pages 108, 123.

and refreshment for this yeare; and that incase the said Barstow shall neglect soe to doe, that then the Court will take some other course about the same." This he immediately did. He, his son Joseph and his grandson kept the tavern for years which is so frequently mentioned in Judge Sewall's diary and was the place of temporary abode of judges, lawyers, commissioners, dignitaries and others travelling between the two colonies.

William Barstow was a selectman; a highway surveyor and member of the committee to perambulate the patent line in 1666. For this latter service, most creditably performed the Court awarded him between forty and fifty acres of upland upon the river which were afterwards used as a shipyard.

Upon the advent of Phillip's War when Joseph Barstow was keeping the tavern, the Court ordered a garrison to be kept at his house "both in respect to the towne of Scituate and the country." This action and the presence of the twelve men who constituted the garrison saved the bridge in 1676 but sent the Indians to Greenbush where the death and destruction inflicted by them have already been described.

THE BAILEYS

Like so many other Scituate families, the Baileys were of good estate and in comfortable circumstances when Thomas, the American ancestor of the Scituate branch, came to Boston and thence to Weymouth in 1630.

Some writers have placed John Bailey the first of the name in Scituate, here in 1670 and have called him the son of Thomas. Barry † says this is *probably* the fact, but it is evident that he makes the statement on the authority of Deane ‡ that "he (John) married Sarah White (perhaps of Weymouth)." Savage says that he does not know who the father of John was but he was probably born in this country.

William H. Reed, Esq., of Weymouth, in an address before the association of Bailey Families at their fourth annual gathering held at Rowley on August 19, 1896, states that John Bailey of Scituate was a grandson of the original Thomas. This evidently is correct and is pretty clearly shown from an examination of what data is available at the present day. The will § of Thomas Bailey of Weymouth is dated May 23, 1681 and was proved and allowed before Governor Bradstreet and John Hull, Assistant, on October seventeenth of that year. It contains this bequest:—

"Item. I give and bequeath unto my eldest and beloved son John Bailey 2-3 of all my right title and interest in my dwelling house, barns, outhousings, orchards, errable lands, goods, chattels with 2-3 of the appurtenances unto said housing and lands belonging, together with the 2-3 of all my Lotts in Weymouth woods belonging or in any wise appurtaining. Also I give and bequeath to my said son John 2-3 of my movables within dore and without, of whatever quan-

---

† Barry's History of Hanover page 199.
‡ Deane's History of Scituate page 213.
§ Suffolk Probate Records No. 1197.

tity or quality soever they bee and my will is that in case my said son John decease before his wife Hannah then what movables of mine is remaining and extant by inventory at my son's decease shall be to the use and for the proper behoof of my daughter and Thomas Bailey equally to be divided the one-half to the one and the one-half to the other, to be of them and their children according to their discretion."

The "eldest son" John mentioned in the above testament was not John Bailey of Scituate because the latter's wife was not Hannah above named, but first Sarah the daughter of Gowan White, and second Ruth Clothier. Again, John Bailey of Scituate had been living here since 1663 when as a youth he was in the employ of John Williams and in common with many others quarreling † with him. He married here in 1672; was admitted a freeman in 1684 and "took up" the farm at Great Neck which belonged to John Williams and was afterwards devised to him by the will of that eccentric planter. All this must be conclusive that John Bailey of Scituate was not the eldest son of Thomas of Weymouth. Finally, as is correctly asserted by Mr. Reed, the eldest son John had a son of the same name who married Sarah White.

Other writers have made the equally egregious mistake of assuming that John Bailey of Scituate was the grandson of that Thomas the brother of Reverend John Bailey, the great non-conformist. This statement also must fail. John Bailey the eminent Congregationalist divine was born

---

† "5 October 1663. John Bayley complaineth against Ensigne John Williams, in an action of slander and dafamation, of one hundred pounds x x x x he the said Bayly obtained a verdict of ten pounds and charge of the Court". Plymouth Colony Records Vol VII Pages 110-113.
 "March 1, 1663-1664. Ensigne John Williams and John Bayley for breaking the peace by striking one another, fined each oo : o3 : o4". Plymouth Colony Records Vol IV Page 50.

near Blacburn, Lancashire, England on February 24, 1644.†
He was offered, in case he should conform to the Established church, a duke's chaplaincy, with a deanery and a bishopric, whenever a vacancy should occur, but rejected the offer. He was twice imprisoned on account of his Congregational principles, notwithstanding his irreproachable character. No release was granted until he promised to leave the country, which he did in 1684, accompanied by his younger brother Thomas, who also was a minister. ‡ It is obvious that "younger brother Thomas," driven out of England in 1684 was not the grandsire of John Williams "ancient servant" who occupied Farm Neck in Scituate in 1674.

Yet they had some traits in common—each was stubborn. When John Bailey of Scituate was fined three shillings and four pence for his altercation with his employer the latter paid. Not so John Bailey. He refused to be mulcted for a fight in which he was not the aggressor. For fourteen years this amount was annually carried upon the books of the colony treasurer as due "the countrey." In 1674 mention of it ceases but the credit side of the ledger does not record that it was paid.

In all his life he was appointed to the performance of but one public duty. He was sworn as one of a jury to examine into the death of Joseph Ellis, a neighbor. Here is what he reported:—

"Wee, whose names are underwritten, being impannelled on a jury the 29th of July 1676, by Mr. Nathaniel Tilden, the constable of Scituate, to view the corpes of Joseph Ellis, of Scituate, by intelligence understanding that he went in to the harbour at Scituate, to swim or wash himselfe, with John Vaughan and Daniell Hickes Junior: whoe doe affeirme, that the said Ellis made the first motion soe to doe, and tosin past his

---

† Sprague—Annals of the American Pulpit.
‡ Address of Rev. A. F. Bailey at the Bailey-Bayley Family Association at Andover August 16, 1894.

depth, cryed for healp; and the said Vaughan did the best hee could to healp him, but could not save his life: and wee judge, that the water in the said harbour was the sole meanes of his death." †

A descendant of the same name and in the sixth generation was a Quaker preacher and lived at Hanover Four Corners. He was a famous clock maker and manufacturer of compasses.

In his day and generation Deacon Joseph Bailey was by far the most prominent member of the Bailey family. He was a grandson of John, born of the former's second son (third child) Joseph, in 1704. He married Elizabeth White in 1732 with whom he was prominent and active in church affairs for half a century. At the age of seventy he was appointed a member of the first committee of Inspection and Correspondence and later did the best work of his life on the draft of the vote prepared by the committee of which he was a member, and reported to and passed by the town upon the question of the adoption of a state constitution.

The Baileys were large factors in public affairs at this time. With Deacon Joseph in the first committee of Inspection and Correspondence was his nephew Paul, then but just of age. On the same committee, appointed in 1777, was his brother Caleb and the rolls, as the war for independence progressed, bear the names of many another of the family who fought for the principle involved in that struggle.

---

† Plymouth Colony Records Vol V Page 225.

THE OLD SCITUATE LIGHTHOUSE.

Discontinued Nov. 15, 1860, by authority of the Act of Congress approved Sept. 28, 1850, on establishment of Minots Ledge Light. From the original negative in the archives of the Lighthouse Service, Washington, D. C.

THE BARKERS

John and Robert Barker, brothers were living at Jones' River (Kingston) in 1638. John was a bricklayer and in the year above named his brother Robert had just completed his apprenticeship with William Palmer, carpenter.

In 1632 John had married Anna, the daughter of John Williams, Sr., and had carried on his trade at Jones' River during all the time up to 1641 when he bought the ferry over the North River which is now Little's bridge. He was drowned there on December 14, 1652.

He had one son, John, born in 1650, who upon the death of his father was taken first to Barnstable and then to the home of his uncle Capt. John Williams in Scituate. The difficulties between these two as the boy grew to manhood and after were frequently aired in the colony court and are more particularly related in pages which follow. Deane says that he "is mentioned as a lawyer in the colony records in 1674;" but this is error and probably grew out of an examination of and hasty misconception by the author, of the following entry:

"27th October 1674. Whereas att the last Court John Barker, attorney to Samuel Hieland, as attorney to the said Hiland, by process of law obtained a verdict and judgment of fourteen pounds of Israell Hubert †, eight pounds whereof is by the said Hubert already payed; and that some way the said Barker hath procured the bill by which the said sum was demanded; this Court hath ordered, that the remaining six pounds remaine unpayed untell the said bill be delivered to Captaine Cudworth, appointed by the Court to receive it."

This did not mean that young Barker—he was then but

---

†Israel Hobart a shipbuilder at Hobart's Landing on the North River in 1676. At the date above named he lived in Hingham.

twenty-three years of age—appeared before the Court as an attorney-at-law. Hiland had merely attorned to him. He was the former's proxy. Having in mind that at the time the action was brought Hiland had already received more than one-half the amount of his bill it is not surprising that he preferred to attorn to another than to appear personally.

In July 1676 Barker joined his uncle's company as a sergeant and accompanied him to Mount Hope where he was wounded in the last battle with King Phillip and returned home. He was a man of wealth and some learning but never held public office except one term in the General Court in 1706.

The inventory of his estate filed in 1729 shows:

"Plate £15. Divinity, Law, History, School Books, Latin, Greek and Hebrew £53. Silver tankard £26 Silver Cullender and three silver spoons £8. The best bed and furniture in ye Easterly Chamber £10. The bed and furniture in ye Great Lower room £13. Napkins, table cloths, sheets and pillow coats £12. Another bed and furniture in the West Chamber £10. An oval table of black walnut and another small ditto. Several chests with drawers and a carpet."

Altogether these contents of his dwelling were appraised at three hundred and seventy-five pounds. He left one son Williams Barker, the devisee of the Cedar Point farm. Samuel, a son of Williams above named, married the daughter of his grandfather's second wife by her first husband and after the death of his father took up his abode in the homestead which had been built about the old garrison house.

During his occupancy in 1765 he had a negro man servant named London who had married an Indian woman called Martha Ned. They lived together in a small house on the farm. There was a feud between London and two other negroes named "Port Royal" and "Polydore," slaves of Capt. Barker's neighbor Benjamin House. The antagonism became so bitter that Port Royal and Polydore made a violent and very effective attack upon their racial brother and his red wife and their dwelling. The story is interestingly told in a recital of the proceedings of the Superior Court of Judicature at the May term 1768:

"Port Royal, a negro man of Scituate in the County of Plymouth, Laborer and servant for life to Benjamin House of said Scituate, yeoman, and Polydore a negro man of said Scituate yeoman and servant for life of said Benjamin House, being indicted (at May Term 1765) for besetting the dwelling house of Martha Ned of said Scituate, an Indian woman and wife of London a negro man of said Scituate and servant for life to Samuel Barker of said Scituate two several times and for breaking the door and window of said house and for pulling down one end of the said house and for tearing off great parts of the roof of said house and for taking, stealing and carrying away from thence sundry goods of the value of £5 :16s :, the goods and chattels of said Martha Ned as in said indictment is at large set forth the said Port Royall and Polydore are now brought and set to the bar and arraigned and severally plead not guilty. A jury is thereupon sworn to try the issue Mr. Josiah Cushing foreman and fellows namely, David Damon, William Warren, Jona Carey, Ichabod Wood, Uriah Wadsworth, Elisha Stetson, Elisha Bisby, Recompense Magoun, Ebenezer Briggs, Amasa Thompson and Peleg Stetson, who having fully heard the evidence, upon their oath say that the said Port Royall is guilty of the two trespasses charged in the Indictment but is not guilty of the theft; and the said Polydore is guilty of two trespasses aforesaid but is not guilty of the theft."

As will be seen three years elapsed between the time of indictment and trial. It was not however until 1773 that Pelham Winslow of Plymouth, King's Attorney, having in the meantime tardily discovered that one of the petit jurymen had also been a member of the grand inquest which found the indictment, *nol pros'd* it.

His sons were the last of the descendants of William Barker to dwell there. It was still kept in the Barker family however being purchased by a descendant of Robert, brother of the first John.

JOHN WILLIAMS

The ship "Charles" from Barnstable, England, when it arrived at Boston in 1632 had on board John Williams, his wife Ann and four children, Ann, John, Edward and Mary. His destination was evidently Scituate, whence he immediately came and built a home on the north side of the harbor over-looking Cedar Point. His farm was in the Conihasset tract and upon the purchase from Hatherly he became one of the partners. He was early propounded and admitted as a freeman and at once began to take an active part in municipal affairs. In 1640 he was chosen, with Edward Foster, Humphrey Turner and Richard Sealis, as a deputy from the Colony Court and re-elected in the years 1643, 1644, 1647 and 1648. In 1641 he was the surveyor of highways.

Although not of the colonial council of war, he saw the importance to the little community of the site upon which he had built his home and he fashioned it with port holes after the manner of the "garrison" or "block" houses, which the Pilgrims found so essential to their defense against the Indians. A portion of it is standing to-day; although the outer walls have been covered with shingles and the inner re-inforced with brick. A brick floor takes the place of the original and the ancient pitch roof has been remodeled. It forms the ell of the present building. Like his neighbors he was hardworking, and frugal. He found his new acres thickly covered with cedar, with little meadow, but his own efforts and those of his two sons rapidly broke them up and reduced them to cultivation. From time to time he had his allotments in the division of Conihasset lands and when he deceased, it was a well cultivated farm of generous proportions that he left to his son John. The eldest child Ann married John Barker, then of Duxbury, later of Marshfield, in the same year her father came to

Scituate. Nineteen years later her sister Mary married Anthony Dodson, the surveyor of the Conihasset Partners. Both of the daughters reared families and have left numerous descendants, but John and Edward though each married, died without issue.

It was this second John Williams who kept the family name very much in evidence before his colonial neighbors between the time of his being made a freeman, and his death in 1694. His nature was a peculiar one. Industrious, wealthy, as material prosperity in those days went, yet he was a hard task master. He readily loaned money to those who applied for an accommodation, but their "bill of hand" or "specialty" always bore a generous interest. Brave to recklessness, as ensign and later captain of the military company, he was a natural leader in warfare and an uncompromisingly stern disciplinarian. He was early a constable of the town. In his home he was overbearing and quarrelsome to and with those who dwelt beneath his roof either as wife, ward or servant. His sister's son, John Barker, who was after the death of his father by drowning, early apprentised to him, later engaged in business ventures with him and frequently had occasion to sue him, bears witness however that he was kindhearted. In 1677 the two were engaged in logging on joint account. The timber was sawed into boards at the Stockbridge Mill on the First Herring Brook. Williams anticipated trouble and took the precaution to have the testimony of Charles Stockbridge, sworn to before James Cudworth an Assistant, perpetuated upon the records of the Court at Plymouth, as follows:—

"I, the deponnent, doe hereby testify that on the accoumpt of sawing of pyne timber, or loggs, into boards, which Capt. John Williams, and his reputed cosen †, John Barker brought to the mill, as they told mee, as co-partners, in the year one thousand six hun-

---

† Why "reputed cosen", is not clear. Barker was the only son and oldest child of John Barker of Marshfield who married Williams' sister, Ann. Winsor's History of Duxbury page 224.

dred and seventy and five, the sawing of which, as appears by my booke, according to my agreement, came to a just sume of four pounds and fourteen shillings and five pence halfepeny, and after the said logges were sawne, I saw the said Williams and Barker dividing the boards which were made of them, and one layed one part one way, and another the other part another way, the whole pay for which sawing above-said I have had of the said John Williams, concerning which the said John Barker asked me since if that I were payed, and I told him that his unkle had payed mee the whole pay, and he said that he was a good unkle. †

The trouble feared by Williams developed. Barker sued him for an accounting of his guardianship and let it be known among those who eagerly listened that "the said Williams is the wickedest man that ever was upon the face of the earth." Later, his uncle sued him for this defamation but did not put the slanderer to the proof. He permitted himself to become non suit.

Williams had as a member of his family, beside his nephew John, the latter's sister, Deborah. She was a posthumous child, born after her father had been drowned. At the

---

Williams was also his guardian. "Att the court of his Majestie holden att Plymouth, for the Jurisdiction of New Plymouth, the fifth day of March 1677-8 John Barker of Barnstable, complaineth against Captain John Williams of Scituate as guardian and receiver of the rents and proffits of the lands of the said John Barker during his minoritie, in an action of accoumpt, to the damage of two hundred pounds, for that the said John Williams as guardian in socage tooke into custody the said Barker, in the month of March, in the year 1657, and from the said time received the rents and proffitts of the said Barker's lands, in the townshipp of Marshfield, from the several yearly tenants of the same, until the said Barker did arrive at the age of twenty-one years, which was in the year 1672, being fourteen years compleat, and thereof hath not rendered an accoumpt to the plaintiffe to this day, notwithstanding the said guardian hath not improved the estate in educating and well bringing up the said heire, but contrariwise did improve the said heire as his servant, about the said Williams his own servill imployments." Plymouth Colony Records Vol VII Page 209.

---

† Plymouth Colony Records Vol VII page 212.

age of six or thereabouts she went to her uncle's to live. She was as Goodman Bird of Scituate told the Court "weake and infeirme" through the "hard usage" which she had received at her uncle's hands. Williams denied both these accusations and produced "many evidences to cleare his innocency in the premises." This he accomplished to a degree. Not so successfully, however, but that Governor Prence, John Alden, William Bradford and Josias Winslow, who sat in judgment upon the matter, determined to appoint Bird her guardian. They admonished him to take her home to live with him and "to endeavor to procure meanes for her cure."

In early life he married Elizabeth, the daughter of Rev. John Lathrop the first pastor of the First Church. Their married life was unhappy. His treatment of her was inexplicable. He may have been jealous, but this would not excuse the charges of incontinence which he made against her or "his abusive and harsh carriages towards her both in words and actions, in speciall his sequestration of himselfe from the marriage bed   x   x   x   x   and that especially in reference unto a child lately (1665) borne of his said wife by him denied to bee ligittimate." Her brother Barnabas took this charge up and complained to the Court. This body "requested Isaac Buck † to be officious therein, and so dismissed them from the Court for that time."

It was only for "that time." Buck's officiousness did not work "for the recovering of peace and love between them" as the Court had hoped. Instead, Williams persisted in his accusations and brought an action in Court against one Thomas Summers for "intollerable trespass in wronging and abusing the said Williams, by inticing his wife, from him, and for unlawfull dalliance with her." He did not bring it to trial but entered into an agreement, in which he renounced his accusation and "all which, together with all

---

† Isaac Buck was an intimate of Williams, a member of the 'train band' with him, and the person who first put him at the head of military company when Cudworth was deposed.

other surmises or charges to that purpose, or of that nature, I doe cleare, acquite, release and discharge the said Summers." This, of course did not satisfy Mrs. Williams or her relatives. She, and they, insisted that her good name should be cleared. The Court responded at once to this demand. Its proclamation was a complete refutation of the ugly slander. It is worthy of repetition here in full:—

"Whereas Elizabeth, the wife of John Williams, hath bine openly traduced and scandalized in her name, and by false reports and reproaches rendered as if shee were a dishonest woman, and that the child she brought forth into the world was not legitimate, these are to declare openly before the country, that the Court, having had sundry occations to hear and examine particulars sundry times relating to the premises, can find noe cause of blame in her in such respects, but that shee hath behaved herselfe as one that hath faithfully observed the bond of wedlocke."

Contemporaneously the much disturbed Bench took this action against him:—

"John Williams, Jr., for his disturbance and causing great expense to the countrey, in reference to the case about his wife, as is extant in the records of the Court, hee is fined to the use of the countrey the sum of £20."

In addition brother Barnabas brought other charges against Williams relating to the treatment of his wife, "to which the said Williams, though seeming to desire tryall of such his guiltiness or not guiltiness might bee put on a jury of his peers, yett afterwards refused it when granted him by the Court."

The Court treated him with manifest consideration, it "being earnestly desirous of a renewed closure of his hart and affections to his wife, and that his future conversation with her might bee better than his former, were willing to extend what lenitie might bee, and in reference thereunto, with exhortation of him to amend his wayes."

Neither leniency nor exhortation were of avail. He did

not mend his ways. The suffering and patient wife was finally forced to bring an action herself, asking for separate maintenance and support. She charged him with "defaming her; carrying bitterly against her in many respecte; witholding necessary comforts and conveniencyes suitable to her estate from her" and "whereas he should have been a shelter and a protection unto her, hath endeavored to reproach, insnare and betray her."

Upon this charge he got a trial by jury—"a jury of his equalls" which convicted him. The Court no longer dealt easily with him. It found that,—

"it is not safe or convenient for her to live with her husband, but do give her liberty at present to depart from him unto her friends until the Court shall otherwise order or he shall apply himselfe unto her in such a way as shee may be better satisfied to return to him againe, and doe order him to apparell her suitably att the present, and furnish her with a bed and beding and such like necessaryes, and to alow her ten pounds yearly to maintaine her while shee shalbee thuse absent from him, and for performance hereof doe require that hee put in cecuritie or that one third part of their entire estate bee cecured for her livelihood and comfort."

In addition, the Court pronounced this judgment.

"2ndly. For that hee hath greatly defamed and otherwise abused his said wife as in the premises, wee adjudge him to stand in the street or markett place by the post with an inscription over him that may declare to the world his unworthy carriages toward his wife."

To the great heartedness of this worthy and much wronged woman is due the fact that this sentence was not carried out. A marginal note made by the clerk says that:

"Att the earnest request of his wife, this part of the centance was remited and not executed."

He however was amerced in the sum of twenty pounds.

It is not recorded that she ever lived with him again. For over twenty-five years, she found it necessary to resort to the Court at intervals in order to obtain the annual stipend which it had awarded her. As late as 1691 when he was at an advanced age (he died in 1694) she was still living with her brother Barnabas. On the sixteenth day of June in that year he, "in behalf of his sister Elizabeth Williams, relating to her yearly maintenance formerly ordered by the General Court to be paid unto her by Capt. John Williams her husband," applied to the Court for assistance in its collection. Wearied, no doubt, by the stubbornness of the still recalcitrant Williams, to whom for almost a quarter century it had given good advice, exhortation, persuasion and punishment all to no avail, this body declined further jurisdiction and resolved "that ye tryall of that case doth now properly belong to a county Court." †

Deane ‡ has fallen into two errors concerning this trouble between Williams and his wife. He has mistaken Ensign John Williams of Scituate for John Williams of Barnstable and has construed the above proceeding to be a decree of divorce. The latter error may have arisen from the fact that Dr. Shurtleff, the editor of the Colony Records published under the order of the Legislature in 1855, so treats it in the index §. But the only cause for divorce in the Plymouth Colony in 1666 was adultery, and this charge made by Williams against his wife in defence of his abusive conduct towards her, he was unable to sustain. The fact that Isaac Buck was appointed by the Court to act as mediator between the two, indisputably identifies the John Williams named in the record as Ensign Williams of Scituate. Indeed, he is so-called in the record of the proceedings of October third, again as John Williams, Jr., in the same record, and as Captain John Williams in 1691. John Williams of Barnstable was not the son of John Williams, senior, of Scituate, nor was he an ensign. He divorced his wife,

---

† Plymouth Colony Records Vol IV pages 93, 107, 121, 125, 126 and 191 Vol VI page 267. Vol VII pages 110, 113, 125, 138 and 141.
‡ History of Scituate page 385.
§ Plymouth Colony Records Vol IV Page 106.

Sarah, in 1673. At about the same time, John Williams of Scituate as Executor of the will of his brother Edward, was litigating with some of his neighbors over claims due the latter's estate, and in the last order made by the Court with reference to his wife's maintenance, the ensign is described as John Williams, Jr., of Scituate.

These errors, very naturally, led him to a third—that of supposing that Ensign Williams' wife was a daughter of Barnabas Lothrop; not his sister. The will of John Lothrop a brother of Barnabas † is conclusive to the contrary. It is dated April 7, 1715, probated eleven days later, and provides that if his only son Joseph, die, being survived by the widow then the rest and residue (after making small legacies to the First Church in Boston and Rev. Benj. Walsworth, its pastor) "to be equally divided.

One-half to go to my welbeloved wife Esther; the other half to my brother Barnabas and sisters, namely:— Mary, Martha, Elizabeth, Hannah, Abigail and Experience."

This treatment by Williams of his wife did not seem to destroy his usefulness in public affairs. He soon got to be the head of the military company, was a selectman, a member of the Council of War, a grand and petit juror and twice a deputy to the Colony Court. The service which he rendered in Phillip's War was of the same high and courageous character as that performed by his neighbors, Gen. Cudworth, Capt. Michael Peirce and Lieut. Isaac Buck. At its close, he received "£4:04s: from the Colony in gratifycation for his services in the late warr."

Combativeness was a dominant trait in his character. When he could not find Indians with whom to battle, he fought with his neighbors. He was engaged, either as a suitor or sued in sixty-three law suits between the years 1648 and the time of his death. Many of these seem to have been brought for the mere love of being in litigation.

He would become non suit in an action only to petition for

---

† Suffolk Probate Records No. 3739.

a review by the Court at its next sitting. Appeals from the Selectmen's Court were many; his recoveries few. Likewise he was a frequent defendant upon the criminal side. He was fined forty shillings for harboring a Quaker. A like penalty was imposed for working on the Lord's Day; and shortly before his death he was fined five pounds for "selling severall potts of cyder to the Indians."

It is not to be understood from the foregoing that Capt. Williams was at all times quarrelsome and agressive. He had a distinctly different side to his nature. He was impulsive, ready at once to become surety for a neighbor who was in trouble; the next day to combat with him. This is well shown in two instances. On one occasion as ensign he had laid a fine on Humphrey Johnson for not training in the military company. The latter sued him, alleging that this was unlawfully and maliciously done; and yet not many years after when Johnson was in one of his numerous troubles, Capt. Williams became surety for him. On another occasion Capt. Cudworth had hired an Indian to cut his winter's supply of wood on the Gulph Island. The redman erected a wigwam there for his shelter. Something in this which angered Williams, impelled him to go upon the island and tear down the habitation. This brought about a suit between Cudworth and Williams in which the former was awarded five pounds. This was just before the beginning of Phillip's War. The two had already clashed in Court several times, yet Gen. Cudworth had no more loyal supporter, no more obedient officer, than this same Capt. John Williams during the years when, under his command, they both were warring with a common enemy in Phillip's War. In that struggle Capt. Benjamin Church, knowing that it was Phillip's custom to be foremost in the fight, when he was about to re-engage him at Rehoboth "went down to the swamp and gave Capt. John Williams of Scituate the command of the right wing of the army and placed an Ensign and an Indian together, behind such shelters of trees as he could find, taking care to place them at such distance that none might pass undiscovered between them. † When the struggle ended Williams took two of the captive Indian boys into his home and service. In his will he appropriately restored to them the share of the Indian lands at Showamet given to him as the "part due unto (him)" for his services in that bloody conflict.

He left a large property which he divided generously, yet with discrimination.

The will ‡ is carefully and skilfully drawn. It is in the handwriting of Samuel Sprague, his long time friend, whom he remembers in it, and who was Register of Wills for the County of Plymouth at the time. It is dated October fifteenth 1691, and was evidently executed at Sprague's home in Marshfield the witnesses being all Marshfield—not Scituate—men. Excerpts from it follow:

"I, John Williams of Scituate in the County of Plimouth in New England being at this present, weak of Body and under ye chastising hand of God yet of sound memory and competent understanding x x do therefore hereby make and declare this my last will and testament in maner and form following:

Imprimis. I commit and commend my eternall concernments to the mercy of God in Jesus Christ and my body to decent burial, as to my executor and christian friends shall seem meet.

Item. To Williams Barker the son of my nephew John Barker of Marshfield all that my ffarme in Scituate on which I live and dwell, that is to say my two hundred acres of land formerly purchased of Mr. Timothy Hatherly and all the meadow at Cedar Point and that called the wash house meadow and that at Musquashcut pond to be enjoyed by him when he shall reach the full age of 21 years." Until then the farm to be occupied by his father "he employing the rents and pro-

---

† Hubbard's Indian Wars Vol I Page 271 note.
‡ Plymouth Colony Records (Wills) Vol I pages 200-205. The original much worn and partially lost is in the present files No. 23033.

fits thereof for paying such legacies out of said farm as I shall hereafter appoint. If Williams Barker shall die or depart this life without issue lawfully begotten then my will is that Samuel Barker his brother shall have and enjoy said farm, x x x he then giving himself and being thenceforth called by the name of Williams Barker."

"Item. To my well beloved nephew John Barker £30." His son John £10: his son Samuel aforesaid £30: and each of the daughters of John Barker £10. "All to be paid in convenient time out of the profits of said farm."

Item. Further to nephew John "one moiety or half share in Conihasset undivided lands."

Item. "To my well beloved nephew Abraham Blush of Boston," house and lands in Scituate which formerly "was my brother Edward Williams deceased & my two remaining lots in Conahasset and my lot there which I purchased of Richard Sillis. He paying £60 to certain legatees."

"Item. To my good friend Samuel Fuller of Middleborough £10: to Sarah the wife of Thomas Stetson £10. To the children of Abraham Blush £40 to be equally divided between them."

"Item. To my well beloved nephew Jonathan Dodson all my lands in Freetown and meadow at Sippecan and on Taunton river."

"Item. I give and Bequeath to my Ancient servant John Bayley of Scituate All that my ffarme on which he now liveth with all my upland, meadow land or marsh lying near adjacent to the same vizt that in Conihasset neck and that at or near ffane Island and said Islands with my meadow in the sixty acres of marsh so-called, and also one moiety or half a share of Conihasset undivided land, to hold to him his heirs and Assigns forever; provided he shall pay and I hereby order him to pay out of it or the rents and proffits thereof in Good merchantable pay to such of my Legatees as I shall nominate the sume of one hundred pounds and to pay the same at ten severall times of payment in equall proportions, that is to say, ten pounds per year every year till the whole is paid."

He gave to his sister Mary Dodson ten pounds and a like amount to each of her daughters, Margaret, Bethiah and Eunice Dodson, Mary Booth and Patience Pierce on condition that they deliver to his executors "a bond or bill obligatory on which I stand charged as debtor to the estate of my late father John Williams in the sum of £40." These legacies were to be paid by John Bayley.

Item. "To my nephew John Barker my common purchase right in Conahasset and the Township of Scituate."

Item. "I give and bequeath to my two boys and children George and Thomas whom I obtained with my sword and with my bow and whom I will that they be sirnamed after my name vizt: George Williams and Thomas Williams, I say I give to each of them as followeth that is to say:—I give and bequeath to the said George Williams one whole share of land at Showamet both divided and undivided, that is to say more particularly one lot lying next to the lot of Lieut. Little and one lot in the outlet being the first and second lot next to the neck and one lot of five acres in the Little Neck called Boston Neck with a share of ye undivided land as aforesaid."

Item. "I further give and bequeath to the said George Williams the Bed and furniture whereon Richard Cox usually lodgeth and one of my guns which he shall choose and my black horse which he useth to ride on and the sum of £10 x x x I further give to the said George Williams the sum of £20 to be paid to him by John Bayley £10 within seven years after my decease and tother £10 within eight years."

Item. "I give and bequeath to Thomas Williams all that my corne mill and lands that I have within the township of Middleborough excepting that given to my kinswoman Mary, now wife of David Wood x x x I further give to said Thomas Williams my three score acres of land that I purchased of John Hammone deceased lying in ffoards farms so-called. Further I give and bequeath to the said Thomas Williams one whole share of land in Showamet both divided and undivided that is to say, two lots of upland lying together at a place called Labour in Vain and one five acre lot in said Boston Neck; with one whole share of undivided lands at Showamet with what meadows I have in at or near said place called Labour in Vain."

Item. "I further give to said Thomas Williams the sum of £20 to be paid by the said John Bailey £10 in nine years after my decease and £10 in ten years; further I give the said Thomas Williams the bed I usually lodge in with ye furniture belonging to it. I also give him the mare that is usually called his and her colt, and two cows and the two stiers that I hired to John and Stephen Burdere and £10 in money all to be paid to his order or guardian."

Item. "I further give and bequeath all the rest of my meadow on the Taunton River that is not before given to the aforesaid George Williams x x x x and if either the said George Williams or Thomas Williams happen to die or depart this life without issue that the survivor of them enjoy the portion or legacy of the said deceased; and if both of them shall die without issue that then my will is that my servant Tom Bailey have and enjoy the portions given to them."

Item. "I give and bequeath to my servant Tom Bailey one whole share of land at Showamet aforesaid that is to say my lot lying on the southerly side of Lieut Little's lot there and my lot that I purchased of Captain Church in the Great Neck, with a five acre lot at or near the Little Neck called Boston Neck also purchased of said Church and one whole share of undivided land in said Showamet   x   x   x   x   I also give him one horse."

Item. "I give and bequeath to my servant Will one horse and the bed and furniture whereon he usually lodgeth and half a share of land at Showamet which said half a share I purchased of Daniel Hicks   x   x   x   x   and one-half a share in the undivided land of Showamet with about ten acres more of the said undivided land which I also had of said Hicks."

Item. "I hereby release and set free and at Liberty my said Boys George Williams and Thomas Williams, and my said man servants Thom. Bayley and Will, hereby ordering that every of them shall be free from servitude immediately after my decease."

Item. "I do hereby commit the Inspection care and oversight of my said boy Thomas Williams unto my friend and Neighbor Joseph Woodworth of Scituate hereby impowering him as a Guardian to said boy, to receive his portion afore given to him and to take the rents and profits of his lands and to Improve and dispose thereof for the good of said Boy in Bringing of him up in the nurture and admonition of the Lord, and to learning of the tongues, arts and sciences."

To his friend Joseph Woodworth he gave five pounds and all the rest of his undivided Conihasset lands. He gave his kinswoman Deborah Burden of Middleborough and each of her children five pounds; to Anna Pratt another relative and each of her children the same sum; to Mary Wood of Middleborough who he also styles a kinswoman "my twenty sheep which are now in her possession," and to each of her children five pounds; to Rebecca the wife of Samuel House one cow and a heifer and to her daughter Rebecca five pounds; to Peter Wortheylake of Scituate five pounds; to Robert Stanford the same sum and a release and acquittance of "whatsoever debt or debts he oweth me;" to Richard Cox and John Hoskins five and four pounds respectively and "to my much esteemed friend Samuel Sprague of Marshfield fifteen pounds and my third part of my book of Statutes which is now in his possession."

Item. "I do hereby further declare it to be my mind and will that if any of my said legatees shall not take up and rest satisfied with this my will and the legacies hereby given to him or them, but shall endeavor to alter, defeat or make void my said will, every such dissatisfied legatee opposing this my will as aforesaid shall have no benefit by the same but shall lose the legacy hereby given to him or them the same to be equally parted amongst such of my legatees as shall acquiese and rest satisfied with this my said will."

The much beloved nephew John Barker was made executor.

"And I do hereby request my above named friends Samuel Sprague and Joseph Woodworth to be the overseers of this my will and to use their utmost care that the same be in all points performed according to the true intent and meaning thereof."

A memorandum added after the will had been thus far written but before signing was as follows, viz:

"I further give and bequeath unto my said sister Mary Dodson £10 to be paid to her when she shall give up the bond aforesaid "and whereas it is before expressed that I give to each of the children of Mary Wood the sum of £5 my meaning is excepting those children she had by her husband coombs, whom I have formerly taken care of and provided for."

Item. "I give to Ruth the wife of Joseph Garret £5."

Item. "I give to James Doughty £5."

Signed in presence of
    Samuel Little
    Valentine Diecrow
    Benjamin Phillips

JOHN WILLIAMS

In all the will there was neither mention of, nor provision for the widow Elizabeth, who was still living at Barnstable, on the day of his death June 22, 1694. The inventory † of personal property alone, and not including the "three indian servants, Will, George and Tom" who had been given their friedom footed up £449:085:06d. When the instrument was offerred for probate before William Bradford, son of the former Governor, Mrs. Williams was represented by William Basset of Sandwich who appeared by special power of attorney and claimed not only her dower rights in the large estate of her husband but also "all and every such debts and sums of money as are now due to me from my husband in the month of March last past and what hath since become due unto me for non-payment of the same." He died still in arrears for alimony. She made no contest. Her dower rights were preserved to her in the decree setting up the will.

---

† It was made by Thomas Hyland, James Briggs and Nathaniel Turner on November 14, 1694 and shows "corn growing on ye land £1.10s".

OTIS

John Otis was born on the banks of the Taw, at Barnstable in old Devon in the same year that the Pilgrims sailed away from Plymouth. When he was fifteen years of age his father, impelled by the same motives which actuated Carver, Bradford and Winslow, sought and found a new home near another tidal stream—Weir River in Hingham. Here the boy lived and married Mary, the daughter of Nicholas Jacob, his father's neighbor in 1653. He lost his mother by death and his father removed to Weymouth the same year.

Hingham continued to be his home until 1661 when with the oldest child, also named John, he moved to Scituate and took up his abode on the driftway. The second son Stephen came into being here soon after. James, Joseph and Job were born respectively in the years 1663, 1665 and 1667.

Of the eldest son John, who staid in Barnstable after his father had completed a temporary residence there, no mention will be made in these pages. As the ancestor of James Otis of Boston his place is secure. His brothers who lived in Scituate gave to the town, colony and province, progeny no less worthy and able than that of their elder kinsman but less conspicuous perhaps because of environment and of inequality of opportunity.

The first John Otis lived in Scituate for twenty-three years. The family home under Coleman's hills was occupied for a time and then a new and more commodious one was built on Otis hill, overlooking the beaver dams on Satuit brook. His life in the town was not different from that of others of his same standing—he was a freeman, a grand and petit juror, a constable and served upon inquests. All these services denote the superior man of the community. Many of the inhabitants of the colony originally came thence as servants. Others, as Bradford complained, had been thrust upon the Pilgrims, and their immediate followers, by the financial sponsors of the colonization for the latter's personal gain. They wanted able-bodied persons capable of endurance and toil; and they found many willing to emigrate who were without either religious zeal or moral restraint. The colonists during the first century would no more have thought of electing one of these to civil or military office than they would of choosing him a deacon of the parish. † Therefore the occupancy of office, the designation to officiate in however small capacity in the enforcement of the Pilgrim's rule of civil polity carried with it the badge of superiority.

Only once did John Otis the father of these boys fall below the standard set for him by his neighbors and by himself for himself. In October 1671 he was fined £2 for selling cider without a license but then the devout Cudworth had done the same thing and brave John Williams was punished for a similar offence not long afterward.

Stephen, the second son was a Conihasset partner. He was commissioned a captain of grenadiers at the age of thirty-seven. At the outbreak of the French and Indian War he was put in command of an expedition to L'Accadie, Nova Scotia being ordered to "enlist forty or fifty Indians" on that side"‡ A letter to Governor Dudley from his son in command at Province Galley in June 1707 speaks of their hardships:—

"We are willing and ready to return to ye Camp with a good reinforcement, notwithstanding all our Difficultys and their thirty-two pounders, which we were somewhat used to at last, we had one man killed in our Ravage up the river, and the man wounded of

---

† One exception should be made to this statement. In the efforts to banish the Quakers, the instrumentality chosen for that purpose was George Barlow of Sandwich the marshal, than whom a greater rascal did not live in the colony.

‡ Province Laws Vol VIII pages 241 and 683.

Otis Company Dead since our Passage. For want of good Discipline and Order our Officers and men were soon Discouraged, altho we had Deserters trying every day to escape to our Camp, and two poor men Endeavoring were executed in our sight, and not having our Mortars, Artillery &c to defend us and offend the Enemy caused such speed and hast in our Retreat which was performed without the Least Damage."

Returned from the war he operated a tannery up to the time of his death. He was succeeded in this business by his son Ensign (so named for his mother who was Hannah, the daughter of Thomas Ensign), who served as a representative to the General Court in 1751, 1752, and 1753. Two other sons were physicians—Dr. Isaac who graduated from Harvard in 1738 and practised in Bridgewater and Dr. James in Scituate. Dr. Cushing Otis the son of Dr. James Otis and Dr. Ephraim at Assinippi were also descendants of Stephen.

Joseph Otis the fourth son like his eldest brother in Barnstable was a judge of the court of Common Pleas for his county. He married Dorothy, a daughter of Col. Nathaniel Thomas of Marshfield. He assumed his judicial duties in 1703 and served for eleven years, being also elected to the General Court in 1710. Contemporaneous in service with him on this bench were his father-in-law Judge Thomas, John Cushing of Scituate, James Warren of Plymouth, grandfather of him of Bunker Hill fame, and Isaac Winslow of Marshfield son and grandson of Plymouth Colony governors. Only one of these men—Judge Thomas —was bred to the law but the possession of "universal confidence and esteem, integrity fortitude and humanity" according to the Boston Evening Post † was an equivalent to knowledge of the law for service in the judiciary in these years. It may fairly be assumed that Joseph Otis possessed at least some of these.

He did not however possess the esteem or confidence of

---

† Obituary on Judge Winslow, December 1738.

Judge Sewall of the Superior Court of Judicature. A controversy was litigated in this court sitting at Plymouth, over some land claimed by one Thompson of Middleborough. A deed of the parcel was introduced in evidence bearing the attesting signature of Joseph Otis. He testified at the trial over which Judge Sewall presided. The latter, prone to jump at conclusions, immediately conceived the belief that there was fraud in the transaction; that Otis was its sponsor and was in some way to profit by it. No record is extant to give either particulars of or the result of the suit. A criminal action involving the same facts was brought against Otis in which he was acquitted. Judge Sewall was much incensed at the result. The following entry in his diary evidences his feelings:—

"March 27, 1716. † (At Plymouth) Court held by 4 Justices March 31. Great storm of snow on the Ground and falling and Jury not agreed; yet about Noon got away the weather clearing. To Mr. Joseph Otis, brought in Not Guilty! I said, The providence of God in clearing you will I hope melt your heart; for what you did was notoriously criminal."

Whatever may have been the moral obloquy of Otis— it would be unsafe to assume any upon the unsupported accusation of the erratic and impressional Sewall—the latter's attempt later to oust him from his position on the bench of the lower court by secret accusations to Governor Dudley, which Otis had no chance to refute is most despicable. That Judge Sewall did this there is no doubt. He unblushingly and with apparent satisfaction makes this entry in his diary:

"Feby 12, 1708: I went to the Gov. at Maj. Winthrop's house, and told him I could be glad Mr. Higginson might be brought into Superior Court. Advised that Mr. Winslow might be brought into Superior Court of Plymouth and Mr. Otis left out: Col. Tho. son-in-law. Told him of the fraudilent deed complain-

---

† This date is taken from Mass. Hist. Coll. Vol VII Page 76. It must be wrong and is probably 1706: See post page 445.

ed of by Mr. Tomson of Middleborough; that the said Otis hand was to the fraudilent Deed as a witness, has now a part of what was granted by it; and was probably the Adviser in the whole matter. Told the Govr. I intended to wait upon his Excellency on Wednesday; but was hindered by the Storm. Note. The Gov'r us'd to tell the Councilors how acceptable 'twould be to him to be discours'd in privat about such matter." †

The note following this entry indicates that Judge Sewall himself felt that he had done something not quite honorable. True, as a member of the Council he had the right to advise the Governor when important public appointments were to be made. But Otis was already upon the bench and councillor Sewall's advice was that he be "dropped" and another put in his place. The reprehensibility consists in the fact that this effort was made by him privately. He may have had this action of his own in mind when charging the grand jury at the first term of court held in the new Town House on May 5, 1713:—

"You ought to be quickened to your duty in that you have so convenient and august a chamber prepared for you to do it in, and what I say to you I would say to myself, to the court, and all that are concerned, seeing the former decayed building is consumed, and a better built in the (its) room, let us pray that God would take away our filthy garments and clothe us with a change of raiment, that our sins may be buried in the ruins and the rubbish of the former house and not be sufferred to follow into this: x x x Let this large transparent costly glass serve to oblige the attorneys always to set things in a true light." ‡

Whatever may be said of the conduct of Judge Sewall in the manner of making his accusations against Judge Otis to the Governor, the charges themselves were of no avail for he continued to serve until 1714.

† Mass. Hist. Soc. Coll. Vol. Page
‡ Mass. Hist. Soc. Coll. Vol Page

THE VINALS

Ann Vinal, widow, with her children Martha, Stephen and John came to Scituate from England in 1636. She had but recently been bereaved, through the loss of her husband, and, possessed of a comfortable competence, much thrift and enormous energy, she took up her abode in a house which she built at Greenbush. Her daughter Martha was in her teens; Stephen was six; and John three. It was not to be expected that she would support this small but husky family out of the income to be obtained through tilling the unresponsive soil at the First Herring Brook. She had no notion when she left the home on the other side of the water, that it should be supported by any such means. She was an accomplished spinster, and brought with her, from England, the spinning wheel, hand loom, and a stock of woolen yarn and "coarse threads" with which she immediately began to supply the needs of her neighbors, in exchange for those necessities of life which she could not supply herself.

It is a little singular that she did not re-marry. Second and third marriages among the early pilgrims were frequent and a fourth and fifth search for connubial happiness, not unusual. If she had the opportunity, she did not grasp it, but stuck steadily to her loom and her children. She saved scrupulously, and continually added to her stock of home-made fabrics. She bought the same interest in the Conihasset lands as her male partners and chose her "lay out" shrewdly when the first allotment was made.

Her daughter Martha married Isaac Chittenden the son of her fellow weaver and Conihasset Partner, Thomas Chittenden, in 1646. Stephen and John continued to live with their mother. When the former married Mary, the daughter of Rev. Nicholas Baker, he took his bride to live at his mother's home.

But three years passed before Ann Vinal, still a comely widow in her fifties, died. Stephen and Mary then succeeded to the "estate." Stephen and his brother John were administrators. This inventory which they filed, bears out the assertion that she was not only a skilled spinster but a thrifty woman as well.

	L	S	D
"Wearing apparel	13:		
In money	6:	13:	04:
Two cows, one heifer and calf	10:		
One mare and two colts	12:		
Three swine	03:	10:	
Woolen cloth & linsey woolsey and cotton and linen cloth	08:	09:	
Six yards of cloth	00:	04:	06:
Five pairs of coarse sheets and an odd sheet and an odd sheet and 4 yards and 1-2 linsey woolsey	03:		
Bedding and sheets belonging to it	07:	08:	
14 yards of cloth and 3 yards of cotton and linen cloth		17:	
Fine linen	01:	09:	
Corn	02:		
Coarse linnine		10:	
A winnowing sheet and bags	01:		
Furniture for a bed, taut rope and a bed cord	01:		
Woolen yarne and coarse thread		16:	
Tallow candles and tallow, tallow riband and tape		08:	
Brass vessels	03:	10:	
Pewter	01:	04:	
One leather vessel		10:	
Iron vessel and other iron goods	02:		
A table, forme and wooden vessels	01:	10:	
Working hooks	01:	15:	

Books	05:
Syder apples and a yard of calico	12:

                                          157: 10: 10:
Nicholas Baker   This is a correct inventory
Nathaniel Baker   excepting the land"

The land excepted from the above was the homestead and one-thirtieth part of the Conihasset tract. Stephen took both. Later he became clerk to the partners. He was admitted a freeman in 1658; was a surveyor of highways in 1662 and 1673, and a member of the grand jury in 1658, 1679 and 1682. He frequently sat upon the coroner's inquest, a duty which only the best men in the community were called upon to perform. He appears to have led a peaceful life, full of modest usefulness to the community.

John married Elizabeth Baker, a sister of his brother's wife. He was admitted a freeman in the same year that his brother took the oath, was chosen a constable and like Stephen served as the highway surveyor. He was apparently not of robust health, as he neared the half century of his life, and was freed from training in 1683 on this account. He died three years later.

Litigation which took place over his will, discloses a circumstance, the like of which not infrequently arises to vex the genealogist and antiquary. As is stated above, he married Elizabeth, the daughter of Rev. Nicholas Baker. His children were John, Elizabeth, Hannah, Jacob and Grace, born in the order named between the years 1665 and 1672. There is no record of any other marriage and yet; —let the record † tell the rest of the story:—

"Att a Court of Assistants held at New Plymouth, the first Tuesday in July, 1686.

Mrs. Elizabeth Vial ‡ relict of Mr. John Vial, deceased, appearing at his majesties Court held at Pli-

---

† Plymouth Colony Records Vol VI Page 199.
‡ In the early days the name was interchangeably spelled, Vial, Vyal and Vinal.

mouth ye first Tuesday of June, 1686, producing an instrument said to be the will of her late husband, and offering a probate of the same. But Mr. John Vial, the eldest son of sd Mr. John Vial, deceased, in behalf of himself and others of his brothers and sisters, entered a caution with the Court, and gave some reasons for it, and made his request to the Court that the probate of sd will might be suspended to this Court. Said Mrs. Elizabeth Vial at this Court appeared, and urged the sd will might be proved; and Capt. Anthony Checkley, as attorney, and in behalf of sd. Mr. John Vial, eldest son of the above said John Vyal, deceased as alsoe others of the children of sd deceased, appeared and produced his reasons, and gave in sundry testimonys to make appeare the will to be uncertaine, unreasonable, &c, and not be allowed, but made null by this Court. This Court having seen the sd will, and heard what was said, and considered what was produced by both party's, and finding uncertainty in said will in most parts thereof, whereby the mind of the testator cannot be well understood, and considering that by reason of alteration of the estate since sd will was first made, there is nothing really given to *the children he had by his first wife,* doe therefore not admitt the probate thereof, but judge it voyd. Yett in the disposall and settling of ye estate do judge meet that there be respect had as much as may be to the mind of the deceased in the writing presented as his will."

It may be that his wife Elizabeth (Baker) deceased after the birth of his last child. There is no record available to determine the date of her demise. In this event, correctly assuming that the Court was right in stating "that by reason of the alteration of the estate since sd will was first made, there is nothing really given to the children he had by *his first wife,*" he must have married another Elizabeth

---

† The italics are mine. Author.

for his second. It is not going far afield to assume that if so, the new wife prevailed upon him to make a will in her favor to the exclusion of the children. The action of the Court seems to bear out this conclusion, especially, as out of consideration for the widow, the recommendation was made "that there be respect had as much as may be to the mind of the deceased in the writing presented as his will."

The Vinals have always been prominent in Scituate. They have performed useful service in the settlement and development of other communities as well. Vinalhaven on the Maine coast is named for a descendant of Ann Vinal. Major William Vinal, another member of this family, built a shipyard at the confluence of Quincy Town river and Weymouth Fore river in the latter part of the eighteenth century and built up Quincy Point to an industrious community.

Gideon Vinal, of the fifth generation from Ann, was a representative to the General Court, in the years 1766 to 1774 and in the latter was chosen a member of the Provincial Congress which met at Salem. His cousin Israel, was one of the delegates to the Convention at Cambridge, which prepared the state constitution in 1779, and in 1783, 1784, 1786 and 1791 was a member from Scituate to the Great and General Court of Massachusetts. His brother Jonathan graduated from Harvard College in 1751, and became a preacher.

The Vinals took a conspicuous part in the town's activities immediately preceding and during the Revolutionary War. Ignatius and Issacher were both on the committee of "Correspondence, Inspection and Safety;" Israel assisted in drafting the patriotic resolutions which Nathan Cushing presented to the Assembly; he was a member of the first Committee of Inspection and a captain of the military company. Calogus as a Minute Man marched to Lexington in Capt. William Turner's Company, and afterward served in the Continental Army for nine months from June 9, 1779. Benjamin was a Sergeant in Capt Nathaniel Winslow's company and Stephen (there has always been a Stephen in the family) and Joseph, Jr., were privates. The former was disabled in the service and drew that always-deserved and well-merited American reward of valor—a Revolutionary pension.

THE TILDENS

Joseph Tilden of Tenterden in Kent, England, was one of the Merchant Adventurers of London who stood steadfastly by the Pilgrims in the many disagreements which existed between the forefathers and their financial promoters, until the purchase of all the interests of the latter by Hatherly, Andrews, Beauchamp and Shirley. Two of his brothers, Nathaniel and Thomas were in Plymouth Colony before 1628, the former at Scituate, the latter at Marshfield.

Nathaniel brought with him from the old country his wife, Lydia and children Joseph, Thomas, Mary, Sarah, Judith and Lydia and built his home on Kent Street between Greenfield lane and the Driftway. Here Stephen, the youngest son, was born. In addition to the land upon which this house was placed he early had allotted to him arable land on the Third Cliff to which he frequently added by purchases from John Emerson, Henry Merritt, William Crocker and other neighbors, until he possessed much of the upland and adjacent marsh in that locality. He was among the wealthiest of the early planters of Scituate and owned large land areas along the North River, in the New Harbor marshes at Scituate and in Marshfield. He had left a comfortable, not to say pretentious home in England † for a rude dwelling here, that he might obtain the greater spiritual solace of an unhampered devotional. He was the ruling elder of the first church gathered by Mr. Lothrop in 1634. During the six years prior to its establishment when Annable, Gilson, Cobb and the others had been "orderly

---

† In his will he gave to his wife who after his death married Timothy Hatherley, "the benefit of one house with lands thereunto belonging, wherein one Richard Lambert now dwelleth, being in the parish of Tenterdem in Kent in Old England, during the term of her natural life. After the decease of said Richard Lambert, then my mind and will is that my two youngest children, Lidea and Steven shalbe maintained both for meate, drink and apparel and lodging by mine executor hereinafter named yet

dismissed" from the Plymouth Church "in case they join in a body at Seteat," he was active in the religious life of the dwellers on Kent Street, when meetings were held in the house of James Cudworth. It was during this period that Giles Saxton although not regularly established as their pastor preached to them, and Nathaniel Tilden "being also qualified in some degree to teache" † assisted him or taught in his absence. It was most natural that having so officiated he should have been made the ruling elder" of Mr. Lothrop's congregation. He was all devotion to his religious principles, yet in nowise a fanatic. An interesting side light is thrown upon his character and one which perhaps affords the reason for his settling in Scituate rather than in Plymouth by a retrospection of affairs ecclesiastical as they existed in the latter town. Robinson, though in far away Leyden, denied through the machinations of some of the Adventurers who forced John Lyford upon the Pilgrims, was still the pastor of their church. He was represented in Plymouth by Elder Brewster, who could not however ad-

---

so as my aforesaid wife shall have the education and disposing of them". He also gave his wife "all her wearing apparell, both linen and woolen, also one bed furnished, which she shall please to take also the great trunk, also I give unto my said wife three pairs of sheets and two pairs of pillow coates, which she shall please to take, one long table and cloth, one square table and cloth, one dozen of middle napkins and one half a dozen of other napkins, two long towels, twelve peices of pewter, which she shall please to choose and of wooden vessels so many as she shall think convenient for her use, also three silver spoons and two of my best spoons, also I give unto my said wife one piece of white fustoon (fustian) also my two shoates, also tenn bushels of corn, five of English and five of Indian, also my will is that she shall have the whole benefit of my white faced cow and the calves which she shall have during the term of her natural life to be maintained and kept for her by mine executor.

---

† Mere ruling elders—who are to help the pastors in overseeing and ruling; that their offices be not temporary as the Dutch and French churches but continual; and being also qualified in some degree to teach, they are to teach occasionally, through necessity or in their pastors absence or illness; but being not to give theselves to study or teaching having no need of maintenance". Prince's Annals page 777.

minister the church sacraments. † Lyford har been summarily dismissed and, "this year (1628) Mr. Allerton brought over a yonge man for a minister to ye people hear, wheather upon his owne head or at ye motion of some friends there, I well know not, but it was, without ye churches sending; for they had been so bitten by Mr. Lyford, as they desired to know ye person well whom they should invite amongst them. His name was Mr. Rogers; but they perceived, upon some triall, that he was crased in his braine; so they were faine to at further charge to send him back againe ye nexte year." ‡

Both of these miscarriages of efficient teaching of the faith at Plymouth had undoubtedly discouraged but not disheartened Tilden and he came to Scituate in the same year when Mr. Rogers being put upon "some triall" was found to be "crased in his braine." It is not improbable that he hoped thus early to bring about an eventual settlement at Scituate, with the aid of his brother Joseph, or Mr. Lothrop whom he had known as a sound preacher in the nearby parish at Egerton. Thus he gathered about him Foster, Rowley, Annable and Lewis and their families and became in effect a ruling elder until the advent of Mr. Lothrop made him one in fact.

He stood firmly with the remnant of this first church when its teacher and a majority of its members removed to Barnstable.

There is no record that at any time he held civil office in either town or colony. He devoted himself to clearing and tilling the lands which he acquired and stocking them with cattle, hogs and bees. He died in 1641.

---

† "Now touching the question propounded by you, I judge it not lawful for you, being a ruling elder, as Rom. XII 7, 8, and 1 Tim. V17, opposed to the elders that teach and exhort and labor in the word and doctrine to which the sacraments are annexed, to administer them, nor convenient if it were lawful".
Letter from John Robinson to Elder Brewster December 20, 1623—Young's Chronicles page 477.

‡ The Bradford History page 292.

Joseph his eldest son, readily took up the church activities which the father had laid down with the second parish however. When he removed from the house on Kent Street built by his father, he married Elizabeth Twisden and made a new home near the First Herring brook and the mill which he erected there under a contract with the town. He had already succeeded to the major portion of the lands owned by his father in Marshfield and Scituate and began the acquisition of large tracts for himself. He bought fifty-nine acres of upland and marsh adjoining the North River from Samuel House of Cambridge, more of Manasseth Kempton of Plymouth and William Hatch of Scituate and increased his ownership at the Third Cliff by purchases from Thomas Richard and John Hanmore. When Hatherly died and Tilden became his residuary devisee, he was one of the largest individual owners of land in the Colony. Much of it was improved land which he cultivated extensively. His business at the mill was also large. Its product found a market at Boston whither it was conveyed by water. The management of his private affairs apparently left him little time for public employment or it may be that like his father he was disinclined toward the latter. It may also be that with the exception of Hatherly, he was not on cordial terms with the men who constituted the Court in the decade between 1644 and 1654. In the former year he was expelled from the Grand Jury "for misdeamnor amongst them." What his action was which displeased the Court is not known It could not have been a serious breach for he was many times a member of that body in after years. Yet it was substantially the same bench—Bradford, Prence, Collier, Hatherly and Alden which ten years later tried him upon the presentment "for taking a false oath att March Court last, about barley received of John Ramsden, affirming it to be delivered him for his own use, which is proved to be delivered him for Mr. Ramsden's use." He was found guilty and fined ten pounds, "Although we conceive," says the record, "hee was drawn into it by the base and ill carriage of John Ramsden." It is not to be supposed that a man of the strong character of Deacon Tilden would rest content with this action even though the Court softened its decree with censure of Ramsden. Tilden sought and obtained a review. In his petition for review he attacked the Court itself. Humphrey, Johnson and Gilbert Brookes were then appointed "as attorneys in the behalfe of the Court to appier in the case." Neither was a lawyer and that was no reason that they should act for the Court in prosecuting Tilden unless it existed in the fact that Johnson was known to be hostile to him. Tilden had caused a defamatory letter concerning Johnson to be read, publicly, and they were litigating before this same Court in an action for the alleged libel in which Johnson sought to recover damages which he placed at one hundred pounds. It is not too much to assert that Humphrey Johnson brought to his task as public prosecutor in this case something more than the public interest. When a final hearing was had the tribunal backed completely down. On March 1, 1658, it made this record:—

"Whereas the Court have granted unto Mr. Joseph Tilden a further hearing in the matter of his presentment about his oath, they having spent much time in hearing of such debates and pleas as might any way tend to the clearing up the truth in that matter, being of nothing more desireouse than to vindicate the innocent, and settle the blame of any former transactions where it is most just to rest, the matter being referred to the determination of the Bench, they conclude, that all former transactions of Courts relateing heerunto are not fully justifyable; nor may wee fully cleare Mr. Tilden from all blame about the same. It being long since these things were first in agitation, and some evidences that then passed in Court not now appearing, yett principally minding such new evidences as have now been produced, both to the taking of some former testimonies, and alsoe further clearing of his innocency that what hath formerly appeered, we doe acquitt him of his former charge of censure for a falce oath, because not grounded upon sufficient testimonies, and doe further order, that his presentment being taken out of the records, this our finall determination about the premises bee in his vindication recorded, and, lastly, doe agree, that Mr. Tilden bearing the charges of his friends in this tryall, the countrey shall alsoe beare the charges of their attorneys and evidences aded heerunto; that the said Mr. Tilden is to bee cleared by open proclamation att the General Court to bee holden att Plymouth in June next." †

After this complete victory over the Court he had nothing more to do with it up to the date of his death except once at the instance of his sister Lydia who was the widow of Richard Garrett for years town clerk of Scituate. She had been left with four small children upon his death and "upon the motion of Mr. Hatherly and Mr. Tilden, in the behalfe of the widdow, Mistris Lydia Garrett of Scituate, to have liberties to sell stronge liquors, in regard that sundry in that towne are oft times in nessesitie thereof, this Court doth give libertie unto the said Lydia Garrett to sell liquors, all waies provided that the orders of Court concerning selling of liquors bee observed, and that shee sell none but to house keepers, and not lesse than a gallon att a time."

He died June 3, 1670 leaving a family of nine children about whose education he was very "urgent." His personal estate was valued in the neighborhood of five thousand dollars and out of it the Court allowed their mother a generous sum "upon her petition for the nessesary apparrelling of her children, and for their maintainance three yeares, of five of them in diett and clothing," and "£12 payed by mee for the schooling and boarding my 2 sonnes, which my husband was urgent with the captaine to undertake" and "out of the estate before it be divided is to be taken 20 £ for Rebeckah, and a bed furnished; 18£ and 20£ in money for Elizabeth and Lydia." A legacy of two hundred pounds was left the wid-

---

† Plymouth Colony Records Vol III Page 156.

ow. The account which she filed contains much evidence of the business dealings of her husband with Boston shipbuilders in his lifetime. There was a debt of £44 due from Benjamin Gillam the shipwright who lived on Cow Lane near Summer Street, and owned the bark "Lidia:" Thomas Hawkins who had a ship yard near his home on Salem Street owed Tilden's estate £34:18S:09d; and the widow of Nicholas Upsall the Quaker keeper of the "Red Lyon Inn" £7:17s:04d. In another part of the same account the Executrix objects to being charged with a part of the debt due from Hawkins which she "conceived to be very doubtful whether ever it wilbe payed." William Boylston was another Boston business man to whom the product of Tilden's mill was regularly sent for many years.

(THE END)

INDEX

Adams, John, 197, 204.
Alden, John, 20, 28, 31, 58, 95, 98, 116, 117, 156, 169, 171.
Allen, (Allin) John, 43, 78.
Allen Joseph, 94.
Allen, William, 92.
Allerton, Isaac, 17, 18, 19, 100.
Andrews, Joseph, 38.
Andrews, Richard, 20, 23.
Andrews, Thomas, 17, 19, 21, 42.
Annable, Anthony, 20, 25, 26, 28, 64, 66, 102, 109, 114, 128, 144, 181.
Arnold, Benedict, 166.
Aspinwall, Williams, 35.
Austin, Anne, 87.

Baily, Abner, 208.
Bailey, Amasa, 198.
Bailey, Benjamin, 206.
Bailey, Ebenezer, 181.
Bailey, (Bayley) John, 75, 77, 181.
Bailey, Dea. Joseph, 190, 198, 203.
Bailey, Paul, 197, 198, 208.
Baker, Nicholas, 73, 79, 82.
Baker, Winsor, 209.
Balch, 80.
Barker, Barnabas, 192, 198, 206.
Barker, John, 53, 62, 109, 178, 188.
Barker, Samuel, 126, 181.
Barker, Williams, 205.
Barlow, George, 123.
Barnes, Rev. David, 86.
Barnes, David, 208.
Barrell, James, 206, 209.
Barrel, James, Jr., 209.
Barrell, Noah, 206.
Barrell, William, 207.
Barstow, Jeremiah, 175, 178.
Barstow, John, 77.
Barstow, Joseph, 113, 174, 206.
Barstow, Nathaniel 206.
Barstow, William, 58, 59, 124. 131, 132.
Base, Edward, 18.
Bates, Ebenezer, 208.
Bates, Guy, 207.
Bate, Reuben, 192.

Bates, Seth, 208.
Beauchamp, (Beacham) John, 16, 18, 19, 20, 21, 23, 42.
Benson, Joseph, 206.
Besbeach, (Bisby), 65.
Bird, Thomas, 25, 26, 130.
Booth, John, 46, 53, 56, 78.
Bourne, Ezra, 126.
Bourne, Deborah, 126.
Bourne, Rev. Shearjashub, 82.
Bowker, Bartlett, 206.
Bowker, Calvin, 280.
Bowker, David, 206, 207.
Bowker, Edward, 206.
Bowker, Gershom, 206.
Bowker, John, 207.
Bowker, Joshua, 207.
Bowker, Lazarus, 206.
Bowker, Levi, 209.
Bowker, Luke, 207.
Bradford, Robert, 82.
Bradford, William, 4, 7, 20, 23, 36, 38, 40, 62, 74, 98, 100, 101, 109, 116, 135, 152.
Brewer, Thomas, 17.
Brewster, William, 3, 7.
Briggs, Abner, 207.
Briggs, Benjamin, 192, 193, 208.
Briggs, Daniel, 208.
Briggs, Elisha, 205.
Briggs, James, 85, 137.
Briggs, James, Jr., 197, 198.
Brigg, Capt. John, 22.
Briggs, Joseph, 207.
Briggs, Mary, 118.
Briggs, Walter, 118, 132, 140, 175, 184.
Brooks, Luther, 208.
Brooks, Nathaniel, 208.
Brooks, William, 206.
Brown, 20, 28.
Brown, Bela, 209.
Brown, Calla, 209.
Brown, Ensign, 208.
Brown, Isaac, 209.
Brown, Jonathan, 208, 209.
Brown, John, 209.
Brown, Joseph, 206.
Brown, Knight, 208.
Brown, Samuel, 207.
Browne, John, 95, 116, 117.
Browning, Henry, 17

Bryant Elijah, 207.
Bryant, Ira, 206.
Bryant, John, 58, 73, 109, 137, 144.
Bryant, Thomas, 110.
Bryant, Zenas, 207.
Buck, (Bucke) Isaac, 109, 116, 117, 118, 128, 137, 144, 151.
Buck, John, 78, 175.
Buck, Lieut, 56, 75, 79, 151, 168, 175.
Burrill, Colburn, 206.
Burrow, Jeremiah, 166.

Carver, John, 7, 20, 100, 152.
Chamber, Thomas, 109, 130.
Chauncey (Chauncy), Rev. Charles, 30, 31, 43, 46, 47, 55, 59, 66, 67, 69, 71, 72, 73, 124, 142, 143, 148.
Checkett, Josiah, 128.
Chiteenden, Benj. 175.
Chiteenden, Henry, 78.
Chittenden, Isaac, 26, 47, 75, 102, 109, 113, 172, 175.
Chittenden, Israel, 53, 59, 137, 177, 181.
Chittenden, Luther, 207.
Chittenden, Nathaniel, 206.
Chittenden, Thomas, 43.
Church, Capt. Benjamin, 178, 193.
Church, Charles, 209.
Church, Thomas, 208.
Clapp, Abijah, 208, 209.
Clapp, Bela, 206.
Clapp, (Clap) Constant, 198.
Clapp, David, 207.
Clapp, Elijah, 208.
Clapp, Galen, 83, 195, 198, 200.
Clapp, Increase, 198, 200, 203.
Clapp, James, 208.
Clapp, John, 192, 193, 195, 200, 204, 205.
Clapp, Joshua, 206.
Clapp, Michael, 208.
Clapp, Nathaniel, 83, 195.
Clapp, Capt. Roger, 41, 209.
Clapp, Samuel, 22, 54, 78, 109, 110, 137, 181, 193 198, 206.
Clapp, Dea. Stephen, 181.
Clapp, Sylvanus, 208.
Clapp, Thomas, 109, 110, 126, 128, 137, 148, 181, 184, 193.
Clark, Nathaniel, 23.
Clarke Thomas, 175.
Cobb, Henry, 25, 28, 64, 102.

Cole, George, 207.
Cole, William, 199,
Collamore, Anthony, 207.
Collamore, Benjamin, 206, 207.
Collamore (Collimore, Collymore, Collamer), Capt. Enoch 181, 206.
Collamore, Peter, 78, 124, 128, 130, 144.
Coleman, Joseph, 49, 128.
Collier, (Collyer), Isaac, 57, 207.
Collier, Jonathan, 208.
Collier, Margaret, 108.
Collier, William, 17, 20, 21, 28, 54, 95, 98, 129.
Colman, Joseph, 92, 141.
Compsett, Josiah, 209.
Combs, John, 116.
Cook, Nathaniel, 209.
Cooper, John, 28.
Cooper, Lydia, 108.
Copeland, Ebenezer, 206.
Corlew, Daniel, 209.
Corthell, Theophelus, 208.
Costo, D 207.
Cotton 36, 74.
Cousing, Israel, 56.
Cowan, Israel, 208.
Cowan, Joseph, 175.
Cowing, Gethelus, 206.
Crage, Elizabeth, 138.
Crage, Lydia, 138.
Crage, Robert, 138.
Crage, Ruth, 138.
Crocker, Elijah, 205.
Crocker, William, 26.
Cudworth, Israel, 53.
Cudworth, James, 25, 26, 28, 43-47, 64, 66, 73, 75, 80, 94, 97, 98, 102, 109, 114, 128, 131, 132, 139, 142, 152, 157, 166, 171-174, 176, 178, 194..
Cudworth, John, 181.
Cudworth, Jonathan, 53, 77.
Cudworth, Mary, 95, 96, 205.
Curtis, Abner, 208.
Curtis, Benjamin, 207.
Curtis, (Curtice) Charles, 195, 199, 207.
Curtis, Eli, 198.
Curtis, Elijah, 199, 206.
Curtis, Gamaliel, 207, 208.
Curtis, James, 199.
Curtis, John, 78.
Curtis, Peleg, 208.
Curtis, Reuben, 208.

Curtis, Richard, 78, 166.
Curtis, Samuel, 206.
Curtis, Thomas, 184, 208.
Curwin,   , 85
Cushing, Adam, 208.
Cushing, Elijah, 126.
Cushing, Francis, 206.
Cushing, Hawke, 83, 200.
Cushing, James, 110, 137, 207, 209.
Cushing, Rev. Jeremiah, 82.
Cushing, John, 22, 54, 56, 109, 126, 131, 137, 146, 182, 185, 205, 208.
Cushing, John, Jr., 109, 126, 193, 195, 198.
Cushing, John, 3d, 110, 137, 185, 206.
Cushing, Judge John, 182.
Cushing, Joseph, 110, 148, 184, 185, 198.
Cushing, Lemuel, 148, 184, 205.
Cushing, Matthew, 59.
Cushing, Nathan, 110, 126, 148, 185, 195-198, 200, 201, 205.
Cushing, Nathaniel, 206, 207.
Cushing, William, 126, 182, 198, 201.
Cushman, Robert, 6, 7, 15, 184.
Cushman, Thomas, 116.

Damon, Edward, 205.
Damon, Eells, 206.
Damon, (Daman) Daniel, 78, 110, 203, 206.
Damon, Hannah, 25.
Damon, John, 25, 43, 59, 109, 137, 175, 206.
Damon, Joseph, 208.
Damon, Reuben, 206.
Damon, Samuel, 206.
Damon, Simon, 208.
Damon, Stephen, 206, 207.
Damon, Sylvanus, 207.
Damon, Zachariah, 175, 181.
Damon, Zadoc, 206.
Danforth, Thomas, 171.
Darby, Rev. Jonathan, 86.
Davis, Sergt, 165.
Davis, Capt. William, 171.
Dawes, Rev. Ebenezer, 83.
Delano, Benjamin, 208.
Delano, Elijah, 208.
Delano, Oliver, 208.
Dimmon, Zachariah, 78.
Dingley, E., 208.

Doherty, John, 206.
Dodson, Anthony, 45, 78.
Dodson, Gersham, 176.
Doggett, John, 184.
Doty, Edward, 140.
Doughty, James, 124.
Doughty, Roberty, 119, 120.
Dudley, J., 62.
Dimbar, David, 192.
Dunbar, Amos, 207.
Dunbar, Daniel, 208.
Dunbar, David, 207.
Dunbar, Edward, 207.
Dunbar, Elisha, 209.
Dunbar, Ezekiel, 207.
Dunbar, Hosea, 207.
Dunbar, Jesse, 205.
Dunster, Henry, 72, 73, 98, 142.
Dwelley, Abner, 207.
Dwelley, Richard, 175.
Dwelley, William, 207.

Eames, Anthony, 41.
Eames, Marke, 22.
Eddy, Ebenezer, 206.
Edenden, Edmund, 109.
Edmunds, Capt. 175.
Edwards, Daniel, 206, 207.
Eels, Rev. Nathaniel, 56, 84, 85, 86, 181, 206.
Elliot, Rev. John, 70, 156, 168.
Ellms, John, 207.
Ellms, Joseph, 207.
Ellmes, (Ellms) Rodolphus, 42, 53, 59, 94, 118.
Endicott (Endicote), John, 36, 38, 40, 94, 95, 98, 118.
Ensign, John, 175.
Ensign, Thomas, 43.
Erskine, Robert, 209.
Ewell, Henry, 128, 158.

Farrar, Thomas, 208.
Fish, Charles, 207.
Fish, Jonathan, 199.
Fish, Stephen, 207.
Fisher, Lieut. Joseph, 41.
Fisher, Mary, 87.
Fitsrandal, Nathaniel, 92.
Fitzgerald, Richard, 148, 184.
Ford, David, 208.
Ford, John, 157.
Ford, Peleg, 184.
Ford, Richard, 208.
Foster, Edward, 25, 28, 32, 102, 109, 114, 120, 130, 144, 158.
Foster, Elisha, 206.

Fox, George, 87, 92.
Foxwell, Richard, 26.
Frazier, Michael, 207.
Freeman, Asher, 208, 209.
Fuller, Samuel, 26, 28, 128.

Gannet, Benjamin, 207.
Gannet, Joseph, 175.
Gannet, Matthew, 78, 113.
Gannett, Joshua, 209.
Garnet, (Garnert) Francis, 61, 62.
Garrett, Richard, 44, 137.
Gaunt, Goodman, 123.
Georges, (Gorges), Sir Ferdinand, 8, 15, 19, 151.
Gibbs, John, 208, 209,
Gibbons Gen., 167.
Gill, John M., 209.
Gilson, (Gillson) Wm., 20, 25, 26, 28, 34, 66, 102.
Gray, James, 206.
Gray, Samuel, 206.
Grose, Elisha, 207, 209.
Grose, Joshua, 207.
Grose, Thomas, 208, 209.
Grosvenor, Rev. Ebenezer, 82, 83.
Gurney, Isaac, 118, 119.

Hammond, Benjamin, 207.
Hammond, David, 207.
Hammond, Frederick, 208, 209.
Hammond, Robert, 122.
Handmer, John, 27.
Hatch, Benjamin, Sr., 204, 206.
Hatch, Benjamin, Jr., 204.
Hatch, Jeremiah 78, 109, 137.
Hatch, Josiah, 208.
Hatch, Thomas, 78.
Hatch, William, 26, 28, 102, 115, 116, 118, 122, 128, 130, 157, 161, 175.
Hatherly (Hatherley) Timothy, 17, 19, 20-23, 27, 28, 32, 34, 35, 42, 43, 45, 47, 50, 55, 56, 57-60, 67, 69, 70, 71, 94, 98, 102, 108, 109, 116-118, 131, 132, 144, 154-157, 159, 160.
Hathmore, Col. 84.
Hawes, Edmund, 158.
Hayden, Bela, 207.
Hayden, Elisha, 208, 209.
Hayden, Ezra, 208, 209.
Hayden, Joseph, 199, 207.
Hayden, Peleg, 209.
Hayden, William, 207.

Henderson, Frederick, 195, 199.
Henley, John, 207.
Henley, William, 207.
Hewes, John, Sr., 26, 102, 130.
Hewes, Samuel, 59.
Hicks, Samuel, 96.
Hicks, Thomas, 141.
Hiland, Thomas, 43.
Hill, Hercules, 158, 160.
Hinds, Micah, 206.
Hinckley, Samuel, 26, 74, 102, 128.
Hinckley, Thomas, 23, 95 142, 184.
Hoar, (Hoare) John, 42, 45, 50, 59, 121, 122, 132, 144, 156, 157.
Hobson, Henry, 95.
Holbrook, Josiah, 207.
Holbrook, Samuel, 78.
Hollet, John, 43, 47, 128, 129, 130, 144.
Hollowell, Nathaniel, 207.
Holmes, Benjamin, 206.
Holmes, Elizabeth, 118.
Holmes, Thomas, 206, 207.
Holmes, William, 43, 115, 116, 118, 144.
Hoskins, William, 199.
House, Abner, 208.
House, Nathaniel, 207.
House, Nehemiah, 206.
House, Peleg, 208.
Howland, John, 20, 28.
Hoyt, Simon, 26, 102.
Humphries, James, 83.
Hutchinson, Gov., 30.
Hyland, Amasa, 205, 209.
Hyland, Benjamin, 207.
Hyland, Elisha, 208.
Hyland, Samuel, 205.
Hyland, William, 205, 206.

Ingham, Thos., 124.

Jackson, Jonathan, 56, 77, 175, 178.
Jackson, Samuel, 59.
Jacobs, Asaph, 209.
Jacobs, Benjamin, 199.
Jacobs, David, 80, 181.
Jacobs, Dr., 184.
Jacobs, Elisha, 206.
Jacobs, John, 59, 146, 198, 204.
Jacobs, Joseph, 181, 199.
Jacobs, Joshua, 181, 204.

Jacobson, John, 205.
James, Benjamin, 199.
James, Benjamin, Jr., 199.
James, Elisha, 203, 205.
James, John, 182.
James, William, 56.
Jeffreys, James, 207.
Jenkins, Calvin, 206.
Jenkins, Daniel, 82.
Jenkins, Edward, 43, 59, 113, 128, 144, 207.
Jenkins, Geva, 207.
Jenkins, Gideon, 206.
Jenkins, James, 206.
Jenkins, John, 123.
Jenkins, Nathaniel, 207.
Jenkins, Samuel, 44, 198.
Jenkins, Thomas, 53, 56.
Johnson, Humphrey, 128.
Johnson, Nathaniel, 61, 62.
Johnson, Nathaniel N., 61.
Jones, Benjamin, 209.
Jones, Ezekiel, 207, 208.
Jones, Dearing, 207.
Jones, Nathaniel, 208.
Jones, William, 207.
Jordan, David, 206.
Jordan, Nathaniel, 209.
Joy, Elisha, 207.

Keane, Robert, 18.
Kempton, Ephraim, 128-130, 144.
Kendrick, 64.
Kennerick, (Kinrick), George, 26, 28, 102, 109, 128, 158.
King, John, 207.
King (Kinge), Sara, 67.
King, Elder Thomas, 65, 67, 69, 70, 73, 75, 109, 137.
King, Thomas, Jr., 136.
Knight, John 17.

Lafayette, 209.
Lambert, Zaccheus, 207.
Lapham, Asa, 208.
Lapham, Isaac, 208.
Lapham, James, 208.
Lapham, Lemuel, 207, 208.
Lapham, Nathaniel, 207.
Lapham, Thomas, 65, 67, 69, 70, 208.
Laud Archibishop, 66.
Lawson, Rev. Deodate, 84.
Layonne, Signor, 209.
Leonard, Josiah, 209.
Leverette, Gen., 171.

Lewis, George 26-28, 64, 102, 144.
Lewis, John, 27, 102, 128.
Lincoln, Benjamin, 82.
Lincoln, James, 206.
Lincoln, John, 207.
Lincoln, William, 208, 209.
Litchfield, Abner, 208.
Litchfield, Amos, 208.
Litchfield, Barnabas, 208.
Litchfield, Caleb, 208.
Litchfield, Charles, 207, 208.
Litchfield, Daniel, 208.
Litchfield, Eleazor, 197, 208.
Litchfield, Eli, 209.
Litchfield, Elisha, 207, 208.
Litchfield, Ephraim, 207.
Litchfield, Israel, 110, 203.
Litchfield, James, 207.
Litchfield, John, 208.
Litchfield, Josiah, 208.
Litchfield, Lawrence, 206.
Litchfield, Lot, 208.
Litchfield, Lothrop, 207.
Litchfield, Nathan, 207.
Litchfield, Nicholas, 45, 54, 110, 193.
Litchfield, Noah, 206.
Litchfield, Samuel, 207.
Litchfield, Thomas, 207.
Little, Barnabas, 184, 195, 197, 198, 203.
Little David, 53, 81, 82, 184, 185, 199.
Little, Warren, 209.
Lombard (Lumbard) Bernard, 26, 28, 102.
Lothrop, (Lathrop) Barnabas, 126.
Lothrop, John, 175.
Lothrop, Rev. John, 26, 28, 30, 64-70, 75, 161.
Lusher, Maj. Ebenezer, 41.

Mann, George, 209.
Mann, Jonathan, 208.
Mann, Josiah, 207.
Mann, Richard, 42, 144.
Mann, Thomas, 198.
Mann, William, 209.
Manson, Nehemiah, 208, 209.
Manson, John, 181, 207.
Mather, Cotton, 142.
Mayhew, Israel, 209.
Mayhew, Lemuel, 207.
Mayhew, William, 207, 209.
McNevin, William, 209.

Melville, Andrew, 63.
Merritt, Consider, 206.
Merritt, David, 207.
Merritt, Daniel, 205, 207.
Merritt, Ezekiel, 209.
Merritt, George, 208.
Merritt, Henry, 43, 130, 144.
Merritt John, 47, 54, 207.
Merritt, Joshua, 207, 208.
Merritt, Melzar, 208.
Merritt Nehemiah, 207.
Merritt, Seth, 208.
Merritt, Zaccheus, 207.
Mighill, Rev. Thomas, 75, 84.
Mitchell, John, 207.
Moate, Nathaniel, 166.
Moore, George, 140, 141.
Morton, George, 198.
Morton, Nathaniel, 108, 158.
Morris, Judge, 105.
Mott, Edward, 205.
Mott, Micah, 206.

Nash, Israel, 208.
Nash, James, 206.
Nash, Joseph, 207.
Nash, Levi, 208.
Nash, Noah, 207.
Nash, Samuel, 158.
Neal, Henry, 120.
Neal, Job, 207
Newell, Increase, 156.
Newell, Levi, 208.
Nichols, Caleb, 206, 207.
Nichols, Noah, 207, 208.
Nichols, Samuel, 207.
Nichols Thomas, 209.
Nicholson, Noah, 207.
Nicholson, William, 209.
Niles, Rev. Samuel, 190.
Northey, Abraham, 184.
Northey, Eliphalet, 207.
Norton, Humphrey, 88.

Orcutt, Seth, 209.
Otis, Charles, 206, 207.
Otis, David, 199.
Otis, Ensign, 181.
Otis, Ephraim, 184, 192, 195.
Otis, Ignatius, 198.
Otis, James, 126, 184, 192, 195, 198.
Otis Job, 199.
Otis, John, 59, 80, 126.
Otis, Joseph, 109, 126, 193.
Otis, Noah, 198, 200.
Otis, Prince, 199.

Otis, Stephen, 53, 56, 62, 184.

Palmer, Ephraim, 206.
Palmer, John, 198.
Palmer, Josiah, 78.
Palmer, Stephen, 206.
Palmer, Thomas, 78, 81.
Palmer, William, 144.
Parker, William, 49, 97, 128.
Parsons, Chief Justice, 49.
Peabody, (Paybody) William, 22, 54.
Peakes, Benjamin, 206.
Peakes, Eleazer, 206, 208.
Pedcock, George, 144.
Peirce, Augustus, 207.
Peirce, Calvin, 198.
Peirce, Hayward, 206.
Peirce, John, 8-15, 19, 56.
Peirce, Mathew, 208, 209.
Peirce, Michael, 137, 151, 168, 174, 175.
Peirce, Sylvanus, 206.
Pemberton, Rev. Ebenezer, 85.
Perry, Amos, 209.
Perry, John, 175.
Perry, Joseph, 175.
Perry, William, 173, 178, 209.
Pidcote, (Pitcoke) George, 113, 114.
Pierce, Benjamin, 53, 56, 62, 78.
Pierce, Calvin, 206.
Pierce, Hayward, 205.
Pierce, Samuel, 206.
Pincin, Simeon, 207.
Pincin, Thomas, 131, 144.
Pincin, William, 207.
Pinchin, Thomas, Sr., 77.
Pitcher, Rev. Nathaniel, 82.
Pocock, John, 18.
Popham, George, 5.
Pratt, Samuel, 176.
Prence, Gov., 20, 28, 54, 66, 94, 95, 135, 169, 171.
Prence, Thomas, 98, 116, 160.
Prince, 21.
Prince, Thomas, 108, 109.
Prouty James, 206, 207.
Prouty, John, 207.
Prouty, Joshua, 206.
Prouty, Richard, 175.
Prouty, Simeon, 206, 207.
Pynchon, Thomas, 128.

Ramsdell, Edward, 207.
Ramsdell, Samuel, 208.
Randall, Job, 85, 173.

Randall, William, Sr., 78, 124, 125, 128, 130.
Rawlins, Henry, 43.
Rawlins, Lydia, 117, 118.
Rawlins, Nathaniel, 117, 119, 120.
Rawlins, Thomas, 118, 130.
Rayner, 66.
Reade, William, 128.
Revell, John, 17.
Richard, Thomas, 140.
Robinson, Isaac, 27, 28, 65, 97.
Robinson, John, 166.
Robinson, Rev. John, 4-7, 65.
Robinson, Thomas, 128.
Robinson, William, 88.
Rogers, John, 140.
Rose, John, 175.
Rose, Laban, 207.
Rowley, Henry, 25, 26, 28, 65, 66.
Ruggles Thomas, 208.
Russell, George, 128, 130, 166.
Russell, John, 209.
Russell, Samuel, 176.

Saffin, John, 121, 126, 132, 144.
Sampson, Nehemiah, 208, 209.
Saunders Edward, 166.
Savery, Thomas, 176.
Sealis, Richard, 43, 109.
Sears, Peter, 205, 207.
Sewall, Judge Samuel, 84.
Sexton, (Saxton) Giles, 64, 65.
Sharp, Samuel, 17.
Simmons, Barnabas, 207.
Simmons, Samuel, 207, 208.
Shirley, (Sherley, Shurley), James, 18, 19, 20, 21.
Smith, Francis, 166.
Smith, Capt. John, 35.
Souther, Nathaniel, 101.
Southworth, Theopilus, 207.
Southworth, Thomas, 95.
Sparrow, Edward, 205.
Sprague, Joshua, 208.
Sprague, Laban, 207, 208.
Sprague, Samuel, 209.
Sprout, Robert, 140.
Stacy, Daniel, 77.
Standish, Josiah, 22.
Standish, Myles, 7, 17, 31, 100, 151, 152, 156, 159, 160.
Standlake, Daniel, 27.
Standley, Jabez, 207.
Stedman, Isaac, 26, 102, 131, 144.
Stetson, Amos, 207.
Stetson, (Studson) Benjamin, 109, 193, 199.
Stetson, Christopher, 206.
Stetson, Elisha, 208.
Stetson, Ephraim, 206.
Stetson, Gideon, 209.
Stetson, Isaac, 184, 200, 206, 207.
Stetson, James, 209.
Stetson, John, 181, 199.
Stetson, Joseph, 198, 205.
Stetson, Matthew, 206.
Stetson, Nathan, 208.
Stetson, Cornet Robert, 41, 58, 73, 96, 109, 128, 131, 132, 137, 139, 151, 172, 175, 181.
Stetson, Samuel, 199, 207.
Stevenson, Marmaduke, 88.
Stoddard, Elijah, 208.
Stoddard, H., 208.
Stoddard, Isaiah, 208.
Stoddard, Noah, 208.
Stoddard, Samuel, 208, 209.
Stoddard, Simeon, 209.
Stockbridge, Anna, 67.
Stockbridge, Dr. Benj., 182, 184, 199.
Stockbridge, Dr. Charles, 182, 183, 184.
Stockbridge, Charles, 78.
Stockbridge, James, 206, 208.
Stockbridge, John, 43, 114, 118, 128, 130, 144.
Stockbridge, Samuel, 205.
Stockbridge, Sarah, 85.
Stoughton, Israel, 36, 38, 40, 41.
Strong, Justice, 49.
Studley, Abial 208.
Studley, Benjamin, 53, 54, 208.
Studley, John, 208.
Studley, William, 206.
Sutton, Abner, 206.
Sutton, Abraham, 128.
Sutton, Henry, 207.
Sutton, Jesse, 208.
Sutton, John, 137, 206.
Sutton, Zeba, 209.
Sutton, Gen., 128.
Sylvester, (Silvester) Dinah, 118.
Sylvester, Elisha, 85, 208.
Sylvester, Israel, 85, 208.
Sylvester, Isaac, 206.
Sylvester, Joel, 208.
Sylvester, Joseph, 109, 119, 177.
Sylvester, Lemuel, 207.
Sylvester, Richard 118.

Sylvester, Zebulon, 181.
Symmes, Timothy, 184.

Taft, 85.
Tarte (Tart) Edward, 123.
Tarte, Richard, 166.
Tarte, Thomas, 42, 59.
Thacher, Oxenbridge, 81.
Thaxter, John, 59.
Thayer, Richard, 152.
Thomas, Nathan, 208.
Thomas, Nathaniel, 176, 177, 208.
Thomas, William, 156.
Thorne, Joseph, 178.
Thrasher, John F., 61.
Ticknor, William, 56.
Tilden (Tildin) Elizabeth, 78.
Tilden, John, 56, 184.
Tilden, Joseph, 43, 45, 47, 58, 124, 125, 157.
Tilden, Nathaniel, 25, 26, 28, 35, 46, 128, 137.
Tirrell, Job, 192.
Tolman, Elisha, 83, 203.
Tolman, Joseph, 83, 195, 198.
Torrey, Caleb, 110, 181.
Torrey, George, 206, 208.
Torrey, Isaac, 208.
Torrey, James, 44, 58, 59, 96, 109, 137, 144, 157, 193.
Torrey, Lieut. 131.
Torrey, Warren, 208.
Totman, Charles, 208.
Totman, Ebenezer, 208.
Totman, Stephen, 206.
Totman, Thomas, 206, 207.
Tower, Benjamin, 207.
Tower, Nathan, 208.
Tower, Stephen, 208.
Turner, Abiel, 198, 209.
Turner, Abijah, 208.
Turner, Amos, 110, 204.
Turner, Asa, 207.
Turner, Benjamin, 188.
Turner, Charles, 110, 198, 208.
Turner, Consider, 206.
Turner Elisha, 192, 199.
Turner, Humphrey, 25, 26, 27, 28, 32, 69, 102, 109, 126, 128, 130, 144, 157, 182, 205.
Turner, Israel, 208.
Turner, Jacobs, 206.
Turner, John, Sr., 74, 78, 166.
Turner, John, 126, 128, 131.
Turner, Jonathan, 205, 206.
Turner, Joseph, 173, 199.

Turner, Nathaniel, 78, 83, 200, 208.
Turner, Samuel, 190.
Turner, Thomas, 110, 185, 193.
Turner, William, 110, 148, 184, 195, 198, 204, 205, 206.
Twisden, John, 67, 70.

Vane, George, 159.
Vassall, Benjamin, 206.
Vassall, Judith, 67.
Vassall, Williams, 29, 30, 31, 32, 55, 65, 67, 69, 70, 71, 72, 131, 143, 160.
Vinal, Ann, 43, 46, 49, 181, 193.
Vinal, Benjamin, 206.
Vinal, Calogus, 207.
Vinal, Gideon, 110, 196.
Vinal, Israel, Jr., 195, 198, 199.
Vinal, John, Sr., 56, 173.
Vinal, Joseph, Jr., 208.
Vinal, Robert 208.
Vinal, Stephen, 205, 207.
Vinal, Stephen, Jr., 44, 193.
Vinal, Stephen, Sr., 44, 49, 53, 78, 128, 131.

Wade, Abdenego, 207.
Wade, Benjamin, 207.
Wade, Issacher, 208.
Wade, John, 207.
Wade, Joseph, 175.
Wade, Josias, 208.
Wade, Levi, 208.
Wade, Nathaniel, 181.
Wade, Nicholas, 113, 181.
Wade, Stephen, 207, 208.
Wadsworth, Christopher, 113.
Wanton, Edward, 89, 92.
Ward, Thomas, 17.
Wardwell, Lydia, 88.
Waterman, Anthony, 184, 195, 198.
Waterman, Nathaniel, 198, 203.
Webb, Barnabas, 208.
Webb, Thomas, 181, 206.
Weston, Thomas, 6, 7, 16, 17, 19.
Weyborn, (Wyborne) Thomas, 166.
Weymouth, George, 5,
Wheelwright, 35.
Whitcomb, John, 43, 144.
Whitcomb, Robert, 95, 96.
White, Gowan, 43, 144.
White, John, 17.
White, Joseph, 78.
White, Peregrime, 160.

, Timothy, 178.
ston, John, 43.
hitcomb, John, 205, 208.
Wilcomb, William, 176.
Wilder, Edward, 59.
Williams, John, 43, 51, 52, 53, 97, 109, 118, 131, 174, 175, 176, 181, 205.
Williams, John, Jr., 59, 128, 131.
Williams, Capt. Jno., 60, 61.
Williams, Roger, 94, 159, 166.
Willis, John, 130.
Willitt, Capt. Thomas, 95.
Wilson, Deborah, 88.
Wilson, Rev. John, 71.
Wing, Ebenezer, 208.
Winslow, Anna, 205.
Winslow, Edward, 20, 30, 36, 38, 40, 129, 159, 160, 204.
Winslow, John, 193.
Winslow, Josiah, 41, 74, 154, 173.
Winslow, Josias, 94, 95, 98, 169.
Winslow, Nathaniel, 204, 205.
Winter, Christopher, 166.
Winthrop, Gov. 30, 171.
Wiswell, 74.
Witherell, Prince, 208.
Witherell, Sarah, 85.
Witherell, Serg't. 178.
Witherell, Richard, 208.
Witherell, Theophilus, 173.
Witherell, William, 72, 73, 74, 75, 83, 84, 142.
Wollaston Capt. 155.
Wood, Thomas, 78.
Woodfield, John, 43.
Woodward, Walter, 130.
Woodworth, Benjamin, 78, 175, 182, 184, 207.
Woodworth, Isaac, 209.
Woodworth, Joseph, 78.
Woodworth, Walter, 26, 75.
Wormell, Joseph, 128.
Worthylake, Peter, 78.
Wright, John, 173, 206, 207, 209.

Young, Samuel, 206.

BIOGRAPHICAL SKETCHES

Baileys, The	345 to 348
Barkers, The	349 to 352
Barstows, The	342 to 344
Clapps, The	306 to 313
Cudworth, James	210 to 235
Cushings, The	259 to 283
Damons, The	337 to 341
Hatherly, Timothy	284 to 305
Otis	369 to 373
Peirce, Michael	325 to 329
Saffin, John	236 to 258
Stockbridges, The	330 to 336
Tildens, The	380 to 386
Torreys, The	322 to 324
Turners, The	314 to 321
Vinals, The	374 to 379
Williams, John	353 to 368

www.ingramcontent.com/pod-product-compliance
Lightning Source LLC
Chambersburg PA
CBHW070057020526
44112CB00034B/1420